THINKING IN A NEW LIGHT

THINKING IN A NEW LIGHT

HOW TO BOOST YOUR CREATIVITY AND LIVE MORE
FULLY BY EXPLORING WORLD CULTURES

Brian Holihan

Full Humanity Press
Sunnyvale, CA

Published by Full Humanity Press
P.O. Box 70015
Sunnyvale, CA 94086

Although the author and publisher have made every effort to ensure the accuracy and
completeness of the information contained in this book, we assume no responsibility
for errors, inaccuracies, omissions, or inconsistencies herein.

First Paperback Edition

ISBN-13: 9780692542415
ISBN-10: 0692542418
Library of Congress Control Number: 2015916087
Full Humanity Press, Sunnyvale, CA

Editing: Rachel Blackbirdsong
Photography: Brian Holihan

For information, please contact the publisher:
info@fullhumanitypress.com

CONTENTS

THE JOY OF EXPLORING OTHER WORLDS

PREFLIGHT CHECK-IN

I FELL IN love with exploring different cultures when I was seven. My father subscribed to *National Geographic* and bought the Time-Life series of books on the world's countries, and I experienced one Wow! after another. Egyptian pyramids, Angkor Wat, ancient Greek temples, the Taj Mahal, Chinese pagodas, Gothic cathedrals, and narrow boats gliding through Bangkok's canals—what inspired so many different art forms?

My parents often took me to San Francisco's airport to watch the never-ending streams of people and planes. I found the women in sparkling red saris boarding an Air India flight especially intriguing. The vibrant hues and swirling forms seemed a world away from the jeans and short-sleeved shirts in my neighborhood. Since those days, I've always enjoyed airports as hubs where folks from all over the world, with their different mindsets, come together.

So in 2007 I jumped at a chance to leave Silicon Valley's high-tech workforce and travel around the world. I journeyed in Southeast Asia, Africa, and the Middle East, and since many of their cultures are not as well-known as the West and China are, I found that humanity is much richer than a small number of traditions. Traveling through one under-appreciated society after another made me think: This must be what heaven is like. One perspective after another opened up to me, and I was free to compare them in any combination I chose. All cultures seemed to shine on each other in a field of connections that became increasingly luminous and pervaded with love as the trip progressed. I realized that the world has so much cultural wealth that we can bring earth and dreams of heaven together. At the same time, we can enhance our creativity by accessing an ever-widening range of ideas. This book explains how to do both.

But the world is currently rough for many, largely because people make it that way for each other. Political corruption, corporate greed, ecological destruction, prejudice, and terrorism run rampant. But if societies see paradise on earth as a basic concept, we're on our way to living in it. More people will treat each other kindly, respect the ecology, and study and expose all cultures' beauty. Parents and schools will teach children to see and share the world's positive aspects, and people will forge public policies to develop them further.

However, academic and scientific conventions say that we cannot discuss paradise because it's too vague. Knowledge can only be about facts, which people can verify in laboratories, quantify, and store as bits of information in databases. At the same time, many people in today's hyper-competitive digital economy only have time to focus on making ends meet. A friend recently told me, "Most people today are in survival mode." Our current economic trends and intellectual conventions imprison us in a self-reinforcing cycle: Because paradise seems too remote to be found in the world and discussed, people hold onto a world-view that keeps it distant.

So this book flouts precepts that say that we are less than we can be. Since it's about increasing your happiness and creativity by exploring multiple cultures, we will attempt the most inspiring vision that we can. We'll soar as high as possible here by exploring places that I've journeyed through. Seeing several cultures back to back during my trip transcended perspectives bound to conventions, not by one step, but by gleefully skyrocketing beyond them. I'll share this experience with you in the following pages.

To give you my full experience, this book mixes cultural depths of the places I toured with my travel tales. My journey wasn't a typical sightseeing jaunt because I had studied the histories and traditions of the societies I visited before leaving home. Seeing their pasts reflected in the present made my travels more rewarding than they would have been if I had only focused on current events. Because it added more depth to my experiences, we'll delve into the roots of the cultures I explored and attain perspectives that can reveal their full richness.

I also often carried a guitar and played it with people. I've found that music is one of the best ways to immerse myself in other cultures because it allows me to share people's feelings more deeply. It was the combination of all these types of experiences (emotional and intellectual, traditional and contemporary, imaginative and earthy) that made me feel that this trip was like paradise. It was so full and wide-ranging that my journey transcended all categories so that everything around me seemed to glitter.

I discovered a method for finding paradise in the world. It's very simple—you can summarize it in six letters and put them on a T-shirt. It shows a way in which all people and cultures are connected that hasn't been taught in schools, and how we can think about this connectedness in optimal ways for our well-being. I'll detail it later, but not until the middle of the second part of this book because this method isn't an immediate fix. You have to appreciate multiple cultures in order to make it work for you. But we'll have enough material by the middle of Part Two to apply to it. By the time you finish this book, you'll find that paradise is right here and that you can help expose it further so that it will be a daily experience for you and the people you're close to. The manual at the end details how to do this.

In *Guns, Germs, and Steel,* Jared Diamond asked why history happened as it did. Why did the West become the world's most dominant culture between the 18th century and the end of the 20th? This book asks: How can history be more rewarding for everybody? What way of looking at the world can promote the most well-being for the most people and allow all cultures to appreciate each other's most inspired creations to the greatest extent? We'll see how all societies can highlight each other's positive sides, and how their people can combine such a big range of perspectives that creative breakthroughs can become so easy that you can have them whenever you want. As you do, your view of the world will keep growing bigger and more inspiring.

But I don't gloss over any ugliness that I found on this trip. I wanted a full romance with the world. Other than the worst human behavior, I wanted to see and feel as much as possible, and this meant feeling some pain at times. I saw many scars from the Khmer Rouge's regime in Cambodia, and it was gut-wrenching to witness hoards of begging children with hopeless eyes. All the countries I traveled in have immense gaps between the rich and poor, and more political corruption than any city dump can hold.

However, I found that the cultural wealth in all these countries was thousands of times worth the heartaches. As I ventured to study humanity's better side, it seemed as though the world was opening more of its splendors to me. My trip usually felt like a dance with the entire globe that was sheer electricity. This book is my gift back.

CHAPTER 1

ENCHANTMENTS OF SOUTHEAST ASIA

I KNEW I was entering a different world as soon as my flight reached Southeast Asia. I first jetted from Hong Kong to Bangkok to change planes for Siem Reap, where Angkor Wat and scores of other proud Khmer monuments stand. While approaching Thailand's capital, I surveyed a cheerful carpet of light green fields. They were long, narrow, and straight as joss sticks. The land looked settled. But when I reached the city, the view became chaotic. Skyscrapers, single-family homes, and golden-roofed temples jostled in a metropolis of more than seven million souls. Old timers reminisce about the Venice of the East, with its limpid canals and long, slender boats as elegant as gondolas. But the cityscape I saw looked as though a million buildings of every shape and size were randomly mixed and dumped on tropical rice fields. Goodbye logic.

The entrance into Cambodia was even more dramatic. I changed planes, from the regal 747 to a twin-prop bird. Half way to Siem Reap, the view shifted from straight light green fields to dark jungle with no break except an occasional river snaking through the trees. The foliage was so thick that the rivers seemed to struggle to flow through it.

Siem Reap appeared suddenly. Most buildings I saw were small wooden houses on stilts. I felt as though I was traveling 1,000 years back and into the lives of the ancient Khmers who erected the monuments that I would explore for the next two weeks.

The middle of town was more modern. Siem Reap became safer in the 1990s (after being plagued by the Khmer Rouge's atrocious reign and its aftermath), and its number of tourists had grown more than 30 percent per year for several years. My plane had not flown over its central area, which was crisscrossed by straight streets with shops and sidewalk restaurants in stately French colonial buildings. Surrounding them were wooden homes, mom-and-pop grocery stores, and trees. Bikes, pedestrians, dogs, and cars shared the roads so that all meshed into a smooth and gentle flow. The town's atmosphere reminded me of a previous trip in central Java. Both places had a soft color scheme. The faded yellow and blue buildings and the golden skins and light clothing of the locals mingled with an endless variety of green hues. The foliage wasn't overpowering in town. All colors melded into a flow of life's energies that was both vibrant and soothing. I had missed this ambience when I left Indonesia and returned to Silicon Valley's anthill vibe. While riding from Siem Reap's airport I thought, Yeah! I'm back!

That trip to Indonesia (back in 1991, when I was at a highly impressionable age) was my first time in Southeast Asia, and it hooked me on the region. I went to Java and Bali in a four-person group on an artistic heritage tour. In our first morning, we walked through Yogyakarta's outdoor bird market and main bazaar. They were so different from my California suburb that I felt like I had just landed on another planet. Elderly women sat on the ground displaying spices, vegetables, and fruit. A small grey-haired man sold monkeys, and a young man with a four-foot iguana crawling up his chest encouraged us to photograph him. We then sauntered through lines of hanging wicker bird cages. This profusion of life forms seemed unreal.

I began to feel at home by the afternoon. We stopped for a rest under a small public pavilion, and a few young local men soon squeezed into it and sat down with us. They were so relaxed. All spoke with soft voices and never fidgeted, and their faces were as reposed as Buddha statues. The men's gentleness fused with the abundance of life forms and colors. The English language doesn't have a word for this combination of civility and exuberance. But this fusion of moods, which Anglo-American culture has trouble categorizing, bestows an endless variety of pleasures on people who live in it.

I missed it when I returned home from that first trip, but I could at least read about Southeast Asia and discover more of its societies beyond Indonesia. These studies and five later visits taught me that many cultures in the region have organized themselves with these patterns for more than 2,000 years. (Populations of the largest cities have mushroomed since WWII and this has created stresses that, along with today's pop cultures and digital economy, have been weakening these patterns in urbanized areas, especially among the young. We'll examine these developments in later chapters, but they have been relatively recent so we will first explore the traditions that have long preceded them.) Most visitors find the area mysterious. Bangkok's urban sprawl and Cambodia's jungles seem to hide bottomless intrigue. The smiles and pretty colors often conceal hidden meanings. The historian Craig J. Reynolds noticed that many Westerners have described Southeast Asian cultures with vague words, including *mixing, blending,* and *eclecticism,* which don't reveal much about what it's actually like to live in them. Even Google's search box can't help people grasp the region's societies because they combine experiences in ways that transcend the words people commonly search.

So we will delve into Southeast Asian cultures in this book and see how rich this little-known part of the world is. We'll compare our discoveries with Western traditions, and then plug both into the method for finding a bigger and happier human landscape than conventions have appreciated. The rest of this chapter will give you an introduction to traditional Southeast Asian societies so that you can see how rewarding they are to explore. Then I'll resume the story about my own trip in the following chapter.

Southeast Asia's natural landscape is both gracious and cruel. Succulent fruits grow in abundance, many fish streak through the rivers, ravishing flowers bloom, and birds sing in an avian orchestra that fuses with the joyful colors. But a flood can suddenly overwhelm a village. So can an enraged volcano. The lush growth harbors disease-carrying insects, and malaria and dengue fever still plague much of the region. I collected my share of mosquito bites but I was lucky. However, a young British man that I met in Cambodia had just left the hospital after battling dengue fever. "I was in a bad state!"

The region is blessed with abundant fish and gorgeous beaches, but the shores have exposed people to invaders and tidal waves. Like the land, the sea is as giving as a mother and as ruthless as an angry spirit.

Not all of Southeast Asia is lush; many areas in uplands away from coasts receive little rain so that farmers struggle to scratch livings from the arid land. The places that do receive the monsoons' blessings depend on them so that their failure to arrive has sometimes been catastrophic. Nature is often generous and beautiful, but the withholding of its gifts has always been a danger that people have feared.

Southeast Asia's geography is different from Europe's. The Mediterranean is special. As a single body of water which southern Europeans, Levantines, and northern Africans have shared, it helped unify the Greco-Roman world over 2,000 years ago by allowing ideas and art forms to be widely shared. Roman-style buildings still dignify the backs of America's five, ten, twenty, and fifty dollar bills. Ancient Roman architecture also influenced the dome on the Capitol Building in Washington, D.C. and the one that crowns St. Peter's in Rome—it has shaped buildings of the West's most prestigious political and religious institutions. Greek sculpture's realistic human figures, Greek temples' proportioned forms, Christianity, Judaism, Islam, and myths about Greek gods and heroes have given people around the Mediterranean many points of contact. So did urban Roman institutions, including civic forums, libraries, theaters, public baths, and civil law.

A person in 1 CE (the Common Era—formerly known as AD) could have sailed from Rome to towns in the Middle East and felt that he was in the same world. After the Southeast Asian part of my 2007 trip, I explored an ancient Roman city in Jordan called Jerash and admired its theaters and main street, which colonnades and stone temples lined. Their stately and regular shapes stood out from the arid, khaki-colored natural surroundings. They made a resounding statement to the locals about the ubiquity of Roman urban life, and architects throughout Europe and America have imitated their forms ever since.

But Southeast Asia's coasts lack a common body of water. Its mainland twists into many shapes which border several seas and oceans so that its image on a map resembles its dense foliage. This has allowed much cultural diversity, but people have lacked a common classical heritage to share meanings within. Indians came to trade in the late first millennium BCE, and they imported writing and universal religions. But what they gave was varied, including several forms of both Hinduism and Buddhism. India thus added even more diversity to the region. Locals then assimilated its influences according to their own mindsets and combined their own traditions with them.

The degree of Indian penetration in Southeast Asia has also varied. Vietnam was much more influenced by China, and the Philippines experienced relatively little contact with outside cultures until Muslim traders began to establish themselves there in the 14th century. Although the majority of Southeast Asian countries did imbibe a lot of Indian culture, it usually planted deeper roots in lowland rice growing areas while many societies in the uplands continued to focus on their own local traditions (uplands are home to a glorious diversity of minority cultures; we'll visit some later).

Some cultural patterns are more common in Southeast Asia than in the West, but they're too diverse to be fully expressed in a few forms. Its people developed different ways of integrating their world than a shared classical tradition, and I've found them just as creative and enduring. Exploring them has been a constant source of pleasure for me.

Because Southeast Asia's environments can be kind and then deadly, people have often used politeness, rituals, and art to render them safe. Indigenous Semai people in the mountains of peninsular Malaysia stress gentleness by smiling and speaking softly. Many have associated emotional outbursts with the sudden onset of particularly violent thunderstorms in which lightning streaks through the blackened sky and winds batter homes so hard that they sway. The anthropologists P. D. R. Williams-Hunt and H. D. Noone found Semai gentleness so irresistible that they married local women and settled into their communities.

People in another indigenous culture in peninsular Malaysia, the Temiar, believe that they can get sick or suffer an accident by laughing long or loudly at another person, eating an animal that was laughed at while being killed, or imitating the cries of certain animals and insects. Rude acts like these can cause thunderstorms, diarrhea, and tiger attacks, so people try to be gentle with each other.[1]

The Temiar also try to avoid startling each other and thus announce themselves while passing behind someone who is sitting. If they don't, the seated person's body odor can become startled and make them ill. In addition, they avoid naming foods across categories while eating. For example, saying "game" while eating rice, fruit, or vegetables can offend the soul of the food that's being eaten, and this can cause diarrhea. Many things in the environment have souls, including odors, foods, plants, animals, birds, mountains, and thunder. Within this copious world, all things must be kept in harmony and treated with politeness.

The anthropologist Marina Roseman felt that their rituals also emphasize this politeness. People maintain harmony with spirits by conducting trance dances in which a medium communicates with them. During the ceremonies, women often dance with supple motions that the Temiar associate with a woman's curving body, wavy hair, and relaxed walk, and with rustling palm fronds and gentle breezes.[2] This network of associations helps render a potentially scary natural environment livable and beautiful.

I got lost in a village in central Java's mountains in 1991. As I walked down the main road, all the locals popped out of their houses, waved, and said, "Hello!" with a smile. One man hustled over to his cow and proudly insisted that I photograph him.

A much cuter picture would have been of the two-year-old girl hiding behind a rough-hewn chair—her eyes were bulging over its backboard as I walked by. But alas, she screamed when I aimed my camera at her. Her big sister trotted over and smiled at me as she picked her up.

We all had fun but the experience also had a serious side. As a Westerner, I was from a region that many Southeast Asians associate with power. Being nice was the safest way to deal with a mysterious Caucasian man.

Rituals for maintaining safety have abounded in many traditional Southeast Asian societies. Supernatural beings must be pleased. The Thai spirit house is a famous example, which I saw all over its country. People install a miniature residence for the land's spirit in front of homes, offices, restaurants, gas stations, and even car dealerships. They place flowers, food, and drinks in it with pristine politeness to keep it happy. This adds artistry to the neighborhood, which sometimes extends beyond. I saw enchanted cities of spirit houses just outside of towns' entrances. Some people think many spirits hang around communities' entrances and that these places harbor unusual amounts of unseen power. The mélanges of shrines to keep the spirits mellow projected so many vibrant shapes and colors among the greenery that I often stopped to enjoy them for a few minutes. The locals had rendered potential danger beautiful.

Spirit houses also added charm to many neighborhoods I've walked through in Vietnam, though the surroundings would have been appealing enough without them. Swaying palm trees surrounded light blue, yellow, and pink homes of local people. These buildings and their yards alternated with small open fields where cows grazed. The spirit houses were mounted on walls of homes and fences. With straight walls and a single gabled roof, they were plainer than the Thai versions, but they still added to the profusion of forms and colors. By resembling the local homes, they made it seem that many types of souls blended into a luxuriant environment.

Throughout traditional Southeast Asia, spirits in the land, rivers, mountains, and trees must be respected. Souls of people who have passed away need to be kept happy. The gracious rice mother, who gives birth to the crops that nourish people, must be thanked. Thai ceremonies are numerous and beautiful. So are Balinese, Javanese, Cambodian, Malay, Vietnamese, Laotian, and Burmese. This region has turned rituals into some of the world's finest artistic traditions.

In Bali in 1991, I watched a ceremony to straighten out the world. People conducted a long procession to the sea to leave offerings because they have traditionally believed that this calms a giant turtle under the land who can cause earthquakes when moving. I leaned against a building on a town's main street and savored the colors as the cortege passed. Slender women in long white gowns balanced bamboo baskets full of flowers, banana leaves, and fruit on their heads. Men paraded in shiny blue and pure white silk shirts, and teams of them carried gleaming bronze gongs on poles. The feast of hues conjoined in a flow that was both lively and relaxed. It was all so pretty that the unseen spirits which can enrich or harm a community must have enjoyed it too.

A person with a strictly modern mindset might scoff at this way of thinking. Don't animism and rituals for placating spirits represent a primitive mentality? Where are the scientific explanations? Furthermore, Southeast Asian countries have produced far less literature than India and China have. Are Southeast Asian cultures less advanced?

These questions come from modern Western and traditional Indian and Chinese perspectives, but Southeast Asia is best appreciated on its own terms. It has its own logic—people there have traditionally held their own assumptions about how the world is integrated, and about what mental associations promote the most well-being. Folks often perform rituals with beauty that defies Western classifications. Flowers, sumptuous arts and crafts, music that is equally energetic and calm, aromatic food, and elegant clothing mix in a stream of grace, liveliness, and tolerance that's as good an ideal for civilized life as a Western civic forum. India has been called an assault on the senses; much of Southeast Asia is a massage for them.

During my artistic heritage tour of central Java, we ate dinner and had a gamelan lesson in a 150-year-old home that was built around a small courtyard. A gamelan is a traditional Indonesian ensemble of instruments that people have played in temples, royal courts, and village ceremonies. No two orchestras are exactly the same, but the most predominant instruments are bronze xylophones, gongs, and kettledrums. Flutes and stringed instruments that people bow are also common. All tones mesh into an atmosphere that seems both spiritual and sensual. As we dined, the musicians practiced and the notes from the xylophones and gongs chimed through the warm evening air. They blended with the flickering torches so that all impressions seemed to fuse into animated energy that pervaded our surroundings. The chicken satays with thick, tangy peanut sauce and the eggs which had been cooked in spicy chili sauce had flavors that also seemed both animated and suave. The slinky cats slipping around our legs hoping for handouts added to this feeling that all life forms intertwine in a field of energy that is both potent and graceful.

We then proceeded to the instruments for the lesson. Our host told us to avoid stepping over them because each has a spirit that requires respect. I walked around one of the xylophones and sat on the reed mat behind it, and the lead musician explained that all of its keys are numbered. He played a sequence of notes that made up a melody and told us to practice it together. I had been used to playing guitar as a solo performer and in rock and jazz bands in which each musician could be heard clearly. For me, listening to each person express his own personality has been one of the most enjoyable things about American popular music. But all the gamelan instruments melded into a larger whole which none of us stood out from. All our notes merged and filled the entire courtyard, and they resonated with the torchlights and the aromas of the food. I was sitting next to the leader; whenever I hit an incorrect note he softly sang the numbers of the proper ones, "Three-two-three-two," in the same slow and steady rhythm that the orchestra played in. Though the music seemed energized, I found it warm and welcoming because I felt unconditionally accepted by the whole community and its traditions.

Many traditional Southeast Asians have considered their etiquette and rituals hallmarks of civilization. The artistry and frequency of rites remind them that they live in an integrated society and that social obligations are precious. Some of them consider Westerners, Indians, and Chinese loud. Some Thai artists before the 20th century portrayed Westerners with beer-bellies and bulbous noses, and Indians with hairy faces. Both have gaping mouths as though Thais imagined noises booming from them that would have scared off every fish within a mile.

In 2012 I watched a line of monks and novices begging for food in the morning in the historic Laotian town Luang Prabang. This is a daily ritual all over Buddhist Southeast Asia. The holy men in cascading orange robes slowly walked in a long line down the street. Secular folks kneeled in a row to place small packets of rice in the monks' bowls as they passed, and the religious procession rippled as gracefully as the Mekong River three blocks away. The line of holy men slowly moved past the line of locals so that both looked like two longboats flowing past each other. The lay people received merit for a better life and afterlife, and the monks were able to eat. These gracious little acts and this pretty ritual help society cohere.

Southeast Asian rituals are often fun. The locals in Luang Prabang quietly chatted and giggled before and after feeding the monks as though it was an opportunity to enjoy each other as much as a way to gain merit. In Thai New Year water fights, people toss etiquette out the window and douse each other. Many people before modernization in the late 20th century believed that the surges of water magically encouraged the monsoon to come, and everybody had laughs in the process.

People can even have a good time when political elites show off their authority. Rulers from Thailand to Indonesia have sponsored dances, theatrical performances, and processions for more than 1,000 years to project their power. Some have displayed themselves in elephant parades, with the majestic animals draped in fabrics that radiate red, gold, and silver. Equally regal are boat processions with long, narrow royal barges, whose bows and sterns curve upwards as gracefully as a royal court dancer's fingers. Artists often carve the bow to resemble the head of a fish, a dragon, or a *naga* (a serpent from Indian mythology which locals combined with their own snake cults, and with dragon lore from China—it's often associated with fertility and nature's power, and can thus bring crops and wealth to people who respect it and harm to those who don't).

Spectators lining streets and rivers wear their best clothes, gossip, crack jokes, and savor delicious recipes.

But rituals in Southeast Asia often have serious sides too. Many people believe that they're infused with supernatural power. Since ancient times people throughout the region have felt that the king and other eminent people wield it. The historian Tony Day, in *Fluid Iron*, noted that some artworks portray violence because religious art and rituals are associated with prime energies in nature, which both establish political states and generate life. They can strengthen the order of society, but their power has no bounds and it can destroy as well as create. Be on good terms with it or else!

I witnessed this side of rituals during my 1991 Indonesian trip. Three other Americans, our local guide, and I drove to a central Javanese village in the evening, and we sat in a line of chairs in the central square. Two xylophone players began to repeat two notes half a tone apart to induce a hypnotic state. Eight other men went into trances and began to dance. Suddenly other men plunged a foot-long spike through each one's cheek, and the well-traveled Manhattan attorney on my left gasped. We shook hands with them afterwards and they were entirely gentle—their grips were soft, their eyes were warm, and their faces showed no tension. The performers briefly brought potentially destructive forces into the community and then controlled them. Traditionally, people have felt that this kind of event can increase the political and metaphysical power of the person who sponsors it, as well as strengthen village harmony and its land's ability to generate crops.

Rituals in Southeast Asia reflect its rich cultural and natural landscapes. They mix a wide range of experiences and messages, including political authority, social cohesion, spirituality, fun, artistry, and fear of unseen dangers. Rituals' associations range from refined aesthetics to political contention. They also vary from spiritual and social connectedness to raw power. Many types of messages and sensibilities are interwoven in ceremonies, and this has inspired endless varieties of art. While some Temiar trance dances have emphasized soft swaying motions, the performance I saw in Java became violent for a while, though peace was restored in the end. Yet many other traditional Javanese dances are known for being slow and refined. Southeast Asia never settled on a few simple forms, like ancient Greek temples' colonnades and the Christian cross, as models of eternal truth. No single form can encompass its abundance. Tolerance of diversity and enjoyment of the moment have helped its cultures hang together, and this engenders much beauty and fun.

I've often found combinations of elegance and fun in people's behavior. In the first Thai restaurant I ever ate in, a Caucasian-American man at the next table asked the waitress if the meat was fresh and she chirped, "Yes. We just killed the dog!" When she went back to the kitchen, he told his friend, "That lady's a joker!" Yes, but I noticed that she gently caressed the backs of the empty chairs she passed, and her hand flowed in the slow, fluid motions of a court dancer. Shifts between esprit and refinement in Southeast Asia happen in endless varieties.

I walked through a temple in Chiang Mai and spotted a man painting one of the sculpted elephants on its main shrine. He quietly consented when I asked if I could photograph him, but then climbed onto the elephant's back and hammed it up by waving and flashing a big smile. Elephants are traditionally considered sacred in Thailand, but so is having fun. Apparently he didn't think he was being disrespectful.

While I was buying silver in a shop outside of Yogyakarta, the two women behind the counter and I conversed in the little Indonesian that I knew. They asked me the standard questions people ask visitors from other countries, like, "Where are you from?" Both smiled and spoke softly. My tour guide had told me the Javanese word for "Thank you" and said that using it would surprise people, so when I bade them good-bye I said, "Matur nuwun." Both women's mouths popped open and their eyes widened with joy. One spritely exclaimed, "Matur nuwun!" After I had walked away from the counter area, I could still hear them singing it in jubilant tones.

I had a racier encounter with a shop-woman on the way home from that trip. The plane stopped on an island called Biak, which is a little north of the Indonesian side of the New Guinean landmass. Our guide had told us that shops there sold penis sheaths, which are made out of gourd and painted. Men in many traditional societies in New Guinea have worn them. It seemed like a good conversation piece to take home so I looked for one, but couldn't find any. I finally asked the young woman from Java who managed the shop. Being a bit bashful about the subject, I spoke quietly and she misheard me. "Peanuts? You want to eat?" I said that I wasn't hungry in Indonesian, but my vocabulary quickly thinned when I tried to tell her what I did want. I thought of drawing a picture but couldn't figure out what to do without being obscene. I finally just pointed straight down. She burst into a smile and said, "Ya! Ya!" and blithely led me to a box under a bottom shelf. I chose one and she wrapped it in a newspaper while still smiling. What impressed me was her perfect mixture of joy and elegance. She obviously had fun but retained all the composure that traditional Javanese value.

Figure 1. Thai lacquer painting, like much other traditional Southeast Asian art, is both animated and graceful.

Most traditional Southeast Asian art isn't as linear or as focused on static geometric shapes as classical Western styles are; it expresses a different world instead. It often depicts flows of animated energies in the environment. Ideas of energy flows have inspired a lot of creativity in the region because people have associated them with many experiences that have been common there since ancient times. All experiences together make Southeast Asia unique:

- A river's flow. Southeast Asians have migrated and formed communities along rivers for thousands of years. Several great rivers on the mainland begin in the Himalayas, and when their snows melt in the spring, the waterways begin to swell. People in the lowlands have often experienced this as a surge of life that bestows fish and nourishes crops.

  Travel along rivers has often been easier than slogs through jungles teeming with tigers and thieves. Many people have thus conceived their landscape as a flow on waterways that undulate rather than as a line between Point A and Point B. Even their boats embody these forms—many are long, narrow, and curvy.

  I took a two-day boat trip along the Mekong, from Luang Prabang to the Thai border, and I felt as though I was enveloped in nature's energies. The mountains that rose on both sides formed a continuous wave of peaks which seemed to wriggle like a snake. Above them, the clouds billowed in these forms.

- Nature's life forms. During that Mekong journey, the trees and plants on both banks didn't stand out as distinct entities. All their foliage blended into vibrant rivers of green between the waterway and the mountains beyond. While walking through jungles, I often noticed that trees' branches and roots curved and twisted as they spread out. Water, land, wood, greenery, and sky undulated, and all together often seemed to fuse into a flow of nature's power.

- Snakes have had special meanings in cultures all over the world because they're easy to associate with nature's energies. They slither into and out of the earth, through trees' foliage, and in rivers. They also shed their skins whole. Their movements thereby seem to transcend all limits, and their shapes and sliding motions make them easy to associate with sex. People have thus identified serpents with primal energies which generate life.

Many Christian traditions have demoted snakes, insisting that only God and Jesus hold ultimate power over nature. In Genesis, Yahweh condemned the serpent to crawl on its belly and took away its ability to speak for tempting Eve with a fruit. But people in many traditional Southeast Asian cultures have felt that their environment has too many life forms to be completely subjected to one being who lays down the law for everyone (the Malay world, however, later embraced Islam—we'll explore this fascinating subject later). Nature is pluralistic, and snakes have retained their proud places in the scheme of things. Many Thai and Laotian Buddhist temples have foundation myths about the land's naga (a mythical serpent) being given a gift before people began to build. From then on, the Buddha respected the naga and it protected the temple from evil spirits. Nature's many souls operate in harmony.

Another popular myth that expresses this harmony is about a naga protecting the Buddha. The latter was meditating when a heavy rain started to fall. The naga spread its hood over him so that he could continue without being interrupted. I've seen hundreds of sculptures of this scene in Cambodian, Thai, and Laotian temples. The serpent's hood (often with seven heads) surges over the Buddha so that it resembles the power in the growth of nature's life forms. But at the same time, the hood forms a graceful arch that softens nature's vitality.

Snakes resemble rivers, fish, branches, vines, roots, mountains, and clouds. They all assume wavy forms that are sometimes graceful and sometimes gushing with power.

- The annual rice growing cycle. In the summer and fall, the monsoon unleashes the sky's might on the land and fertilizes it. I was riding a bike in Hue, Vietnam during the rainy season in 2012. The grey sky had been threatening all morning, but I wanted to savor the relaxed historic town. Around noon it began to sprinkle. I didn't mess around when the rain increased—I shot under the first awning in sight. Two young men ran a custom window shop there and they invited me inside to wait out the storm. The water was now coming down in sheets so that three seconds outside would have drenched me like a river rat. Southeast Asians learn that they can't impose their wills on nature, so they cooperate with each other to make its bursts of energy livable and fun.

Figure 2. Stylized nagas slither down the roofs of many temples in northern Thailand.

Between the storms, farmers all over Southeast Asia grow rice in fields with raised edges that hold the water. Wet rice farming requires a lot of coordination between people, and the work is painstaking. Fields need weeding, water must be allocated to each paddy, water levels need to be kept at the right level for the rice as it grows, fields have to be drained before the harvest, crops must be quickly harvested, and threshing has to be done. All able-bodied people share these labors.

Figure 3. The foot of the main stairway to a temple in Laos.
A naga forms the entire banister on each side.

So sometimes life's tempos are slow and repetitive, and they're sudden and dramatic in other times, but people experience them together. Life is traditionally communal. People's lives flow together within nature's rhythms.

- Religious ceremonies and processions harmonize communities with spirits and nature's energies. People often amble slowly in them, and in this way, they resemble the rivers that their ancestors settled by thousands of years ago.

All these experiences together have encouraged ideas that reality is an abundant field of energy, which people communally live in. Their societies have been different from ancient Athens, where columned temples and stoas embodied simple linear forms as ideals of eternal order. Natural environments in Southeast Asia seem infused with power, which generated all the densely intermeshed life forms. This energy bestows rains, pregnancies, crops, and fish, but it can suddenly become deadly.

Southeast Asians have thus created countless art forms that express energy but soften it with grace. Artists portray nature's unpredictable powers in ways that render them safe enough to live with. Throughout the region, wood carvings, batiks, dances, processions, temples, mosques, palaces, and statues of gods and the Buddha appear both animated and gentle. All these arts balance both senses of the world.

Thai art emphasizes long, slender, and curvy forms. They grace everything from temples and Buddha statues to furniture and silverware. I find it some of the most enjoyable art in the world (we'll savor it in Part Two).

Many Thai restaurants' servers' eyes widened when I said that I didn't want rice. A lot of traditional Southeast Asians consider rice sacred. It's the ultimate gift from nature. In parts of Indonesia and the mainland, people have avoided harvesting with the sickle because its imposing blade seems harsh. Instead, they hide a small knife in the palm of the hand to avoid scaring the gracious rice goddess. People deal with the flow of life by being polite.

Traditional Malay cuisine also often treats rice as the essence of civilized living. The Malay academic Zainal Kling wrote that the most important part of a meal is boiled rice and that all other foods are side dishes (*lauk*).[3] Rice and *lauk* should be eaten together, and a person who only eats *lauk* (whether it's beef, chicken, or fish) is sometimes called a cat because only a carnivorous animal would consume meat by itself.

It can be easy for a Caucasian man to idealize Southeast Asian cultures, and people there have told me that they're not always as nice to each other as they are to me. Most of their societies are hierarchical and folks in them often compete for status. Sometimes people behave politely to mask competition beneath the surface. A Laotian man that I met complained that people organizing a Buddhist festival at their local temple spent more time vying for authority over the proceedings than arranging them.

Andrew Walker, in *Tai Lands and Thailand,* wrote about residents of a northern Thai village gossiping about the local abbot's fondness for alcohol, cigarettes, and women. When young women gathered at the temple to take part in a religious ceremony, one pointed her rear end at an imaginary camera and invited the abbot to have a good peek while the others giggled. Walker noted that rituals and sacred places can be sources of tension in Thailand because people unify their worlds with them.[4] Because they're the venues in which folks come together, disputes and rivalries can break out in them.

Smiles in Thailand are not always happy. I was eating in a Thai restaurant in California when a short thirty-something man introduced himself as the owner. "I hope you like our food." I told him that I did but he still seemed nervous, perhaps because his restaurant was brand new. I tried to put him at ease by adding, "I like all Thai food. The only bad Thai restaurant I've ever been in was up in Berkeley." He smiled the second I said *bad,* as though the word carried harmful magical effects that he wanted to neutralize. Many smiles in Thailand are used to avoid confrontations.

Contrasts between graceful surfaces and potential conflicts beneath them encourage people in many Southeast Asian societies to emphasize self-discipline and the avoidance of intense expressions of feelings. The anthropologist Clifford Geertz noted that traditional Javanese have stressed a distinction between being refined and rough. The former, *alus,* means being polished, subtle, and spiritual. The latter, *kasar,* is voraciousness, crudeness, and loudness, and it's the antithesis of politeness, which human societies require in order to function.[5] I watched two women having a dialog in a TV commercial in central Java. An obese middle-aged black woman was fretting about the mosquitoes while frantically waving her hands. A slender and comely young Javanese lady with a gentle smile then told her about an insect repellent. In the next scene the first woman was joyful and waving her hands as much as before. I was struck by this sharp contrast between emotional extremes and control—the latter is considered Javanese. The grace is usually delightful to see but it's not always carefree, and it can be used to justify the social hierarchy and confirm prejudices against people that are labeled as outsiders.

The shifts between esprit and refinement that I've enjoyed watching are thus expected to be done with discretion. The anthropologist Nancy Eberhardt studied Shan villagers in northern Thailand, near the Burmese border, and she noted that parents there sometimes call young children *hai*. This word in this context means *wild* and *uncontrolled*, and it's sometimes applied to spirits in the forest. People sometimes use it for a baby's leg kicking and impulsive grasping for things within arm's reach. Eberhardt said that parents tolerate this kind of behavior in young children, but they expect them to slowly gain control over their appetites.[6] Polite expressions and respectful salutations for elders are thus often among the first words and gestures that children learn.

I always enjoyed seeing two-year-olds in Thai temples placing the palms of their hands together and bowing in front of the main altar. Eberhardt said that children who refuse to join their hands to thank an adult for a gift often provoke remarks that they must be from the mountains. I was impressed by the graceful, fluid motions of such young kids as they bowed; Thais learn from an early age that this is one of the main aspects of being human.

Expressions of graceful animation thus have many levels of meaning in Southeast Asia. These expressions infuse art, rituals, livelihood, and etiquette, and they combine ideas of personhood, morality, supernatural power, danger, political authority, social hierarchy, beauty, fun, and abundant nature. This mixture cannot be reduced to one image or represented abstractly, but it connects many experiences in a logic that's uniquely Southeast Asian. It must be lived rather than shoehorned into a formula. It's experienced in the wealth of lively folk arts, pretty food presentations, infinitely varied flavors, winsome smiles, spirited rituals, floral temple offerings, and graceful Buddha statues. Then there are the soft and cheerful voices, clean and well-behaved children, and elders with soft-spoken dignity. There's also the competition for social status behind the smiles. The glimmering temples and mosques, singing birds, flowing rivers, pounding monsoons, innumerable shades of green, and all-enveloping tropical sun add even more abundant life. All meld into endless varieties of the flow of nature's energy, and they allow people limitless ways to enjoy it if social higher-ups don't victimize them.

On the other hand, many people fear stepping outside of what's polite and familiar. Most areas outside of Southeast Asia's biggest cities were sparsely populated before the 20th century (Vietnam's Red River area and some parts of Java and Bali were exceptions). Villages are often cozy but they used to be surrounded by hinterlands which tigers and bandits prowled in. Many folktales reflect centuries of needing to be alert at all times. An old Cambodian story warns people to avoid talking to their spouses in bed at night. The careless husband blabbers and a thief crouching under their stilt home overhears where their jewelry is hidden and scurries off with it.

Many traditional Southeast Asian societies have sharply distinguished what is safe from what's dangerous. People associate the former with the family (especially Mother, who is often seen as a model of virtue), the temple, and the rice farming community. They envision them within a circle of safety and identify the latter with zones beyond its embrace, particularly the howling forests and mountains. Three people who sent me emails after my 2007 trip (two Cambodians and one Thai) told me that they worried about me because I traveled too much. One said, "You should rest at home for a while."

Violence can erupt in many Southeast Asian countries with astonishing speed and ferocity, and Thailand has frequently had a high homicide rate. Thais often don't have the room to express wrath that Westerners do. We can sometimes do it gradually—first with a frown or a raised voice, then with a warning, and then with a push. Westerners can do several things to settle arguments without maiming each other. But many Thais lack these ways to express anger because they've been taught to avoid conflicts, so they can let emotions build up until they boil over. William J. Klausner, in *Reflections on Thai Culture*, wrote that he often saw a dramatic leap between a smile and a knife thrust, and that many people gossip and backbite because they only have these indirect outlets for repressed aggression.[7] Some people who feel cheated in business or romance use guns to settle the score. Political conflicts in many Southeast Asian countries have sometimes turned deadly quickly. Life in many areas of the region often alternates between graceful flows which people try to maintain and sudden turmoil.

In 2010 Bangkok became a battleground between the army and pro-testers against the government, and 1,800 casualties resulted. The modern white buildings and sparkling golden-roofed temples were suddenly enveloped in black smoke. However, I saw no signs of the violence when I returned in 2012. The lines of street food vendors and crowds of shoppers meshed as smoothly as ever and nobody mentioned the recent past. People stayed in their safe worlds as though they wanted to prevent it from returning.

But violent rallies burst out again in late 2013 and they resulted in over 400 casualties. The demonstrators were accusing the prime minister of corruption and they insisted that she resign. The military ultimately staged a coup and detained hundreds of politicians, journalists, and professors. Many journalists have said that Thai politics became increasingly contentiousness within the last ten years. This problem has been fueled by wide gaps between the rich and poor and by stresses of modern life which have made it harder to uphold the old etiquette and to appreciate the traditional art and rituals.[8] Some journalists worry that the country is now politically unstable. It has been more peaceful since the coup, but this might be because the junta has cracked down on demonstrations and suppressed criticism.

Political corruption in Southeast Asia makes life trying for many of its people. The journalist Joel Brinkley wrote that a lot of Cambodians must pay bribes for basic schooling and medical care while their government's ringleaders party on in Phnom Penh mansions as big as 60,000 square feet.

In 2012 I met a former teacher in Phnom Penh who said that his ex-colleagues were paid so little that some sold students answers to tests. High school toughs told him, "If you don't give me a good grade I will hurt you." Powerless against students whose dads had political clout, he left the profession and became a taxi driver.

A teacher in a monastery in Vietnam invited me into his classroom and asked me to join his students at their desks. They were all males in their late teens. When the guy on my left started thumbing through my *Lonely Planet* guidebook on Vietnam, I picked up his textbook. Each chapter began with a picture of a political figure, and Ho Chi Minh's face dignified the first one. I figured that the students were being fed political orthodoxy. A short middle-aged man suddenly barged in and gravely said something to the teacher. The latter immediately told me with a meek smile, "You need to go." I headed for the door and the Party lackey looked at me with a "What the hell are you doing here?" expression. Vietnam's government seems to keep a tight rein on what's taught so that nobody will challenge it.

Several Southeast Asian countries are plagued by governments that enforce status quos in which a small percentage of elites lord it over the rest. Most people underneath them must scratch for livings. This region has a long history of colonial and local regimes exploiting its natural bounty and using their wealth on display items like sprawling villas to project their own prestige instead of diversifying their economies so that more people can thrive.

China has already constructed several dams along the Mekong, and it plans to build many more in order to garner hydroelectric power for its mighty southern cities. The governments of Laos and Cambodia are also planning to build dams along the lower Mekong, and much of the hydroelectricity will be sold to Thailand and Vietnam to provide power for their growing urban centers. Ecologist worry that flattening the river's natural ebbs and flows will disrupt migratory and reproductive patterns of the fish that over 60 million people in the region live on, and that this will threaten the existence of many villages.[9] Palm oil plantations and government-sponsored logging have despoiled a lot of forests in Southeast Asia—profits usually flow to cronies and corporations, and many locals have had to leave their ancestral lands for the swelling cities.

Southeast Asian societies are thus complex. Some of the most ravishing beauty in the world and social hierarchies that are often exploitive intertwine in them. Exploring the region has given me many of the most savory moments of my life, and it's immersed me in some of the most memorable human drama I've ever seen.

I often felt as though I was seeing two different realities in all the countries I visited during my 2007 trip. One seemed like paradise and the other was crammed into political and financial systems with narrow mentalities and sharp distinctions between haves and have-nots. This second reality prevents people from finding the first, but the amount of enchantment I saw around the world taught me that the more cultural wealth people discover, the more their perspectives can expand beyond one-dimensional views of humanity that are based on status and money, and into a world in which all societies and people expose each other's full wealth.

Each chapter in this book will thus open horizons into other ways of seeing the world so that the perspective will be as large as possible before you reach the method in Part Two and the manual after the conclusion. In the first two parts of this book, you will see how Southeast Asia's little-known cultural wealth can help people think in ways that they are not currently used to. You'll also tour better-known societies in Europe and explore their histories. By journeying in familiar and less familiar places and times, you will be able to appreciate any view of the world, and then expand beyond it so that you can always enjoy ever more creative vistas.

I made this book longer than most in order to fully share my experience of exploring so many places and times through several media, and to show how much potential for creativity and well-being people have when they're not oppressed, attacked, or facing an environmental catastrophe. Since our world is now globalized, this is an optimal time for a big picture of how rewarding our human landscape can become, especially when political, economic, and ecological problems are so pressing that it can seem impossible to see beyond them. Looking to the highest levels of well-being that we can aspire for can enable us to think beyond conventions and find new solutions, and inspire us to work cohesively to implement them.

By exploring an unusual mixture of cultures and temporal periods, we can enhance our abilities to enjoy the world for the rest of our lives. We'll experience a way to see it that's not bound to one convention or culture. This book shows, not a mere new perspective, but freedom from any perspective, and the ability to always create bigger views which can deepen happiness and help us surmount problems. Instead of strictly being servants of one dominant system of ideas, we can realize our full human potential and enjoy an endless love affair with the world.

PART ONE

CAMBODIA

SECTION ONE

EXPANDING HORIZONS INTO ANOTHER WORLD

CHAPTER 2

THE DEPTHS OF ANGKOR WAT'S SOUL

THE BALMY AIR embraced me as soon as I stepped from the plane onto the runway of Siem Reap's airport. I crawled into a little taxi and the driver, with thinning grey hair and a voice as quiet as a zephyr, said, "Welcome to Cambodia." Both gentle greetings immediately made me feel affection for this ancient land and its people.

At seven o'clock the next morning, I darted down to the hotel's front desk and hired a driver to take me around Angkor for the next two weeks. We drove over Siem Reap's dusty roads and passed lines of children riding old black bikes to school. Mom-and-pop grocery shops, wooden homes, and faded French colonial buildings joined the greenery in a relaxing ménage of colors. The rolling rhythms of soft hues felt like caresses as we rode by.

The town's genial feel quickly changed to dense forest. Khmer kings erected breathtaking temples there for five centuries to command an empire that they hewed from the jungle. This area had loomed in my imagination since I was a boy. Angkor Wat is so big and its system of towers, courtyards, and sculptures is so intricate that it seems more like a dream than a building that people constructed back in the early 12th century. I always wondered how they lived and how they saw the world.

As monumental as Angkor Wat is, it's only the tip of the pyramid (I won't say the more conventional *iceberg* because that's the last thing you'll find in Cambodia's steamy climate). Angkor was once the largest city in the world, and many other kings besides Angkor Wat's builder, Suryavarman II, erected huge temples there. They spread over the plain by Lake Tonle Sap's north shore and greeted the water as it rose each year to irrigate the crops.

While Suryavarman II reigned, France's King Louis VI and Abbot Suger constructed what many art historians consider to be the first

Gothic building, the choir and west façade of the basilica of St. Denis, which rises a little north of Paris. Khmers couldn't build arches or fashion stained glass windows, and thus didn't create the large inner spaces and glorious light shows in cathedrals. But their temples' sizes, complexity, symmetry, balance between elegance and grandeur, mixtures of Indian and local ideas, and varieties of sculpture make them as engrossing. Both types of buildings integrated different but equally rich perspectives of the world.

Angkor Wat emerged as suddenly as an apparition. Its towers punctuated the dark foliage like diamonds and soared above the treetops.

Its visage intensified as we approached the parking lot across the road. The massive grey walls seemed to spread over the whole earth, and the towers in the center thrust into the heavens. Angkor Wat looked like a city and a mountain range at the same time.

It seemed too supernatural to be categorized, and the king probably wanted it that way. He built this frontage to overwhelm all who would see it. Farmers tending their rice fields and cozying in their stilt homes would have had no doubt about its sacredness or who was the boss.

Historians have seen different reasons for its construction. It was likely a mausoleum for Suryavarman II and a temple for the Hindu god Vishnu (Suryavarman's soul supposedly joined his when he passed away). The building faces west but most Khmer temples point to the east. Khmers associated the west with both Vishnu and the afterlife. The king might have assumed Vishnu's role in the Hindu Trimurti as the sustainer of the universe, between Brahma the creator and Shiva the destroyer—a dream team to identify with if you want to run an empire.

Other historians say that Angkor Wat's measurements correspond with astronomy and Indian myths about gods. They concluded that it might have been both an observatory and a giant map of the universe. The art historian Eleanor Mannikka wrote that the sun rises over different towers on important days, including summer and winter solstices.[1] Ancient Indians and Khmers identified Vishnu with the sun, so Angkor Wat was probably related to its movements.

But people at Angkor Wat probably did more than observe the sun. Mannikka found several repetitions of the numbers 28, 32, 45, and 108 in its measurements. These numbers symbolized Hindu ideas of gods and movements of stars, planets, and the moon. She also noted that the creation of the universe was carved on the temple's eastern side, where the sun rises. Angkor Wat's plan thus might have integrated the cosmos, the forces that created it, the state's order, and the king's power. If so, it was the center of the whole shebang as the Khmers saw it (some of Mannikka's ideas are controversial, but since these numbers occur several times, they probably did express Khmer ideas of the universe to some extent).

Others have seen Angkor Wat as a spiritual quest. A walk from the entrance to the center might symbolize the soul's journey towards the source of creation.[2] The main tower represents Mt. Meru, which ancient Khmers and Indians saw as the center of the universe, where the rain-bringing god, Indra, presided in his bejeweled palace. A procession to the temple's center might be a journey to the most meaningful and powerful place in the universe.

This temple has many facets because the Khmers were unifying their perspectives of the world with it as their empire was growing. It expresses the scale of their kingdom during its glory days.

A broad flight of stairs lifted me from the road to the bridge that crosses the more-than 650-foot-wide moat. I then gazed across the moat at the more-than 700-foot-long entrance of the first enclosure. Three multi-tiered towers crown its central section, long columned corridors project from each end, and a stately pavilion with a gabled roof climaxes the far end of each corridor. The whole section is large and symmetrical, but the towers and reliefs of Hindu gods and female dancers embedded in dense vegetal patterns (which are carved on walls, columns, and lintels over doorways) are elegant. This structure impeccably combines power and refinement.

I entered this building's central section through a portico fronted by a colonnade and crowned with stacks of tiled roofs, but the darkness that suddenly enveloped me contrasted with the opulent exterior. A long, cavernous gallery extended from each side of the entrance hall. Priests in the galleries accepted offerings and recited prayers for worshippers who respectfully kneeled. The smell of incense, the dusky interior, and the huge stones meshed in an aura of mysterious power.

I walked out the other side and into the main courtyard and found it even more dramatic than the first enclosure's entrance. The central towers loomed ahead and a broad and straight causeway with naga-shaped balustrades on each side led towards them. This was an ideal place for royal processions. The blazing sun must have given them even more luster. The power that I felt from it can encourage people to think that the spires transmit the energy that created the universe.

The excitement kept growing after I crossed the courtyard. I arrived at the steps of a large cross-shaped terrace in front of the central towers. This platform punctuates the transition from the causeway to the main section. It would have been ideal for ceremonies, which thousands of people might have gawked at. The historian L. P. Briggs felt that people conducted public rituals there. Female dancers might have performed with sparkling crowns and tinkling jewelry. They couldn't have had a more stirring backdrop.

After crossing the platform, I ascended the middle section's front steps, entered its portico, and reached two corridors that branch off to each side. They make up one of the four passageways that form a rectangle around the center. My procession had abruptly changed from the huge open courtyard to long covered corridors that surround the main towers. I was about to enter another world.

All four walls around the towers are covered with stone friezes in a style that's elevated far above the lives of the farmers who lived nearby. The faces of the figures are so aloof that they seem too superhuman to notice ordinary people. The carvings are about 6 1/2 feet high, and they extend about 2,000 feet around the temple. The sculptures illustrate four themes: battles between Hindu gods and demonic beings opposed to them, epic battles between warriors for the throne of India, the creation of the universe according to Hindu mythology, and Suryavarman's authority. These whopping subjects and the enormous space they cover make the carvings seem regal rather than intimate. The friezes are key messages that the great king wanted to give all who enter.

The raised floor makes the friezes even more sublime. It's about eight feet above the ground, and the space between the carvings and outer edges is wide. To see them from the soil, I had to stand several yards away, but I couldn't observe details from there. The reliefs were not made for casual viewing; they demand full attention. It's not known whether only priests used the corridors to perform rituals, or if a larger public was allowed in. But whoever walked through them must have felt deep reverence.

Plays of light animated the corridors even more. Many shades of green foliage flickered behind the outer columns as I walked through. The pillars created shifting combinations of light and shade on the friezes and floor as the sun blazed. The creative forces of nature seemed to energize the mighty carvings. The sculptures don't just tell stories— they radiate power.

People have usually read the carvings counterclockwise in the last 100 years, but the Angkor Wat specialist Vittorio Roveda said that this is only a convention. Scholars don't agree about the direction or the starting point, but since the action in the carvings moves counterclockwise, I followed the herd and began at the entrance portico. I thus turned right and explored the southwestern wall. It features a mythical battle in which two armies fight for India's throne. Closely packed lines of soldiers march, chariots race, furious horses and elephants charge, warriors stab with spears, and bodies pile up. Burly men close enough to hug thrust their spears at each other. The huge panel crowded with intense action can make visitors wonder if they will disintegrate before finishing the circuit.

But the pavilion at the end of the corridor has a rarity at Angkor Wat: a scene of ordinary people's lives. It's a celebration with dragon-headed boats rowed by oarsmen, possibly on Tonle Sap. On the shore people dance energetically, a woman cradles a toddler, and two ladies under a pavilion take food from a kneeling servant. Here is that timeless mixture that's common in Southeast Asia: a religious festival, fun, food, families together, and ideas that they are all associated with spiritual power and political leaders. Glory to the gods and the king!

When I turned the corner, I was back to more serious business because I was approaching the great Suryavarman II. Every important type of person in that time is carved in an epic procession. Ministers, princes or governors, religious ascetics, and upper class women make it grand enough. But the army marches in it too, with commanders presiding on top of elephants (their ranks are identified by the number of parasols raised over them). The king sits on an elaborate throne with naga-headed feet. He is on a larger scale than everyone else, and he's giving orders to officials and holy men while attendants fan him. Everyone kneels around him as he sits under 14 parasols (a number that signifies his supreme rank).

One group of soldiers stands out from the others. They sport long and wild hair, and they have often been called Thais because the word *Syam* is inscribed near them. The Khmers might have been distinguishing themselves from people they considered less civilized. But Roveda wrote that *Syam* might have referred to dark-skinned people in general, and that these soldiers were probably mercenaries or Khmer residents of a neighboring land which may or may not have been where Thailand later developed as a nation. Whoever they were, the striking differences between types of soldiers highlight the army's size and the procession's scope—the army is cosmic rather than local. The parade is on an epic scale that reinforces Angkor Wat's larger-than-life grandeur.

Suryavarman II appears a second time, grandstanding on an elephant and surrounded by a forest of parasols (15 this time) and soldiers carrying long spears. He's on the same superhuman scale. Historians say that this wall has the first Khmer pictures of a known person in a sacred setting, but Mr. Big's features look more idealized than realistic. This early portrait shows the king rivaling the gods in majesty.

The second major panel on this wall stupefies even more than the first. It depicts souls in heaven and hell. The blessed occupy the top and the damned suffer on the bottom. In the center, the Hindu god of death and judgment, Yama, sits on his ugly buffalo and wields clubs with his enormous number of arms. He directs the souls' fates at the moment of death. Yama dominates the panel in this Khmer Divine Comedy, as Suryavarman II rules the first. Both are associated because they stand for the social and cosmic order. Whoever walked through there got a resounding message: Obey the king and heavenly bliss is yours; disobey and be vanquished. Extremes of grace and cruelty are close on this wall. Don't make the king mad.

Inscriptions list sins and the tortures that they earn. Thirty-two hells await specific types of miscreants. Twelve are reserved for thieves, and stealers of land, horses, footwear, and rice have their own real estate.[3] Many punishments are also given to people who disrespect priests and religious rituals. This focus on crimes against property and religious majesty suggests that Suryavarman's court emphasized the political order and distinctions between elites and commoners. Adultery isn't mentioned nearly as much. The carvings stress social hierarchy and the sacredness of rituals. In contrast to the Christian tradition which Europeans followed at the same time, the friezes aren't particularly concerned with pleasures of the flesh. Khmer rulers seemed more preoccupied with obeying authority and more willing to allow enjoyment as long as it didn't compromise their positions.

Transgressors in the reliefs are stabbed by deer horns, mauled by lions and dogs, crushed under rollers, flogged by demons, and pulled by ropes through their noses. Nobody just gets a fine or a warning. Above them, elegantly crowned elites under parasols, wearing flowing skirts called *sampots*, amble in a procession to heaven. People only receive the ultimate punishments or rewards. There's no middle ground.

Both panels on this wall are on an imperial scale, and the second thrusts a stern message about obedience in viewers' faces. There is no Jesus, St. Francis of Assisi, or Dante's Beatrice and Virgil to humanize the grandiose for the common person. People are seen in terms of these sweeping perspectives which struck me as aloof and sometimes harsh. I felt relieved to reach the end of the gallery, sit in one of the southeastern pavilion's window frames, and enjoy a soft breeze.

How do you fathom this place? It's spiritual and brutal. It's elegant and forceful. It floats in the heavens and commands the entire earth. More mysteries quickly followed.

The panel on the east wall portrays the universe's creation, and it is one of Angkor's most famous works of art. Its 150-plus-foot-long carving shows gods and demons (*asuras*) pulling a giant serpent from both ends. In Hindu mythology, this tug-o-war churned the sea of milk at the beginning of creation. Vishnu became incarnated as a tortoise to support the mountain that the serpent wrapped itself around. By pulling its body, the gods and *asuras* rotated the mountain.[4]

This panel is so symbolically rich that it has been read in another way. Though some see it as another message about Suryavarman's power, others think that it has a more spiritual meaning and that the viewing of all the walls might begin with this scene.[5] If so, the judgment of souls on the previous wall might climax the end of a cycle of creation and destruction. The process then begins anew with the churning of the sea. The suffering in hell and the horrific battles on the west wall represent the cosmic transformation as one era ends and its material structures dissolve.

But why stress the cruelty of the hells' torments so vividly if they only illustrate a cyclic change? The graphic punishments provoked the historian Tony Day to see Angkor Wat as both beautiful and violently centralizing. He noted that Suryavarman II's reign was taxed by wars with two powerful eastern neighbors, the Dai Viet in northern Vietnam and a federation of people in southern Vietnam called Chams. The latter soon invaded Angkor, and they might have conquered and sacked it. They at least took over much of the empire's eastern territory. Suryavarman II needed to marshal as many troops as possible to march in the searing heat and risk having their stomachs ripped open with spears. Does Angkor Wat embody spiritual growth or violent politics?

I think it expresses both. This culture saw the world less in terms of precise definitions according to Aristotle's law of the excluded middle (P is either A or not A, but it cannot be both) than Westerners have. Khmers thought more of the harmony of the whole universe and society, and they often fused several meanings. To them, the king's key role in the cosmic order and his honor on the battlefield were inseparable. Both ideas blended in images of Suryavarman defeating disorderly forces and restoring prosperity. He had deposed and killed his uncle before taking the crown, and thus might have used scenes of Hindu gods overcoming demons and establishing the dharma to justify his own rule. I've found Angkor Wat captivating because it projects incontestable power and ethereal grace at the same time. You can see it in either way and be equally awed.

The carvings on the rest of the walls are mostly of battles between Hindu gods and their foes, and they include one of the most violent scenes in Asian art. This depiction of the *Ramayana's* final combat climaxes in a whirl of destructive energy that flings bodies around like twigs.

Female dancers who entertain gods balance the war scenes. Some are called *apsaras* and they reside in the heavens. Others are called *devatas* and they stand rather than fly. Both are the height of elegance, and they adorn courtyards, walkways, and towers throughout the temple. Hundreds are unique, with different hairdos, crowns, and outfits. They have narrow waists, slender limbs, round breasts, and the coquettish grin of a teenager who just discovered that she can turn the head of every male in the room. Some might have represented real dancers at the Khmer court.

But they must have had more spiritual meanings because they catered to the gods. Paul Cravath and Denise Heywood noted that dance was a key art form for the Khmers. Performers might have enacted archetypal patterns of creation and honored ancestral spirits at temples and the royal palace.

Cravath, in *Earth in Flower,* wrote that Angkor's dancers regularly performed to help usher in the monsoons each year. Khmers associated female dancers' movements with feminine patterns of energy that bring fertility to rice fields. He said that Angkor's king represented masculine power, and that the court dances harmonized the feminine and masculine aspects of nature. He also wrote that Khmers staged dances to commune with ancestors and nature spirits. So ritual performances integrated many domains and types of beings that enabled society to flourish. These carvings impeccably balance sensual beauty and celestial grace, and they're justly some of the most popular Khmer works of art.

Back at the entrance portico, I ventured closer to the source of creation by ascending the stairs towards the central tower. This was a key transitional zone—I was leaving the area where worldly images predominated and entering more mysterious domains.

At the top of the stairs, I entered a square courtyard with a large pool in each corner. Colonnaded walkways lie between the four basins and form a central cross. The columns create interplays of light and shade that would have danced in the sparkling waters and on the walkways. The pools were dry when I was there, but locals had placed large arrangements of orange flowers and banners in front of Buddha statues because Angkor Wat is now a Buddhist temple. The bright colors of ancient religious rituals and the interplays of light, water, and stone must have made this a ravishing place.

I then climbed a long stairway to one last corridor that surrounds the central towers. Its halls lack carvings and they are narrow and enclosed—they're darker than the first corridor. Mannikka proposed that their circuit around the center represents the moon's orbit and the constellations. Khmers believed that the central towers symbolize the universe's center, which the heavenly bodies orbit. The halls' dimness heightened the splendor I was about to bask in.

I walked out the other side of the corridor and looked up at the celestial towers that have been the most famous images of Angkor. The sudden change from darkness to sunlight was stunning, and some art historians have thought that this shift is supposed to inspire a spiritual experience.

The towers rise from a 40-foot-high platform—a spectacular climax of the journey which began on the road. Even the most level stairways ascend at a 50 degree angle. Here the path is so steep that it seems as though only gods belong at the top.

I ascended the stairs that soar to the southwestern tower. "Wow! I'm at the top! I'm finally here! This is one of the most magnificent human-made places in the world!" I proceeded through the doorway to this most sacred realm, and . . .

SPLISH!

"What the hell is . . . ?"

I looked up as I wiped the mysterious clear liquid from my face and glasses. I was just christened by a bat relieving himself who, along with several buddies, hung from the ceiling. They sometimes congregate in temples in southern Asia. During a later trip up there, I heard an English-speaking guide warn his group, "Be careful or the bats will drop you something."

The summit immediately made me think of the glory of the gods and the king. The place is stunningly symmetrical, with four corner towers that surround the central spire. They are supposed to represent peaks that encircle Mt. Meru. Colonnaded passageways line all four outer walls and run through the corner towers. Perhaps priests once walked through them with incense, chanting hymns to invoke the cardinal directions and the gods that represent them—holy men might have harmonized cosmic powers before approaching the central tower.

Each quadrant has a dry pool that's four to five feet deep (like the lower courtyard, but the upper basins are larger). They probably symbolize oceans that surround Mt. Meru. A colonnaded walkway projects from the middle of each passageway lining the outer walls, proceeds between the two pools that adjoin it, and ends at a shrine in the central tower.

Vishnu's statue no longer presides in the central tower, and its chamber was sealed in the 14th or 15th century when Angkor Wat was converted into a Buddhist temple, but I saw wonders on the upper terrace that even Suryavarman's architects didn't imagine. Languages of visitors from around the world mixed with ornate carvings of gods, stacks of tiled roofs, lilting devatas, the chirping of birds and bats, and soft breezes rustling through the window slats. Thousands of forms and the sounds from nature and cultures from all over the globe comingled.

Gentle Cambodian families enhanced the harmony. Two local women and two five-or six-year-old children sauntered around the central tower, on top of the plinth that it stands on. Both kids smiled at me when they noticed that I was watching them. The conviviality, elegant architecture, breezes, and sunlight made everything around me sparkle. Even the bats were beautiful now (sadly, there was a 30-minute time limit on the upper terrace when I returned in 2012—increasingly large crowds were clogging the steep stairways and making them dangerous).

This monument displays contrasting personalities so well that you can spend years savoring it. On one hand it's full of graceful and spiritual images that include elegant floral patterns that adorn lintels, lithe devatas that sway on walls, towers that rhythmically balance each other, and the top level embodying paradise. But its massive frontage and violent reliefs project centralized power with a jackhammer force. Suryavarman II extended the Khmer empire farther than any previous king had—all the way to the fringes of the Burmese empire. He went over the top to express its sacred and lordly sides in the same monument.

Angkor Wat is symmetrical, but not in the way that ancient Greek architecture is. Later in that trip, I visited several ancient Greek cities on Turkey's west coast, including Miletus, where the first known Western school of philosophy emerged in the sixth century BCE. The temples and stoas that surrounded its two agoras immersed people in an order that inspired dialog (the extant buildings are from Hellenistic and Roman times because the Persian Empire leveled Miletus in the 490s for leading a rebellion against it). Those open spaces with clear vistas of pro-portioned colonnades and human-sized buildings encouraged Greeks to feel that the world is fathomable, and that everyday language can express its fundamental order. These assumptions are key foundations of Western civilization and modern science.

But Angkor Wat's symmetry is so complex and its scale is so vast that it silences people. It only could have been built by beings with far more power than my puny biceps can muster. Its regularity and the refined carvings may reassure folks that the kingdom is in harmony, but it seems like an order centered on gods and the king. I often felt mixed emotions there because the building was both inspiring and oppressive.

The reliefs' styles also mix grace and force. Angkor Wat's sculpture has been called classical because it's elegant and elevated above daily life. Devatas are suave and charming, and some warriors in battle assume postures from classical Indian dance. But other figures have angular faces and they seem absorbed in their mythic worlds and detached from our concerns. Trees in many scenes bristle with dense and animated foli-age as though they're full of nature's energy. The carvings are thus both courtly and infused with mysterious power.

This power envelops many senses. When I was leaving the temple at sunset during the rainy season in 2012, it became noisy with crickets. They weren't concentrated anywhere, but instead pervaded the whole area. Birdsong filled it during other visits. These all-encompassing sounds, along with the tropical heat and the monsoons, meshed with the overpowering architecture and sculpture to create a feeling of energy coming from the center of the universe.

Angkor Wat radiates both divine grace and bone-crushing authority. The variety of scholarly interpretations of it reflects this diversity—it's too big for one view. You can see it from many perspectives, and they're all magnificent. Approach this embodiment of the Khmer universe closely enough and you may either feel transported into the heavens, or pulverized by its size and power.

I found equally dramatic contrasts in the local people. When I walked back across the bridge over the moat and towards the car, many families sat on mats and blankets by the water. All the tourists made bee-lines across the road to their busses and cabs, but I turned right and was alone with the Cambodians as they enjoyed their heritage. Groups of children played along the shore. I could imagine ancient Khmers relaxing by the water because reservoirs, canals, and Tonle Sap surrounded Angkor with it. The tourists didn't know what they were missing.

One man invited me to join his family. I took off my shoes and sat on their straw mat. He had a wife and two daughters; one appeared to be five and the other about two. The five-year-old frequently smiled at me, but the younger one was bashful. The temple's towers were silhouetted against the indigo evening sky, and the darkening water gleamed like a bed of sapphires. I felt transported back to Angkor's zenith.

Well, sort of. The man was a taxi driver. He might have been panning for more business, but he never asked me to become a client. He offered me a roasted corn cob and his wide smile often flashed.

After we parted, I crossed the road and several begging children converged on me in the dirt parking lot. I walked briskly and tried to keep an emotional distance, otherwise the number of them would have been overwhelming. But one girl who was about ten asked me where I'm from. I said, "California." She exclaimed, "I know California! Arnold Schwarzenegger is your governor. George Bush is your president." Since she was bright and cheerful, I let her walk with me to the car.

"Are you married?" she asked. I said that I wasn't and she said, "Adopt me as your daughter and take me to California. I will help you find a wife!" She spoke with a smile as though she knew that this was an unrealistic request, but it hurt to realize that the biggest thing on the mind of this girl with a beautiful smile, sparkling eyes, and intelligence was finding a secure home.

I often saw reminders that Cambodia is one of Asia's poorest countries and that politicians have exploited it so that they can live like kings. The government recently forced long-time Phnom Penh residents from their homes which were located around a popular lake. It gave them little compensation but allowed its cronies to develop upscale properties for themselves. According to the *Washington University Global Studies Law Review,* the government and private companies have forced thousands of people from their land in order to take advantage of rising real estate prices, and the government has used threats, violence, and police detention to suppress community resistance.[6] Today's fun-loving youths face political corruption and an underdeveloped economy. This scenario reminded me of the contrast between the beauty of the devatas and the harshness of the hells on Angkor Wat. Grace and ruthless authority were often juxtaposed during my stay in Cambodia.

But I mustn't oversimplify this land with more than 2,000 years of history and a great empire's legacy. The Khmers didn't portray people in only one way. Angkor developed at least 14 styles of sculpture during its sway; Angkor Wat's is only one. A type that preceded it, called Baphuon (after an enormous temple about three miles away), is known for lively figures of people and animals. A woman plays with a puppy that a girl has handed to her; a rat climbs a tree trunk; birds and monkeys on the branches enjoy fruit; a baby crawls into a kneeling woman's lap; and a woman nurses a baby and wears a soft grin that's as gentle as any Buddha statue's smile. Cambodia is a land of diverse ideas, images, and art forms which can inspire her people and the rest of the world.

However, I saw enough of a tug-o-war between beauty and cruelty to wonder, With energetic young people eager for fun and prosperity, toiling in an economy that corrupt politicians have been milking, and in a society haunted by the Khmer Rouge, will today's cultural scene coalesce more around a brilliant heritage or recent brutality and poverty? Will Cambodian society reach the potential that its illustrious past can inspire or repeat past traumas?

The journalist Joel Brinkley concluded that Cambodia is cursed. He found that its people hold fatalistic beliefs that they're destined to suffer. The first of Buddhism's four noble truths is: Life means suffering. Brinkley said that this idea has combined with the miseries that the Khmer Rouge caused and with today's poverty. In 2012 the movie *The Killing Fields* was playing on the TV in my hotel's dining room while I ate dinner. Several locals and Westerners were glued to it. I found it especially hard to see a scene of a crying child with a mangled body on the operating table. I wondered why anyone would want to watch, but I understood that reliving a trauma is part of the healing process, and it's far from over.

Brinkley said that Cambodians are dour people. That's crap. They're cheerful and fun-loving when allowed to be, and amazingly so in these trying times. I walked through a village south of Phnom Penh during the rainy season in 2012 and met four teenage girls relaxing under a small bamboo pavilion by a lakeside, as their Khmer ancestors did. A golden-roofed pagoda rose across the sparkling water. All the girls were bubbly and they often burst into laughter. Back at my Phnom Penh hotel, I placed my guitar on the bar after playing it. A server soon picked it up with a huge smile and strummed it even though she had never played an instrument before. This is Southeast Asia—fun is part of its ancient heritage and Cambodia's exuberant natural landscape often inspires joy. Brinkley focused only on today's problems.

We can help Cambodians recover their glory by exploring their heritage and appreciating their country's creative potential. A deep journey into their history will show that Cambodia is also a rich country that can inspire the rest of the world if it becomes better known. If we spread ideas about this nation's richness, more people will study it, share their discoveries with their families and friends, and become inspired to help improve its people's lives. By doing so, we will improve our own lives by enjoying cultural wealth that is rarely taught in schools. We will also gain a bigger range of ideas to boost our own creativity. Exploring Cambodia's past is win-win for everyone involved.

Angkor Wat is just the surface of a much deeper past. We'll delve into Cambodia's roots in the next chapter and find that it emerged in one of the world's most creative cultural crossroads.

CHAPTER 3

⌒

GOING DEEPER:
SOUTHEAST ASIA'S ANCIENT SOIL

THIS HOUSE ISN'T as big as Angkor Wat, but in its own way it's as impressive as its descendant.

Figure 4. Home sweet home in a Laotian village.

It represents one of the world's most widespread lifestyles. Most people have not had the opportunity to discover how fertile Cambodia's roots are, so we'll explore them in this chapter. They emerged in a crossroads that now encompasses about one fourth of the world's population. Learning about it has been one of my all-time favorite journeys.

The archeologist Charles Higham studied mainland Southeast Asian sites where hunter-gatherers lived more than 4,000 years ago and found that many people lived well. They enjoyed an abundance of fish, game, fruits, and vegetables. Higham concluded that most were well-fed, though some bones show evidence of anemia. He also discovered cowry shells at inland sites, so communities traded or carried luxuries over long distances. Even then, people enjoyed the land's bounty.

However, life expectancies in commonly studied areas averaged only about 30 years from birth.[1] Many archeological sites show no evidence of warfare—there were few broken bones. Did a high percentage of people contract diseases from insects and other pests?

Some of Southeast Asia's most common thought patterns thus might have already formed by 2000 BCE. Even then people probably relished nature's copiousness, enjoyed the moment when they could, and feared sudden misfortunes.

With so much natural abundance, Higham wondered why locals adopted the rigors of rice farming and concluded that it allowed more people to live in the same settlements. It supported higher populations, but once they became dense enough, they depended on it. He wrote that farmers probably moved in from the north by the early second millennium BCE and intermarried with locals.[2] However, others think that locals began to farm rice on their own, and that this might have happened in northern Thailand by 4000 BCE.[3]

Rice growing communities had formed in southern China along the middle and lower Yangtze River by 6000 BCE.[4] The area's many low wetlands with lakes and marshes made it ideal for pioneering irrigated rice farming. People there began to construct paddy fields bordered by low earthen dykes that optimized the distribution of water. All had to cooperate to take advantage of each phase of crop growth. They worked together in the searing heat, with mud squishing between their toes, piling up earthen banks, planting stocks, coordinating the flow of water, and harvesting. This toil within tightly knit communities became one of the most common experiences in Southeast Asia.

The labor-intensive work required big families or large clusters of households, but the growing communities needed more and more rice. So as ancient populations grew, people fanned out and established more villages that farmed. They moved south along rivers that flow into the Yangtze, and into Vietnam, Laos, and Thailand. Some sailed to Taiwan by 3000 BCE, and from there and China's southeastern coast, people migrated all over island Southeast Asia.

Whether locals in Southeast Asia began farming by themselves, or if new arrivals from lands around the Yangtze introduced agriculture to the region, both areas' lifestyles fused. One of the most widespread ways of living in human history emerged. Villages with

- Stilt homes,
- Rice paddies,
- Water buffalos and pigs,
- Limber boats used for transportation,
- Close-knit communities that emphasized the group,
- Religions that extended the group into the spiritual world by stressing a multitude of souls in communication with each other and with the living

spread through the peninsula and ultimately over half the earth's circumference, from Polynesia to Madagascar. They covered much of southern China too (mainstream Chinese societies were concentrated in the north then; their people began to migrate in large numbers to the Yangtze area after the Han Dynasty broke up in 220 CE, and they gradually made their cultures dominant there). I asked a young woman from Shanghai that I met in Siem Reap what she thought of Cambodia's countryside, and she said that it reminded her of the village where her grandmother had lived.

I find Southeast Asian villages uplifting. The generous growth of life mixes with the community's intimacy. People are usually gentle and welcoming when I enter, and I always enjoy the soft colors around me. The warm tans and browns of bamboo and wooden homes with thatched roofs, the narrow earthen footpaths between the houses, and the vegetable gardens in front of homes feel like a cozy embrace in the midst of the profuse greenery surrounding the village. Women prepare meals and sew, children play, elders gossip, ducks waddle around, and dogs sleep. These places attract pests too—rats, mice, and mosquitoes thrive on their high concentrations of food. Everyone is in close quarters. The unwanted species and lack of privacy are often annoying, but when people go to bed at night they know they're not alone. When they can take a break from work, they often have fun with each other.

This lifestyle still thrives and it's flexible enough to adapt in many places. Houses can be disassembled and carried to new locations. Traditions of appeasing many spirits can add more cults as people move to new lands, or as migrants settle into an established village. This mode of living thus assumed many vibrant varieties as it spread to more places. It appears humble on the surface, but its flexibility always allows more cultural fusions, and this has generated a wealth of great art, from graceful ceremonial dances to Khmer sculpture. It's also savory when times are good and people can enjoy nature's beauty together.

However, village life can also be trying. The work is hard, its repetitiveness can be boring, and droughts and floods sometimes occur. Many people in modern times have thus left for the excitement and variety in cities. I met a young woman in a village in southern China who migrated to Shenzhen when she was about twenty. She said that she enjoyed the big city more because there was more to do there. But she decided to move back after her first child was born because the countryside seemed better for raising kids. Though life in Southeast Asian villages can be restricting, people are intimate with each other and the environment.

Many Asian urbanites long to reconnect with this way of life. I saw part of a Vietnamese movie on a bus from Phnom Penh to Ho Chi Minh City in which a middle-aged farmer in the paddy fields was carrying a duck in each hand, singing to them, and laughing with untrammeled joy.

I saw romanticized views of pre-industrial Asia in China too. In 2012 I was walking between two villages in Yunnan, near Dali, and came upon two empty tour buses that had stopped by the roadside. I found their passengers, who were Chinese, romping through a rice field and snapping photos of each other between the tall green stalks that swayed in the breeze. Some young women got into the spirit by raising their arms, looking up to the sky, and smiling from ear to ear as though they were communing with the basic forces of nature.

The relationship between people and buffaloes is hallowed in much of rural Southeast Asia, and a man in a village near Yangshuo, China wanted to show me. He was swimming in the river as I explored the countryside. A buffalo suddenly lumbered towards me. It was big and ugly, so I backed off. The man got out of the water and came over to demonstrate that the beast was friendly, and he asked me to pet it. The hairs on its head were as thick as an elephant's, but it enjoyed the rubbing. I guess it just wanted some love, and its owner went so far out of his way to show me that he must have identified with this animal which people in his region have worked closely with since ancient times.

The buffalo is also highly honored in Vietnamese culture. The image of a child on a buffalo's back has symbolized peace and prosperity in Vietnam. These are blessings that people in this stunningly beautiful land have often lacked because of invading foreigners and its own rapacious politicians. One of the most ancient images of wellness in Southeast Asia consists of a man on one end of a plow and the strong, docile animal on the other. In lands full of mysterious energies, the buffalo has represented civilized life. So I will tell you a buffalo story from a Laotian creation myth.

Once upon a time, the supreme deities, who presided in the sky, ordered all the people to give them offerings during every meal. But the people, being human, disobeyed. The gods caused a flood that submerged the whole earth and drowned almost everyone. But three elders saved themselves, their wives, and their children by floating on a raft. So far, this isn't too different from the story of Noah's ark in Genesis, but they sailed up to the gods' kingdom and lingered there for a while. When the water receded, the king of the gods returned them to earth and gave them a buffalo. They began to plant rice with the help of their new partner.

Three years later the noble beast died. A vine grew from its nostrils, and three enormous pumpkins emerged from it. The elders pierced them and humanity sprung into the world from them. The elders taught the new people how to cultivate rice and build houses, and explained the importance of marriage.

Humanity's birth from pumpkins issuing from a dead buffalo makes this story different from the Noah's ark tale, but it expresses experiences that have been common in Southeast Asia. In the Bible, Yahweh created Adam directly from the soil's dust. But the Laotian myth says that we emerged from an animal and a plant—we're embedded in nature, and its energies generate many life forms which are intertwined.

Of course we didn't come from just any animal. We issued from a creature that our ancestors have produced crops with since ancient times. Civilized life is thus close to the forces of creation.

Though I was raised as a Christian, I'm attracted to this optimistic view of the world which affirms all of nature. Life forms are embedded with each other in a harmonious ecosystem. Southeast Asia's lush green fields, profuse jungles, and sinuous rivers have inspired this view of the world.

Changes accelerated around 500 BCE, which was the beginning of the century when Athens built the Parthenon. People in mainland Southeast Asia started to smelt iron for farming implements and weapons.[5] This process requires high temperatures, but once smiths mastered it, the metal became cheaper than bronze because it was abundant in the region. It's also harder and stronger than bronze. People could now fell more trees, clear more brush, and plow their new fields more easily to amass rice surpluses. The more efficient food production liberated some workers from farming and allowed them to specialize in making things, including tools and jewelry. Others conducted long-distance commerce. With Indian states, they traded their own forest products, gold, and bronzes for glass beads, agate, and carnelian. Many communities in Southeast Asia grew and they constructed systems of earthen walls and moats surrounding a central area. Local villages probably began to pay them tribute for protection. Port towns emerged along coasts and consolidated trade between Southeast Asia, India, and China. Larger and more complex communities began to emerge and develop into centralized states—Angkor Wat's roots grew.

Increasingly wealthy rulers collected luxury goods such as jewelry and bronze ritual drums, and they could use food reserves to attract even more followers. Their increasing flamboyance and political clout must have encouraged their subjects to identify them with the land's power to generate life. Many of their homes and courts became ritual centers, which people treated as intersections of supernatural powers. Tony Day wrote that ideas of spiritual potency were associated with them.[6] Older folk cults for ancestors and nature spirits thus became integrated with the prestige of the ruler, who now had food surpluses and luxury goods to enhance his own charisma. People associated courts with a network of ideas that included safety, the spirit world, crop growth, and social hierarchy.[7]

Then by 200 CE, people in southern Cambodia and southern Vietnam established the first known big state in the region, Funan. At least Chinese travelers called it a state, but many historians think it was a network of smaller communities interlinked by canals. Its location near the sea enabled it to prosper from maritime trade in an economic system that integrated Rome, India, and China in an unprecedented increase of prosperity and political organization. While Rome erected its great forums and public baths, Funan dug a network of canals to connect its major towns with each other. Commerce between India and Southeast Asia increased, and Cambodians imbibed more influences from India. A creative explosion followed.

As Southeast Asians and Indians sailed to each others' lands, Southeast Asian rulers, merchants, and artists learned about Indian alphabets, rituals, religious ideas, and art forms. Because Hinduism and Buddhism spread through most of India, Southeast Asians discovered both faiths around the same time. They would mix aspects of both in their art and rituals, and this gave them more scope for creativity.

The period from 200 BCE to 100 CE was a watershed for civilization. Rome and China's Han Dynasty consolidated huge empires, and the world between them became more integrated than ever. The Silk Road emerged up north and soon cities with bazaars teeming with camels, merchants, and missionaries from several faiths enlivened the arid wind-swept lands. Down south, Romans joined the growing emporia along India's coasts, and archeologists have dug up Roman coins as far east as Vietnam and Canton (modern Guangzhou). Romans exported so much gold to India that Emperor Vespasian (r. 69–79 CE) stopped the practice to protect the treasury. The large courtyard houses in Pompeii, with their lavish wall paintings and colonnaded gardens, show off the new wealth from this trade.

Southeast Asian states grew and consolidated with combinations of local and Indian ideas. These mixtures became so pervasive that they still influence people's thoughts throughout the region. The fusion of Southeast Asian and Indian civilizations has made up one of history's greatest crossroads. Cambodian culture developed in it.

India had so many currents to share that becoming exposed to them was like standing in a rushing river. Its ideas about both spiritual and worldly matters were already highly developed, and Southeast Asia was about to get blasts of both.

- Buddhism was branching into several traditions, most notably the Theravada and the Mahayana. The former follows the Buddha's original teachings about overcoming attachments to the world and living a simple and ethical life to build merit for a better rebirth, and ultimately nirvana (liberation from the whole cycle of births).

  The Mahayana (Great Path) is more ambitious. It emerged in the first century CE, and it teaches that all beings are interwoven. Because of this, people must try to liberate others as well as themselves. It also says that souls called bodhisattvas have already earned liberation, but they have delayed it to help free other people from their past karmic chains. The Mahayana thus sees more potential in people, and it appeals to many mindsets. High-flying ones can focus on the idea that everyone can attain spiritual perfection and become a bodhisattva while ordinary folks can pray to elevated souls for help in their daily lives.

  The Mahayana imagination populated the universe with many enlightened souls, and thereby added more figures for artists to depict. It also expanded the cosmos from one Mt. Meru at the center into innumerable world systems. Most of them are Buddha-fields (*buddhaksetra*) in which a Buddha spreads law and compassion.[8]

Theravada followers have found these ideas a world away from the Buddha's original teachings about simple daily life, but these expansive visions created a wealth of subjects for artists. Many Southeast Asian rulers identified with a bodhisattva to increase their own prestige, and sculptors and painters portrayed them wearing the bodhisattva's clothing and jewelry. Both forms of Buddhism spread to Southeast Asia—an immense windfall of ideas to receive at the same time. Cultures in the region would fuse aspects of both traditions in their own creative ways.

- New styles of sculpture helped bring religion down to earth. Two Indian artistic centers emerged by the first century BCE (Gandhara and Mathura), and they created ways in which artists throughout India and Southeast Asia have portrayed the Buddha and Hindu gods ever since. These iconographic traditions rendered divine souls more tangible for a wider public than the airy speculations from earlier literature rooted in the Vedas, such as the *Upanisads*. The latter say that reality is unified in a way that is too subtle to be expressed. That may be fine for guys in loincloths living in forests and meditating all day, but what about the rest of us? The new art expressed spirituality in more human terms, and it allowed Buddhism and Hinduism to spread more widely in India and Southeast Asia in this time of increasing commerce.

- The *Bhagavad Gita* was India's first major literary expression of *bhakti* (devotion) yoga. This text mixes a focus on love for a divinized being with meditations on cosmic unity. Christianity was becoming the West's central faith around the same time and it also made love a core value. Both East and West saw movements that emphasized spiritual devotion as their material wealth increased. The new ostentation didn't warm all hearts and it was unevenly distributed. Both areas also suffered economic downturns at times, so their prosperity wasn't always stable. But Krishna had an answer for the distressed.

His disciple Arjuna was a master archer, and he was on the verge of entering an epic battle between two branches of the same family for the throne of India (this fray was carved on the first panel that I saw at Angkor Wat). But unable to bear the thought of killing his relatives, he withdrew from the fight. Krishna, in the guise of his charioteer, told him that there really is no killing because souls are eternal. He then explained the structure of the universe, but in the 18th and final book of the *Gita*, he told him to forget the order of things and just think of him with constant devotion. "Do not think of the fruits of your work; just work out of love for me, and take refuge in me alone." The battle resumed and Arjuna and his brothers ultimately won after nearly everyone else was slain.

Personally, I'd only have two words for someone who tells me to hurt anyone in my family, but love for a spiritual being became a major part of Hindu culture in India. From the sixth through the ninth century, poets sang about their devotion to Vishnu (Krishna was an incarnation of him) and Shiva, wandering throughout the land and inspiring kings, merchants, and farmers. They added emotional fire to Hinduism.

This *bhakti* movement had Indian traits which were different from Christian devotion. Indians' imaginations weren't hemmed in by a single church, doctrine, or liturgy. Poets sang what they imagined and felt, including tales about Krishna's impish boyhood and girl-charming adolescence. He stole sweets and played by the river with scantily clad women with long, silky hair and water drops glistening on their full breasts in the moonlight. This was way beyond Christian decorum, but anything in India's immense mythological landscape was acceptable as an illustration of spiritual love. The heart knows no bounds; it sees the beloved in everything.

These poems still inspire people. I lived in Chennai in 1996, where a man named Subramaniam invited me to his mother's apartment for lunch. A young Swiss woman, a young Belgian woman, and two other young southern Indian men were with us. We sat in a circle in the front room, and Subramaniam wanted each person to sing a song before lunch. The women and I would perform first because we were the guests. With a voice that will never be confused with Pavarotti's, I felt a bit self-conscious. The Swiss woman also seemed uncomfortable when her turn came. The Belgian was an actress with a pretty voice, so she did well, though she didn't express much feeling while singing. But the Indians were transported into a different world when they performed devotional songs. With eyes closed, body swaying, and hands waving, each seemed completely absorbed in the emotion.

The *bhakti* movement inspired more religious sculpture, temple construction, dance performances, and processions. Vishnu incarnated many times—Rama and Krishna were only two of his embodiments. He also came to earth as a fish, a boar, and a lion. As a turtle, he supported the mountain that the serpent carved on Angkor Wat's east wall wrapped around. Stories emerged about all of his lives, and artists gleefully portrayed the immense variety of forms.

Westerners have seen Jesus' life as a one-time occurrence, and before modern times most saw it as the central narrative in history. But Indians' imaginations flew far beyond one time, place, and biography, and this engendered a vast profusion of stories, art forms, and rituals. All of these reinforced the sense that abundance, rather than simple abstract forms that ancient Greeks focused on, is basic in the universe. Emotions, myths, rituals, art forms, and temples have seemed like manifestations of nature's copious flows of energy. This sense of profusion developed in many media, and merchants, Hindu priests, and Buddhist monks brought them to Southeast Asia as its states continued to grow. Southeast Asians, already used to pluralism and flexibly blending traditions, were able to adopt them and modify them in their own ways.

- But as spiritual and artistic flights were soaring, the caste system became more rigid. Brahmin priests composed *The Laws of Manu* to regulate Hindu life and substantiate their own authority. This text has stressed keeping the lowest classes in their places. In modern times a low-caste man in India toiled for many years to save money for a small plot of land to grow crops, but his neighbors beat him up every time he tried to plough it. This oppressive mentality solidified around 2,000 years ago. Thankfully, Southeast Asian's didn't adopt the caste system nearly as much.

- While Indian culture was advancing on both high and low roads, its two main Sanskrit epics, the *Ramayana* and the *Mahabharata*, synthesized a common mythology that everyone could share. Tangible stories of gods battling demons, princes fighting over India's throne, and fashionable heroes now fleshed out the older Upanisadic meditations. Sculptors produced images of them to appeal to more people. This tradition inspired many of Angkor Wat's friezes.

  Some of these friezes are furry as well as fleshy. Angkor Wat's west wall's ultra-violent battle scene from the *Ramayana* includes monkeys. Muscled simian warriors joined this battle, and many Indians still revere their commander, Hanuman, for helping Rama to rescue his wife from a king who had abducted her. They might have come from folk tales that got absorbed into the epic narrative, and they added sizzle to it. The monkeys on Angkor Wat flex, snarl, bite, and stab. The imaginations behind Indian stories gave Cambodia's kings emotionally engaging ways to project their own rule.

- Other Indian traditions gave growing Southeast Asian states yet more ways to project kingship. The concept of the *Chakravartin* was especially influential. It referred to the most renowned king, who was the center of society. *Chakra* means *wheel* in Sanskrit, so the monarch is the hub of order. Southeast Asians could easily associate this wheel with their homegrown ideas of the royal court as a central zone of spiritual power and communal safety.

  India provided many other ideas for kings to consolidate their growing states with. They used Indian calendars to organize administration and rituals, and they also imported their alphabets and adapted them to their own languages. Landscape features were named after mythic places in India, and Mt. Meru became one of the most popular. Many Southeast Asian societies had already envisioned a sacred hill where sky and earth meet, and where ancestors and nature spirits reside. This idea became more magnificent with the addition of Hindu gods, stone temples, and royal rituals in which bearded Brahmin priests chanted sacred texts in a mysterious language.

One of the most prevalent art forms that Southeast Asians imported was the Shiva linga, which is a stone phallus associated with Shiva's power. Cambodians installed it in the center of temples as a key state cult and on hilltops, and they associated it with the king's potency, the land's fertility, and the sky's fertilizing monsoons. Divinity, political order, nature's power, and crop growth were thus expressed with this simple image which could be replicated easily. Most Khmer kings before Suryavarman II (Vishnu's follower) worshipped Shiva, and they installed lingas in key places in their land to bring order to the realm.

Shiva lingas and nagas' bodies are different from abstract lines which Westerners have assumed to be most basic. Instead of being straight and eternally motionless, they're surging, undulating life forms swelling with nature's creative energies. Since they are less geometrically precise, artists could vary them in many ways. Because both are easily reproducible, they spread all over Southern Asia, and the locals created many new varieties of them.

What inspired ancient India's profuse creativity? One source was its diversity of life forms, from elephants to ants. I brought a box of sweets to an office in Chennai in 1996 and placed it on top of the refrigerator. I thought they would be safe there, but an hour later they were covered with ants, which were much smaller and faster than the docile breeds in Silicon Valley. Other species I've seen are almost an inch long. Nothing stays uneaten for long in India. Life transforms quickly there.

"You're gonna do it aren't you, Brian!" How can I refuse when a woman asks this? We were in a group of Americans on an elephant safari in Nepal in 1994, in the lowlands next to the Indian border. A trainer had just given us an elephant riding demonstration. A small, wiry young man stood in front of a pachyderm's face, pulled her ears forward, placed his foot on her trunk, and pushed. She lifted her head and he sailed over it, turned around in midair, and landed with his legs around her back.

The trainer told us we could try it. "But remember, you fall at your own risk." I gingerly approached after three others had gotten on top of her.

I grabbed her ears, pulled them forward, placed my foot on her trunk, pushed, and flew up in the air—and landed on my stomach on top of her head, with my feet sticking over the front. I squirmed and finally made it to her back and sat—facing the wrong direction.

I wiggled around until I faced the proper end, and then draped my legs over her back, which was so high and wide that I felt like I was sitting on a house. The trainer said, "If you put your feet behind her ears and push them together, she will walk." As soon as I did, she pranced off into the jungle, and kept going. I yelled, "How do I get her to stop?"

The trainer jogged over and she halted and kneeled down so I could easily dismount. She never made a jerky or unnecessary movement while I was on her. I'm sure she could sense my fear because it was emanating from every pore of my body, but she was perfectly gentle.

Elephants and monkeys are more intelligent than the West's beloved dogs and cats. Yahweh told Adam and Eve to dominate all the beasts in nature, and ancient Greek artists after the Minoans portrayed humans more than animals. In the West it's easy to think that we're categorically above all other creatures. But because elephants and monkeys approach our level of intelligence, it became easier in India to think that life is one continuum. This profusion of life forms—from insects up—makes people think that the river of life is incalculably abundant.

It's a short mental step from there to thinking that species transmute into each other in a vast chain of lives which are determined by karma (the sum of your current and previous lives' thoughts, deeds, and emotional attachments). Many Indian religious traditions have thus taught that all beings are unified. The *Upanisads* have said that the essence and energy of the whole universe (*brahman*) is within each person, and that if you meditate on this unity, you can liberate yourself from the cycle of rebirths.

More worldly people revel in India's sensual abundance. They're transfixed by nature's diversity, the profusion of art forms, and the power of the sun and monsoons. The whirling saris, the shimmering jewelry from toe rings to bangles, the fragrant spices, and the upper class pageantry also bedazzle. The parrots, peacocks, monkeys, elephants, pariah dogs, rodents, and insects also join the kaleidoscopes of densely packed and ever-shifting energies and forms. Mark Twain wrote that India was the one country that he longed to see again because it was full of life. From spiritual ideas to earthly pleasures, India was an inexhaustible fountainhead, which Southeast Asia, with its own diversity and vibrancy, was ready to absorb. You can spend many lifetimes savoring the ways in which these regions have fused, without even mounting an elephant.

But Southeast Asians didn't just passively ingest Indian culture; they did unique things with it. Within their own rich and flexible cultural landscapes, they shaped what they took from India in their own ways and often added grace to it.

Buddhist stupas (monuments that house relics of the Buddha and other revered people) in Thailand and Burma became more elongated and flowing. Many Southeast Asians smoothed out transitions between stupas' different zones so that the whole edifices seem to ripple like rivers.

Borobudur, the most famous Southeast Asian temple other than Angkor Wat, stands on a small hill in central Java so that it overlooks the treetops and rice fields, and it was built more than 300 years before Suryavarman II's monument was. It combines a symmetrical Buddhist map of the universe with a folksy style of sculpture. The carvings wrap around the monument as the friezes on Angkor Wat do, but their size isn't monumental, and they grace several terraces that rise towards the center. Buddha statues on the top are sheltered by small stone latticed stupas that are bell-shaped. Stilt homes and chubby faces in the lower friezes mix with the big picture of the universe in an expression of the Buddha's compassion. I enjoyed Borobudur as much as Angkor Wat because it's more consistently gentle.

Southeast Asians were especially imaginative with shadow puppetry. They used it to dramatize the two Sanskrit epics and their own myths and folk tales, and each culture developed its own style.[9] Many central Javanese performances are slow and stately. Their royal courts espoused a value called *lango*, which meant refined allusiveness. Instead of directly stating ideas and feelings, artists and courtiers hinted at them with poetic language.

A ballet dancer from San Francisco named Terry led the tour in Java that I joined during my first trip to Southeast Asia. He had watched a classical Javanese dance in California 16 years before and thought it was the most graceful thing he had ever seen. He immediately migrated across the Pacific and hooked up with a dance master, but found himself in a different world than he had expected.

Many classical dancers in central Java spread yellow-gold powder on their skin to make it shine. Terry tried it but it turned his pale Irish face pink. He later found out that people giggled during his performances because they thought he looked like a monkey. Folks were quick to have fun in their sacred ceremonies.

Later in that trip I attended one of statelier traditional dances in Bali, called Ardja. The lead dancer was a young woman who swayed her head, torso, and every limb independently. She must have begun training as soon as she could walk. I had never seen anyone move so elegantly and I couldn't take my eyes off her. Afterwards the performers faced us in a line and we all shook hands. She coyly lowered her head and eyes. When we clasped hands, I said "*Indah*" (beautiful), and she looked into my eyes with a warm smile.

Several Southeast Asian cultures have made the ancient Indian epics feel homey by adding their own stories, which often provide comic relief. A popular Javanese character called Semar is a rotund clownish figure. The audience laughs as he jokes and stuffs himself. Because he's identified with abundance, he has also been considered Java's guardian spirit, who carries the fertilizing power of the mountains and imparts timeless wisdom in his wisecracks.

Performers often conduct comic scenes in everyday language and enact epics in speech that's so archaic that nobody understands it. Many have believed that the old language has supernatural power that can enhance a community's well-being. Perspectives thus shift. Projections of political authority mix with the fun stuff, and power is rendered loose enough to live with.

Friends that I made during the Malaysian phase of my 2007 trip drove me to the outskirts of Kota Bharu in the evening to see a shadow puppet show. We sat on the ground, in the middle of a crowd of children and parents. All the kids were clean and well-behaved. One friend told me that the comic characters were the puppeteer's own inventions, and that he was making up parts of the plot. This ancient art is a living tradition, and youngsters still learn about the need to harmonize with the community and spiritual powers through theater that mixes morality, animism, fun, and vivacious art.

India was very diverse, like Southeast Asia, and its art came from several centers, including prosperous merchant communities on the southeastern coast. The Satavahana state built the great stupa at Amaravati (in modern Andhra Pradesh), which housed some of ancient India's finest sculpture (many works from this shrine comprise one of the British Museum's star attractions). Its carvings portray scenes from the Buddha's life and they're packed with densely intertwined life forms. Crowds of people filling the scenes, full-breasted women with bodies gyrating in S curves, and animals make the images so sensual that they bespeak a love of abundant life, even though the great teacher emphasized nonattachment to the world.

The Pallava kingdom, which bustled farther south (around modern Chennai), was one of the most influential societies in southern India's history. The luxurious lives that its prosperous merchants enjoyed were described in the *Cilappatikaram*, which is the most honored epic in the Tamil language. They played vinas (southern Indian stringed instruments with tones that are warmer and lusher than the better-known sitars from northern India) on the upper terraces of their tall houses, which lined streets that headed for the ocean. Women with perfume in their hair danced in groves by beaches strewn with flowers. In sight were ships full of goods on their way to Southeast Asian ports. Its bazaars overflowed with grains, pastries, fish, salt, betel leaves, incense, pearls, coral, sandalwood, sandalwood paste, scented powders, flowers, silk and cotton clothes, perfumes, and oils. Coppersmiths, painters, sculptors, goldsmiths, jewelry merchants, and butchers hawked their goods amid the colors, scents, and sounds. Pallava sculpture reflects this epic's love of life. One frieze in Mahabalipuram (which is about 40 miles south of Chennai) shows a man milking a cow while she licks her calf. This gentle realism reminded me of the serene cows on India's streets today.

Traditions also came to Southeast Asia from many other Indian states, including:

- The Gupta and post-Gupta dynasties in the north,
- The Vakataka Empire, which succeeded the Satavahana state and spread across central India,
- The Chalukya Dynasty in the central and western parts of the south,
- Mathura and Ghandara in the northwest (the latter is now in Pakistan and Afghanistan),
- The Pala kingdom in Bengal.

Each place had its own artistic styles that pollinated Southeast Asia. Many art forms and ideas from several places in India thus entered a region that was very diverse to begin with. Southeast Asia became even more joyfully abundant than it was before.

China also inspired some of Southeast Asia's art. It ruled Vietnam for more than 1,000 years, and by the fifth century CE, Chinese merchants were shipping goods to India rather than hauling them over the old Silk Road. Ports on the Malay Peninsula thus grew. The art historian Hiram Woodward found more Chinese than Indian influence in some of Cambodia's earliest sculpture.[10] He also felt that China might have inspired square and rectangular architectural forms of Khmer temples that preceded Angkor Wat. Rectangular royal palaces as large as a city dominated great Chinese capitals like Chang'an (modern Xi'an) and Luoyang. Beijing's Forbidden City continues this ancient tradition.

The square temples at Angkor were probably also inspired by India's main school of sacred architecture, Vastu. This tradition divides a building into 81 squares. Different Hindu deities inhabit certain squares. Encompassing the whole area is the *Vastu Purusha*, the site's presiding deity, who animates the entire building. He lies across the whole floor, with his head in the northeastern corner. This is no Parthenon—abstract lines and static ratios aren't central ideas in this architecture. Vastu reflects Indian ideas of the primary importance of spiritual energies which infuse all life forms and sacred art. Eleanor Mannikka wrote that it likely influenced Angkor Wat's design.[11]

Many Indians still honor Vastu. Two Indian women at a table next to mine in a Berkeley café were wondering about a strange architectural form projecting from the inside balcony of the upper floor. One said, "I think it's a Vastu thing." The idea that strangeness is a Berkeley thing didn't seem to enter her head. But in a real Vastu design, the whole structure is a spiritual map of the universe. The gods are in their places and their energies are harmonized with the building. Many buildings in modern India have been designed according to its principles.

Southeast Asians' heritage of flexibly fusing different cultures was already ancient by the first millennium CE, and they now regularly interacted with two enormous civilizations. This has allowed yet more cultural variety to flourish, and I've found each society savory because it's unique and brimming with life-loving art forms.

Because the region's limitless human variety can always encourage new art forms and ideas, the vitality of societies can always regenerate after the worst catastrophes. The enormous diversity of images and ideas that fertilized this area since ancient times can encourage new views of the world. This variety is a bottomless well that we all can drink from.

Many great cultures developed in this crossroads, including Cambodia. It has reveled in this crossroads' profusion of forms, as other societies have, including Burmese, Thai, Vietnamese, Malay, Javanese, and Balinese, but it has also been unique. In the next chapter, we'll see how Cambodia became Cambodian.

CHAPTER FOUR

ROOTS OF GLORY:
THE KHMER EMPIRE'S GENESIS

THE FUNAN CULTURE preceded Angkor Wat by 1,000 years, and it influenced all later Cambodian kingdoms. What was Funan life like? Chinese traders gave glimpses of the people in this seminal society, and I find their environment appealing. They lived in wooden and stilt homes on earthen mounds by an extensive network of canals. Some of their houses sported carvings. Rice grew in abundance and marshes full of reeds flourished beyond the villages. Homes must have looked like islands in a sea of green. People probably lived like these kids that I met while walking down a country road in southern Cambodia.

Figure 5. Funan fun

They were fishing with a big net and seemed like they were always quick to have fun. They immediately waved at me and invited me down to the shore.

On drier land in Funan times, bananas, oranges, and pomegranates grew. Scented woods like sandalwood also thrived. Since people lived downstream from the mighty Mekong, they had plenty of fish. Elephants lumbered along and people domesticated some as pack animals. Political rulers rode them for prestige.

Funan people thus had many items to trade with other lands, along with plentiful food, vibrant vegetation, and rousing pageantry, to make their lives prosperous and happy. They made boats up to 90 feet long, with bows and sterns in the shape of a fish's head and tail. Thailand's famous royal barges follow this ancient art form.

Chinese writers who visited Funan said that its people integrated their society with a lively naga myth. Once upon a time, a naga king ruled a local state. He had a beautiful daughter who married an Indian Brahman called Kaundinya. Many kingdoms in Southeast Asia and southern India emphasized myths about the union of a naga princess and an Indian Brahman producing their royal lines. These stories had sticking power because they blended the forces of nature with the prestige of local kings and Indian priests. This was an ideal combination for ensuring stability. Many states conducted rituals that symbolized the marriage of the king with a feminine spirit that could help bring rain and fertilize rice crops.

The ancient Funan city of Oc Eo was special. As a densely populated settlement that focused on making goods for international trade, it manufactured glass beads, pottery, engraved jewelry, and gold ornaments. The historian John N. Miksic wrote that Oc Eo thrived from 100 CE to 600 CE.[1] Archeologists have found brick foundations there that had gold plates with embossed and etched images of Vishnu. A large canal connected the city with an area called Takeo, which some archeologists think contained a key Funan port. Craftspeople and merchants in Oc Eo might have lived apart from the farmers, but both types of workers seem to have often lived well.

But dangers abounded. Crocodiles hunted in the delta while tigers, boars, and wild buffalos roamed dry ground. Snakes slithered through the rushes and trees. The land must have harbored its share of disease-carrying insects. From this luxuriant growth, death could suddenly strike. This contrast between benevolence and danger must have reinforced mixtures of ideas that are still common in Southeast Asia:

- Enjoyment of the moment's fun and fear of the unknown,
- Distinctions between the familiar community and the wild outside,
- Attraction to rulers who display their power, and wariness of that power's dangers,
- Art and rituals that embody animated energy and tame it.

These already ancient ways of relating to the world, which had emerged in villages in many areas in Southeast Asia, were now given more luster by the first large states. Royal pageantry, Hindu statues and temples, and Indian priests chanting in an exotic language made the old associations more magnificent. They helped unify perspectives in the increasingly large political world in Cambodia, and in many other places in the region.

Cambodian culture soon flowered into unique varieties which added more roots that the Khmer Empire emerged from. Around 600 CE, communities in the north built a kingdom, or a network of independent towns, called Chenla, which traded goods and arts with Funan. Many Funan people were now migrating north. Contemporary Chinese chroniclers wrote that Chenla vanquished its southern neighbor, but recent research suggests that the migrations were peaceful. Sailors had discovered how to travel directly from India across the Bay of Bengal with the annual monsoons' winds, which helped them avoid the longer task of hugging the coasts. They also established routes farther east, between Indonesia and southern China.[2] Merchants bypassing Funan ports meant less international trade for people in Cambodia. Funan residents might have been impelled to move north and focus more on agriculture and land-based trading networks.

However, John N. Miksic wrote that Funan commerce was still robust in the middle of the first millennium, and that people might have moved north for cultural reasons.[3] Miksic said that the southern people might have found more security in a state organized around farming. The reasons for this lifestyle change remain a mystery, but this cultural shift endured for 1,000 years. Farming would dominate Cambodia's economy and society throughout Angkor's history.

I made a deal with a driver to take me to the best-preserved Chenla capital. It's a little less than 100 miles east of Siem Reap, and it was called Isanapura in its day, after the king who probably built it, Isanavarman. Today its remains sleep by a little town called Sambor Prei Kuk. Though Angkor Wat grew from some of its art forms, the site has plenty of its own merits.

My driver suddenly had to rush to the hospital to see his son, who had just fallen at his school. His older son met me in the hotel lobby and introduced himself as the day's driver. He had just married and asked if his wife could join us. They seemed well-matched—she was bashful and quiet, and he was gabby, with a mouth that stretched from ear to ear. The newlyweds played cassettes of slow, romantic Cambodian pop songs all the way to the site.

The drive took us back to ancient Khmer times. We traveled across flat plains dotted with stilt homes. Large open spaces had been cleared for rice fields, so we peered across an orderly land that contrasted with the surrounding jungle. This was the same landscape in which Angkor Wat's builders lived. Morning mists at the far ends of the fields made them seem mystical, as though gods had created them.

We left the main highway for a dirt road that wound for the last ten miles to the site. Small clearings for homes alternated with jungle— there were no more large open spaces. The area looked wilder. Chickens, dogs, playing children, and relaxing elders enlivened the yards. The homes were humble; each was raised on stilts, with one or two rooms and no windows. Though plain, they seemed like safe enclaves within the dense woods.

The ancient site was full of strikingly handsome buildings. It was probably Isanavarman's ritual center, and it consisted of three nearly square sets of temples.[4] Each group was dedicated to Shiva. The grounds contained little else—there were no stores or restaurants, only jungle and a few locals selling drinks. My driver and his wife seemed disappointed. They stayed in the car and were as silent as stone sculptures.

If they had expected another Angkor Wat, these structures must have seemed like matchboxes. But they're splendid in their own way.

Each set of buildings is composed of several brick shrines. The biggest temples contain one large chamber for a god's statue, and the tallest buildings rise about 50 feet. They would have impressed the ancient farmers, but they weren't overwhelmingly large. Some are octagonal, some square, and others oblong, but all their forms are well-proportioned. Their symmetry perfectly balances strength and elegance.

India's magnificent Gupta dynasty probably influenced the buildings' forms. This was the largest Indian kingdom in the fifth century CE. Gupta artists fashioned simple and balanced forms that have been compared to classical Greek art. Many styles soon emerged throughout India that elaborated the shapes into the multi-leveled temples and many-limbed gods that most people associate with Hindu art. But the Chenla capital kept the basic forms. Its kings might have used them as models of order as they turned jungle into rice fields. Rulers probably integrated rituals with the growing seasons.

An ancient brick wall surrounds one of the compounds, and it contains a row of large circles that frame lively carvings of people and animals. A man fights a lunging lion in one of them. Cambodians loved action scenes long before Angkor Wat's extravaganzas. Chenla established a blend of symmetry and exuberant carvings which the Khmer Empire inherited and fused with Funan cultural patterns.

Today the jungle has taken over the area. Tree roots have grown so deeply into several temples that the structures would crumble if people were to remove them.

A thin elderly man who was practically toothless joined me when I started to explore the place. When I realized that he was acting as a guide, I tried to ask him to let me be alone, but he stayed with me and I didn't have the heart to be gruff with him. He turned out to be helpful because one of the complexes is a bit distant from the others, and the thick jungle could have made finding my way around difficult. He smiled a lot and said little. His calmness and the site's serenity complemented each other. So did his age and the buildings—they were weathered, yet retained their dignity. A herd of cows calmly grazed nearby. They were too content to notice us.

The drive back rudely interrupted this peaceful mood. We returned to the main road and a calf wandered onto it alone, probably searching for his mother. My driver slammed into him at 60 miles per hour though he had time to veer to the side. I glanced back and saw the poor guy lying motionless on his right side, sliding off the road like a slab of meat. The driver's wife screamed just before the collision, but neither one showed any other emotion. He expressed no more remorse than a person would after running over a dead leaf. What a contrast with the romantic cassettes that they had played in the morning.

When he pulled into my hotel's driveway, the only thing he was upset about was the big dent in his father's car. I wondered if Cambodia's present traumas encouraged his hardness.

But beauty always resurfaced quickly in Cambodia. Siem Reap's center was both relaxed and lively; locals and tourists mingled in its market's enormous pavilion. Fruits, vegetables, T-shirts, shoes, wooden sculptures, small electronic gadgets, sellers, barbers, manicurists, and customers were crammed as densely as the jungle outside of town.

Young men smoking cigarettes lingered in a small CD shop next to the pavilion. All the products were Cambodian. Slow and romantic songs from soft-voiced singers breezed from the speakers. All the videos I saw in Cambodia had boy-meets-girl themes, with accompanying slow music. The couples in them often flirted or cuddled by a lake or in a garden.

The town and its surroundings did have some Wild West roughness. One man advised me to avoid staying out until the nightclubs closed because local gangsters hit the streets drunk and eager to fight. But the neighborhood was peaceful whenever I was out late. The few people outside walked slowly, without any jerky movements that suggested anxiety, so they seemed to be unafraid. But in early evenings, prostitutes accosted passersby in front of a grocery store, and an endless barrage of young men on motorcycles looking for passengers called out, "Hello, motorbike?" One night two suddenly began an all-out fistfight. The combination of poverty and the rising number of tourists in Siem Reap brings people in search of quick money and thrills. Some are shady while others are desperate. Though back street affairs were evident, Siem Reap still felt safe.

The one scare I experienced happened in the ancient city. While exploring an extensive temple called Banteay Kdei, a policeman approached, showed me a fake silver medal, and insisted that I buy it for ten dollars. I gave him the money, since no one else was in sight, but he noticed more cash in my wallet and demanded some. I loudly said, "No!" and walked away. He didn't follow me, but I explored the whole complex while realizing that he was lurking around the entrance. Because I feared that we would meet again on the way out, it was harder to enjoy the sacred art. I found myself wondering, How forceful can I be without getting arrested? I was able to sneak away, but felt cheated out of fully appreciating the temple.

Visitors can lose a lot more than a few bucks if they're careless. The Khmer Rouge planted thousands of landmines in the area around Siem Reap, and I saw fruits of this evil sowing in some of the larger temples. Traditional Khmer orchestras of five or six men who had lost a limb or two played near the entrances and sold CDs of their music. Half of them looked sullen and the others seemed resigned to their disabilities. None showed any joy in performing in front of an audience.

But we have only seen a fraction of Cambodia's wonders. More emerged when the area around Angkor became a state at the beginning of the ninth century. It synthesized Funan liveliness and Chenla love of symmetry and made them spectacular.

Chinese sources say that royal succession crises had split Chenla apart shortly after its heyday.[5] A ruler named Jayavarman II then moved northwest to where Angkor would eventually be built, and in 802 CE, conducted a ritual in its northern hills to become the *Chakravartin*. He now had Shiva's power at his back and could use the old associations of royalty, the sacred mountain, animated forces in nature, and Hindu gods to project himself as the leader of this plain. Historians say that the meaning of the ceremony back in 802 is actually not known, so we don't know if he had that network of ideas in mind. But later Khmer kings did, and they saw him as the founder of their empire.[6] They would carry these ideas to new political reaches and artistic heights.

However, some kings would express power in heavy-handed ways, with imposing temples and stiff statues with facial expressions that made them seem too aloof to care about ordinary people. Trends in both elegance and force existed throughout Angkor's history, and much of its art reflects tension between them. These two personalities alternated from the ninth to the 14th century, and they created an artistic feast.

All the same, kings erected increasingly grandiose buildings as time went on. The land became loaded with huge piles of stones and laterite that required more and more people to labor for their upkeep. Several features of Angkor encouraged a taste for magnificence, and they made Cambodian culture unique:

- Central Javanese temples might have first inspired the Khmers to build big. Borobudur was erected in the late eighth and early ninth century by the Sailendra kingdom. It's much larger than earlier Southeast Asian stone temples, and historians have speculated about its influence on Cambodia. In the 800s, the Khmers began construction projects that outsized their own earlier works by many factors.

    But Khmers increased the scale of their buildings to otherworldly dimensions and burdened the earth with many of them. Both civilizations advanced in different ways. Javanese constructed only two enormous temples: Borobudur and Candi Prambanan. They built many kingdoms that rose and waned over the centuries. Their long, thin island has rich volcanic soils, but mountains separate them into pockets, and different areas held the most powerful states in different times. The Khmers were usually governed from Angkor, and many of their opuses got bigger and bigger. If they had early inspiration from Java, they mixed it with Indian currents (many societies in India built stone temples in the first millennium CE which embodied Hindu views of the universe) and their own aesthetics, and buffed it up by many factors.

- Angkor's unique geography was probably one of the biggest reasons why Khmers built to awe people. The city presided on a flat plain by Tonle Sap's northern shore. It was bordered in the north by the Phnom Kulen hills, where people quarried sandstone for the monuments, and where Jayavarman II had conducted his ceremony. The Mekong flows 150 miles to the east. Snow in its Himalayan source melts and the summer monsoon rushes in at the same time. The Mekong swells to a torrent which surges into the river that Tonle Sap flows into and forces its current to reverse. Water thus rushes into the lake every year so that its area increases fourfold and the surrounding plain is inundated. When the current reverses again and the water recedes, millions of fish become trapped within the locals' reach. This probably seemed as miraculous to the Khmers as the Nile's annual flooding did to ancient Egyptians.

The monsoon which arrives around May also seemed divine. It comes during the hottest time of the year, often beginning gradually and becoming increasingly intense during the summer until it drenches the earth with bursts of potency and grace. The rains usually last from May to November, but little falls in the other months and the contrast between wet and dry seasons is very sharp. My 2007 visit was near the end of the latter. The flat land's reddish brown dirt was completely dry. Dead leaves and thirsty beige grasses crackled when I stepped on them, and the air was dusty. Because Angkor is inland, it doesn't get as much rain as the Mekong delta and other coastal areas in Southeast Asia do, so it's not as lush all year. Khmer kings who were associated with nature's sudden bestowal of waters thus must have seemed like gods to many people.

The gods granted this energetic grace when I returned to Angkor in the late summer of 2012. At first I hesitated to go during the rainy season, but I found nature's life force exhilarating. Contrasts between the sky and land were so striking that only deities could have created them. The swelling clouds stood out from the flat rice fields as dramatically as the great temples did. The swirling greys and the sudden downpours made it seem that the gods were empowering the sky and fertilizing the earth.

The water in the rice paddies reflected the animated sky and the stately trees so that the views were luminous. Everything seemed to reflect everything else, and the images shifted every few feet as I walked. The whole landscape shimmered.

- Monarchs built awesome temples to associate their own might with nature's exuberance. But they had to go over the top to match it. Khmer kings constructed huge reservoirs (called barays) and canals that channeled water from the northern hills when the monsoons came. The east and west barays are more than four miles long and over a mile wide. Barays and the network of canals that linked with them could fertilize more land for rice farming. Their oceanic scales must have made them seem as otherworldly as the annual floods.[7]

- Like the Chenla state, Angkor was inland and distant from international maritime trade. Rice dominated the economy, which lacked a common currency—most people bartered.[8] Kings, their extended families, people that the monarchs appointed to oversee provinces, and elite priests controlled most of the wealth. Rice was the only major game in town, and its big leaguers portrayed themselves as divinely sanctioned.

- Cambodia's dense forests probably strengthened the love of elite ostentation. The Mayan rulers in Central America, who also built states in jungles, thrived on it too. Heavily wooded environments are hard to construct cities in because the land has to be intensively cleared and manipulated. Because of the manpower requirements, control is often forced from the top, with flamboyant elites displaying sacred authority. Khmer and Mayan rulers projected themselves dramatically, with ornate stone temples and awe-inspiring rituals.

  However, Angkor was different from the Mayan world. The latter was fragmented into many states and ecological zones, and it lacked a geographic feature to help unify all of it (like one central great lake or river). Because there was no single place from which one kingdom could consolidate the whole area, no Mayan city's population or construction came close to Angkor's in scale.

- The area's climate probably strengthened the Khmers' focus on centralized power and its sensational displays. The weather was certainly hot when I was there, but not in India's horrendous three-digit summertime temperatures, and it wasn't as oppressive as inland Florida's humidity which made me feel like I was breathing through a sponge when I attended a July conference at Disney World. I rarely felt uncomfortable in Cambodia. I paced myself and always carried a water bottle. The easiest way to live in its climate is to work in a steady, unhurried flow. Stay within the system's rhythms and don't question or try to outpace them.

This collective tempo easily meshes with the rice growing cycles. The agricultural seasons usually follow the same relaxed annual rhythms.[9] Khmers shared the same flow of time and tended crops in the midst of family and community, surrounded by forest and enveloped in heat.

Khmers subsumed the steady pace of life and the local village under the glory of the king, other elites, and the gods. Their horizons probably often shifted between their villages and dazzling displays of political power with Hindu rituals and imposing architecture. Most Cambodians still honor local spirits (which they call Neak Ta), and I often saw little shrines for them by trees and in Buddhist temples. Many communities in ancient Angkor clustered around ponds, and their residents must have honored spirits at shrines. Some historians have said that Khmer peasants' mindsets were largely focused on their small local worlds, but the regal temples loomed in the background, reminding them of the glory of kings and Hindu gods every day.[10] The rhythms of village life and the splendor of royal and religious monuments were often experienced together so that the latter probably seemed to add immense power to the former which helped to safeguard it.

- In this relatively two-dimensional perspective of the world, kings, elite priests, and administrators formed a network that ruled the land and took most of its wealth.[11] China honored Confucian literature until its imperial court was overthrown in 1911. It stressed values that all people, including the emperor, were bound to. Benevolence and sincerity hold the world together, and a ruler is supposed to personify them. If he fails, Heaven may mandate that his followers depose him (at least in theory). But Khmers lacked a voluminous literary tradition in their own language which yoked people in all classes to one system of ethics. Surviving inscriptions in Angkor are largely about the glory of the king and the gods (usually in Sanskrit), and the founding and administering of temples (usually in Khmer). Khmer literature was less able to provide perspectives that transcended the power of the king. More often than not, it glorified it. The Khmer state wasn't held together by a Confucian literary canon, but by personal loyalties between kings, other elites, and the under classes.

- Many royal successions became rats' mazes. Khmers lacked a constitution that said how the next ruler should be chosen, so violent rivalries often erupted. Kings had several wives, and inheritance passed through both male and female lines. A monarch's death often left several relatives to dogfight for the title (Suryavarman II killed his uncle in order to take the throne). The winner had extra motivation to build enormous temples to show that he was on top of the heap.

  Even when the king was strong, powerful families often conducted political intrigues, and governors of provinces sometimes tried to break away. A monarch could never take his rule for granted. The idea of divine kingship was thus projected with as much gusto as possible.

  Several succession crises beset Angkor right after Suryavarman II died. A later king named Jayavarman VII then built even more than he did (we'll explore his stupendous legacy later). Much Khmer construction happened in this pattern of political turbulence followed by a grand building program that outdid the past. Instead of establishing a stable dynasty, the Khmer monarchy had dramatic ups and downs and projected its own splendor whenever it could to make people believe in its strength.

Several factors thus encouraged displays of centralized power that could overshadow the subtle sides of Khmer art. The need to tame the dense forest, the economy's focus on rice, the balmy climate, the annual monsoon, the flooding and receding of Tonle Sap, frequent succession crises, and possible early inspiration from Java converged to encourage hypnotic displays of top-down authority and ideas that magnificence encourages well-being.

So is Cambodia cursed, as Brinkley said? Are her people destined to be exploited by the wealthy few? Not necessarily. Khmer art often mixed power and delicacy, and many exquisite varieties of both blossomed throughout its history. I saw many examples of the latter, which I found as enthralling as Angkor Wat. The interplay between these moods fostered centuries of some of the most enchanting art in world history.

Cambodia emerged in one of humanity's most fertile cultural crossroads, and it became one of its most influential varieties. Khmers mixed expressions of force and elegance in ways that varied throughout their empire's more-than 600-year history. This engendered a sinister side where absolute power was extolled, but the country and its people emerged within a much larger and more ancient field of cultural patterns. Appreciating this field is a great way to lighten the influence of that one side of Khmer history and help restore Cambodia to its old splendor.

As Chapter One concluded, you can enhance your creativity and ability to find paradise around you by seeing the world become bigger and bigger. This increase isn't tied to just one variable, like size or power. It comes from appreciating all aspects of human experience, and from multiple cultures sharing their heritages with each other. Because this kind of bigness has many dimensions, it can increase without a final limit, and without oppressing anyone.

Khmer society displayed power as magnificently as any culture ever has. It's easy to ignore the subtler sides of Khmer art because they exist in the shadows of the great temples, but we will explore the flowering of Cambodian society in the next chapter. Angkor created one of the most stimulating fusions of Indian and Southeast Asian abundance. The next chapter shows that its cultural wealth is far greater than what we have seen so far. Prepare to meet the Khmers as they march into their glory days.

PART ONE

CAMBODIA

SECTION TWO

THE FULL FLOWERING

CHAPTER 5

BUILDING FOUNDATIONS FOR THE GODS' PALACE

ANGKOR WAT IS the most famous Khmer monument, but I found the first big temples in and around Angkor as rewarding to explore. Khmers in the ninth century established artistic standards and ideas about the world for the rest of their empire's history. King Jayavarman II opened that century with his *Chakravartin* ceremony in the northern hills, where he built a city with a terraced temple in its center. Later kings used his ceremony to reinforce old associations between the sacred mountain, Hindu gods, royal authority, and local spirits. By erecting even larger temples down on Angkor's plain around 900 CE, they made this mixture of ideas sensational.

The material foundations of the Khmer Empire might have gotten a boost in the ninth century. The historian Victor Lieberman wrote that rainfall might have increased then and that many people were migrating into Angkor's area to take advantage of its augmented fertility.[1] Most newcomers probably came from the Mekong area and southern Laos, trekking with all their possessions on bullock carts, hoping for a secure life on Angkor's spacious plain next to fish-bestowing Tonle Sap. King Indravarman I (r. 877–889) and his son, Yashovarman I (r. 889–about 910), could marshal enough workers to build cities and temples that embodied some of the key ways in which Khmers thought about the world.[2]

Indravarman finished his royal cult temple in 881. It's called Bakong and it presides in Rolous, which was where the capital was back then (it's about eight miles southeast of Angkor). Because it is closer to Tonle Sap's shore than Angkor is, it was an optimal place for Khmers to begin creating fields for wet rice farming.

A previous king might have already begun Bakong, but Indravarman at least finished it and dedicated it to Shiva.[3] It symbolized Mt. Meru, as

Angkor Wat would 250 years later. Five nearly square and increasingly small levels of sandstone stand on each other, and they embody five levels of existence. The realm of the nagas is the lowest, and the world of the maharajas (great kings) hovers above the other four. An ascent to the top is a thus a journey from earth to the supernal realm. I stood on the summit and looked over the treetops and off to the horizon which merged into the sky warmed by the resplendent sun. It seemed that I really was on top of the universe's central mountain.

Indravarman made Chenla symmetry more dramatic. A stairway ascends each side of Bakong, and stout sculptures of elephants guard the corners. The temple's northern and southern sides have matching systems of shrines and long covered galleries, and two moats surround the whole complex. The outer moat measures about 900 meters on one axis and 700 on the other. A linga for Shiva presided on the temple's summit. Bakong's stately proportioned forms projected the strength of the king's royal cult, and its symmetrical buildings and expanded concentric enclosures became models for Angkor Wat.

The sky was clear before I climbed the temple during my 2012 trip, so I didn't bring an umbrella from my tuk tuk even though the rainy season was in full majesty. Dark grey clouds soon rolled in and the heavens were infused with the life force that irrigated the rice fields that Khmers had created. How many priestly ascents up the great temples coincided with a sudden downpour? Ancient Cambodians must have associated one with the other.

But nobody put priestly finery on me when I returned to earth. Instead, I scuttled back to the tuk tuk just in time to avoid getting firehosed, and remained in awe of how nature and Khmer culture converged to help create thought and art that have inspired people ever since.

Indravarman built two other great monuments, and all three formed an archetypal trio in Khmer culture. He dug the first great baray, which probably bolstered his image as a bringer of rains. It was 2.3 miles long and half a mile wide, and the fourth largest baray ever built in the Angkor area.

The third construction, Preah Ko, wins most hearts, including mine. It embodies the side of Khmer aesthetics that stresses elegance, and it took it to a new level.

Indravarman dedicated it to his ancestors and Shiva in 879 (two years before Bakong was consecrated). As his private family temple, it elaborated on old mixtures of royal spirits and a Hindu god. He thus honored his forbears before finishing his own public cult temple.

The towers represent ancestors, including Indravarman's parents. The males form the front row, and the queens line the back. The illustrious Jayavarman II occupies the central building in the front. All the shrines stand on a four-to five-foot-high rectangular platform. Preah Ko was a major step from the single-room Chenla shrines towards Angkor Wat's complexity.

The art historian Michael S. Falser admired Preah Ko's humanity. Two walls surround it and he felt that they balance space because they're not large enough to dominate the whole temple. They are in harmony with the empty zones between them so that positive and negative volumes complement each other.

The central towers were smaller than I had expected from pictures in books. Like the Chenla temples, they didn't make me feel as small as a dust mite. They're so close to each other that walking between them felt like being in the midst of a family. Perhaps Indravarman imagined his ancestors talking to each other when he paid his respects there.

Preah Ko's sculpture is equally exquisite and it inspired artists throughout Khmer history. Carvings of foliage and male and female guardians adorn the sides and doorways of the central towers. The guards project the vigor and poise that Khmer elites wanted to be associated with.

Lintels are decorated with imaginative vegetal patterns. A thick garland emerges from each side of the mouth of a *kala* (a monster with bulging eyes who guards doorways). An imaginary beast with a lion's head and an elephant's body springs from the other end of each garland. The whole design is both energetic and elegant. Classical Greek columns and lintels are dominated by clear lines, but these blocks brim with abundant life forms animated by nature's power.

Figure 6. Door lintel at Preah Ko.

Designs in many doorways show people intertwined with dense vegetation (Figure 8). Khmers would fashion these lively vegetal images for the rest of their history.

Doorposts are equally ornate. Many levels of octagons, cubes, and disks are stacked on each other so that the entire column is a profusion of forms instead of one line. This was already common in India, but the Khmers narrowed the posts, making the copious flow of forms elegant.

So while constructing this temple, Indravarman looked both backwards and forwards. He honored his parents but built on an unprecedented scale and created new standards of refinement in Khmer art.

Figure 7. Close-up of the same lintel.

Figure 8. Nature's exuberant energies on a door pattern
in a late ninth century temple called Lolei.

His three monuments synthesized symmetry, grandeur, and upper class refinement. This combination of impressions probably encouraged the growing labor pool to associate royalty with the state's order and nature's power, which brought the annual monsoon and flooding of Tonle Sap to irrigate crops. Indravarman could link this trio of constructions with local spirit and ancestral cults to provide an overarching order for people as they settled into Angkor, cleared land for fields, and planted rice.

Indravarman's son, Yashovarman I, also built these three types of monuments (a family temple, a royal cult temple, and a baray), but he outdid his father. He solidified these three constructions as central in Khmers' ideas of the world. He also founded the city of Angkor as the new capital.

Yashovarman paid his father homage before relocating by building an ancestral temple, which was his own version of Preah Ko. It's called Lolei and it only had four towers instead of six, but the pious son constructed it on an island in his father's baray. The water is long gone now, but the little towers once resembled blooming lotuses on it.

The new king must have felt satisfied with this tribute to the man who had been the Khmers' most illustrious builder. He respected his family's lineage and then carried it to new heights that rivaled Indra's celestial palace on Mt. Meru.

But Yashovarman's accession was violent—he had taken the throne from his brother, the crown prince. This might have impelled him to establish a new beginning that was more splendid than the past. He surrounded his new city with an earthen bank that measured four kilometers on each side, but he was just getting started.

The new king strengthened Khmer intellectual roots by building the other two types of monuments, but on an even grander scale. He first dug the largest baray made so far, which is more than four miles long and over a mile wide. People standing on its shore saw the water rippling towards a barely visible tree line. It must have seemed that only a god could have made it.

Yashovarman then worked on his city's centerpiece, his royal cult temple, which still looks down on Angkor Wat. He followed some of his father's ideas when he built Phnom Bakheng. Like Bakong, it housed a linga, was modeled on the cosmic mountain, and was constructed as increasingly small platforms standing on each other. But it is much more eminent than Bakong.

Yashovarman built it on a 220-foot-high hill. This lofty base enhances the feeling that the temple is the center of the universe. It's just down the road from Angkor Wat, and I could look down on its pineapple-shaped towers from the summit. Yashovarman's baray spread out in the opposite direction. Its glimmering surface under the ebullient sun stood out from the forest and fields.

Forty-four brick towers surround its base, and sixty more punctuate its terraces. On the summit, four towers surround the central shrine (the current one was built in the 12th century). The numbers 44, 60, and 4 add up to 108, which is a sacred number in Hindu and Buddhist cosmology. It often symbolizes the totality of creation. Phnom Bakheng is thus more complex than Bakong, and it's a microcosm of the universe. It thus portended Angkor Wat, but it rises higher. Yashovarman's spirit seems to remind Angkor Wat's builder, "Good job kid, but you still must respect me."

So Yashovarman extended ideas and aesthetics that his father expressed and made them even more prominent in Khmers' views of the world:

- Temples' combinations of symmetry, size, and elegant carvings, which highlighted the power and refinement of gods and kings,
- The temple-mountain as the center of the cosmos and royal cult,
- Associations between the royal cult, a linga's power, the annual rains, and the flooding of Tonle Sap.
- Fusions of local ancestors with Hindu gods,
- Numerical symbolism that correlated the royal temple with the universe,
- An enormous reservoir that connected the king with the annual monsoon and Tonle Sap's flooding.

Yashovarman made these ideas and patterns more magnificent by increasing the scale of his constructions, and this helped solidify their importance in Khmer thought up through Angkor Wat's time and then through the 13th century (when Jayavarman VII built more than any other Khmer king did). They structured the sense of nature's abundant energies into symmetrical and elegant patterns that symbolized order for the expanding state.

I ventured into the jungle in the hills north of Angkor and became immersed an environment that the Khmers knew when they constructed their first monuments and rice fields. The endlessly varied shades of green and dark brown and the fleeting views of the sky through the rare openings in the foliage flickered as I walked so that everything seemed animated. The friezes of garlands with men and animals sprouting from them, which Khmers carved over temple doorways, made sense because twisting and intertwined branches and vines always surrounded me. As above, so below—roots followed this pattern too, and they spread so profusely that I always had to watch my step to avoid tripping. Cambodians lived near this wild growth when they created rice fields. I had the impression that they felt they were incorporating its power into the temples that they were building and then ordering it with their symmetrical designs.

The temples impressed people in other ways besides visual forms. While descending the hill that Phnom Bakheng rises on, I became captivated enough by the loud mixture of birds and crickets pervading the trees and bushes to stop and listen. As they chirped the dense canopy of leaves enveloped us. Instead of one sight or sound to focus on, there was an all-pervasive vitality. When I reached the bottom, a traditional band played stringed instruments and a hand drum. Their sounds were as energetic but more ordered, as though the forces of nature were made refined and mystical. Ensembles like this performed in the courtyards and open pavilions of ancient temples and palaces (they were depicted in some temples' friezes).

Musicians that the friezes represented probably accompanied dancers who were enacting rituals to bring rains and commune with ancestors of royals and with other spirits. The dancers would have added more refinement to the vigorous mixtures of impressions in and around the monuments. Paul Cravath, in *Earth in Flower*, wrote of another idea which the symmetry of the temples might have expressed: male and female energies balancing each other and encouraging rains and crop fertility—he felt that the dances embodied this harmony. If so, this balance would have been easy to associate with the ideas in the above list, and it would have added more enrapturing beauty to them.

The common people who lived around these temples had many ways to enjoy them, even if only elites were familiar with the Hindu myths that they embodied. I was exploring another monument that Yashovarman built, Phnom Krom, during my 2012 trip. The locals were finishing their work for the day and returning home for dinner, and they brought the old stones back to life. The sparkling waters that surrounded us and the jubilant sun that had appeared from behind the clouds had raised everyone's spirits. Children in the village played and were quick to laugh. Adults exploring the temple on top of its 400-foot hill greeted me. The bubbling emotions I saw in the village and on the hilltop were probably similar to ancient Khmers' exultation when the rains came.

The surroundings matched the festive mood. The life-giving water rose around the house stilts, the fresh sun shined, and the rice fields glistened under the caressing waters as though they were smiling out of gratitude. The dramatic temples and the sacred power that infuses the natural environment when the rains come encourage joy. Khmer art and aesthetics didn't just trickle down from the top when kings conducted rituals. Nature's dramatic growth, the liveliness of the arts, and the people's eagerness to celebrate good times must have reinforced each other.

Times weren't good for everyone though because Khmers used a lot of slave labor to construct their monuments. It's hard to imagine all of their builders reveling in their beauty. To the under classes, their size and regularity probably symbolized incontestable power. People seem to have felt both the hard and soft sides of Khmer art as soon as Angkor was built.

The elegant side of Khmer art fully blossomed shortly after Yashovarman's reign. Many visitors to Angkor give the beauty prize to a temple called Banteay Srei. A man named Yajnavaraha (who was one of the king's counselors and priests) and his younger brother erected it in the late 10th century. Vittorio Roveda thinks several later kings or elite officials modified it up to the 14th century.[4] Yajnavaraha later became the guru of King Jayavarman V, who was known for religious tolerance—both Hinduism and Buddhism flourished under his care. So this shrine was erected by a religious man for his own devotions rather than by a king projecting his own power.

As my driver and I headed for Banteay Srei (it's about 13 miles north-west of Siem Reap), the surroundings switched back to thick forest enveloping stilt homes. But the dirt lot near the temple was crammed with more than its share of cars and Korean tour busses which jolted me back to the present. The inner temple's small size must have complemented the piety of a local elite family, but the groups of chattering tourists made me feel that the whole Hindu pantheon was marching through it in broad-brimmed hats, toting cameras. Yet its elegance still shone around the densely packed bodies.

Banteay Srei was built from pink sandstone, which is soft and easy to carve. This helped Khmers develop new standards of realism in their friezes. Faces have more intense expressions, which add an inner dimension to them. Two monkeys from the *Ramayana*, Valin and Sugriva, viciously fight; they project enough rage to make people shutter. The figures are so deeply carved that they seem about to leap from the walls.

The sandstone also allowed sculptors to carve larger narrative scenes, and thus take a major step towards Angkor Wat's huge panels. Banteay Srei's images are also from myths of Hindu gods directing events with cosmic importance. Khmers were now able to put the vast panoramas from Indian myths on their temples. Although Banteay Srei wasn't a royal shrine, its builder had to make his art conform to the court's prestige. Its sweeping perspectives of gods ordering the universe complemented ideas of the king as the hub of the empire.

Sculptures of female deities balance the big perspectives, as Angkor Wat's devatas do. Their gentle faces crown their bare upper bodies, which are round and soft-looking. But their elegantly flowing *sampots* and their jewelry refine the eroticism. Throughout their history, Khmers made statues of women that impeccably balance sensual beauty and respect for their dignity. The lines of the deities' garments on this temple flow in ways that mimic the vegetal patterns carved around them. Locals later named this shrine Banteay Srei (Citadel of the Women) after them. Doorposts, lintels, plinths, and rooflines are as finely sculpted as jewel boxes. Banteay Srei's carvers made every inch glitter.

The people I met there made the place even more savory. One was a tall, fast-talking fifty-something New York construction worker, who introduced me to his much quieter companion, a young Cambodian man who ran a local orphanage. The latter's soft voice and clear eyes exuded peace. The New Yorker described the enormous amount of work that his friend did, who seemed too modest to explain it himself. The Cambodian's smile and the construction worker's outgoing personality formed contrasting examples of graciousness.

A long line of vendors in the parking lot sold T-shirts. The girl that I bought mine from wore a jacket, scarf, and straw hat in the 95-degree heat. Maybe her employers made her wear them to model some of the goods. "You buy everything from me, okay?" she said with a cheerful voice and radiant smile even though she might have been uncomfortable in the searing heat. During both of my trips to Cambodia, I noticed that many females kept their dignity in trying circumstances.

I took a walk during a break in the middle of the ride back to Siem Reap, and pretty melodies from a bowed stringed instrument breezed through the foliage. The player was excellent; he put the maximum amount of feeling into every note. I had to accompany him with a guitar that I bought in town and had placed in the back seat of the car.

He was about forty-five, with dark green tattoos that covered his bare chest and arms. Since ancient times, many Southeast Asian societies have thought that tattoos give their bearer magical protection. He was polite when we met, but he said and smiled little. He would have been a teenager during the Khmer Rouge's regime, and this made me wonder if he had lived in a world of forced labor and mass starvation at an age when more fortunate people experience their first romances. His stern face seemed to extend his protective armor from head to toe. His stiffness contrasted with his music. We jammed for about 20 minutes. He bowed what sounded like folk songs, and I alternated between strumming chords and playing melodies. About half a dozen times, his mouth widened into a smile and his eyes glowed with warmth.

As time went on, the subtle artworks had to compete for people's attention with grander expressions of centralized control. The balance between elegance and power often tilted towards the latter.

A key shift towards the bigger bang occurred during Rajendravarman II's reign (944–968). The empire had split into two capitals before his rule so that a rival king presided in a ritual center that he built at Koh Ker (it's about 70 miles northeast of Angkor). This center and many small temples that dot the countryside around it are fairly well-preserved, and they're known for especially lively sculptures. After its founder died, Rajendravarman centralized the kingdom again at Angkor and brought new levels of organization to the realm by replacing local lords who owned their own land with appointed officials that reported to him. He also established more ritual centers in the provinces.[5] The Khmer state consolidated into an empire that would rule much of mainland Southeast Asia for the next 300 years. The king built monuments that matched his imperial ambitions.

Rajendravarman erected a huge state temple called Pre Rup near the southern side of Yashovarman's baray. It was another step towards Angkor Wat, with five towers looming on a high central platform—they're in the Mt. Meru form, with the highest tower in the middle, surrounded by the others at the corners. He constructed a similar temple called East Mebon on an island in the middle of the baray. Both have door lintels in Preah Ko's pattern of mythical creatures issuing from garlands, but they're more formal. The vines' flows are straighter and stiffer, almost like a military march. Rajendravarman tightened art forms after the looser experimentation at Koh Ker as though he and his master builder told the artisans, "Stop messing around! We have an empire to build."

In the 11th century, Suryavarman I took the throne after a long war with a rival prince and extended the kingdom into much of where Thailand later emerged as a nation.[6] He also built Angkor's biggest baray about three miles west of the former champ, near the back of the royal palace. The historian David Chandler saw this as a sign that more people were living in Angkor, and that the empire was becoming more bureaucratic and centralized. The number of places Khmers called cities increased from about 20 to 47 during his reign. L. P. Briggs felt that Suryavarman was a great king because he unified more territory and ran it relatively smoothly. However, Chandler wrote that kingship intensified, meaning that royal power was more centralized, extensive, and sensational.

Suryavarman II also grabbed the throne violently, by killing his uncle, Dharanindravarman I. He bolstered his own image by building Angkor Wat. He also invaded Cham states (in central and southern Vietnam) and the Dai Viet (in northern Vietnam), and expanded the empire through more of Thailand. Things were happening on a larger scale under both Suryavarmans. The territory and the magnitude of wars increased, and larger monuments projected the glory of the men who directed epic events.

But Suryavarman II wasn't the most prolific Khmer builder. Jayavarman VII, who reigned from 1181 to about 1220, earned that honor. The period between Suryavarman's death in 1150 and his accession must have been traumatic because several violent succession crises beset it and the Chams launched a major invasion. Jayavarman then headed a march into Angkor, took over the throne, and piled more lordly constructions on the earth than any other king had. His buildings represent the height of Khmer power. Walks through them gave me unforgettable glimpses of Khmer civilization during its political zenith.

We will explore them in the next chapter and immerse ourselves in Khmer culture during its apex. Having examined its foundations in this chapter, we're ready to approach it during its heights.

Europe also reached one of its creative peaks during that time. The most admired Gothic cathedrals were built while Jayavarman VII reigned, and some of the greatest literature in Western history was written in the 13th and early 14th centuries. We'll enter this society in the next chapter too. Comparing both civilizations will prepare us for exploring the method for finding paradise in the world. Each culture's ideas and art emerged in larger settings with many facets. Appreciating these environments can lighten tendencies to be overawed by elites' projections of power. The larger cultural landscapes and their diversity can provide bigger Wows, which can be directed at all of us instead of only the people in power. Following these Wows around the world can take us to paradise.

CHAPTER 6

THE PAGODA AND THE CATHEDRAL: THE KHMER EMPIRE AND MEDIEVAL EUROPEAN SOCIETIES COMPARED

MANY CAMBODIANS HONOR Jayavarman VII as the greatest Khmer king. A hospital that I drove by in Siem Reap bears his name. This was fitting because he founded over 100 places that catered to the infirm. Thousands of people were picked to supply them with food and medicine. Each hospital employed two doctors, several assistants, two cooks, and many temple servants who conducted rituals for giving offerings to the Buddha.

Jayavarman adopted a different religion than the former kings' Hinduism. The old forms of worship identified rulers with Shiva or Vishnu, and often made them aloof and mysterious. But Jayavarman VII embraced a form of Mahayana Buddhism that stressed compassion.

The royal workshops sculpted statues of Buddhas, bodhisattvas, and royals that come down to earth from the unsympathetic Angkor Wat friezes. Many resemble real Cambodians, with features that are less stylized and angular. Their lowered eyes and gentle smiles suggest meditation, but their square faces and solid torsos project strength. The old Khmer use of symmetry to fuse energy and grace assumed one of its most splendid varieties.

However, some historians have seen a sinister side of the court's compassion. Jayavarman began a construction binge that seems maniacal, and he built more than any of his predecessors had. Thousands of farmers and slaves were forced to toil under the scorching sun. The king's building program seems self-contradictory because it expressed his compassion by burdening his people. L. P. Briggs felt that it took a strange and megalomaniacal mind to conceive temples and hospitals to

make his subjects' lives easier and then inflict miseries on them in order
to build them.

Claude Jacques said that some of the construction traditionally
attributed to Jayavarman was done later. Khmers continued to erect and
modify monuments in the 14th century. However, even Jacques noted
that the unprecedented amount of building began with Jayavarman as
the driving force—he made his people construct more than Khmers
ever had before, and all the later Khmer kings combined didn't come
close to matching his amount of building.

Jayavarman's four most famous monuments at Angkor project both
compassion and command. They represent the height of Khmer power
and wealth, and I found them breathtaking. Like Angkor Wat, they're
both elegant and imposing, and people can spend years enjoying their
different meanings.

Jayavarman began a massive reconstruction of Yashovarman's royal
city. Like his predecessor, he wanted to establish a new and bigger
beginning.

My driver followed the road past Phnom Bakheng to its walls. They're
almost two miles long on each side, about 25 feet high, made from laterite,
and surrounded by a moat. Their most intriguing parts are the five gate
towers. Each has four giant faces (one on each side) above a corbelled
arch over the entrance. They smile a bit, without showing any teeth. Their
square forms project the unmovable strength that Jayavarman's Buddha
sculptures exude. They express both compassion and incontestable
power, and they made me wonder what splendors awaited behind them.

Our car inched towards one of the gates because traffic was jammed
near its narrow archway. The turtle's pace increased the drama as we
approached the faces over the gateway. Many art historians have thought
that they represent Lokesvara, a bodhisattva who embodies the Buddha's
compassion. He protects the world between the Buddha's death and his
future incarnation as Maitreya. Others have written that they might be
portraits of Jayavarman and that he fused his identity with Lokesvara's.
Other identities have been surmised, but whoever they were, the mighty
walls and unflappable faces projecting order throughout the land would
have awed a Khmer peasant walking behind his bullock cart towards

the kingdom's center. The faces on the towers gazed into the infinite distance as he ambled to the slow rhythm of clip clopping hooves. Commoners felt a striking contrast between their little stilt homes and the political and religious center.

Jayavarman wanted all comers to feel this contrast. A long sculpture of a snake being pulled in the same fashion as the giant one on Angkor Wat's frieze lines each side of the the bridge. Gods do the work on one side and demons labor on the other. Many historians think these works either portray the creation of the universe, as Angkor Wat's scene of the giant serpent does, or Indian myths of a naga bridge that leads to heaven. In either way, the statues make it clear that a visitor is approaching the most potent place in the world.

We then rode through dense forest to the Bayon, which many people consider Angkor's most fascinating monument besides Angkor Wat. Jacques called it one of the most powerful religious buildings in the world. It occupies the symbolic center of Jayavarman's city, and some historians have seen it as a model of the universe. Walking through the Bayon immersed me in Khmer thought during the height of Angkor's glory, and it illustrated key changes since Angkor Wat's construction.

The Bayon's soft grey hues and weather-beaten visage give it a wistful air that could have made a poet from Europe's Romantic era swoon. But it must have sparkled when it was new. Enclosing walls and dozens of towers with an enormous face in each cardinal direction rise towards a central spire that was about 150 feet high before its top collapsed. The whole edifice must have looked like a giant wedding cake, but the face towers made its outline even more complex.

I first passed through ruins of an outer nearly square enclosure of galleries that once housed shrines for dozens of gods and ancestors. The statues are long lost, but a few elderly women burned incense for people who gave offerings. Since the Bayon is a Buddhist temple, locals go there to worship, and a few were relaxing in the outer enclosure. Two young men sat in one of its shrines, and both smiled and said, "Hello!" Though I received a friendly welcome to the Bayon, its inner area still seemed mysterious.

I then reached a key transitional area: the outer wall of the temple's central section. It's nearly square and, like Angkor Wat's middle corridors, emblazoned with carvings on all four sides. But these reliefs are so different from Suryavarman II's visions that they approach a revolution in perspective.

Like Angkor Wat, the Bayon has its share of marching soldiers—Khmers still loved action scenes. These images include a sea battle which might represent troops driving the invading Chams out of Tonle Sap, though other interpretations have been proposed.[1] But the clashing armies are mixed with views of daily life that come down to earth from Angkor Wat's regal scenes. Women in their homes prepare meals. Men haul goods on ox-pulled carts. A man and woman walk behind a cart, a child rides his shoulders, and baby goats trot beside its wheels. People in a pavilion help a woman in labor. A crowd watches a cockfight. Men fish with nets and women sell food in a market. The perspective of the king and his armies has expanded to the rest of the people.

A second enclosing wall, which is closer to the center, also teems with carvings, but many project a more sublime atmosphere (they were largely carved after Jayavarman VII's reign, in the late 13th century). Gods, soldiers, and smiling mystics with long beards dominate this wall. Several friezes show a Hindu god surrounded by worshipers. Sometimes he is in a shrine that floats on lotuses, and elegant court women outflank it so that these scenes are both otherworldly and sensual.

But the atmosphere becomes more solemn on the other side of the wall. The enclosure brackets the area around the central tower's platform, and many thick square columns cram the space into narrow passageways. Some of the galleries were built later, in the late 13th century. A Hindu reaction against Buddhism flared up then, many Buddhist images were defaced, and new structures were added (Hindu gods on the second enclosing wall were carved around that time). The effect is claustrophobic. I could barely squeeze through some of the walls and pillars. The narrow, musty corridors invoked images of chanting priests and aromas of incense. A pungent smell would have carried well in this place, and it would have made the temple seem even more powerful and sacred. When I was on the west side, the odor of urine wafting through one of the passages was almost unbearably strong. I wanted to escape the combination of ancient mystery and present squalor.

I felt liberated when I ascended the steps to the top level. I was now surrounded by the face towers. Their lips turn up at the corners into Mona Lisa smiles so that they look both reserved and enigmatic.

Though some guidebooks have said that the faces portray Jayavarman in the guise of Lokesvara, other interpretations have been proposed. One of the most interesting is detailed in a recent book, *Bayon, New Perspectives*. One of its contributors, Peter D. Sharrock, has seen Tantric influence in this temple. Tantric Buddhism fused the Mahayana tradition with Hindu ideas that saw creative sexual energy pervading the universe's abundance of forms, and it flourished in northern India by the late first millennium CE. It emphasized yogic techniques for becoming conscious of the unity of all things and reaching enlightenment. According to Sharrock, the face towers depict, not the king, but a Tantric deity called Vajrasattva. The profusion of faces thus might represent him emanating throughout the universe so that his nature permeates every inch of it. The Bayon's wedding cake form might symbolize a spiritual universe before it condensed into solid matter.[2]

Sharrock argues that the faces on the towers don't look like Lokesvara or Jayavarman VII.[3] The latter's surviving portraits show a sturdy ex-military man with a bull neck and the paunch of a middle-aged king who had substituted banquets for battles. His cheeks are fleshy, but the ones on the Bayon are more elegant. Its faces seem more idealized, but Jayavarman's made me imagine his wife teaching the old warrior about compassion with a few playful pinches.

Many ascetics in Northern India practiced Tantrism when Jayavarman took the throne, but in the 1190s, Islamic armies from Afghanistan swept through the land, ransacked Buddhist monasteries around the Ganges, and butchered many of their monks. Some who escaped fled to Southeast Asia and they might have influenced Cambodia's king. Khmers were long used to synthesizing images and ideas from India with their own royal cults.

It is not even necessary to posit Tantric influences to see the Bayon as the Buddha permeating the universe. In the 1930s, Paul Mus said that it might embody a miracle he performed to convince skeptics that he could help liberate them from their karmic chains. He manifested himself in infinite images from all angles, and they rose to the highest heaven. Mus felt that the Bayon's multitude of face towers reproduced this captivating mythic image in stone.

Other art historians see the Bayon as a Khmer map of the world, which combined local cults with ideas from India. The temple contains inscriptions that identify deities, prominent Khmers, cities, and provinces, and it used to house at least 117 statues (they were later stolen). The Bayon thus seems like a microcosm of the empire and the heavens. If the temple represents a shift to Tantric Buddhism, it synthesizes it with local ideas of geography, ancestral cults, royals, and Hindu gods. This is Southeast Asian syncretism at its finest.[4]

I then approached the center of it all. A line of connecting rooms enters from the east and they lead to the middle chamber. The room is circular and it once housed a 12-foot-tall statue of the Buddha until the Hindu reactionaries smashed it and threw it down a well. A narrow corridor wraps around this space, and two circles of 16 rooms project from its other side like lotus petals. Some historians have seen this configuration as a mandala, which is a circular diagram of the cosmos emerging from the center. These chambers thus might be the first forms of the universe's emanation. It's a pretty design, but the interior was dark and constricting, with an uneven floor, stuffy air, and bats darting overhead. A priest sat in the middle and took offerings from a few locals.

So my progression through the whole temple alternated between compassion and mysterious power. The carvings on the walls project both. Their style is named after the Bayon, and it's folksier than Angkor Wat's. Some fans of Khmer art say that its quality is lower than its predecessor's, but the figures are easier to relate to. They look more like real people and express a wider range of emotions. But though the reliefs expand perspectives to commoners, they still focus on centralized power. The people are not differentiated from the temple. The carvings aren't portraits by Titian or Rembrandt that meet your gaze with dignity as individuals who have deep inner lives. Instead, they merge into crowded scenes and alternate with many images of marching soldiers and battles. Some warriors kneel and raise severed heads over themselves. In an image of a naval battle, a crocodile chomps on a human corpse. All the people seem like cogs in a larger scheme in which the universe's energy is more important. No scene stands out from the others. All wrap around the temple as though the grand system is its main concept.[5]

Jayavarman built the Bayon in a time of crisis. According to inscriptions from his reign, Cham armies sacked Angkor, and he took the throne by force and defeated them near the royal palace. Recent scholarship has questioned the sacking of the city, but it agrees that the Chams invaded the eastern part of the empire, and they might have conquered and ruled Angkor for a while. Being in the midst of invading armies and lacking a strong king, Khmers might have thought that the universe was in turmoil. Claude Jacques felt that Jayavarman VII's power was fragile because his enemies were near. David Chandler saw his regime, with its manic building program, as an attempt to break with the past after he violently assumed leadership and drove the Chams out. Maybe he projected his authority with so much construction because it was dicey to begin with.

The Bayon expressed both openness to new perspectives and a desire to assert centralized power as ardently as ever. It expanded horizons to common folks and Mahayana ideas, but used them to give cosmological backing to a new king after a turbulent time. Jayavarman seems to have deployed the full range of ideas that Khmers held to secure his kingdom in every possible way.

But the Bayon surpassed its maker. The Hindu reaction in the late 13th century was unprecedented. Religious intolerance had never surfaced in Angkor before (at least not on a large scale), but so much Buddhist sculpture was destroyed there that a king likely gave the order. Since the Bayon was Angkor's symbolic center, it was converted into a Hindu temple, and more friezes and inner corridors were fashioned.[6] Like Angkor Wat, it's so intricate and multifaceted that it elicits several interpretations and all are awe-inspiring.

I met a group of four monks while walking around the top level. Their bright orange robes stood out from the dark grey late afternoon shadows that engulfed us. We sat between the face towers and one described the rigors of their practice. They rose at an hour when most of us are barely half way through the night's sleep, begged for food in the morning, and were not allowed to eat in the afternoon or evening. They usually had to labor and read scriptures in their monastery and thus probably welcomed their sojourn as a break. One did all the talking; the others were shy and passive and rarely smiled. Many young Cambodians endure barren monastic lives because they have no alternatives in their impoverished country.

A small elderly woman sat in a corner pavilion and burned joss sticks for worshipers. She smiled, but more meekly than joyfully. She was probably a survivor of Pol Pot's regime who had found this a safe little niche. She silently sat between the thick walls and seemed as passive as the three monks. Their narrow worlds contrasted with the old grandeur that surrounded us.

The palace grounds sprawl next to the Bayon, and they comprise one of the best places to imagine what the glory days were like. What was there before Jayavarman VII beefed up the area was already dazzling. A temple called Baphuon shone next to the royal compound; it was the largest monument in Angkor when it was built in the 11th century. The top soared about 150 feet, and it was probably plated with gold leaf or copper leaf (it was called the Tower of Bronze after the Bayon was built, which was called the Golden Tower). The tropical sun beaming on it must have made it seem like a dynamo of cosmic energies.

Just beyond Baphuon is a huge parade ground (1,800 by 656 feet), which stretches between the royal palace (on the left) and a group of ancient official buildings. The Khmers displayed themselves here in full splendor. Religious festivals enlivened the calendar, and crowds assembled to watch parades, fireworks, and elephant and boar fights.

Royal processions from the palace included soldiers, musicians, drummers, and people carrying banners. A group of 300–500 dancing women wearing flowers in their hair and holding burning tapers joined them. The female palace guards also promenaded, and they toted lances and shields. Dignitaries on elephants rode in front of the king, and they were surrounded by more red parasols than a Chinese political envoy named Zhou Daguan could count when he lived in Angkor in 1296 and 1297. The king's wives, concubines, and servants rode next; some sat on horses and elephants while others reclined in palanquins and carts. More than 100 gold filigreed parasols sheltered them. The king came last, standing on an elephant and brandishing the sacred sword under more than 20 gold filigreed white parasols with handles made of gold. Soldiers and more pachyderms surrounded him.

A late 12th century stone terrace extends in front of the palace, forming a fitting frame for these spectacles. It is almost 1,000 feet long, and its height varies from 10 to 15 feet. Carvings of nearly life-size elephants in hunting scenes fill it with regal energy. Men positioned on their backs chase tigers, buffaloes, and boars. This wall, called the Elephant Terrace, was probably the base of royal reception pavilions where the king and courtiers watched the festivals.

The palace was the largest in Southeast Asia. A laterite wall about 1,900 feet long, 800 feet wide, and 15 feet high surrounded it (its shorter side faces the parade ground). A grand stairway with elephants carved on each side still leads from the parade ground to the Universal King's house.

A multi-tiered pyramid called Phimeanakas punctuates the middle of the palace's compound. A Khmer legend said that the king slept with a courtesan in a room on the pyramid's summit every night. She represented a naga princess who transformed into a beautiful woman. Some Khmers and Chinese residents believed that this ritual fertilized the kingdom because it was a meeting of the ruler's celestial power with earthly energies. But if it was enacted on this pyramid, it wasn't a casual fling. The room at the top is about 50 feet above the ground, and the steep stairs render the climb and descent a bit dangerous. I found it surprisingly small. There's no area for frivolities, but only enough space to lie down. If the legend was true, a royal rendezvous must have been conducted with the formality of a state ritual. The ceremony might have only occurred in folk tales, but the building formed an august center of the palace ground.

Some people might have taken this tale seriously, since many Southeast Asian societies held myths about a high-caste Hindu man and a local naga princess begetting their royal dynasty. Funan did too. The Khmers might have made the old story more splendid by associating this monument with it.

Other remnants of the palace's past glory also tantalized me. Five enormous pools once gleamed within its walls. Historians think that they might have been used for both ritual cleanings and pleasure. As many as 3,000–5,000 female servants, including concubines, are supposed to have lived within the compound. If they frolicked in the waters, they might have made kings and courtiers imagine devatas.

I trampled through the area, imagining how Khmer royalty lived. A terrace with friezes of birds rose between two of the pools. Perhaps dancers and orchestras with tinkling gongs performed on it. Long rectangular foundations of royal apartments and storerooms spread between the pools. Spaces in the palace alternated between commanding halls and open areas with sparkling water.

But court life seems to have been stilted. The king gave audience twice a day when Zhou Daguan lived in Angkor. Servants blew into conch shells to signal the ruler's arrival, and he appeared in a golden window. Two women pulled a curtain back to reveal him as he held the sacred sword, and all in attendance had to put their hands together and bow to the ground. They could only raise their heads after the horns stopped.

Even Zhou Daguan was impressed with the rooms, and he hailed from mighty China. They had enormous pillars and beams that were carved and painted, and they alternated with long corridors and high towers.

I found the buildings on the other side of the parade ground as engrossing as the palace. Twelve laterite towers line it, and two long single-story buildings called khleangs stand behind them. Inscriptions from the time say that dignitaries stayed in the khleangs while visiting the capital. I found these structures stately. Their walls are high and thick, with a central room and a long, narrow chamber branching from each side. The buildings are formal and symmetrical, so they were fitting places for distinguished guests.

Different theories have been proposed for the towers' functions. People might have watched processions from their tops, or acrobats might have walked on tightropes between them. Zhou Daguan said that when two people had a public dispute, each sat in a tower and emerged one to four days later. The one who was wrong was always sick. All three explanations sound far-fetched to me because none seems like a sufficient reason for building them. Whatever their purposes were, the towers and khleangs complemented the elephant terrace and palace. The buildings surrounded parades with aloof majesty.

Only the stones and laterite remain, but these edifices once framed festivities that would have made the Super Bowl seem boring. Bright flags and tents, bursting fireworks, shrieking conches, booming drums, lithe dancers with sparkling jewelry and tiaras, and regal elephants glittered between the monuments. Racing chariots, grunting wrestlers, and men on horseback fighting with spears rumbled through there. Acrobats and jugglers added lilt to the muscle. The sense of fun and the sublime power of the king and the gods must have blended to an extent that's hard to imagine today. In this mixture of cheer and awe, how could people have doubted that the combination of the king and the deities was the source of their well-being?

Khmers fused local spirit cults, harmonious village life, symmetry, elegance, royal majesty, Hindu and Buddhist deities, Indian traditions of expressing abundance, their own love of fun, and Angkor's dramatic natural landscape into some of the most spirited art anyone has ever created. This mixture of ideas and sensibilities might seem muddled to moderns, but we have to see it through Khmer eyes to fully appreciate its richness. We'll do this more deeply by immersing ourselves in Medieval Europe and comparing both societies. They can shed light on each other because both emerged and waned around the same time. Seeing both together can enlarge our worlds by showing how unique and multifaceted every culture is.

MEDIEVAL EUROPEAN REFLECTIONS

Khmers made the majesty of royalty and gods a central focus, but Jayavarman VII's European contemporaries lived in a different cultural setting. Medieval Europeans shared many ideas that separated kings and godliness, and they invoked them with zeal. The Christian Trinity of Father, Son, and Holy Spirit was delineated at the Council of Constantinople in 381 and expounded as the only divinity. Jesus lived only one life, and he is the only son of God. He is unique, rather than incarnated many times, as Hindu gods and the Buddha were. These strict theological limits prevented kings from choosing the deity that best complemented their authority.

Medieval Europeans did associate kings with sacredness. Many felt that their monarch was God's earthly representative. The French anointed their kings in Reims Cathedral from a little vial that they believed a dove had brought for the baptism of Clovis I in the fifth century CE (Reims is about 80 miles northeast of Paris). Norman churchmen also felt that the king was God's anointed, and by grace, godlike himself. But monarchs still had to follow theology that the Church approved. Popes insisted that the king's power is only over his earthly realm.

The papacy had reformed the Church and strengthened itself in the middle of the 11th century, and it was resolved to restrain kings from claiming enough power to challenge its own prestige. Popes were now elected by cardinals rather than appointed by emperors, and the papal administration grew into a bureaucracy with lawyers, financiers, and notaries. The papacy formed a state over towns near Rome and they swore allegiance to it—it was becoming its own independent sovereignty and claiming that no worldly monarch could impose on its authority.

Pope Gregory VII and Germany's emperor, Henry IV, were headstrong men. Henry was exercising what he thought were his royal prerogatives by choosing his own bishops and giving them the ring and crozier that signified their rank. Gregory was outraged. Both were about to knock heads with a bang that thundered all over Christendom.

Gregory protested and Henry called a conference of bishops in Worms in 1076 (a city on the southern part of the Rhine River), where he declared that Gregory's election was null and void. The pope responded by excommunicating him and absolving his subjects from loyalty to him. Henry then scampered south and waited in the snow at the gates of Canossa, where the pope was resting. Gregory pardoned him, but only after three humbling days.

The Khmers didn't have a powerful spiritual institution that was distinct enough from the king for a prolonged period to formulate a theology that established permanent limits for him. Their monarch could identify with Shiva, Vishnu, or any Mahayana deity he fancied. Europe had a separate church, which defined orthodox thought. Cambodia's kings could mix ideas, faiths, and images more freely.

Popes also found their own authority contested. The Orthodox Church in Greek-speaking Byzantine lands denied their supremacy. Its patriarchs felt that their own form of worship was the oldest and purest. Those Latin upstarts were imposing their own interpretations on God.

Some Christians in lands that followed the pope challenged him too. In the 12th century, some of Rome's residents began to identify with ancient Rome, and they felt that the papacy was less important than its secular institutions, such as the senate. The 14th century legal scholar Marsilius of Padua complained that popes were too worldly. They behaved like kings by luxuriating in palaces and directing armies. He asserted that the pope is supposed to live in humble poverty, as early Christians did, and leave statecraft to secular men. Ghibellines (supporters of the Holy Roman Emperor in his tussles with the pope) in Italy and kings and dukes in France, Flanders, and Germany shouted, "Amen!" Europe had so many sovereignties and voices that anyone's assertion of divine authority over the whole pot of stew would have had his neighbors up in arms.

That neighborhood was increasingly noisy. Towns had been growing in Europe since the late 10th century. The barbarian raids (Viking, Saracen, and Magyar) had subsided, and people were improving farming methods. They made heavier ploughs that dug deeply into hard northern European soils. The newly adopted harness enabled horses to pull plows by putting the stress on their shoulders instead of their windpipes—this multiplied their pulling power. It also enabled more inland trade by making large horse-drawn carts possible. Farmers developed a three-fold system of crop rotation that produced more from the land by using two fields each year and letting the other lie fallow and replenish. People also used more manure to fertilize soils. Watermills were being built in northern Europe, and they allowed grain to be ground more efficiently than older mills powered by animals or humans. Communities cleared forests and drained marshes, putting more land under cultivation. All these quiet labors enabled a steady population increase, and some historians have found evidence that Europe experienced a general rise in temperatures which would have prolonged the growing seasons. Its population growth created profound social changes.

The historian Victor Lieberman, in *Strange Parallels*, wrote that Southeast Asia might have received more rainfall during that time, and that this fostered higher populations and encouraged the growth of more complex political states—Angkor's Rajendravarman II and Suryavarman I extended the Khmer empire and organized it more tightly as Europe grew. But the population growth in the West created a seedbed for an urban revolution that formed a contrast with the Khmer world.

Towns throughout Western Europe received their own charters for governance by the 13th century, and in many, a person could become free after living there for a year and a day. The population rise created competition for land. Younger sons in noble families who couldn't inherit the family estate had to make a hard choice: Let your older brother wipe his feet on you because he came out of the womb first; fight that bastard to the death; find religion and live a dull life in a monastery; or move and forge your own place in the world. Many young men chose the last option.

So did many in the under classes. Nobles competing with each other were squeezing all the goods they could from their peasants. So both callous-handed farmers and angry younger sons packed their bags, hit the roads, and headed for the town gates. Money was increasingly used, and this allowed many serfs (or their new urban patrons) to buy their freedom from the old feudal bonds.

Others came too. Semi-professionals, such as notaries, looked for employment. The more enterprising landowners were enticed by business opportunities.

As the cities grew, they became more complex and created spaces for more types of people to settle into. Many came, including traders, artisans, entertainers, wandering scholars, itinerate preachers, orphans, and prostitutes. Proud and independent merchants emerged and displayed their new wealth with multi-story homes, sumptuous tapestries and gowns, banquet tables piled with beef and venison, courtly dances, glittering rings, and prancing horses. They resented tax-happy kings, popes, and lords. All these classes of people jostling each other in the dense streets forged identities that were increasingly independent from royalty.

People specialized in different trades and formed guilds. Many of today's common English last names emerged from them, including Smith, Clark, Baker, Cook, Miller, Hunter, Barber, Carter, Wheeler, Mason, Tinker,

Weaver, Potter, Tanner, Farmer, Fisher, Chandler, Page, Foster, and Roper. Others were named after their towns, such as York, Lincoln, Dover, Wells, and Winchester. Some people were named after places where they lived or came from, like Hill, Wood, Rivers, and Dale. Others received last names based on personal characteristics, including Sharp, Fox, Dull, Armstrong, Little, White, Brown, Black, Long, Short, and Freeman. People's own identities apart from royal majesty were strengthening.

The growing towns did allow kings to gain power at the expense of the landed nobility. The latter relied on their own lands for wealth and didn't participate as much in the growing monetary economy. As more money went into circulation, they were hit by inflation at the same time that they were losing laborers to the towns. But monarchs relied on urbanites for their taxes and administrative skills. Kings were able to marshal more resources, but because they relied on townspeople for money, they had to respect them. Urbanites had good reason to be proud.

In 2010 I immersed myself in medieval town life in Regensburg, Germany, which is one of the best-preserved northern European towns from the 13th century. It stands on the Danube in an area that has been a ritual center and trading hub for at least 3,000 years. The town became the seat of the Bavarian dukes in the sixth century, but they moved west to Augsburg in the 14th century, and Regensburg became something of a backwater. I felt lucky because its medieval townscape didn't get the Renaissance makeover that Augsburg had in the 16th century. I wandered through it, surrounded by narrow winding streets with tall wood-framed houses on each side, crowned by steep gabled roofs. A few homes are square stone towers over 100 feet high. Some of the town's wealthiest lounged in their upper chambers and looked down on their neighbors.

Urban streets back then were elbow to elbow with hawkers, urchins, preachers, laborers, and cut purses. Dogs, cats, pigs, rats, mice, and fleas shared the same space with them. There was plenty of dung to step in. Germany had a bedbug epidemic when I was there, and I often had to stop to scratch the fiery bites swelling on my shins. I thought, Hey! This is too much immersion!

Fortunately my medieval immersion was incomplete. Homicides were common back then. Town registers all over Europe brimmed with accounts of deaths from fights that flared from insults in taverns and disputes over the prices of goods. Blood feuds often raged as well.

But people kept coming to the cities anyway. They considered the liveliness and freedom worth the dangers. Cathedral squares bustled with markets, ballgames, acrobats, and plays. Some actors carried a bucket of blood from a local butcher to make scenes more real—*Saving Private Ryan* is gory, but medieval special effects included real goo and smells. In morality plays, actors playing devils ran through the crowd, pinching spectators.

On the surface medieval Europe might seem cruder than Angkor, but people synthesized its many contentious perspectives into some of the finest art and literature in world history. Literacy spread beyond monasteries and royal courts, and texts in common tongues flowered—writers began to express sophisticated town and court life in languages that people spoke in their homes instead of Latin. Some authors updated older Celtic myths for urban audiences, including the King Arthur tales. These texts mixed ancient pagan lore about heroes and magic with newer images of upper class banquets, chivalrous knights, refined ladies in flowing gowns, personal spiritual quests, and castles well-supplied with tapestries and precious tableware. People were getting bored with older sagas of sweaty men hacking each other with broad swords. Tastes were becoming more refined.

No text is more refined than Dante's *Divine Comedy*. He composed it in the early 14th century in his native Tuscan language, which modern Italian descended from. This masterpiece presents a panoramic view of the medieval universe, from the bottom of hell to the Trinity. Everything is in its place in a geometrically ordered hierarchy. On the surface it sounds like a literary version of Angkor Wat, but it expresses the West's unique cultural wealth in the Middle Ages.

Dante detailed historical predecessors and his contemporaries so well that the great literary scholar Erich Auerbach called one of the poem's episodes an early modern portrait. Dante met a pair of lovers named Paolo and Francesca in hell. They were eternally blown by winds (this was symbolic because they had been blown around by their passions in life). While still alive they were alone, reading a chivalric romance, and in the heat of the moment, life imitated art. Francesca told Dante that as they read, their eyes met and their cheeks began to change color. As she described their current plight, Paolo cried his eyes out and Dante swooned with pity. The poet portrayed this whirlpool of passion to vivify its place in the larger cosmic system—those who couldn't control their lusts in life occupy one of hell's circles. However, he showed the characters so realistically that many readers sympathize more with them. Dante made them lifelike to make the levels in the cosmic hierarchy seem real, but he did such a good job that many readers' sympathies are more with the people in it. They're so tangible that Auerbach said that he created a new way of seeing the world. Dante gave people more flesh and blood than Jayavarman VII did on the Bayon. The *Divine Comedy* is one of the West's greatest literary works because it's both a highly developed medieval vision, with its hierarchy of beings, and a preview of the modern world, which has focused more on individuals. It integrates a multitude of perspectives that no Khmer text includes.

I explored Dante's neighborhood in Florence in 2008. The multistory stone homes standing against each other invoked a secular society of merchants and bankers building their financial empires and neighbors competing to erect the tallest house. But a little church where Dante as a boy might have heard of horrendous tortures in hell and the beauty of paradise is half a block from his reconstructed home.[7] The imaginative youth saw moneyed men parading in fine gowns and heard priests threatening eternal torments for the seven deadly sins on the same day and street. He could integrate these two worlds with impressions of Beatrice (he met her at a May Day festival when he was almost nine) as the ideal of feminine grace leading him towards salvation. He had literary models for this, since idealized images of women had infused Europe since the 12th century through troubadour poetry and the new popularity of the Virgin Mary. Medieval European towns had many currents. No wonder why countrymen were abandoning their ploughs for them.

The Khmer literature that survives praises the king and gods and deals with the donation and administration of territories and temple properties, but doesn't focus on much else.[8] Inscriptions in temples say that the king could vanquish one thousand armies and outwrestle any monster.

Swinging his mighty sword, he removed the enemies from the world and bestowed order. I'm impressed, but where's someone I can relate to?

Angkor's texts also proclaim that Lord Shiva is the universal soul, the source of all knowledge, and the developer of the world, whose lotus feet are poised on the heads of the other gods. Other texts eulogize people who gave large donations to temples, praising their genealogies and good works. But the surviving writings don't include other voices or daily life—no ordinary guys are stumbling through their first romances and shoving their ways through city streets. The old inscriptions are beautiful though. They radiate with passages about how great the king and gods are as centers of cosmic and political order. They are as ornate as the temple carvings and as exultant as the festivals. No competing voices restrain them from linking the king and the gods with everything good and glorious. Because the surviving Khmer literature lacked Europe's clashes between perspectives, it portrayed the earthly and celestial rulers in a way that reflected the temples and ceremonies—with untrammeled exuberance. It expressed a different world from Medieval Europe.

Western traditions of focusing on distinct domains and highlighting contention between them were already ancient in Dante's day. Ancient Greek literature was full of debates. Homer's *Iliad* begins with a row between the general, Agamemnon, and his best warrior, Achilles. The former took the latter's war booty, a woman named Briseis. Achilles then deserted his comrades in a huff, and the war dragged on, and on, taking many lives. The *Iliad's* first book ends in a quarrel between the gods—as below, so above. Zeus and his wife, Hera, went at it until he threatened to rough her up with his hands, which no seasoned warrior had ever withstood. This is hardly ennobling stuff, but arguments in the Homeric epics provided ancient Greeks with ways to debate in their civic centers. Usually lacking kings with centralized royal courts, people advanced in the world by contending directly with each other, and they were proud of not kissing anyone else's feet. The ancient West's most honored literature provided bags of arrows to fire at bullies.

Nobody ever ranted better than ancient Rome's Cicero when he accused his opponent Mark Antony of decadence in the first century BCE. He smeared his personal life to show that he lacked the control that was supposed to be the basis of virtuous Roman life—he allowed other men to use him for sexual pleasure (Romans considered this one of the worst insults), and vomited in his own lap during a public assembly after one of his many drinking bouts. This certainly doesn't resemble Khmer portrayals of their kings.

An even hotter head arrived in Paris in the early 12th century, when Khmers were erecting Angkor Wat. Peter Abelard was born into a minor noble family in Brittany. His father saw the growing importance of literacy and noticed that his son was as quick as a fox. Peter entered Notre Dame's cloister school and caused a sensation.

His teacher, William of Champeaux, was one of Europe's most distinguished thinkers. He was used to getting his respect, but Abelard quickly challenged him and cast diplomacy into the dunghill. He told him that his reasoning was wrong and that his conclusions were ridiculous. Since William's honor was at stake, the two squared off in a debate. The older man believed that the general is more real than the specific. In other words, God created the category *Tree* before He made any single tree. William also thought that the essence of all people is the same so that individual differences are merely accidental. The brash youth bested him. Abelard was more in tune with the increasingly sophisticated world of the growing cities, whose multitude of cultures and nonconforming personalities couldn't be cobbled into a simplistic scheme of categories. He left to start his own school and many of his classmates went with him. Silicon Valley's start-up culture emerged on the medieval Seine.

Abelard was on the vanguard of a movement that sent shockwaves all over Europe. Aristotle was being translated from Arabic into Latin in Spain and Sicily after most of his work had been forgotten in Europe since the sixth century. Bright-eyed young students were discovering the power of his reasoning techniques, and older folks were shocked that they were applying them to the deepest Christian mystery, the Trinity. St. Bernard of Clairvaux proclaimed that faith does not dispute, it believes.

However, much more disputing came. The first European universities were emerging. Scholars had already been congregating for discussions in cathedral cloisters and town squares. As these gatherings became regular, universities in Bologna, Salerno, Padua, Paris, and Oxford were established, and they began to confer degrees. Young men flocked to them from all over Europe. They lived in special apartments, struggled on low budgets, got drunk whenever they could, and developed a reputation for rowdiness. The college experience was born. The Church tried to suppress the teaching of Aristotle's texts, and more than a century of debates about reason versus faith ensued.

Medieval Europe was thus peculiar. People dreamed of a unified cosmos under God but bickered about its nature from many perspectives. I saw this knotty mindset in Regensburg when I stood on the main bridge over the river that the town straddles. I viewed the dense jumble of steep, high gabled homes and could almost hear the shouts from windows, share the excitement of markets and saints' feast days, and feel the fear of epidemic and famine, which lurked like wolves ready to sink their fangs into the townspeople's flesh.

But towering over this jostle of dreams and terror was the cathedral. It is in the classic French high Gothic style, which emerged in towns near Paris when Jayavarman VII built the Bayon. This style emphasized proportioned relationships between buildings' components rather than a dazzling crowd of face towers. People in Europe's growing towns resurrected the classical Greco-Roman love of static ratios, but now used them to express Christian ideas.

Figure 9. Straight lines expressing spiritual ideals in Laon Cathedral, France.

Figure 10. Strasbourg Cathedral's proportioned facade rising over a chaotic street.

In the nave, rows of columns and arches repeat static geometric forms, but they lead the gaze towards the altar and Christ. They thereby highlight his life and death as the central events in history. The perspectives that they encouraged were more linear than the Bayon's portrayal of the Buddha penetrating the whole universe.

Though the part of Regensburg's cathedral that I could see from the bridge (its west façade) was constructed after the 13th century, its geometrically ordered design rising above the chaotic streets was a site that dominated many cities by 1300. Europeans in the 13th century believed that God created a fixed universe with everything in its place in a divine hierarchy. According to this view, nine levels of celestial beings soar above us and the beasts grovel below.[9] The cathedral shows the universe's sacred order in stone, as the Divine Comedy does in words. So I saw two different worlds in Regensburg. In the Middle Ages, motley crowds cluttered winding streets, and God's divine plan arched over them. This sacred order rising above the bustle of everyday life captivated people in the 13th century.

These buildings rose in ways that the Khmers could never have imitated. Gothic cathedrals contained vaults over a broad and lofty nave that was partitioned by a line of arches on each side, which led the gaze to the altar and up into the heavens. Over the arches, sets of stained glass windows depicted Biblical personalities and events. Nobody else in the world came close to erecting such wide and high enclosed spaces with stone and filling them with so many windows that the stones seem to dissolve into colored light. Cathedral builders followed a philosopher from the third century CE named Plotinus, who thought light was an early emanation of God. All worshippers in the building seemed bathed in divine light.

Perspectives of divine order arching over creation were actually deeply entrenched before the first Gothic cathedrals were built, and Henry IV created one of their grandest expressions. Speyer was a bustling city on the southern Rhine and a key node in trading routes between Italy, the northern Rhine, and France. In 1030 Emperor Conrad II began building a colossal imperial cathedral in which he and his successors would be buried. Henry IV raised arched vaults over its nave, making a resounding statement about German imperial might after he returned from his meeting with Pope Gregory VII in Italy. But if he meant to say, "In your Italian faces!" he helped spread ancient Roman aesthetics even more.

Speyer Cathedral is one of the most magnificent buildings in the Romanesque style, which preceded Gothic architecture. It lacks the latter's large windows and delicate, complex linear patterns, but it follows ancient Roman forms more closely, with arches that are semicircular rather than pointed, and by using the horizontal basilica form that ancient Romans developed (a long hall with a semicircular apse at the far end from the entrance, and a colonnade on each side of the hall). The arched vaults that Henry IV added over the nave are repeated with geometric regularity. The columns lining both sides and the arches rising between them are equally regular. Spatial units repeat in proportions that are as stately as those of ancient Greek and Roman temples.

If Henry IV didn't easily feel humble, I sure did when I entered his cathedral in 2010. The nave was enormous and cavernous, and on both sides simple arches presided over the thick, straight pillars that supported them. They led my gaze to the apse at the far end, which was a stately semicircle lined with more arches. At first I enjoyed the building's combination of purity and strength.

I then began to find it heavy-handed, as though Henry was spreading spirituality with a sledgehammer. I finally felt relieved to exit and sit on a bench in a little park next to the nave, watch local children play, and enjoy the late afternoon sun.

Speyer's cathedral is only one example of one of the West's most representative styles of architecture, and I explored many other Romanesque churches that remained savory to the last second. Cologne had been an eminently prosperous city of merchants on the northern Rhine since the tenth century (it was also one of the most important northern European cities when the Roman Empire ruled); they dealt in dried cod, herrings, iron swords, cloth, goldsmiths' work, wine, and English wool. Today it's known for its Gothic cathedral, but 12 fine Romanesque churches form a ring around the city like a garland. This number symbolized Christ's apostles during the Middle Ages, so people thought Cologne symbolized the heavenly Jerusalem, which many believed would appear on earth at the end of time. Merchants sailing to Cologne to unload their boats and folks walking or riding to one of its wall's 12 gates would have first seen the churches' towers to remind them of this vision. One of my all-time favorite Romanesque churches is Great Saint Martin. Its lines of pillars and arches are as stately as Speyer's, but I found them more exquisite.

Its nave is much smaller than Speyer's, and it ends in an elegant three-leaf clover-shaped choir. This design has three small semicircles at 90 degree angles to each other (rather than one commanding semicircle) and each one is lined with arches. This was inspired by the clover leaf shape of the Church of the Nativity in Bethlehem. As medieval Europe grew economically, people made pilgrimages to the Holy Land and this form resonated with them.

I especially enjoyed ambling in Great Saint Martin's choir. The clover leaf is another simple, static form that Westerners treated as a model of eternal truth. Because the church was built on a narrow piece of land, people made it lofty rather than sprawling. As I strolled around the choir, my gaze naturally turned upwards. Great Saint Martin isn't a huge building that makes a thunderous statement about power. It's small and intimate, and it makes the permanent forms and heavenly aspirations seem as gentle as the flowing melodies of Gregorian chants from its time.

Many parts of the church still hold paint from the Middle Ages, and lively reds, yellows, and blues predominate—I imagined that Cologne's worldly merchants could stand only so much contemplation. Everything came together for me: Stately and simple geometric forms, lofty spiritual aspirations, intimacy, gentleness, and worldly bustle mixed into a superb expression of the integration of heaven and earth.

Romanesque style assumed many varieties, and it spread all over Western Europe. At its far end, in northwestern Spain, people built an enormous Romanesque cathedral to honor St. James, and thousands of pilgrims from all over Europe trekked there. Traveling on foot and on donkeys and horses, they followed certain routes, and some of the way stations had Romanesque churches too. The abbey church at Vezelay is considered one of the most beautiful buildings in France in that style, and many people congregated there before beginning the long journey to the west.

A huge Romanesque basilica was built in Reims to honor St. Remi for baptizing Clovis. It's about one mile from the grand Gothic cathedral which was constructed in the 13th century, and people conducted processions between both buildings when a new king was anointed. Though the cathedral is one of the most magnificent examples of Gothic architecture ever built, the basilica is so stately that I felt that it holds its own. In its nave several levels of semicircular arches rise on top of each other as though the simplest static forms are the most fundamental in the universe. They balanced the showier Gothic designs at the other end of the procession.

The Tower of London is a stern version of Romanesque style—William the Conqueror was more interested in command than contemplation. But people in England built many fine Romanesque churches too. Linear designs on some are so exquisite that some Anglophiles claim that Gothic style first emerged there (Durham Cathedral is one of the most admired examples).

A reason why Romanesque style spread so much was it represented an overarching sacred order as towns grew and the Church strengthened its authority. Khmers were also using symmetrical architecture to unify their world, but Romanesque arches were simpler. Ancient Romans had pioneered them and used them to dignify their civic buildings. These arches later mixed with Christian thought. Christian thinking has often been organized around small numbers of key things. The Old and New Testament, the Trinity, the four evangelists, the seven days of creation, and the twelve apostles easily fit into simple architectural forms. For example, the north sides of cathedrals were often associated with the Old Testament while the south symbolized the New Testament—the sun emerges from the south in the spring, when Easter is celebrated, and its renewal was associated with Christ in chilly northern Europe. The four evangelists were painted in the corners underneath some towers and domes.

The Khmers didn't emphasize a universal system of a few precisely defined concepts as much as Europeans did. Instead, they cohered around ideas and art forms that the kings who built the first big temples around Angkor expressed. Many Khmer monuments symbolized four peaks and the oceans around Mt. Meru (including Angkor Wat), Hindu and Buddhist deities, harmony between male and female aspects of nature, and increasingly spiritual levels of existence towards the center (including Bakong's platform's five levels and Angkor Wat's entire lay-out). Later kings, such as Jayavarman VII, added ideas that were com-patible with them. Khmers weren't limited by some of the ways in which medieval Europeans conventionally treated ideas:

- Christian views of time were linear, with creation happening once and for all. Time wasn't a cycle of multiple creations and destructions. Genesis clearly outlined the sequence of days in which God made the world.
- People are born only once; they don't reincarnate into a multi-tude of life forms and spirits.
- Jesus was the only incarnation of divinity; the Church didn't allow the crowded pantheons of Hinduism and Mahayana Buddhism.
- The Bible was the only truly holy book.
- Medieval Europeans inherited ancient Western philosophic tra-ditions of looking for all-encompassing definitions of ideas and things and arguing over them.

Khmers could fuse ideas and images without these concerns. The main ways in which they conjoined them enhanced ritual potency and pro-jected the prestige of elites. The main limit was probably political. For example, Peter Sharrock, in *Banteay Chhmar; Garrison-Temple of the Khmer Empire,* wrote that Jayavarman VII built an enormous temple complex called Banteay Chhmar west of Angkor (near the Thai border), which has Buddhist themes sculpted on its walls which aren't carved in temples in Angkor. Sharrock feels that the established Hindu families in Angkor required the king to be more restrained with Buddhist themes there. But in both areas, he integrated ideas and images from both faiths. He thus seems to have been interested in including all of the ideas that people in their respective regions found most meaningful, rather than asserting one theology as absolute and universal. Cambodians combined kings, Hindu gods, Mahayana deities, local spirits, honored ancestors, and the natural environment without treating a few fundamental ideas as theo-logically limiting.

Khmers had imported Indian ideas that link the cosmos across domains that are vaster than one creation and one lifetime (such as cycles of multiple creations and destructions and ideas that Hindu gods and the Buddha were incarnated many times). The multitude of incarnations of deities allowed people to mix their lineages (Hindus have seen the Buddha as one of Vishnu's incarnations, and some Buddhists have envisioned Hindu deities honoring the great teacher). This gave Khmer kings flexibility to blend faiths, which Western rulers, who were bound to a stricter theology, lacked. A Cambodian king who wanted to show that he was in command of the empire could marshal all the known gods, teachers, and local spirits to get his point across.

Westerners have more often treated ideas as abstractions, which have definitive characteristics and limits that cannot be breached. Khmers instead blended ideas in ways that reflected their own cultural landscape—according to ritual efficacy, social harmony, aesthetical appeal, royal majesty, and nature's abundance (monsoons and profuse foliage were often key themes), without being as concerned about contradictions and all-encompassing definitions as Europeans were.

Things in the medieval West actually weren't as simple as a few preferred ideas and basic forms. There were not only many different voices that tussled over the order of things; equally creative voices were silenced. Jews had played a big role in the initial growth of medieval Europe's cities by acting as bankers, scribes, and middlemen in trade with the Middle East when few Christians outside of monasteries and royal courts could read and write.

Many of the largest European towns had a large Jewish section—so I've read; very little from them exists today outside of museums. But some of the world's most renowned interpreters of the Talmud lived in Europe (the Talmud is a literary tradition of discussions about Jewish law and humanity's relationship with God). Rashi of Troyes (1040–1105) was one of the most illustrious Talmudic scholars in the 11th century. Many towns in France and Germany had Talmudic schools, and they frequently exchanged teachers and letters. One of Europe's largest Jewish communities lived in Speyer, off a street that was within sight of the cathedral's main entrance.

The *Bahir* was published in Provence in the 12th century, and it formulated some of the basic ideas in the Kabbalah, which is the main

Jewish mystical tradition. This ancient text (Aryeh Kaplan wrote that most Kabbalists think that it was first composed in the first century CE in the Holy Land) detailed the first ten numbers, the *sefirot*, as sacred emanations that everything in the universe came from.[10] The patterns that the universe emerged in can be read in the Torah (the combination of the Old Testament books of Genesis, Exodus, Leviticus, Numbers, and Deuteronomy) because each Hebrew letter has a numerical value. Passages in the Torah are thus supposed to have metaphysical meanings that are deeper than literal readings. But Jewish legal and mystical traditions were not encompassed by Christian perspectives, so you won't see them under Romanesque cathedrals' arches or in Gothic stained glass windows.

Though many Jews lived in their own neighborhoods, people of both faiths surely interacted closely every day because medieval towns were crowded. But institutionalized persecutions began in the 11th century. Another town around the southern Rhine, Mainz, expelled most of its 2,000 Jews in 1012. Then during the First Crusade (in the 1090s), Jewish populations in many towns were massacred. St. Bernard opposed the killing of Jews when he spearheaded the Second Crusade (1147–8). However, large-scale persecutions increased in the late 13th century and the 14th century. Many fled to Eastern Europe and again established urban communities and commercial networks. They synthesized the Yiddish language from High German, Hebrew, Polish, and Russian.

Khmers also classified a large percentage of people as rightfully oppressed. Unlike medieval Europeans, they widely practiced slavery, and many slaves had been captured from tribes living in the hills and forests outside of wet rice farming communities. Because these unfortunate people lacked written literature and didn't use money, it was easier to subsume them under centralized political power to the extent of silencing them. But Jews in Europe had an ancient literary culture that valued debate as much as ancient Greeks and Romans did. The West's societies were thus harder to shoehorn into one religious and political system.

European societies from the 11th through the 13th century tried to unify the world with a system of eternal ideas and forms, and they embodied them with Romanesque and Gothic architecture, yet they had a multitude of voices which were too diverse and able to express themselves to be shoved under one simple framework. They tried to define the order of things but were quick to argue over the intellectual status quo. This situation encouraged intolerance at times, but it also fostered a lot of creative art and literature, and much of modern Western culture descends from it. The West has combined the assertion of a permanent, abstract order of all things with open rebellions against it. Many people in modern times have expounded the fundamental laws of physics as the all-ordering principles, yet a wealth of modern artists and poets emerged that have looked beyond rationality and conventions for alternative meanings. They're all following footsteps that our medieval predecessors took in those rambunctious town streets.

The Khmers also built huge shrines that towered over locals' daily lives and ordered them, but they fused these two perspectives in their own way. Villages and magnificent temples in the Khmer world were integrated with rituals, royal and godly majesty, lush art, and feelings of excitement. Cambodians made up for the lack of one consistent doctrine and a multitude of literary voices with exuberance. They couldn't create the large inner spaces and stained glass windows that Westerners did, but their temples meshed with the more tropical climate's blazing sun, monsoons, and abundant vegetal growth. All these experiences and aspects of nature together integrated the Khmer world in ways that were as rich as medieval European culture.

Medieval Europeans used technology more prolifically than Khmers did, and this made it harder to impose one man's glory on them. They either invented or widely adopted clocks, windmills, watermills, more effective ploughs, the harness, the stirrup, eyeglasses, distillation, the crank, the crane, and the spinning wheel. The Church often insisted that free Christians could not be enslaved, so people increasingly relied on working more efficiently. By the end of the 13th century, Europeans (and some people in China) were probably the most adept in the world at using levels, gears, and wheels.

They also increasingly used mathematics. Arabic characters for numbers were replacing the more cumbersome Roman numerals because they made calculation easier. This numerical system allowed people to use money more easily and frequently. Leonardo Fibonacci was the son of a Pisan customs agent who worked in Algeria. The sharp young man learned about Arabic and Indian mathematics and published a book about them in 1202 called *Liber Abaci*. He introduced the decimal system to Europe and illustrated its use for bookkeeping, currency conversions, and interest calculations.

Many Europeans in the 13th century were replacing parchment with paper, and this reduced the cost of storing information. Royal and ducal courts, churches, and merchants could keep more archives, accounting records, and legal documents.

The legal profession grew in the 11th and 12th centuries as people rediscovered ancient Roman law and applied it to their growing towns and monetary economy. Law became one of the main schools in universities (especially in highly urbanized northern Italy), whose graduates joined secular and church governments as administrators. Many folks detested lawyers, but largely because so many prospered from all the business they could do in courts and the growing cities. People trudging through their dirty streets enviously eyed the steeds they rode.

Because Khmer society had fewer merchants, lacked money, and relied more on labor and less on technology, royal power was a stronger conceptual center.[11] New ideas and images, including Mahayana cosmologies, Tantric deities, and Jayavarman's portrayals of compassion, could easily be made into vehicles for its expression.

Westerners might find this focus on central authority simplistic, but it was part of a very rich field of meanings that blended ideas in ways that Europeans didn't. Angkor's thought integrated many ideas, traditions, and experiences, including:

- Hindu myths,
- Indian cosmologies, including ideas of Mt. Meru,
- Ideas of supernatural energies,
- Mahayana deities,
- Royal cults,
- Local spirit and ancestral cults,
- The monsoons,
- The jungle's all-enveloping growth,
- Tonle Sap's miraculous flooding,

- The tropical sun,
- Rice farming,
- Intimate village life.

Because Cambodians weren't as heady as Europeans about precisely defining things and theologies, they fused many different ideas flexibly. Khmers beautified their world with art forms from several Southeast Asian and Indian states, and they spiced it up with some of the most inspired pageantry that anyone on the planet has devised. Liveliness trumped Aristotle's logic.[12]

Angkor's exuberance outshone what we can see today. Only temples' weathered stones and laterite remain, but many were gilded and brightly painted. They shone like jewels over the rice fields, twinkling canals, and expansive barays.

Men and women perfumed themselves with sandalwood and musk, and they loved to bathe. Zhou Daguan said that they refreshed themselves several times a day, and that every two or three families shared a pond. We can imagine them savoring a break from the heat, teasing and splashing each other, wrestling, singing, and flirting. Khmers seem to have been cleaner than medieval Europeans, and they probably would have found their sporadic bathing disgusting.[13]

Every three to five days, groups of women made a day trip from their homes to bathe in the river. Zhou Daguan said that they crowded its bank every day (often in the thousands) and that they took off their clothing before wading in. Male Chinese visitors hung out there whenever they had time. Zhou was from a culture that stressed public honor and which firmly oppressed women (China's previous dynasty, the Song, began foot binding as its political and business leaders looked back to ancient Confucian values and developed ideals of feminine elegance; the women of the prior Tang Dynasty who rode horses and even played polo became distant memories). He seems to have been fascinated by Angkor's freer women, and he wrote a lot about Khmers' erotic customs, but next to nothing about Angkor Wat. Cambodians more freely enjoyed themselves as long as people didn't disturb the social order.

A temple that Jayavarman VII built called Neak Pean was an exquisite place to bathe. It now consists of five square ponds—one in the center and one adjoining each of its sides (there used to be another eight pools surrounding these five). The main shrine rises on a round island in the middle pool. The central pond might have symbolized a Himalayan lake that was imagined as the source of the world's four main rivers, and renowned for miraculous healing because it was pure. Some historians think that people came to this temple for physical therapy. Each side pond is connected to the central basin by a little chapel into which the water might have flowed to patients. Reflecting Jayavarman's compassion, three of the entrances to the island's shrine were walled up and sculptures of Lokesvara, the main bodhisattva of compassion, were carved on them. People who bathed in the cool waters for relief from fevers and aching muscles must have felt that they were receiving grace from the source of life.

Angkor combined cozy groups of homes and ponds, verdant fields, and glimmering canals and barays. Magnificent temples punctuated the vistas. Exultant festivals that mixed pageantry and fun were frequent. Many shrines balanced grandeur and ethereal elegance. All buildings together incorporated a range of styles from more than 1,000 years of cultural exchanges with India and other Southeast Asian lands. This was one of the most beautiful places people have ever created.

So cultures integrate their views of the world in different ways, which have an enormous number of facets. Cultures mix many ideas and art forms, and these fusions are influenced by:

- The natural environment,
- The already rich heritages from ancient times,
- Ways of economic exchange,
- Political institutions,
- Patterns of everyday life (wet rice farming, for example),
- Religious traditions and ideas,
- Other cultures (India and other Southeast Asian societies inspired the Khmers, and the Levant and Mesopotamia influenced ancient Greece).

Ideas and art forms that are treated as basic are given this status within an infinitely abundant cultural landscape. What seems obvious comes from this abundance. Its many dimensions and long history can make people think their fundamental assumptions are universal truths because these assumptions are constantly reinforced. So many experiences strengthen them that it can be hard to see beyond them and easy to become locked into the same biases for life.

But when you appreciate the immensity of the environments that people's basic assumptions emerged in, realize that they're reinforced within these abundant environments, and then discover the varieties of these environments, your old assumptions can become sources of freedom. As you learn how to explore them more objectively, and how to compare them with other cultures, you can fly through one landscape after another so that they all become ever more enchanting. The very ideas that we hold as most fundamental can become launching pads to perspectives that keep getting bigger and more wondrous, in which we can explore an ever-growing range of ideas and synthesize them in any way we choose.

The richness of a culture, however, can become constricting because people can treat its most common ideas as truths that they cannot look beyond. For example, Khmers made royal and godly splendor ever more bedazzling. Jayavarman VII added even more luster to Angkor by building two goliaths next to its center, and they're the other two of his four great monuments there. They were monasteries and centers of learning, but they were very different from Abelard's academic haunts.

Jayavarman built the first, Ta Prohm, in 1186 to honor his mother. He conceived her as Prajnaparamita, the Mahayana goddess of wisdom and the Great Mother in its pantheon. He dedicated the other, Preah Khan, to his father in 1191 and saw him as Lokesvara. He was following an old Khmer tradition (Indravarman honored his ancestors at Preah Ko more than 300 years before), but the new king made it as sensational as possible.

These two places were practically cities. Ta Prohm housed 12,640 people, including 18 high priests, 2,740 other priests, and 2,202 assistants. Six hundred and fifteen female dancers performed. Almost

80,000 people provisioned everyone with food, clothing, and mosquito nets. Nearly 100,000 workers performed services for Preah Khan. These numbers might have been inflated to dramatize the places, but just walking through them can make people boost things to supernatural scales.

I found that the biggest Khmer temples can bring out a person's inner child. They're so much larger than ordinary life and their forms are so ornate that they can overshadow reason. The outer walls of Preah Khan and Ta Prohm enclosed the areas where thousands of people lived (the houses were wooden and are thus long gone), so after walking through each complex's outer gate, I moved through a large open ground before reaching the central section. Anticipation thus built as I proceeded through both places. The architects had a keen sense of drama, as they did at Angkor Wat—Khmers must have designed large temples with processions in mind. I could imagine chanting priests, hundreds or thousands of monks, and elephants carrying the king and his ministers. People's heartbeats must have quickened as they paraded towards the center.

However, the atmosphere transforms quickly at the entrances to the central sections of both temples and Angkor Wat. The construction suddenly becomes dense. The outer section's open space and the middle's gravity contrast with each other. People know they're in a very powerful place when they approach the center.

Both of Jayavarman's monuments amplify the senses. Small orchestras played gongs and xylophones in each temple's outer yard, and I could hear the chiming long before reaching them. The large open area allows notes to travel, and the sounds of these instruments carry well. They pierce the sultry air like bursts of energy from the source of creation. Chants and incense within the inner shrines and corridors must have seemed as potent. Sights, sounds, and aromas in both foundations became superhuman.

But the two foundations aren't all muscle. Soft sides balance their crowded architecture and oceanic spaces. Both contain an assembly hall just in front of the central section (called the Hall of the Dancers), with energetically dancing devatas carved on the pillars and lintels. Each of the four outer walls has an entrance in the middle. Columns flank the wide walkways that lead from each door to a square open space in the center. The pillars are straight and stately, but the hall isn't huge. If dancers did perform there, it gave them a dignified and well-proportioned setting.

Khmers held myths about apsaras (celestial dancers for the gods) emerging from the ocean of milk as the gods and demons stirred it to create the cosmos (many joyfully glide over the snake-pulling scene on Angkor Wat). Khmers thus found it easy to associate dance with the basic patterns of energy that brought the universe into existence. Since the Hall of the Dancers in both of Jayavarman's complexes is east of the central section, the sun greeted it as soon as it rose. But since both establishments were mainly for Buddhist worship, the art historian Hiram Woodward thought that dancers might have enacted the Buddha's birth.[14] Both of these themes are about creation. Dancers might have embodied nature's life-giving energies in these handsome rooms. If so, their symmetry patterned performances in ways that strengthened the empire's order.

The bases of many buildings in both complexes rise in tapering sections with sumptuously carved vegetal designs covering them. This custom of constructing ornate plinths follows Indravarman's Preah Ko. The bottoms of these two temples rise in several curving sections that make them seem to bloom like flowers.

The lower steps of many Khmer temples from Preah Ko to Jayavarman VII's works elegantly curve into a point in the middle so that they resemble lotus blossoms and flames when you look down on them. The architects of these two complexes surely didn't imagine my old sneakers treading on these sacred spaces.

Ta Prohm's inventory included musical instruments which complemented the visual feasts. Both complexes thus used multiple senses to blend opulence and sensuality to the extent of making residents feel that they were in the gods' palace.

But the gods' living quarters were cramped. There was no place within the central section's network of halls and shrines with a view of more than a fraction of the whole complex. After I walked through the Hall of the Dancers, the construction became denser. The central tower isn't nearly as lofty as Angkor Wat's and the Bayon's. The latter two monuments also limit each perspective to a fraction of the whole when you're in one of the courtyards, but they draw your gaze to the middle spire, which symbolizes the heavens. But because the symmetry in Jayavarman's two establishments is strictly horizontal, it doesn't as strongly encourage people to visualize a loftier place that integrates the universe. Both complexes combine regularity with obfuscating complexity and otherworldly elegance. They dazzled the people who lived there while preventing them from viewing the whole area.

The corridors in these two temples are very long and narrow—they're too constricted for groups of students and teachers to saunter and hold informal conversations. They were not meant for free exchanges of ideas and wisecracks. Because they're arrow-straight, the gaze is hemmed in and forced into one direction. They were good areas for solemn processions and quiet meditations rather than inquisitive student life.

The two complexes did blend faiths more tolerantly than medieval Europeans did. Though Jayavarman was a Buddhist, Preah Khan contains large sections for Shiva, Vishnu, and royal ancestors. The king had no qualms about including every religion that his people followed.

Each temple housed hundreds of statues of gods, bodhisattvas, and ancestors, but many of the long, straight corridors meet at 90 degree angles, and their intersections are small rooms that served as shrines that held a statue. The corridors and shrines thus formed a grid of squares and rectangles. This made me wonder if the cults' rituals were tightly coordinated with each other. Jayavarman was open to all religions in his land, but both complexes gave me the impression that he wanted to control them with a firm grip. I felt that the temples that were supposed to embody paradise were equally focused on his centralized power. Since ancient times, Cambodians had mixed many faiths, ideas, and art forms. But Jayavarman VII devoted so many resources to huge monuments that projected his authority that he might have limited his people's creativity by not sanctioning alternatives. The amount of building and the innovativeness of royal art sharply declined after the 13th century.

In 2012 I explored the old northwestern town Battambang and saw some of Cambodia's creative potential when I discovered a group of local artists which is called Sammaki. They showed me their work, and a painter named Theanly Chou then drove me to his home on his motorbike to see his canvases.

Theanly's parents owned an old row house by the river, and he had converted most of the second floor into a studio. He grabbed two aluminum chairs for us and showed me a portrait he painted of one of Cambodia's most honored pop stars from the 1960s. Many Cambodians see that time as the golden era of their pop culture. It was spirited and growing, and digesting influences from all over the world. Sadly, the Khmer Rouge killed its major stars, but Theanly is spreading their legacies in his own way.

Many Cambodians consider Sinn Sisamouth their greatest pop music artist from that time. Theanly played several of his recordings. Nothing seemed very original to me, but Sinn assimilated an impressive variety of styles. Some songs sounded Latin American, and others were mid 1960s-style pop that reminded me of the Beatles in their early days. He also recorded the ballad "A Whiter Shade of Pale." Sinn was also an intellectual. He had studied medicine and learned several languages. He became a professional musician and singer after many years of study, but died during the Khmer Rouge's regime in mysterious circumstances.

Theanly captured both sides of him in a portrait that shows a thoughtful and educated man who's also whimsical. Sinn represented Southeast Asia's ability to fuse multiple influences as well as the Khmer monuments did.

So does Theanly. He showed me a portrait he painted of Audrey Hepburn. Her combination of elegance and sprite, which it showed well, reminded me of Angkor Wat's devatas. Theanly's multicultural blends and their mixtures of refinement and vigor gave me tantalizing hints of Cambodia's cultural potential.

However, David Chandler wrote that more than half of the ancient Cambodians were probably slaves. He said that we have to be careful with the word *slave* because Khmer definitions of it were different from ours. There were many classes of serfs. Some lived horribly. They slept on the ground under the house, and if they angered their masters they were forced to bow their heads and remain still while being caned. But others were dancers and musicians, and some even married members of the royal family. Some even owned their own slaves. Their lives thus varied. All the same, they probably didn't have much leeway to think freely, and the artists must have had to subjugate their creativity to their masters' instructions. Khmer elites only allowed a fraction of Cambodia's creative potential to blossom.

However, Zhou Daguan found Angkor still vibrant when he lived there in 1296–7 (one hundred years after Jayavarman VII's reign). People held a daily market that lasted from dawn to noon. Chinese traders had been moving in and many married Cambodian women. This was a shrewd step since most merchants in the market were women. There must have been a lot of flirting where people bathed, and the local women might have been attracted to foreign businessmen for their wealth. Thais were also coming into the region and some were tailors. So business beyond the rice economy was growing and becoming multinational.

A major festival highlighted each month. In the first, people set up a stage with room for 1,000 spectators in front of the royal palace. They hung globe lanterns and flowers all over the platform and gathered on it to watch fireworks. Zhou thought they were loud enough to shake the whole city. This fair rollicked for 15 days, and the king sometimes came out at night and lit fireworks himself.

Ballgames enlivened the fourth month. In the fifth, people carried Buddha statues from all over the country to the water to bathe them in front of the king (Zhou didn't say whether the water was Tonle Sap, a river, or a pool in the palace). In the seventh month, folks offered rice to the Buddha and ceremoniously burned it outside the south gate. More women than Zhou could number rode in chariots and on elephants' backs to watch, perhaps to increase the land's fertility, since this was a harvesting time. They might have worn their finest fabrics and jewelry to compete with each other in splendor.

Female dancers graced the eighth month by publically performing a dance they did every day at the palace. Elephant and boar fights added spice to the same month, and the king invited foreign envoys to watch. These spectacles went on for ten days.

Khmers still knew how to have a good time. Zhou Daguan noted that invading Thais, who had liberated themselves from them after Jayavarman VII's reign, had devastated the countryside around Angkor, but the city was still wealthy and vigorous enough to impress him.

This splendor raises questions about how Cambodia became mired in poverty and how the Killing Fields happened. The next chapter will conclude Part One by bringing Cambodia's history up to the present. But it will also show how we can help it regenerate and inspire societies all over the world, including our own.

CHAPTER 7

FROM HELL'S BASEMENT TO BUILDING PARADISE: HOW TO RESTORE CAMBODIA'S GLORY AND ENABLE HER TO ENRICH THE REST OF THE WORLD

A YOUNG WESTERN man who stayed at my hotel in Phnom Penh talked nonstop. He also sang—loudly, often, and way off-key—and flirted with the female staff with equal garishness. I thought he was a nice guy, but he seemed to crave constant attention. The young Cambodian woman who managed the place tolerated his chatter for a long time as he sat at the bar, but she finally said, "You shouldn't talk all the time." Though a frown furrowed her face, she wasn't confrontational. Her tone was like that of a big sister giving advice. So many Cambodians impressed me with exquisite combinations of elegance and directness that I wondered how their country plummeted into such misery after its glory days.

This chapter will show why Cambodia's history became so tortuous after its illustrious past. We'll then see how it can overcome its recent traumas and contribute to our globalized world. All countries have tremendous cultural wealth, including those that are the poorest economically. Appreciating and nurturing them will greatly enlarge our worlds and enhance everyone's creativity.

Sixteenth and early seventeenth century travelers found Angkor Wat serviced by priests who used it as a Buddhist shrine. Large sections of carvings were even added to the walls in the sixteenth century. Many horses in battle scenes look like Chinese dragons, and historians have surmised that Chinese or Thai immigrants labored there.

But Angkor's population then is figured to have been only ten percent of what it was during its heyday. The carved horses lack the older friezes' upper class refinement and look more like comic book drawings. What happened?

Historians have suggested several reasons for Angkor's population loss. The National Academy of Sciences recently found that its reliance on the system of canals and barays could have led to it. Deforestation probably created erosion that clogged the canals, since people were cutting down more trees in the northern hills for both lumber and land. Increasing amounts of sediment might have loosened, flowed downriver, and silted up the waterways.

Scientists also found evidence of prolonged droughts in the late 14th and early 15th centuries.[1] At least one major baray was operating below capacity. So, careless soil management and less reliable monsoons might have given Angkor a one-two punch that left it without enough water to irrigate its crops.

Both of these blows could have led to a third. The shallow pools of stagnant water that they must have created would have been ideal breeding areas for mosquitoes. Some historians wonder if Angkor suffered from malaria epidemics when it was already having difficulty maintaining its current population.

Other reasons for the population decline have been proposed. Jayavarman VII's building orgies might have taxed the state's resources. However, not all historians agree. Claude Jacques wrote that the economy remained robust throughout the 13th century, and his opinion is in line with Zhou Daguan's observations.[2] But Khmers never built another large baray at Angkor after Jayavarman's reign, even when water became scarce. Did kings now lack resources that their predecessors could marshal?

Khmers changed their water distribution strategies after Jayavarman VII's rule by building laterite bridges with corbeled arches that were so close to each other that they could be closed to hold the water from upriver. Some historians have thus wondered if centralized control had weakened so that locals were managing the water supply from their own territories.[3]

Thais might have wreaked havoc on Angkor after they freed themselves in the 13th century. The Khmers thereby lost a lot of fertile land, which Thais could now use as bases for launching their own military campaigns. Then in 1431 and 1432, the Thai kingdom Ayutthaya stormed Angkor and carted off artists, ritual specialists, and statues.

However, the impact of the Thai wars has recently been questioned. Claude Jacques wrote that they might not have been as frequent as the Khmer chronicles said, and that until the late 16th century, Khmers often won too. He felt that damage from the Thais has been overestimated. But Zhou Daguan said that much of the land outside of Angkor was completely despoiled because of Thai invasions, and some historians think the Khmers abandoned the city for a while in the 1430s.[4] The effect of Thai wars remains an open question.

Even if Thais didn't destroy much of the city of Angkor in 1431–1432, the loot they carried away included elite priests and artists. L. P. Briggs felt that the Khmers couldn't replace them. The royal and religious institutions that projected society's order might have lost prestige. While Ayutthaya forced Khmers to work on its own temples and irrigation projects, Angkor had fewer people who could glorify its own traditions.

Not all reasons for Angkor's population decline were negative. Novel mixtures of ideas encouraged Cambodian society to evolve in new directions.

For example, by the 15th century Theravada Buddhism became Cambodia's dominant religion. Monks had been preaching the Theravada in Burma and Thailand, and wandering missionaries spread it eastwards. This faith stressed following the Buddha's original teachings to gain a better rebirth. Though Zhou Daguan still saw Hindus in Angkor in 1297, hulking temples had already become less relevant. He wrote little about the monuments, but described the palace, royal court, processions, and economic exchange in detail. The Theravada is supposed to connect people with the Buddha's actual sayings and cut out the later Mahayana flamboyance. It stresses moral discipline and a regulated monastic life, and rejects loose metaphysical speculations and bloated pantheons. Its leaders focused on teaching and doing good works, and they thus became closer to the people than elite priests chanting arcane hymns in imposing temples were. By the 15th century, the royal monuments might have lost spiritual prestige and aesthetical appeal that could have made people resist leaving when ecological problems worsened.

Cultural changes happened in another key dimension. International commerce increased in Southeast Asia in the 14th century, and this created opportunities nearer Cambodia's coast. Towns in Cambodia and in what are now Malaysia, Indonesia, Thailand, Vietnam, and southern Burma became wealthier through trade with China's new Ming Dynasty and with each other. The spice business was booming then and people were trading cloves and nutmeg from the Moluccas all over Southeast Asia and in China, India, and beyond. Locals in many parts of the region increasingly used money. Khmers relocated south, where the Tonle Sap and Mekong rivers meet, to be closer to the action. By the 15th century, inland ritual centers with monumental temples and economies based on rice had become backwaters.

Theravada Buddhism and Islam were becoming Southeast Asia's dominant religions, and they appealed to traders because they emphasize honesty, day-to-day work, humility, and sobriety (much more influenced by China, Vietnam held onto Mahayana and Confucian traditions). The future of most of Southeast Asia was now in states that valued commerce, and which followed religions that stressed morality and industriousness more than gargantuan temples.

So ecological damage, droughts, Thai wars, excessive construction that might have taxed the state's resources, changes in faith, and increasing international trade might have worked together to cause Angkor's population decline. Historians have debated the relative importance of each factor, but recent evidence suggests that ecological harm and droughts were two of the biggest causes.[5]

Though Angkor declined, Cambodia remained vigorous. David Chandler felt that the word *change* describes Khmer society in this period more accurately than *decline*. New cities emerged in the south, including Phnom Penh, Longvek, and Udong. Many cultures rubbed shoulders in the 16th and 17th centuries—Cambodia harbored Chinese, Malay, and Arabic businesspeople, and its capital city had separate quarters for each society. Devout Japanese pilgrims trekked to Angkor Wat. Portuguese missionaries and Spanish adventurers also lived in Cambodia, and one of its kings even converted to Islam when he married a Malay woman in the mid 17th century.

Chandler felt that Cambodia didn't begin to decline until the 18th century, when she was sandwiched between Thailand and Vietnam as they aggressively grew. As more Vietnamese moved south in the 17th century, they took over Saigon (now Ho Chi Minh City) and ultimately built it into a commercial hub that eclipsed Phnom Penh and rendered it provincial. Thailand's new Chakri Dynasty took charge of much of western Cambodia in the late 18th century. Vietnam continued to expand, and it assumed control of Cambodia's eastern area and her royal court. Vietnamese forced Cambodians into unpaid labor in order to develop their own canals, and sometimes suppressed their Buddhist traditions to the extent of desecrating pagodas. Cambodians finally rebelled in the 1840s, but Thailand then increased its control over them and tried to direct their royal court's affairs from Bangkok.

As Cambodia's next door neighbors sapped her international trade and annexed her land, she had less leverage against them. In 1863 she became a French protectorate. Norodom, who became Cambodia's king in 1864, negotiated the deal to relieve her from her Asian bullies. The French ruled relatively loosely at first, but they took tighter control after a national rebellion in 1884. The once proud Khmers remained colonial subjects until gaining independence in 1953.

Cambodians have sometimes been stereotyped as passive in modern times, and thus prone to Khmer Rouge brainwashing. But they launched several rebellions against oppressive rulers. Around 1820 a monk named Kai spearheaded a revolt against the Vietnamese as they exploited Khmer laborers, but Vietnamese soldiers killed him and crushed the rebellion.

Cambodians have remained lively in peaceful ways too. Judith M. Jacob, in *The Traditional Literature of Cambodia*, noted that they enjoy verbal wit and indulge in word-play with puns and rhymes. Contests of one-upmanship that test people's cleverness have been popular activities. Much traditional Cambodian poetry shows a love of nature, with an emphasis on flowers that is similar to what I saw in ancient temple friezes and in some of the romantic pop videos. So though Cambodian society might have become provincial, it was still spirited. People valued bravery, mental quickness, and nature's beauty.

Then how did the Killing Fields happen? It's a huge leap from a stunted economy to one of history's most atrocious regimes. How did a great culture go so bad so quickly?

David Chandler saw connections between Jayavarman VII and the Khmer Rouge. Both severed ties with the past to create an ideal society, implemented grandiose schemes, and stressed their own authority without an independent church or representative government to provide checks and balances.

Tony Day saw similarities between Angkor Wat and the Khmer Rouge because both emphasized centralized power, glorified violence that helped establish the state, and starkly juxtaposed heaven and hell. Guards at S-21 (the interrogation center in a converted Phnom Penh high school where about 20,000 people were tortured and executed) called prisoners "damned souls." Day saw connections between this verbiage and Angkor Wat's heaven and hell scenes.

Yet the mixture of recent stagnation and the old respect for social hierarchy and incontestable power didn't have to create the monsters that took control in 1975. There wasn't a straight line from Jayavarman VII to the Khmer Rouge; other causes converged.

The Vietnam War traumatized the country. In 1970 Cambodia's top politicians deposed Norodom Sihanouk, who was once the king. He had abdicated in 1955 to be free from royal ceremonial obligations, but remained the country's most dominant politician for the next 15 years. However, he often treated Cambodia as his footstool by giving power to his cronies and suppressing criticism. People were increasingly dismayed by the government's corruption, but as discontent mounted in the 1960s, Sihanouk spent a lot of time making movies, perhaps retreating into a fantasy world. But many farmers still associated him with sacredness for helping to free the country from France and for being of royal pedigree (even though he ruthlessly suppressed a peasants' revolt in the province of Battambang in 1967). So for many people, a pillar of order was toppled in a time of upheaval.

But Chandler said that this pillar helped to create the chaos in the next decade. Sihanouk had treated Cambodia as his personal property and its people as his children, and he considered opponents to be traitors. Another historian, Milton Osborne, wrote that his security police hounded his critics. The historian John Tully said that his henchmen hunted down communists living in Phnom Penh and towns, who then retreated to the jungles and became his determined enemies.[6] By retarding the development of pluralism and debate, Sihanouk encouraged his enemies to be equally absolutist when they replaced him.[7]

The Khmer Rouge and North Vietnamese troops waged an especially vicious war with Cambodia's government from 1970 to 1975. Hundreds of thousands of teenage boys and young men, formerly immersed in village and Buddhist traditions from the Middle Ages, experienced freedom and masculine identities for the first time by firing modern weapons at each other.

The war ravaged Cambodia's economy, which was already fragile after the corruption from Sihanouk's time. Inflation spiraled out of control, exports nosedived, roads were ruined, tourism ended, and the little industry there was faced chronic shortages of labor and supplies.

In 1973 Vietnamese forces pulled out of Cambodia; this turned the fighting into a civil war between the government and the Khmer Rouge. Both sides committed atrocities against each other, and this strengthened the tendencies to see each other only as absolute enemies.

As the fighting raged on, Richard Nixon's administration carpet bombed much of eastern Cambodia to stomp out the Viet Cong. Innocent farmers were trapped underneath. The sleepy worlds that they had lived in became a more atrocious hell than the ones on Angkor Wat's south wall. Death came as suddenly as an enraged evil spirit. The B-52s, which could reach altitudes of over 50,000 feet, flew too high to be seen or heard. People only knew they were under attack when the jungle around them was bursting into flames and the sky was billowing with black smoke. The once verdant fields now choked with burning corpses, and screams of women and children whirled through the razed villages. The death toll from the bombings has been estimated to have been between 150,000 and 750,000.[8]

Cambodians traditionally associated well-being with the Buddha, monasteries, social hierarchy, politeness, the family, harmony with spirits, and a strong and benevolent royal court. But the traumas they suffered shattered this world and made young men susceptible to becoming hardened soldiers.

At least half a million refugees flocked from the east to Phnom Penh. The restive throngs fueled the Khmer Rouge's attempt to overthrow the government. The Khmer Rouge took over the countryside, surrounded the capital, and began to shell it. Its soldiers marched into it in 1975. The worst was about to come.

Why did Pol Pot become one of history's worst fiends? Even David Chandler, who wrote a biography of him, admitted to being mystified. People who knew him as a boy or young man found him easygoing and charming. He seems to have been a perfect chameleon who adapted to his surroundings. He had been unassuming as a young schoolteacher and then became ruthless as the political leader.

He lived in Paris in the early 1950s and learned about Marxism there. His extreme interpretation of it was encouraged in a later exile in Mao's China, where he was impressed with the decisiveness of the Great Leap Forward. After assuming power, he mandated unrealistic goals for rice production that caused soil exhaustion and famine. The government sent some of the nation's rice crop to China to buy weapons, and Khmer Rouge members gobbled up much of the rest.

Pol Pot tried to destroy all tradition, as Mao attempted to do during the Cultural Revolution. Teachers and artists were either killed or forced to labor in the fields. The Khmer Rouge abolished families and money, and forced children, parents, and spouses to live apart and slave in separate farming collectives. Buddhist monks were defrocked and forced to push plows, and many were executed. All people were to live as subsistence farmers in a society of equals that embodied the revolution's purest ideals.

So far, Pol Pot could be seen as just an unsophisticated convert to Marxism. Ignorant about human realities (needs for families, fun, intellectual life, spirituality, commerce, art, and recognition), he imposed impossible goals on his subjects. John Tully said that he reasoned that Cambodians could do anything because they built Angkor.[9] But why was he so wantonly cruel? Why force the entire population of Phnom Penh, including the sick and aged, to evacuate and march to the fields within days of conquering it and work 12 to 15 hours a day? Trivial disobediences provoked torture and execution.

The forced evacuation of Phnom Penh was horrendous. Many of the Khmer Rouge who stormed into the city were adolescents from the country who had never seen concrete buildings, running water, soft drinks, or electric appliances. Brutalized by American bombing and by five years of civil war, they unleashed their aggression on the strange surroundings (the Marxism they had imbibed taught that urban life is corrupt and decadent). They forced thousands of sick, crippled, and wounded patients from their hospital beds and ordered them to march out of town. Frail old women hobbled, injured solders struggled on crutches, and some people were wheeled in their beds by family members. Some of the healthy turned back when they reached the outskirts and were immediately shot. Thousands died in the evacuation, and Phnom Penh became a ghost town within a few days.

According to most estimates, between 1.4 million and 2.2 million people were killed while the Khmer Rouge was in power.[10] They died from malnutrition, exhaustion, and the lack of medical care (medical professionals were either executed or forced to work the land). At least 250,000 of the victims died from torture and executions after being identified by Pol Pot's paranoid regime as enemies of the state. A stupefying 30 percent of Cambodia's population perished between the 1970 coup and 1979.

Many events converged to empower the Khmer Rouge and to encourage the cycle of brutality to develop during Sihanouk's reign and escalate in the 1970s, but we may never know what warped Pol Pot's mind. Sadly for Cambodians, he never received the justice he deserved. After the Khmer Rouge was ousted in early 1979 by invading Vietnamese, who had gotten fed up with raids from across the border, he and his army retreated into jungles in the northwest and launched counter attacks. The Khmer Rouge blanketed the area with landmines that have ripped off thousands of civilians' limbs.

In 1997 Pol Pot's comrades arrested him for murdering a senior Khmer Rouge official called Son Sen, whom he had accused of treason, and he died the next year. Though found guilty and sentenced to house arrest, it's not known whether he died from execution or natural causes, and he is reported to have had no regrets. For all the misery he caused, Cambodians have not been able to feel closure. Most surviving Khmer Rouge troops and officers blended back into society. They now plant rice, drive taxis, run mom-and-pop grocery stores, and cook food in restaurants. It's easy to feel that monsters are still lurking beneath the surface of everyday life.

I visited the Killing Fields when I returned to Cambodia in 2012. A roughly equal number of Cambodians and Westerners silently ambled around, each in his own thoughts. We walked past transparent cases that held stacks of skulls and heaps of rags that the victims wore when they were slain. Thin arm bones, a cranium, scattered teeth, and a sandal rested on top of a case so that visitors could caress them and feel closer to the victims. Little banners decorated the Killing Tree to commemorate a spot where goons bashed babies' heads. People who showed disgust were punished for not being enthusiastic about the revolution.

However, I found healing as evident as the horrors. All the guards spoke as softly as the afternoon breeze coming from neighboring rice fields. A tall and thin Thai-style temple housed most of the skulls. Its roof combined sculptures of nagas and garudas. Both are enemies in Indian and Khmer mythology. Garudas are mythical birds and nagas live in rivers, yet they coexist on this building to symbolize harmony.

On the way back to Phnom Penh my driver asked, "How do you feel after being there?"

I said, "Stop the car," and then showed him a picture that I had recently taken of a smiling mother holding her baby and said, "New life."

He immediately repeated, "New life" as though our utterances together would have extra magical power.

I saw a lot of new life during both trips. Performing arts organizations have resurrected traditional music and dance. Buddhism has made a comeback, and politicians sometimes ask monks for blessings.

Many artists call the northwestern town Battambang home. An organization called Our Strength uses a room in Sammaki's house to promote women's health and arts. When I visited it, girls in their early teens were kneeling on the floor, working on their opuses. Some works were about what adolescents all over the world obsess over, romance. They painted people embracing so tightly that their bodies merged. Their work projects the emotional exuberance of ancient Khmer temples.

Wall paintings that I saw in the public assembly halls of many modern Buddhist temples also show old Khmer esprit. The Buddha presides on golden thrones and walks down stairways with the regal bearing of

Angkor's kings. Attendants who surround him are as elegantly dressed as elites in the processions on Angkor Wat's friezes. Celestial women are more decorously attired than devatas, but their faces are as beautiful—some Cambodians still envision heaven in terms of feminine grace. Ancient Khmer art still lives in people's dreams of the highest ideals.

I spotted three teenagers (a boy and two girls) kneeling under a small pavilion that sheltered a Buddha statue in a remote part of Angkor. He was snuggling with one of them. I found this breach of protocol at a Buddhist shrine funny enough to photograph. I discreetly slid my camera from my pocket to sneak a picture from behind, but just before I snapped, the girls turned to me and smiled. This signaled to me that old Southeast Asian mixtures of piety, fun, and civility are thriving again in Cambodia.

However, Joel Brinkley found darker situations there. He wrote that many people's lives are not much better than they were under the Khmer Rouge. Most people outside the Siem Reap-Phnom Penh-Battambang triangle have little access to international travelers, and they're trapped in a system in which politicians and police fleece them. John Tully concluded that Cambodia is ruled by the strongest for the strongest.[11] A roughly twenty-year-old man that I met in the countryside complained that the government had done nothing to pave his village's road. I sympathized with him because rain had turned the dirt into a river of mud, and I had to carefully choose every step to avoid falling flat.

Kalyanee Mam's multi-award winning feature documentary, *A River Changes Course*, details the struggles of rural Cambodians as their government appropriates more of their land for logging and factories, and dams up rivers that their families have called home for untold generations. The film's luscious cinematography shows Kalyanee's deep respect for the natural environment and affection for the people so well that I felt like I was among them when I watched it. One woman described local folklore about butterflies—they fly north to Laos every year to regain their colors and then return to her forest, adding their vibrant hues to it. Sadly, her surroundings have now been so denuded for logging that she and her family are losing their forest, which they depend on for both survival and spiritual traditions. She doesn't want to leave but figures that she will have to because most of her life-long neighbors already have. Her formerly vivacious land has become barren.

The Economist reported that Cambodian politics is in a period of flux. Hun Sen, a former Khmer Rouge member who ultimately defected, has been the most powerful political figure for 30 years, and he has often brutally suppressed opposition.[12] His country's economy has recently grown by seven percent per year, but it has favored people who are already politically connected, and he has given land concessions to Chinese and Vietnamese concerns. Oil has recently been discovered off shore, and real estate prices in Phnom Penh increased severalfold in the last 15 years, but these two industries usually benefit people who are already wealthy enough to buy homes and the machinery for a capital-intensive industry. The textile industry is also prominent in Cambodia, and it also favors people with enough money to build factories while others toil in them for subsistence wages. All three industries feed corrupt regimes in many countries and further marginalize the poor. I saw at least twice as many tuk tuk drivers in Siem Reap during my return visit. All were young men calling to every passerby. The number of begging children at Angkor's temples had increased severalfold so that they were in front of almost every major monument rather than just Angkor Wat. The constant requests for business from drivers and from children desperately trying to sell scarves and T-shirts often made me unable to take the relaxed walks in Angkor and Siem Reap that I enjoyed in 2007.

Older people, who remember the atrocious 1970s and fear the return of the savagery, have repeatedly re-elected Hun Sen. But the 2013 election saw a shift in generations. More than half of the voters were under thirty years old and were thus born after the Khmer Rouge's downfall. They are frustrated with their country's corruption and the greater prosperity that they see its neighbors enjoying. In 2012 I saw Hun Sen's face on dozens of billboard posters. He looked assured and aloof, as though he was posing as a mighty Khmer king. But young people, communicating with cellphones and social media, reduced the impact of the government-run newspapers and TV programs. They voted for change, and the opposition won 55 seats in the 123-seat National Assembly (the opposition claimed to have won the majority and said that the voting was rigged). Sen will now have to respect his detractors' leverage, either by cooperating with them or suppressing them even more. *The Economist* initially wrote that he is likely to do the former because there's too much opposition to control, but it then reported a crackdown on dissent at the beginning of 2014 which left five people dead and twenty injured.[13] For now, Sen refuses to tolerate opposition, but the *The Economist* says that his strong-arm tactics will lessen his popularity, which has already been declining. Cambodians are going through one of their most turbulent political scenes since the Khmer Rouge ruled.

David Chandler wrote that authoritarian politics and traditions of deference have dominated Cambodia's history for the last 2,000 years. Michael Vickery, in *Cambodia, 1975–1982,* said that ruthless suppression of political opponents has been common since ancient Khmer times. These are general trends but they don't comprise a curse. Many young people are aware of other countries' freedoms and economic successes, and they're looking to the future no matter how heavily Hun Sen roosts.

At the same time, ancient traditions of Khmer exuberance and Southeast Asian diversity and fun are resurfacing. Their endless ways of creating beauty and balancing hard and soft power can add to our world's web of cultures. Since the 18th century, Cambodia has been exploited by other countries and its own corrupt strongmen. With a more humane government, and with more people who appreciate its traditions, it can recover its full range of cultural patterns. These include the classical balance of Chenla temples, the refinement and intimacy of Preah Ko and Bantey Srei, Angkor Wat's magnificence, and tolerant blends of faiths. They also include vibrant ceremonies, mixtures of sacredness and fun, the ability to combine ideas and images from many cultures, India's huge heritage, and lively folk religions. These are all great attributes to add to today's world, which the political analyst Thomas Friedman called hot, flat, and crowded. Cambodian culture can make our world more effervescent and fun.

We can help its people by sharing our appreciations of Cambodia with family members and friends. We can post messages on social networking sites to inform others about both the greatness and struggles of this land. More people can thereby become inspired to support schools and artistic organizations. As more learn about Cambodia's cultural wealth and work to improve its people's living conditions, we'll become part of its traditional exuberance. We can help Cambodians reach their potential, and as we do, we will be enriched by its flowering.

This mutual growth is a key part of the method for finding paradise on earth. By studying another culture and exposing its beauty, we can help it develop more, and at the same time, enhance our own creativity by expanding our range of ideas. Everyone's views of the world can thereby become bigger. We can see the world anew on a regular basis by learning about the varieties of ways in which different societies integrate their own perspectives.

As more people share many societies' cultural wealth, we'll gain perspectives of the world which will be head, shoulders, and torso above today's polarized politics and wide gaps between haves and have-nots. Our ability to establish them in the world depends on how many people we inspire to begin exploring societies beyond their current horizons, and how many others they inspire (we can regularly share our discoveries with our families and friends, and in social media). People can synthesize their different cultures into landscapes as celestial as the one I experienced on Angkor Wat's upper terrace. If we get enough dialogs going, we can keep inspiring more people to explore the wealth in other cultures so that we'll all become like candles lighting other candles.

I was a little sad when I rode to the airport to fly back to Bangkok. I still think of Cambodia's warm-hearted people, illustrious monuments, soft colors in towns, and many glorious shades of green and brown in jungles and fields. The country was savory to the last minute. I arrived at the X-ray machine in the departure terminal and emptied my pockets into a tray. A female security guard noticed a wad of cash in my wallet and said, "All that money!" with a flirtatious tone and smile. The Khmer love of fun made me even more reluctant to leave.

But I found Thailand as fascinating. Any Southeast Asian country is only an introduction to one of the world's richest regions. Our flight through our cultural potential is only beginning.

PART TWO

THAILAND

SECTION ONE

EXPANDING PERSPECTIVES FURTHER

CHAPTER 8

TRADITIONAL GRACE AND MODERN LIFE IN THAILAND

THERE ARE NO elephants in Thailand. Thais have traditionally avoided building Angkor Wat-sized monuments that awe people. Instead, they've created an endless variety of graceful forms and emblazoned them with sprightly gold, silver, red, blue, and green hues. Most Thai artworks aren't wham-bam big, but I found many to be some of the most beautiful in the world.

Thai art comingles with a natural landscape that includes teak forested mountains in the north, fertile riverine planes with dancing rice stalks in the center, and sparkling beaches down south. Its land has a captivating variety of trees, flowers, birds, fruits, waterways, and mixtures of human ethnicities. These forms of natural and cultural beauty fuse into an environment that many travelers from the West find so enchanting that they decide to move there.

But my visit began in Bangkok's concrete jungle. I planned to immediately leave town, drift north through Thailand's older cultural capitals, and then fly back down to explore the big city. I could thereby immerse myself in traditional Thai life after seeing Cambodia, and then find out how Thais have adapted to the modern world.

I especially enjoyed discovering Thailand after Cambodia. Though both influenced each other, they're so different that I often felt that I was seeing with new eyes. Both have unified their worlds with unique perspectives and art forms. Comparing both cultures back to back was one of the most rewarding travel experiences I've ever had.

Each country also revealed more aspects of the West, and my later travels in Europe illuminated Southeast Asia even more. All cultures together showed me a way of seeing the world in which all societies can nurture each other. By Chapter 13, we will have enough material to detail the method for optimizing this kind of perspective.

First we'll delve into the depths of a culture that fascinated me long before I visited it. Thailand mystifies many Westerners. It's full of contradictions, including a deep Buddhist faith and tolerance of prostitution. It's also profuse with graceful art and corrupt politics, which became increasingly divisive a few years ago. How do they all fit together?

At the airport, I found a taxi for the 50-mile drive north to the wealthiest former Thai capital, Ayutthaya, which used to be one of the world's most vibrant cities. I followed the driver outside and into what I had imagined my first encounter with Bangkok to be: a mixture of heat, concrete, and gridlock traffic. We needed 20 minutes to squeeze out of the airport, but the cars flowed smoothly on the sleek new elevated highway that ran through the city like a ribbon. It threaded the sprawling central area and gave me a panorama of it.

Bangkok seemed to have its own logic—or illogic. Gleaming skyscrapers were unevenly spread among low-rise apartments, single-family homes, and golden temple roofs and spires. The winding streets looked haphazard. I could see why many Westerners find this city enigmatic. There were no linear perspectives of enough of the whole to give me an idea of how the place ticks. The densely packed mishmash of buildings and undulating streets suggested a different way of thinking. I wondered, How am I going to find my way around here when I come back? My trip through the old kingdoms up north would provide the answer.

As we motored along, my driver tuned the radio to a local rock station. I found the meaty guitars refreshing after all the slow music in Cambodia. He kept the volume low, probably out of respect, so I asked him to turn it up. The band sounded like a Nirvana clone, with distorted guitars that blasted so few chords that I could count them on one hand. But the singer had a soft and happy Thai voice rather than Kurt Cobain's raspy, forlorn tone. Even Thai grunge is sometimes pretty.

But the next bands were much sappier, and I regretted asking him to play the music louder. A lot of Thai pop is as sugary as a bowlful of jelly beans and chocolate syrup, but guys put up with it to please their girlfriends.

Equally suffocating was the thick haze of cigarette smoke in the car. Lots of Southeast Asian males light up. But before the mixture of glib sounds and sour smells became unbearable, the concrete thinned and was replaced by light green fields. Thailand always presented pretty colors and helpful people which lightened its blemishes. This, I was to find out, is an ancient cultural trait.

We rode through the Chao Phraya basin's bounteous green carpet. This area has been Thailand's main rice bowl for many centuries (though many of its southernmost regions have only been farmed in recent times—they used to be marshy, but people filled them in for agriculture and housing projects as Ayutthaya's and Bangkok's populations grew). Nature's rhythms are as unhurried and stately as royal court dances. Year after year, people follow the cycle of wet and dry seasons. The rains usually come in June or July, and rice stalks rise until the land is decked with joyful green. Nature's power and benevolence have returned. The rains subside around November, and the heads of crops turn amber and gold. They are pregnant and it's time to harvest their bounty. Every healthy person treads into the fields to contribute his and her share of the work. After the harvest locals conduct festivals and prepare the ground for next year's planting. This noble cycle has nourished the land for an untold number of generations, though farming has recently become more mechanized and dominated by big businesses.

This basin has also been culturally fertile since ancient times. The Dvaravati civilization emerged around its edges by the seventh century CE and ringed it with large moated settlements that were towns, ceremonial centers, or both. These communities imported Buddhism and Hinduism while trading so much that they issued coins. They exchanged goods with each other, Indian merchants, Cambodia to the east, and societies in Burma to the west. Since this land has been integrated by waterways, its people frequently shared religious ideas and artistic images with each other. Many, perhaps the majority, were Mon rather than Tai (the spelling *Tai* is used for people of that ethnicity before they formed states in the 13th century in what is now Thailand, and for citizens of other countries who are descended from them). Groups of Tais moved in from their ancient homelands in southern China and northwestern Vietnam and mixed with them, but most Dvaravati writings are in Mon. This language is related to Khmer. The tolerance and cultural diversity that many Thais are proud of already blossomed on this plain.

Angkor conquered much of Thailand in the 11th century and ruled there until the 13th, so both areas had much time to share religions, political ideas, and artistic styles. Thailand gave Cambodia Theravada Buddhist traditions and imported the Khmers' lustrous art and rituals.

The Khmer empire wasn't able to maintain its outposts in Thailand after Jayavarman VII's reign. Local Tai strongmen liberated it and established three great states:

- Lan Na in the north; its capital was Chiang Mai,
- Sukhothai in the center,
- Ayutthaya in the south.

Each was unique, but still characteristically Thai. All these kingdoms synthesized multicultural fusions in their own ways, which combined to give Thailand's cultural landscape depth and variety that people can spend their whole lives savoring.

Ayutthaya was founded in 1351, and it became the most powerful Thai state until the Burmese destroyed it in 1767. Thais then established Bangkok as their capital in 1782. Ayutthaya could dominate international trade because it was closer to the sea than the other two kingdoms were. It also had the most flatland for rice farming and could thus support more people. Merchants from all over the known world teemed through its ports in splendid displays of colors that rivaled the vitality of Thai arts. Arabs, Persians, Gujaratis, Tamils, Chinese, Japanese, Malays, Javanese, Bengalis, Portuguese (in the 16th century), and Dutch, English, and French (all three in the 17th century) sold their wares and bought goods there. They loaded their ships with wood, spices, wax, ivory, rhinoceros horns, and hides of deer, buffalo, and cattle. The land's gifts and merchants from every known state converged in this vigorous city.

Ayutthaya exported rice to another great Southeast Asian state that I later explored on the same trip, Malacca. Its capital hugged the western side of the peninsula's southern end in what is now modern Malaysia. Malacca lacked extensive lands to farm but it controlled trade through the straits. This was some of the most valuable real estate in the world because it was one of two places where ships could sail between India and China. The other was off the southern end of Sumatra, which was more out of the way. Controlling the straits gave Malacca a lot of wealth to show off.

Like Ayutthaya, Malacca hosted merchants from every known culture, but Muslim sultans ruled this equally colorful melting pot. They governed from a multi-story boat-shaped wooden palace on stilts that perched on a hill overlooking the harbor and warehouses. Malacca sent luxury goods and cotton from India to Ayutthaya in return for rice. These two business meccas grew up together. Both represented Southeast Asia's new commercial directions after Angkor and Pagan declined, and both added more dazzle to the region.

Angkor also enriched Ayutthaya's cultural synthesis. Ayutthaya adopted some of its royal rituals after taking many of its eminent priests and artists in 1431–2. In the Indravisaka ceremony, the Thai king assumed the guise of the ancient Vedic god Indra to make rain fall. Royalty and the land's fertility were thus linked, and Angkor's hallowed rituals added might to this association. Scribes, accountants, doctors, priests, and astrologers developed a palace language based on Khmer and Sanskrit. So Ayutthaya's kings projected their own prestige with the Khmer court's glamour.

Ayutthaya's cultural effervescence and the land's allure blended in a spellbinding cityscape. The city thrived at the confluence of the Chao Phraya and Lopburi rivers. Engineers dug a canal to make an island and then built the capital on it. They also constructed canals through the city for transportation. The cobalt lanes carrying long, narrow boats were bracketed by trees and pagodas. Some foreigners noted that streets along the canals were dirty and that high water sometimes flooded them, but Dutch travelers estimated between 300 and 450 shrines in Ayutthaya and noted that almost all were gilded. Architects aimed more for grace than bang. Instead of mountains for Hindu gods, Thais built tall, narrow Buddhist pagodas that curved upwards into needle-sharp points which rose above the tree tops and tickled the clouds. An orchard of spires shimmered above the verdant canopy. Spiritual luminosity and natural abundance intertwined and reached the sky.

The land around the island must have been equally enchanting. A 17th century Dutch merchant named Jeremias Van Vliet noted that the island's main streets were uninhabited, since it was the kingdom's political and ritual center. Most people lived in the surrounding area, which bustled with villages, temples, and rice fields. Ayutthaya was thus dominated by waterways, greenery, cozy homes, and tall, lean spires rising over the tree tops.

But the graceful forms masked several tensions beneath the surface:

- Ayutthaya fought about 70 wars during its 416-year life. Its kings competed with other states for Southeast Asia's increased trade.
- Firearm use began in Southeast Asia in the 15th century. Malacca fell to the Portuguese in 1511, and Ayutthaya entered an arms race with neighboring people, including the Burmese. All scrambled for Portuguese, English, Dutch, French, Chinese, and Persian cannons, guns, mercenaries, and engineers. The blasts made warfare deadlier and contrasted with the ethereal art.
- Ayutthaya's court often ruled more harshly than the other Thai states. Beginning in the late 15th century, kings partitioned society into levels that highlighted distinctions between upper and lower classes. Much of the beauty that the nobles created was built on the aching backs of the under classes, who had to perform free labor for the king.
- The kingdom was politically unstable. Like Angkor, it lacked rules for royal successions, and many of them were violent. But people were willing to game for the throne because the king profited from the trade. Millions of elephants, rhinos, and deer were slaughtered, and their pelts and horns were sold to foreign merchants. Noblemen were willing to risk their lives for the rewards from this system which siphoned the environment's wealth.

All the same, the natural beauty, royal glitz, and sleek temples gave locals lots of ways to enjoy the moment and ignore impending political upheavals. As in modern Bangkok, many corrupt and greedy elites masked themselves in a culture that stressed elegance, fun, and smiling complicity. But Ayutthaya was intoxicating during the peaceful times.

The Burmese zealously leveled Ayutthaya in 1767. This orgy of destruction was rare in Southeast Asia, and it traumatized the country so much that it still bears scars. The Burmese destroyed more cities on their way back to Pegu, and large sections of land were depopulated. Hundreds of thousands of people, dazed from wanton pillaging they had never experienced, desperately wandered in search of food. Some Thais still speak of Burma with bitterness. One man that I met called it "the enemy," and several movie makers and modern writers have portrayed its people as thugs.[1]

But the Burmese spared many stupas. They're scattered throughout Ayutthaya, which also has modern wats, museums, and the old palace grounds. Most tourists only see a fraction of what is there. The town's relaxing atmosphere made me glad that I began my Thai journey there instead of Bangkok. The people's amiability and the remnants of past glory gave me an introduction to traditional Thailand that I'll always treasure.

My taxi driver dropped me off at a small single-story hotel that surrounded an intimate patio lined with dense shrubbery. A petite middle-aged woman met me at the front desk. She smiled bashfully as we greeted each other with the traditional *wai* (both hands raised with the palms together—a salutation adopted from India, Sri Lanka, and Cambodia).

I immediately explored the town's gems, beginning with an outdoor museum in the form of a traditional central Thai home. Three wooden buildings arranged in a U shape stood on a stilted platform about eight feet high. The outer walls and roofs were a little concave. Most Thai architectural forms avoid big and flat surfaces; they seem to flow instead. Walls and roofs often curve, doors and lintels are carved in sinuous swirling patterns, and roofs' corners often project outwards and upwards into long winding shapes that end in sharp points. Angkor's temples look more substantial—square and rectangular forms which are often densely packed seem to project energies that order society. In contrast, Thai art forms curve so much that they've been compared to a river's flow and to a boat. Sinuous lines seem to tame energies into smooth ripples so that nature is benevolent. Both cultures have made different forms fundamental in their views of how the world's order coheres.

Figure 11. Boat-like lines under the windows at Wat Chong Nonsi, a temple in Bangkok that was built during the late Ayutthaya period, before the city was formally founded.

I saw a snapshot of today's Thailand in the second museum. It housed a replica of the old royal palace in a ten-foot-square glass case. A middle-aged man was teaching a class of roughly forty kids who were about ten years old. They kneeled in front of it while he lectured at length in a tone as grave as a priest's while expounding the seven deadly sins. No student uttered a word. Many Western visitors are impressed by Thai children's politeness. They show deference to teachers which some Americans would consider fawning. Some people have criticized the Thai education system for stressing passive rote memorization over critical thinking.[2] The kids probably left the museum full of respect for their traditions, but I wondered if their leeway for analyzing their past and identities would be limited.

But I was looking at them through American eyes rather than their own. The modern West put objectivity and freedom front and center. I loved my footloose romp around the world, but most Thais are happiest in a harmonious group. These children were learning to enjoy living together as much as they were acquiring facts and figures. Thais often value group harmony and enjoying the moment's pleasures more than objectivity. Their architecture's flowing forms embody this congenial mindset.

I then visited the real palace. The royal stupas rose just behind the entrance. Three large spires were in a row surrounded by the remains of a rectangular cloister with a long meeting hall at each end. Smaller stupas stood around the cloister so that the whole area was a forest of towers.

The stupa was already an ancient architectural form from India and Sri Lanka when Ayutthaya flourished. It was originally a burial mound and a shrine for spirits. People later adapted it to Buddhism to house relics of the great teacher and his honored followers, but lovers of Thai art feel that Thais made it more graceful.

They imported a common Sri Lankan form that's structured into three main sections. The bottom is bell-shaped, the middle is a square block, and the top is a series of increasingly small parasols that end in a conical spire. These represent different levels of the cosmos, which become more spiritual as the altitude increases. Thais transformed the whole form into patterns as lissome as their domestic architecture. They began to make stupas narrower, and then merged the three sections into a flow of softened energies that ripple like a river. I think this is one of the world's most pleasing art forms, and it takes people into a different way of seeing than the West's emphasis on abstract lines.

As I walked around the palace stupas, some of the smaller spires playfully hid behind the bigger ones and then reappeared. This inter-play kept shifting as I strolled. The curving forms danced in a slow and relaxed tempo.

The three main stupas honor kings from the 15th century. People in Ayutthaya deposited relics of royals in shrines because they associated rulers with the Buddha. To them, monarchs protected the dharma on earth.[3] Ayutthaya fought about 70 wars, but kings projected their rule with soft forms in order to appear benevolent.

I needed a little imagination to visualize the palace after the Burmese leveled it. But modern excavations have revealed the bottom foot or two of the grand meeting halls. There are also models in guidebooks and in the museum, as well as descriptions and drawings by European visitors. While walking through the expansive grounds in the sultry heat, I assembled a picture of the palace when it ruled the realm.

The main buildings had a central section which a tall spire crowned. Two of its sides were adjoined by a long rectangular hall. The other two sides stuck out less so that each building was in a cross shape that was long on one axis and short on the other. Several overlapping gables topped the portico on each side of the building. A stack of curving roofs rose above, which gradually became steeper towards the central tower. The horizontal emphasis of the long halls thus seamlessly transformed into a soaring spire. The shift from the horizontal to the vertical axis was tapering rather than sudden—confrontational forms were avoided. These buildings where the king was enthroned with Khmer rituals that presented him as godlike balanced all their forms and surfaces so that no single one walloped visitors. The two long halls that emerged from the middle displayed earthly power, but the central tower reached for the heavens. In this way, worldly and spiritual realms balanced each other.

Several meeting halls and ponds glittered within sight of each other. Together, they created similar impressions that a walk around the royal stupas provided: a flow of forms and colors that was so ethereal that only a sacred realm could have generated it.

The whole palace was thus like an otherworldly dream. Lofty spires, masterfully designed halls, and rustling trees were reflected in pools. Both this area and the royal stupas created gossamer swirls of forms and colors that blended in limitless varieties in relaxed tempos as people ambled around. Nature's animated energies and alpha-male warmongering were made refined.

Performing arts added even more beauty to the scenery. Dancers and musicians entertained kings and aristocrats in the palace and upper class homes. Poetic forms were formal and elevated above daily speech and folk drama, and spectators sported their finest silk clothing. Some of the most hallowed performances were of the *Ramayana*. Masked dancers and shadow puppets dramatized its most popular episodes, and slender female dancers performed with slow, stylized steps and hand movements.

This super-refined world's art must have encouraged people to forget the cutthroat politics—back the loser in yet another turbulent royal succession and the next rippling pool you'll see might be your own blood. People had to look out for Number One in Ayutthaya's uncertain political climate.

The kingdom lacked a constitution that stood above political frays. Instead, a small circle of extended families tussled for power. The historian David Wyatt wrote that this led to the kingdom's undoing. Ayutthaya was wealthy enough to boot the Burmese invaders out, but its factions didn't put up a common front.[4] Ayutthaya's mixture of alluring beauty and social tensions shattered like a crystal palace before the more determined army.

Yet its ideals of beauty, which emphasize graceful flows of forms and colors, still flourish all over Thailand. They were expressed in many types of art outside the palace, including domestic and temple architecture, ceramics, painting, sculpture, lacquerware, fabrics, and furniture. The aesthetics spread throughout the land and resonated with the people, who already had a heritage of diversity, tolerant mixtures of animism and Buddhism, and an often-generous natural landscape. Political rulers and courtly arts, monks and sacred arts, and common people and folk arts fused into a unique culture.

Two of Ayutthaya's grandest temples highlight its center. Their towers soar across the street from each other, and their location made their forms exemplary during the kingdom's heyday. Wat Mahathat is the elder. The other, Wat Ratchaburana, was established about 50 years after Mahathat. A chronicle from the 17th century said that king Borommaracha II (r. 1424–1448; he was in charge when Ayutthaya plundered Angkor) erected it to honor his two brothers, who had killed each other in a duel over the throne after their father died. Borommaracha thus might have constructed this shrine next to Mahathat to legitimize his own rule. Suryavarman II and Jayavarman VII also built to awe after violent succession crises, but both Thai wats' forms were softened to encourage people to forget the mayhem. They include two of Thai architecture's most distinctive features, and they reveal key aspects of Thai thinking.

One is the main spire. Thais adapted it from Angkor, Sri Lanka, and Burma, but they added their own touch. Many Khmer towers have distinct levels, which look like several increasingly small platforms stacked on top of each other. But Thais often smoothed the levels into one tapering form and made it narrower, as they did with Sri Lankan stupas, while most Khmer towers are more dense and square (as though the power of nature and the gods is concentrated in them). Angkor Wat's corn cob steeples were a transition between both styles because builders placed curving stones in the corners between the levels to create the appearance of one continuous surface. The art historian Betty Gosling, in *Origins of Thai Art*, made a case for Thai influence, since the first major Khmer temples in this style were built in eastern Thailand (there also might have been inspiration from Burma). Ayutthayans made these spires even more lissome, and they downplayed the exuberance which Khmer's often stressed.

The second feature is the assembly hall (the vihara), which is a key center of Thai experience and a major cultural shift from Angkor. One of the temple's most sacred places was now open to ordinary people. Rather than erecting huge piles of stones to honor a god, Theravada Buddhists stressed the assembly hall, where everyone could sit together, hear sermons, admire murals of the Buddha's past lives on the walls, and bow to his statue on the altar at the far side of the entrance. It was built from humble bricks rather than pompous stones and often overlaid with soft white stucco. It's a central place in the community, and people see it as one of the main sources of goodness and order (Cambodians also adopted the vihara after they embraced the Theravada faith).

People's behavior in viharas always impressed me. They took off their shoes before entering and sauntered around. They then sat on the floor and bowed three times to honor the three gems of the faith: Buddha, Dharma, and the community of monks (sometimes the third gem's meaning has been extended to the community of all Buddhists). I never noticed anyone chattering loudly (unlike tourists in Rome's

Sistine Chapel, where deep-voiced security guards had to constantly bellow, "Silensio!" and "No Foto!"). However, people in viharas weren't rigid. Many parents let their children play and even run around a bit as long as they didn't bother others. People were considerate while allowing room for fun. Paintings, gold stencils on columns and the ceiling, long hanging banners, flowers, joss sticks, and golden Buddha statues surrounded us. All these easygoing forms and colors meshed with the genteel people into a model of how the world hangs together. As in architecture, no single form dominated the others. Instead, all flowed together.

People always seemed comfortable with my plopping onto the floor with my cumbersome shopping bags and briefcase. They let me witness their spiritual life whenever I wanted to be with them. The etiquitte that children learn might encourage passivity at times, but the civility and artistry in viharas have traditionally taught people to cohere and enjoy the moment.

A man in a saffron robe at Wat Ratchaburana fleshed out this type of cohesion when we met. He took a folder of pictures from his gown's pouch and showed me his parents and girlfriend. Many Thai men join monasteries for a short time to gain merit for their parents and themselves and then return to worldly life. This man still thought of his secular connections, but he also showed me photos of wats that he had visited all over Thailand. He often smiled while sharing pleasant images of both worlds.

Hundreds of objects were enclosed in Wat Ratchaburana's crypt in 1424, and their cultural variety shows Thai diversity in full splendor. Several coins came from a Kashmiri Islamic state, some amulets were written in Chinese, and images of the Buddha were crafted in India, Sri Lanka, and Tibet. Thai Theravada traditions have been conservative by stressing the Buddha's original teachings, but they have been open enough to assimilate images and rituals from several lands and faiths.

Thais also mixed animistic beliefs with Theravada practices. Some historians think that most people outside elite circles in Ayutthaya's early days were more centered on traditional spirit cults, and that Buddhism only slowly permeated most commoners' lives.[5] Many people today still honor local spirits and believe that misfortunes are caused by witchcraft and sorcery. Some wear amulets to protect themselves from harm. Sellers in outdoor markets display rows of phalluses which embody fertility and power. Hindu gods imported from India and the Khmer Empire also join the inventories. People who hope to win a lottery or land a business deal sometimes worship the elephant-headed Hindu god Ganesha, who bestows wealth. Some in the middle and upper classes see these practices as more widespread among peasants and urban laborers, but people in all levels of society adhere to some of them, and many of the wealthy do so more than they publically admit. Most common forms of Thai Buddhism reflect Thailand's people and art by emphasizing a source of safety (the original teachings of the Buddha) but being willing to adopt features from many cultures and fuse them into vibrant mixtures of forms and colors. Enough liveliness mixes with the focus on staying within known boundaries to make conventions flexible and sometimes fun.

These mixtures even influence people's emotional patterns. While ambling around the grounds of the national museum in Bangkok, I watched kids rehearse for a performance of the *Ramayana*. They played soldiers in Hanuman's monkey army, which Angkor Wat's friezes also portray. I was full of delicious satays and desserts as I watched the dancers' motions and bright costumes blend with the trees and opulent buildings. Thais call this feeling *sabai*. It means a mellow happiness, and it often refers to sitting with friends and chatting after dinner.

Sabai isn't intense. It's not what a rabid football fan feels when his home team scores a game-winning touchdown against its fiercest rival. It's more of a combination of mild stimulation and harmony with the surroundings. Thais have created endless varieties of these mixtures in their architecture, sculpture, theater, painting, and personal behavior. You can't fully express them in one form, like a Greek temple's colonnade, but you can never run out of variations to savor.

What created traditional Thai thought patterns? Everything in the natural and cultural landscape converged to create a unique way of perceiving and thinking. The natural environment has mixed the flows of rivers, the voluptuous heat, and the abundance of trees, flowers, and birdsong. The cultural products have included art that's smooth and rippling, cuisine that blends flavors from all over the known world, spirit cults, pretty rituals, soft voices, respect for the king, forms of Buddhism that combine conservatism and tolerance, and the centrality of the wat and its vihara. All these aspects of nature and society converged into a common way of seeing the world that has been reinforced countless times each day. Thai culture wasn't created by one huge thing, but by the ways innumerable little things have been combined. The media often tout Thailand's beaches and Bangkok's searing nightlife. The digital world speeds up our perceptions so that thought patterns that are slower, but subtle and beautiful, are fading. But travel north if you go to Bangkok, slow down, and open your senses to more nuances. You'll then experience one of the most enjoyable ways of representing reality that any culture has devised.

To explore more of this landscape, I hired a tuk tuk driver to take me to more of Ayutthaya's old temples. One of its most famous monuments forms a great contrast with Khmer art. The Thai king Prasat Thong erected Wat Chai Watthanaram in 1630 where his mother had lived. It represents Mt. Meru, as Angkor Wat does, but in a Thai way. A square wall with a tower in each corner and at each midpoint encloses the loftier central spire, which symbolizes the lustrous peak. The surrounding wall, more walls beyond it, and open areas in between represent the rings of land and oceans around Meru. However, the towers are narrow and they gently taper as they rise. So rather than looking like one huge mass, the wat undulates with steeples that dance as the stupas on the palace grounds did.

The wat's location at the edge of a river that borders the old city amplifies this effect because water reflects the towers. The palace's builders used pools in the same way.

An excellent way to explore Thai wats is to slowly approach them and amble through their courtyards and viharas. This is how Thais have traditionally visited them. There's no vantage point from which people can see the whole. This is so in Jayavarman VII's two big foundations in Angkor as well, but they often straitjacket the gaze into long, narrow corridors and small courtyards. Perspectives are usually freer in Thai architecture. They meander through dancing forms and flickering colors. Boat-like halls, curving roofs, and rippling stupas don't sharply contrast with surrounding spaces. Surfaces and spaces mingle into a happy flow that people can wander through and see from many angles.

Water is often a key aspect of Thai art, and many celebrations include boat processions. The frequent use of water in rituals and daily transportation (at least before the 20th century) has added more lightness, fun, and spontaneity to Thai perspectives. It has also strengthened the relaxed flow of a multitude of forms as a fundamental aspect of reality.

Ayutthaya's stupa for Queen Suriyothai is a marvelous example of how these lilting forms mix. Thais erected it next to a river to honor her for leading an army against invading Burmese in the late 16th century. It's narrower and more elongated than the Sri Lankan bell shape, but it also has several indentations in each corner. The scallops and increasing narrowness towards the top make the whole edifice ripple as delicately as the water that reflects it.

I saw how these combinations of water and lightened forms can become magical when I viewed Suriyothai's monument from the other side of the river. Long, narrow boats glided by. The water, the slender vessels, and the stupa in the background intermixed. Standing on the grounds of a monastery that was full of traditional architecture, I was looking from one jewel, across the serene water, to another. Since Ayutthaya once glittered with spires, monasteries, the royal palace, and waterways, a perspective of the city would have been less of a survey of an abstract grid and more of a meander from one enchanting place to another.

Meandering perspectives have also been common in domestic architecture. Traditional homes in central Thailand are often arranged around a veranda, but not in a standardized way. Every house is unique, depending on the needs of the residents and the structure and size of the family. Because all the homes are different, I always found walks through residential neighborhoods and villages charming, and thus took them whenever I could. Even where people had little money and buildings were small, every structure and yard was a different view and the homes meshed with surrounding foliage. Small spirit houses added glitter. Neighborhoods were refreshingly different from the "little boxes" stereotypes of Californian suburbs.

Verandas comprise much of the space within homes—sometimes 50 percent of larger buildings. Many smaller houses also have large front porches. Spaces between the inside and outside thus aren't sharply distinguished in traditional central Thai homes. This openness allows air to circulate in the hot climate, and it encourages a sense that all life forms flow together. People hear birdsong and crickets as they eat together. Roosters crow in the mornings and dogs sometimes bark. Today motorcycles, trucks, radios, and TVs add to the hum. People on their terraces can look out at the fruit trees around them and at neighbors' homes. Space in living areas isn't compartmentalized; it often flows throughout the neighborhood.

Homes in northern Thailand are usually single units rather than multiple structures around a middle courtyard. But they also encourage this sense of flow because each is still unique. Many have large verandas at the entrance, and a high percentage of houses are raised on stilts. Underneath, chickens cluck, dogs sleep, and men fix their motorcycles. Spirit houses are still within sight of people's residences so that the whole street can seem like one flow which all souls share.

This spatial openness has encouraged people to stress etiquette. Parents have traditionally taught children at an early age to be aware of how their bodies and behavior affect others around them. Kids learn not to shove things in front of people, raise their voices, spit, move abruptly, or walk against others. From an early age, people are taught to distinguish grace from wildness, and they learn to move in ways that gently flow through their surroundings.

Traditions from India were synthesized with this local stress on etiquette as Buddhism permeated daily life. A person shouldn't touch another's head or pass things over it because that's supposed to be the most sacred part of the body. Feet are its dirtiest components, and several travel books warn Westerners that they should never touch people with their feet or point them at them or at Buddha statues when they sit. The left hand is also considered unclean (it's traditionally used for going to the bathroom), so people should use the right hand to pass food to each other.

This plethora of rules isn't as regimented as it might sound. The emphasis on tolerant meanders allows many emotional outlets. One of the most famous Thai words is *sanuk*; it's usually translated as *fun*, but it has many nuances. Western travelers have noticed that people in Thailand like to have fun whenever they can, including when they're working. In Ayutthaya I had just finished dinner in a restaurant and I was about to pour water from one half-full clear plastic bottle into another so that I would only need to carry one. A waitress promptly came over and began to do it for me, but since both containers' ends were small, she had to pour it gingerly. When she finished without spilling a drop, another server clapped and quietly cheered. Thais work as hard as any other people I've seen, but they like to inject fun into the tasks.

The anthropologist Herbert P. Phillips, in *Thai Peasant Personality*, noted that an activity must be *sanuk* in order to be considered emotionally worthwhile.[6] Something is *sanuk* if it has novelty and can be done comfortably and with frivolity. It's also *sanuk* if it can be shared with others, and thus many group activities have this quality. Harvesting rice in cooperative teams, walking to school in groups, and joining religious festivals are common examples. Phillips noted that they're all experienced within teams of people who are loosely coordinated rather than tightly arranged like an assembly line. They all combine the safety and warmth of collective life with some novelty and spontaneity. This mixture mirrors the experience of sitting in a vihara, ambling around a wat, and living in a traditional house.

Unable to find a little-known temple in the northern town Nan, I popped into a small grocery store for a snack and directions. A roughly sixty-year-old man was chatting with the fifty-something man who owned the place, and when I asked them where the wat was, both pointed in opposite directions. I showed them my map and they studied it for a minute or two. They chattered and pointed in various directions, so I pointed to the general area that I thought the temple was in. After we reached a consensus, the sixty-year-old offered to drive me on his motorbike.

We whizzed down narrow roads lined with dark wooden stilt homes that were surrounded by shrubs and trees. He actually didn't live in Nan and he had rarely been there, but he was still quick to offer help. What began as an annoyance for me became enjoyable for both of us. He had *sanuk*, and by doing a good deed he acquired a little Buddhist merit. I had been exploring another wat before reaching the store, so the journey between both temples turned into delightful interactions with two people. Within traditional Thai landscapes, you can have lots of spontaneous encounters that are as lilting as the art forms.

Though Thais learn to control their emotions and behavior, they find many ways to avoid tedium and excessive seriousness. Traditional life is often more of a meander than a military march, and even soldiers can get this idea. I was in another historic northern town, Chiang Saen, and I arrived at its principal wat, Phra That Chedi Luang. About 200 soldiers on a break shared the grounds with monks. Their garb differed, but all were disciplined young men quietly strolling around the temple.

This wat's main stupa's lower section is an octagon, but the shrine's entire form looks less like a static geometric shape and more like a flow of energy from the heavens. It ripples like a river, as though grace is descending from the sky. As I joined the people's ambling, I saw statues of devotees mixing with the trees, and they seemed to glide around the stupa as I walked. Birdsong filled the air around us. Though all the people around me lived in ways that most would consider austere, we melded with these beautiful forms and with each other so that we all seemed integrated in a flow of life's energies, which the Buddha and traditional Thai customs often render gentle.

Perspectives in the West were opening into a new dimension when Thais were developing some of their most enduring art forms, which have expressed how their world coheres. Europe reached another one of its most influential creative peaks: the Italian Renaissance, whose artistic and intellectual leaders developed three-dimensional perspective. This has greatly shaped Western thought and art ever since. Why did it become basic in the modern West, and why did these two cultures emphasize different forms in their art and perspectives of the world? The next chapter will show hidden wealth in ideas that the West has taken for granted.

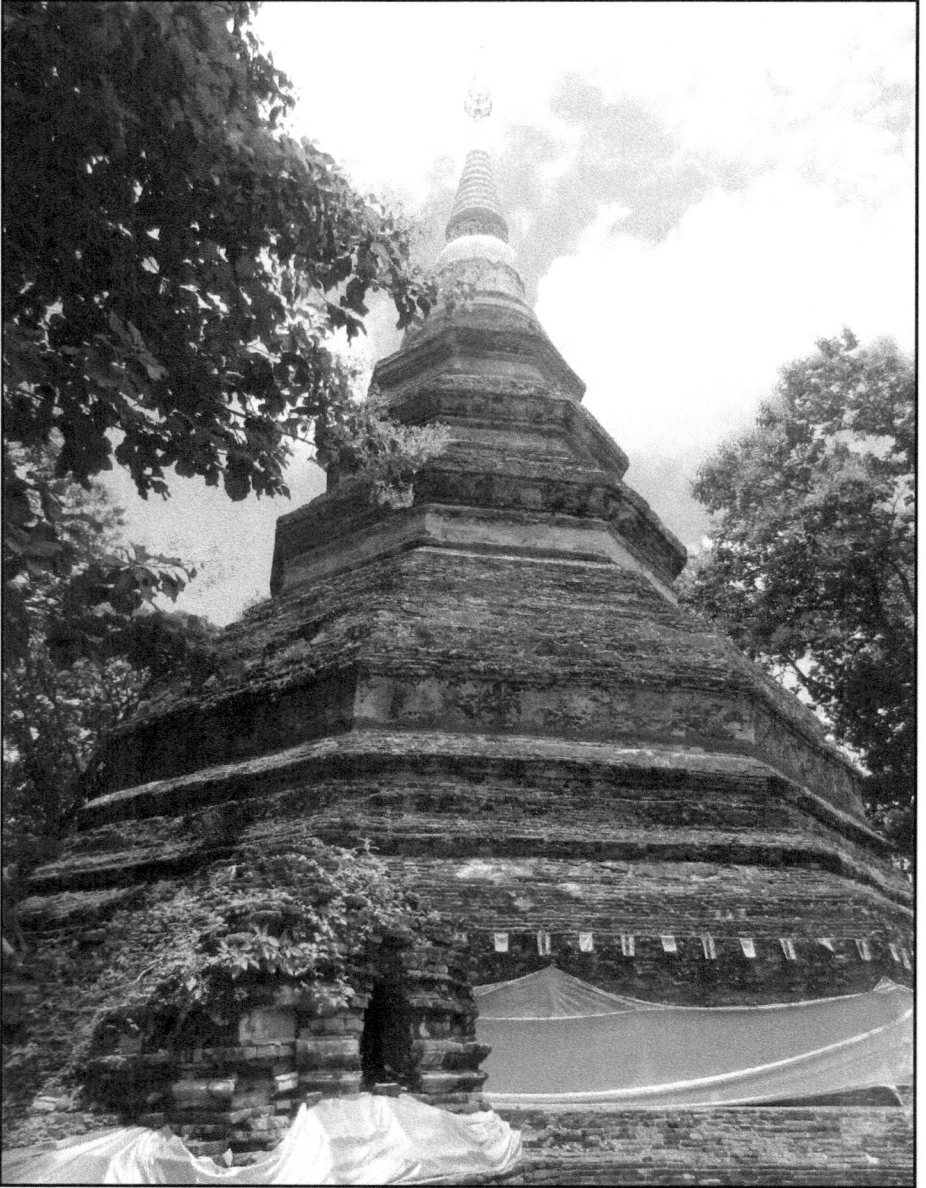

Figure 12. The main stupa in Phra That Chedi Luang in Chiang Saen.

Figure 13. Nature and culture exquisitely mesh in Phra That Chedi Luang.

We'll then return to Thailand in the chapter after the next and explore more aspects of its traditional views of the world. I've focused on the beauty in Thai perspectives in this chapter, but we will see that they have more facets. So does every other culture's perspectives. We will go deeper into how a society develops its world-view by first journeying through one of the most important movements in Western culture, and then we'll compare Thailand with it to attain bigger views of what a perspective is, and of all the world's cultures.

CHAPTER 9

THE WORLD IN A POINT:
THAI AND WESTERN PERSPECTIVES COMPARED

I FOUND TRAVELING through Italy in 2008 especially enjoyable because I could compare some of the West's most influential art with what I had seen in Southeast Asia. Hidden facets of the traditions that I grew up in kept surfacing so that my native culture and Southeast Asia illuminated each other in an increasing variety of ways. These experiences were even more savory than the pistachio gelato that fueled many of my walks.

In Florence around 1410, an artist and architect named Filippo Brunelleschi created a sensation.[1] He had painted an image of Florence's baptistery and the surrounding piazza on a panel that was about 12 inches square, which had a small hole drilled in the middle. He stood about six feet inside the cathedral's entrance, looked towards the baptistery across the street, held the panel up with the painting facing it, and peered through the hole. With his other hand, he held a mirror between the panel and the baptistery so that he was looking at a reflection of his own painting in the mirror. Brunelleschi encouraged his fellow Florentines to gaze through the hole, and they were astounded that the view was the same as it was when they looked directly at the building. To them, it seemed that he had performed a miracle.

Brunelleschi chose a perfect object for demonstrating his discovery of three-dimensional perspective. Abstract lines dominate Florence's baptistery from the ground to the roof.

Its outer shape is an octagon, and each wall is sharply partitioned into rectangles, squares, and half circles by thick, dark lines. He wasn't looking at anything that resembled a Thai wat's multitude of forms and flows and treating it as the most exemplary place to demonstrate a new

Figure 14. The baptistery in Florence, Italy.

way to perceive, even though Florence straddles a river. Instead, abstract lines and static shapes influenced his choice. These forms, which ancient Greeks had established as fundamental in nature, shaped the development of modern perspective.

His friend Leon Battista Alberti wrote a book in 1435 that theorized this perspective, and he translated it from Latin into Italian so that all Florentine artists could read it. Like Brunelleschi, he structured perspective according to Euclidean geometry, which treats the point, the line, and the plane as the basic ordering principles in the world. By standing on a certain spot in the cathedral and looking through a small hole in the panel, Brunelleschi showed that a perspective can be derived from a single point and straight lines.

Alberti explained Euclid's geometry by saying that a point cannot be divided into parts, and that several points in a row form a line. Several lines in a row make up a plane. The sides of the triangle from the eye to the object it views are thus lines, and they comprise the frame of the perspective.

He also wrote that an artist can use points and lines to organize what a person sees. In a painting, all lines that project from the viewer's side converge on a central point. From this point, an artist can draw a series of lines that extend down to the line at the bottom of the picture frame from one lower corner to the other. He can then draw another row of lines that are horizontal, which thus intersect the first lines. All these lines make up a checkerboard pattern on the painted scene's ground. In this way, he can accurately depict complex scenes in which all things are properly placed. He and the viewer thereby command everything in the picture.

This ability to analyze and control appealed to Florentines. Many of their leading citizens were bankers and merchants and they commissioned artists—patrons were already inclined to quantify things. Europeans increasingly adopted this precise three-dimensional perspective over the following centuries.

This perspective doesn't convey all the rich flows of forms and colors in Thai temples, palaces, neighborhoods, and processions. Most Thai art forms are not static like Euclidean geometry. Instead, they flow and gleam as you saunter around them, and they often intermesh. They're often experienced in a relaxed procession or a walk with family and friends.[2]

Both cultures have held different assumptions about what the most exemplary acts of perceiving are. The graceful procession, the river's gentle flow, the amiable group, and the relaxed amble are not reducible to a stationary viewing point that commands the whole scene. They're dynamic—they slowly glide. They don't as strictly focus on objects one at a time and analyze their details as though they're muscles and facial features of a Greek sculpture. The blending of all things into a congenial flow is often more important than the single entity.

Straight lines don't dominate the views in Thai temples, homes, paintings, and sculptures. Many forms bend and undulate, sometimes like gently rippling water and sometimes sharply into needle-like points. Mellow and dramatic energies are thereby balanced. Both cultures have held different assumptions about how things within a scene are connected.

The West's development of three-dimensional perspective mixed with many other currents, and all reinforced each other. One of the most influential was the emerging focus on the body and its physical substance. Thirteenth century Gothic artists had covered the body with flowing robes, and medieval scholastics saw it as the soul's prison. Then several early 15th century Italian sculptors and painters began to portray it as both physical and dignified. This trend climaxed in the early 16th century in Michelangelo's sculpture of David. Florentines were initiating this movement when Brunelleschi demonstrated his new perspective. They were thinking as though the most exemplary things that people view are physical bodies which can be precisely located on an abstract grid, rather than profusions of things and forms in nature's energy flows.

Kings ruled Angkor and Ayutthaya, and they limited merchants' freedom. Because both economies lacked money (though it was increasingly used in Ayutthaya, especially among the growing population of Chinese traders in the 18th century), people had no common standard of value independent from Mr. Glorious. This greatly differed from early 15th century Florence, which was a republic where representatives from its wealthier classes were both elected and chosen by lot to govern.[3] Money and commerce were the kings. Merchants formed seven major guilds and fourteen minor guilds, and they enjoyed voting rights in the city's government. They thus had their own identities, which they were proud of. Each group celebrated its patron saint's feast day, oversaw the finances of churches and hospitals, and commissioned art. They sponsored an artistic revolution that expressed their experiences.

One of Florence's most important buildings was Orsanmichele. This was a multi-story grain market that contained an especially revered image of the Virgin Mary. The building still stands in the center of town, halfway between the cathedral and the main square (everyone regularly saw it). Florence's governors decided that a statue of a guild's patron saint would occupy each niche on its exterior. But by 1400 only three guilds had finished the job.

In 1406 Florence conquered Pisa, which had been a long-time rival. Florentines were jubilant because their city was inland and Pisa was by the sea and had been a powerful maritime empire. Florentines felt that they were entering a new age of glory which could be compared to the ancient Roman past. They resolved to fill all the niches within the next ten years, and they created some of the most influential art in Western history.

The sculptors that the guilds employed made figures that contrast with the meditative faces on the Bayon's towers and the serene expressions of Thai Buddha statues. Some were willful men in the process of lecturing, looking directly at passing citizens in the streets. People then might have imagined their thundering voices.

Donatello first carved a statue of St. Mark. People walking by could see the saint's body outlined under the clothing. Instead of another Gothic figure of a soul in drapery, the sculptor gave his fellow citizens a physical person. But a teacher of Donatello's, Lorenzo Ghiberti, took this realism even further.

Ghiberti's St. Matthew engages people more intensely. His Gospel is open and he's gesturing towards it. He has a message that he wants to give passersby, and he assumes the position of an ancient Roman orator to dramatize the importance of Jesus' life. Donatello's St. Mark looks into the distance, but St. Matthew pulls people into his space. He is more animated and he points to a real text.

Figure 15. Ghiberti's St. Matthew in Florence.

St. Matthew thereby embodied and enlivened a three-dimensional space before Alberti wrote his mathematical theory, and before painters mastered it. By looking directly at his audience, and by gesturing towards a book, St. Matthew directs the focus to two points. He's not contemplating the universe or the depths of his own being, like many Southeast Asian Buddha statues. He is also not serenely merged in a smooth flow of Thai forms. Instead, the focus is on a vigorous spirit that's more willing to confront an antagonist than most Thais traditionally have been. Ghiberti carved St. Matthew for the bankers' guild, and this view of a person involved in the world must have appealed to its members. They had made bookkeeping methods more accurate, and they were acutely aware of the prices of things—by gesturing towards something written in a book, St. Matthew was speaking their language.

This stress on massive bodies engaged in the world spread to painting in the 1420s, and an equally historic artistic revolution occurred. A young man named Masaccio painted scenes from the story of Adam and Eve and the life of St. Peter in the Brancacci Chapel of Santa Maria del Carmine, which stands just across the Arno River from Florence's main buildings. He used contrasts between light and shade to make bodies seem solid and muscular. This technique, called chiaroscuro, became basic in Western painting, and Masaccio used it to give Adam the tan and tone of an Italian charmer on the beach. It also makes bodies seem to project into three-dimensional space.

Masaccio also made the body express emotions. Adam and Eve have been expelled from Eden; Eve cries furiously enough to make viewers weep, and Adam covers his face in shame. But Adam's body is so engaging that it exalts the material world that they're condemned to roam.

Adam's arms are disproportionately short, almost like a lizard's, but Masaccio quickly learned the new perspective and used it to paint a more complex scene in the chapel. He depicted the New Testament story of St. Peter collecting tax money and giving it to the collector in the town of Capernaum by the Sea of Galilee. Jesus and his followers stand in a circle in the center, they have normal limbs, and he tells Peter how to get the money. On the left side, Peter kneels by the water and extracts a coin from a fish's mouth, and on the right, he hands it to the official. This balanced scene of many people is bordered by the sea on the left, and by a building with linearly arranged doors, windows, and awnings on the right. Behind everyone, mountains become hazier as their distance increases. The whole picture thus exists in a three-dimensional space that's so realistic that everyone seems to be on a stage. Ghiberti's St. Matthew implied three-dimensionality, but Masaccio created a whole three-dimensional scene with multiple people and a natural background that recedes into the distance. He pioneered a new way to see the world.

The floodgates quickly opened. The rest of the century was one of the most influential periods in Western art's history. Painters synthesized three-dimensional perspective, corporality, classically proportioned architecture, and scenes from Biblical narratives, and they created standards of realism that artists have followed ever since. Every great 15th century painter was unique. Each approached this mixture with his own background and added more ways to make it appear real. All painters together reinforced the focus on substantial bodies, linear relationships, and three-dimensional perspective—multiple views strengthened this way of viewing, as several types of experiences established Thai ways of perceiving and thinking:

- Fra Angelico was a Dominican monk who lived in the convent of San Marco, which is a few blocks from Florence's cathedral. He used the new perspective to show Jesus and a few saints facing each other across a small space as though they're conversing. Their bodies are covered with long gowns, but their faces are so soft and men's beards seem so real that I almost feel that I can touch them. Fra Angelico applied techniques for representing the world to spiritual realms, making them more tangible.
- Fra Filippo Lippi was a less obedient monk—he ran off with a nun and they had a son. But Filippo was a great painter whose worldly mindset made Biblical stories more realistic. He situated many of his scenes in rooms that look like homes of wealthy Florentines. His *Feast of Herod* contains the standard image of John the Baptist's decapitated head being brought to Herod, but in his version, tables covered with white cloths, bowls, cups, and knives surround the gross-out fare. Painted landscapes cover the walls behind the tables.

    Filippo became known for adding variety to his works so that scenes included much more than Masaccio's stately bodies and buildings. Filippo portrayed children and old people as well as adults in their prime. He also showed his subjects in a greater variety of poses and surrounded them with objects from daily life. Alberti had written about the importance of variety—a painter can make different types of figures complement each other so that the picture is more engaging and the space that its subjects occupy seems real.

Filippo's son, Filippino Lippi, also became a great painter. He added brilliant images of people to the Brancacci Chapel, including a self-portrait. Filippino looks directly at the viewer with confidence. The bastard son has secured his place in the world.

- Piero della Francesca portrayed the recovery of Jesus' cross in a church in the nearby town Arezzo. The static, balanced proportions of its scenes reflect Platonism's ideas that permanent ratios are divine. He was also a leading mathematician who wrote a treatise on solid geometry; his scenes neatly divide areas into different abstract shapes. People on each side symmetrically balance each other, and the colors of their clothing sharply contrast to emphasize the sacred geometry. Platonism became fashionable in 15th century Florence, and Francesca showed the divinely ordered forms in human settings.

- Andrea Mantegna portrayed people with ancient Roman monumentality. He lived in the northern town Mantua, which is near Milan. Mantegna admired statues that the ancients made and developed techniques for elevating people in his scenes above the eye's level so that the viewer looks up at them. Figures project ancient Rome's grandeur. Arrows pierce St. Sebastian's body, but the viewer admires a physique as muscled as a Greek god's. Sebastian stands against a classical column. This outer projection of strength reflects the steadfastness of this man, who survived the attack and remained an ardent Christian.

Mantegna also mastered foreshortening, which allows a painter to show a long object from one end so that it appears short. One of his most famous paintings is of the dead Christ, who is shown from the bottoms of his feet. Some viewers were uncomfortable with this much emphasis on Jesus' physicality.

Another early 15th century painter, Andrea del Castagno, portrayed the Trinity from a perspective that looks down on the head of the crucified Christ. Artists were becoming more adept at showing the body from all angles, and doing so in ways that elicited strong emotions in viewers.

- Paolo Uccello took so much pleasure in solving complex problems in three-dimensional perspectives that he stayed up all night in his study working on them. One night when his wife called him to come to bed he countered, "What a beautiful thing perspective is!" He especially enjoyed painting birds and animals and filled his house with pictures of them. Since *Uccello* means *bird*, even his name conveys one of his favorite subjects. This wealth of life forms allowed him to keep working on the fine points of perspective.

  He painted a stunning scene of the Great Flood in Florence's Dominican church, Sta. Maria Novella, which stands a few blocks from the cathedral and San Marco. He showed nature's raw power so brutally that he included a baby's corpse bloated with the water that he had swallowed. A crow pecks out another body's eyes. Around them, the wind furiously blows and a tree is ripped to pieces.

- Domenico Ghirlandiao painted faces so realistically that some make me feel like I'm looking at photographs from the late 15th century. His *Adoration of the Shepherds* in Florence's Sta. Trinita shows devoted visitors at Jesus' manger with greying hairs, facial stubble, and broad peasants' hands. I've wondered if he used real laborers as models.

- Antonio del Pollaiuolo took the nude male body into a new dimension by painting it in violent scenes. His Hercules's face grimaces in a wrestling match with a giant, and the muscles of warriors in battle ripple and contort. The body has jumped out from its statuesque origins and into the bustling world that Florentines breathed.

- Leonardo da Vinci then integrated three-dimensional perspectives and Pollaiuolo's interest in energy. For him, nature was in constant motion and he enjoyed showing all the ways in which people move. Each apostle in his *Last Supper* reacts in a different way to Jesus' statement that one of them will betray him.

Leonardo thus revealed people's mental states with their postures. He could depict the whole range of human movements and feelings and place them into any setting.

Leonardo also looked deeply into people's bodies and showed bones, muscles, and sinews beneath the skin. He also drew skeletons, nerves, veins, and anatomies of different features and organs. Leonardo also delighted in painting things in the natural surroundings, including plants, animals, rocks, and swirling waves in stormy oceans and rushing rivers. He also drew many machines which he had conceived of, including army tanks and contraptions to allow people to fly. Nothing in the world escaped his curious mind, sharp eye, and fertile imagination.

Many moderns have praised him as a proto-scientist, but Leonardo was even more than that. He perfected a technique called *sfumato*, which applies many different shades to edges of objects in order to blur them. This gives the backgrounds in the *Mona Lisa* and in Biblical scenes a mysterious and spiritual air. His brush could make anything in nature and the mind come to life.

Many approaches to three-dimensional perspective and the portrayal of physical bodies converged during this time. Thais didn't develop any of these varieties because they had their own perspectives and ways of representing the world which were so rich that they were fully absorbed in them.

Traditional Thai paintings lack a fixed perspective with the central vantage point which Alberti theorized. They also do not arrange everything on a precise grid—they don't regiment everyone's experience. The viewer can see a royal audience hall from the front and admire its elegant lines and shimmering golds, and then hover over its courtyard and watch a group of people waiting for the king.

Many fans of Thai painting have praised its appreciation of nature. Images of rivers and verdant hills with birds, monkeys, deer, and fruit trees sometimes surround scenes of palaces and temples. But these natural features and the people in the central stories are often out of scale with each other, and they're not spatially related by precise lines. There is no single perspective that's imposed from above. Instead, viewers can meander from one scene to another, and each person can look at whatever makes her happy at that moment.

Figure 16. Regality and informality in a Thai painting—people, buildings, and natural scenery blend without a unified perspective that pulls all into one system of lines. The viewer can meander instead of adhering to a standardized grid.

Images painted in viharas illustrate exemplary stories from the Buddha's past lives, but people can mosey between the episodes' lessons and enjoy the beauty of the scenery at their own paces. They receive instructions about virtues to uphold, but not in an intense or confrontational way. Instead, people can look at these images in the same way in which they amble around a wat or a neighborhood—they can slowly stroll and enjoy the flow of forms and colors.

The West's own rich idioms kept getting richer. Michelangelo was a younger man than Leonardo, and he considered him his arch rival and enemy. This was no surprise, since the former was hard to get along with. He once got into a fight with another apprentice, who punched him in the nose and broke it. That probably hurt Michelangelo even more internally because he felt that a beautiful body expresses divinity, but he now had a frontage that looked like a banana slug. But his pride and determination to forge his place in Florence's super-competitive artistic community spurred him to create works that honored the body.

People in Rome's Sistine Chapel who only look up at Michelangelo's ceiling miss the full impact of his genius. Twelve large frescos that line the side walls show how painting at the end of the 15th century had evolved. In 1481 Pope Sixtus IV wanted the best Tuscan artists to paint the chapel's walls. One side has six scenes from Jesus' life, and the other has six from Moses's. The painters (Perugino, Botticelli, Ghirlandiao, Signorelli, and Rosselli) synthesized the techniques that artists recently developed and crammed so many details into the frameworks that several frescos seem about to burst in all directions. Many combine multiple stories—Moses appears seven times in one painting.

After admiring them, I looked up and basked in God's power as He created Adam (I had to use binoculars because the ceiling is very high). Though Michelangelo's scene is only 20 to 30 years newer than the wall frescos, the sensibility has changed. The energy of the crowded pictures on the walls is concentrated in these two male figures facing each other.[4] Adam reaches out and almost touches God's hand while looking directly at Him, confident in his own identity as an embodied person.[5] Body, mind, and soul are in harmony in the most perfect human form. Instead of Thai views of creation as a flow of life forms, Michelangelo fashioned a muscled nude man in the form of his creator, who is also a well-muscled man. I find this one of the most powerful images in Western art. Laotian myths said that humanity sprang from a pumpkin that grew from a dead buffalo's nostril. This is a beautiful idea which sees people, animals, and plants within the same flow. But the Florentine artist concentrated the essence of creation into one object, which is proportioned, fleshed out, and serene—divine perfection.

Michelangelo had sculpted *David* a few years before as the strong individual about to vanquish the giant. His heroic spirit is as magnificent as his perfectly proportioned physique. There is no need for Angkor Wat's complexity because the athletic human body is noble enough. *David* would have been just as defiant before Suryavarman II's army, and he looks as though he'd still be standing after the fray.

Equally wondrous things were happening in Florentine architecture in the 1430s and 40s. Brunelleschi was designing the perfectly proportioned interior of the Church of Santo Spirito, which stands just across the river from the main part of town, near the Brancacci Chapel. Instead of using Gothic pointed arches and ornate sculptures, he resurrected Roman circular arches and flat coffered ceilings. All forms are clear, simple, and symmetrical. The floorplan's central square (between the two transcepts) is the building's basic unit, and dimensions of the nave, choir, chapels, and aisles are proportioned according to this square's sides.[6] Florence's new houses of God were now locating divinity where the community gathered as much as in the heavens, in contrast to Gothic cathedrals, whose stained glass windows soared above worshippers as a far more luminous world. Divinity now existed in simple squares, lines, and ratios which the human mind can fathom.

In 1436 Brunelleschi finished his most renowned masterpiece: the dome on Florence's cathedral. Its 140-foot diameter matched that of the largest existing dome, the ancient Roman Pantheon, but its base is higher than the Pantheon's apex, and its angle of ascent is much steeper than the ancient building's dome. Nothing like it had been built before. I found climbing the stairs to its top thrilling. I was high enough to believe that I was looking down on the ant-sized people from a modern skyscraper. I had to remind myself that I was in a building that's almost 600 years old. This use of abstract geometric forms to rise to the heavens must have reinforced the idea that these shapes are divine.

So in the early 15th century, three-dimensional perspective, classical architecture, corporality in painting and sculpture, and the Platonic veneration of permanent forms and ratios were converging. Many painters fleshed out this convergence in different ways, and together they made it seem like reality. The modern West's focus on three-dimensional perspective emerged from many idioms that reinforced each other.

This cultural landscape had yet more aspects, which were very human. In the 1390s Milan's large and aggressive inland empire became even more fearsome. The Visconti family ruled it as aristocratic dukes rather than republican citizens, and they had already established a new standard of ruthless ambition. The brothers Bernabo and Galeazzo were said to have designed a 40-day sequence of tortures for their prisoners. The wheel, the rack, flaying, eye-gouging, and the severing of limbs and parts of the face alternated with a day of rest to maximize victims' agony. Everyone knew not to pique the Visconti brothers.

Galeazzo's son, Gian Galeazzo, murdered his uncle Bernabo and seized power. He then expanded Milan southwards and onto Florentine soil. The duke and his vast army reached Florence's walls, but he suddenly contracted a fever and died in 1402. Though the outcome seemed miraculous to Florentines, the war had been traumatic and it highlighted the perils of an unrestrained autocracy.

Florence's chancellor from 1375 to 1406, Coluccio Salutati, spread the appreciation of ancient Roman literature that focused on civilized urban life, including Cicero's praise of republican freedom. Salutati gathered a circle of younger men around him who shared his passion for antiquity, and they contrasted Florence's values of liberty and good living with Milan's power mongering.

They spearheaded a major change in literary taste by preferring eloquence and style over metaphysics and logic chopping, which the university men in those Gothic cathedrals in the cold North admired. The Florentines' values were more urbane. They believed that a person should become a complete human being by being generally well-read, civic-minded, articulate, and well-acquainted with other worldly people. Salutati brought ancient writings about cultivated secular life into polite circles in the decades before the sculpture on Orsanmichele took form.

Cicero paid dearly for insulting Marc Anthony's alcoholic and sexual license. The latter's henchmen killed him, cut of his head and hands, and fastened them on a public platform in the Roman forum for his inflammatory writings. But Salutati and his friends admired Cicero for defending civic freedom. He used Cicero's literary style for political correspondence. According to an often-told story, even Gian Galeazzo Visconti said that one letter from Salutati was as powerful as 1,000 lances on the battlefield.

Salutati's eloquence came from an already ancient tradition. Ancient Roman literature was fundamental in European schools throughout the Middle Ages. Generations of students learned Latin by studying grammars with passages from some of Rome's most famous writers, including Horace, Livy, Ovid, and Cicero. Roman law became more widely studied in the 11th century as Europe's towns grew again, and this made people more aware of ancient Rome's political history. Cambodia and Thailand lacked a homegrown ancient literary tradition that detailed a rich secular life, but people in Italy became increasingly aware of the West's as their cities grew, and they proudly used Rome's heritage for their own standards of thinking and writing.

Florentines became acutely conscious of a difference between classical and Gothic architecture. The monuments from ancient Rome's past, which included proportioned colonnades, victory arches, friezes of historical events, and open spaces which encouraged worldly discourse, became models of well-being. Leading Florentines began a craze for collecting antiquities and sent men to comb the ruins of Rome for sculptures to bring back to their gardens. Brunelleschi went there to measure and sketch its remains before he designed Florence's cathedral's dome.

This humanist movement received a bonanza from the beleaguered Byzantine Empire. The Ottoman Turks had already reduced it to a small area around its capital, Constantinople, which they would take in 1453. Exiles reached Florence with their books and they began to teach Greek. One of the most famous professors, Manuel Chrysoloras, mentored several Florentine students who later became teachers. They became the first generation of classical Greek scholars in Western Europe since antiquity.

The teaching methods Chrysoloras used reinforced Salutati's. He stressed the all-around education (*enkyklios paideia*) that many ancient Greeks did by mixing a broad academic curriculum with sports, music, and moral training. Both believed that becoming a complete person enables one to be a good civic leader.

Two powerful images were thus emerging just before Brunelleschi and Alberti articulated three-dimensional perspective, and they helped ingrain it into ways people perceived the world and thought:

- The open civic plaza lined with proportioned classical architecture became a model of well-being.
- The community of free people interacting with each other within this space became a model of liberty. They dealt with each other directly rather than under Gothic arches or within a palace. Each was his own node, and they were all related to each other like points linked by straight lines. Gothic cathedrals also emphasize lines, but they lead to the altar, and up to the heavens. Florentines opened linear relationships into the lateral dimension so that interactions between people in the world are as important in the order of things.

However, Mary McCarthy saw darkness in the abstract lines that Florentines focused on and described it in *The Stones of Florence*. She thought violence made people long for an ordered world of static lines and shapes as an escape from their blood-splattered streets. She said that family feuds were endemic to the city and that lineages often aligned behind polarized political parties.

One of the main fracases had roots in that old conflict between the pope and the most honored ruler in Germany. The 11th-century tussle between Pope Gregory VII and King Henry IV hardly ended when the German waited in the snow for forgiveness. Not content with enlarging Speyer's cathedral, he spearheaded an invasion of Italy in which his troops reached Rome and pillaged it. Henry V invaded Rome in the 1110s to enforce his own ability to choose German bishops, and he imprisoned the pope. Many German emperors considered Italy to be their inheritance from Charlemagne's early ninth century empire.

Some Italians supported the pope against the barbarian king who claimed sovereignty over their land, and they were called Guelphs. Others found the pope meddlesome and supported the northern emperor as the liberator from his restrictions, and they were known as Guibellines. The dividing line between both became especially firm and ferocious in Florence. Families sided with and against each other along it even when they weren't disagreeing over that specific political issue. It structured many quarrels so that people were forced to decide which side of the line they stood on. McCarthy said that Florence's murderous conflicts were shaped into this either/or choice. Each party had its own ways of cutting fruit, choosing drinking goblets, speaking, and walking, and infringements often provoked heated arguments. Many experiences thus highlighted this thick division between people, which often turned violent at the drop of a glove.

Florentine men often married late in order to save money for a nest egg, so it was common for husbands to be ten to fifteen years older than their wives. Richard C. Trexler, in *Public Life in Renaissance Florence,* wrote that the average age of males who married in 1427–8 was thirty-four. Many fathers thus died before their sons grew up. Florence's streets teemed with adolescents and young men ready to punch and stab as soon as they were annoyed because they lacked a mature male role model to restrain them.

McCarthy thought that the black lines that demarcate the baptistery's handsome rectangles and semicircles represented ways in which Florentines habitually saw issues. Instead of the Thai flows that harmonize many perspectives, people thought in terms of sharp political differences and often drew blood over them. McCarthy felt that Brunelleschi's perfectly balanced architecture reconciled the oppositions and put them in a peaceful equilibrium. Patricia Lee Rubin, in *Images and Identity in Fifteenth-Century Florence,* wrote that Florentines associated order with status, political grouping, cosmic hierarchy, and the painter's craft, and that they saw chaos, disintegration, and the horrors of Dante's hell as opposites of order. The simple, cultured shapes on the baptistery must have appealed in many ways to citizens.

People built soaring stone tower-houses before a 13th century law limited their height to a little less than 100 feet. Some were higher than 200 feet—the family with the tallest home could drop boulders and burning pitch on rivals. Streets and piazzas often erupted into brawls and knife fights. The ordered public spaces that Brunelleschi created sharply contrasted with the mayhem that they were supposed to replace.

Life in the ordered spaces was sometimes terrifying too. Lorenzo de' Medici established himself as Florence's political leader in the late 15th century, but the Pazzi family resented his prestige. They hired assassins to attack him and his brother Giuliano while they were worshipping under Brunelleschi's dome. The killers chose the most sacred moment in the Mass (the raising of the host) as the signal to draw their daggers and plunge them into the two men. They killed Giuliano, but Lorenzo escaped into the sacristy with a minor injury. The Medicis' supporters rounded up scores of suspects and hung many of them. They first cut off some men's noses and ears. Da Vinci sketched a man who had been hanged. His detached view of the limp body and vacant eyes suggests that he was used to seeing such horrors.

I enjoy comparing McCarthy's and Kenneth Clark's ideas of what inspired Florentine art. The latter, a stately old Englishman from Oxford and a career museum curator, ogled over the generation of great men who brought classical literature to the city. Clark thought it was heroic to slice through the puffed up metaphysical ideas from the Middle Ages and see the essential forms of things.

McCarthy had a knack for portraying maladaptive personalities and dysfunctional families, and she seems to have enjoyed deflating male egos. She saw the violent conflicts between men as some of Florence's biggest artistic inspirations.

I think each saw a different part of the picture, which had many facets. The enjoyment of simple proportioned forms and the fear of violent death were two common experiences in Florence. Both converged to make three-dimensional perspectives seem real and compelling. They dominated Florentine life in different times. The historian Gene A. Brucker said that the tower-houses and brawls characterized life during Dante's time (the late 13th and early 14th century) and that streets became tamer in the early 15th century, when classical sculpture, painting, architecture, and literature were spreading.[7] If Brucker was right, the deadly conflicts that were structured around either/or choices probably helped shape Florentine thought in the earlier period. Then the men that Clark praised refined the forms in many media, and this encouraged more civilized living. Instead of tower-houses, the wealthy were now building palaces with classical forms, and many still project their ordered facades over the streets.

Michelangelo's *David* came to life for me when I returned to Florence in 2013. I was walking from Dante's reconstructed house to the main piazza and heard horns blowing. When I reached the piazza, I joined the crowd that had gathered there, and groups of uniformed men were jogging into the square and stopping in front of the governors' palace. Some wore black, others were in green and khaki camouflage, and all sported hats with black and green tail feathers from pheasants. Some carried red banners and others ported Italian flags. Several men in dark grey and blue suits then formed a line on a platform in front of the palace, next to Michelangelo's *David*. Policemen in black uniforms and horn blowers in long white gowns and red caps joined them. Red flags raised on staffs between the men added even more flash. One of them, a man with a full head of grey hair, in a dark blue suit, spoke about an alliance between Florence and Turin, declaring that it would benefit all of Italy. But I found the crowd more interesting than the political rhetoric.

Nobody seemed to be as interested in listening to the speaker as they were in being with each other. A portly old man and woman next to me each held a toddler. A bald fifty-something man in front of us turned around and caressed one of the kid's cheeks. Several uniformed people started to assemble for group photos. Most were elderly men, but one was a roughly twenty-year-old woman who was about five-foot-ten, with long wavy brown hair, large sparkling eyes, and an ebullient smile. The older men took her picture, and two were poking a young man and smiling, encouraging him to flirt with her. Thin, plain-looking, and pallid, he didn't follow their advice, and I wondered if he felt that she was out of his league. A Chinese couple came over and snapped a picture of the group, and one of the seniors said, "Xie Xie!" His thick jaw, broad hands, and cheerful eyes made him look like one of Ghirlandaio's shepherds. A middle-aged woman carried a grey and white striped tabby cat that looked apprehensive in the midst of the noisy crowd. Someone then fired a gun into the air when the speech ended.

Public gatherings like this in piazzas were regular events in Florence and other Italian towns during the Renaissance. Some were violent—people fought, and militias from all neighborhoods gathered before marching to the battlefield. But many, like the one I enjoyed, mixed politics, fun, and family. Religious processions were also regular in the piazzas, and wardrobes of priests and costumes of people dramatizing Biblical stories and saints' lives were even more colorful than the garb I saw. Piazzas housed all these events and framed them with colonnades, linear rows of windows, and statues that glorified the body. These spaces weren't just abstract; they were full of life which included the violence that McCarthy emphasized, the stately men that Clark admired, and many vivacious festivals. All these experiences together confirmed the Euclidean lines and planes and the realistic statues that surrounded them as the world's main ordering principles by reinforcing them every day.

Figure 17. The perfect body of Michelangelo's David standing over the crowd, projecting idealized order.

Though these classical forms were ideals, political geography was often different from them. Brucker wrote that each of several of the most prominent families clustered its homes in one district—along one street or around one square. The Medici palace was at the corner of two major thoroughfares, near the cathedral, and the residences of other rich bankers and merchants stood in their own areas. Florentines regularly saw contrasts between civic order and familial rivalries. This probably made them continue to look to the ordered forms in piazzas as ideals of well-being.

The West's emerging perspective already had deep roots—it didn't suddenly emerge in the 15th century. Dante vividly described his characters when he wrote his *Divine Comedy* in the early 14th century, and he said that his contemporary Giotto was the world's greatest painter because he portrayed people with more realism than any predecessor had. In a scene that Giotto painted in the Scrovegni Chapel in Padua, an aged Anne and Joachim (the Virgin Mary's parents) kiss and she caresses his bushy grey beard. He was a master of dramatizing Biblical stories with people that were lifelike and monumental. Why was Florence already so advanced in realism?

Florence developed its republican government in the 13th century. Members of the city's guilds were elected and chosen by lot into office, but they held their posts for a very short time to avoid corruption some were in office for only two months. Electoral processes were often complex, and this encouraged people to look beneath impressive facades that candidates and their familial networks projected and analyze the hard facts.

Florence also began to develop its legendary wool industry in the 13th century by importing the raw material from England, washing it in the Arno River, weaving it, and dying it in brilliant vermillion and yellow hues so that it became the most widely desired fabric in Europe. This industry was large, employing 30,000 workers in and around Florence at peak times, and its production process was complex. Wool making had roughly 30 stages, and specialized laborers worked in each one. Sorting the different grades, beating, dying, combing, spinning, and weaving were some of the steps in the making of fine cloth. Many were carried out in large workshops, while spinning was often done by peasant women in their homes in the country. Managing this industry which the city's livelihood depended on required attentiveness to many details.

To manage the wool trade, people entered more business partnerships and set up complicated systems for transportation. People's wills kept pace with their increasingly complex commercial relationships because their assets were distributed in more places. Now that they could sue each other for more reasons, the legal profession grew. Legal conflicts show up so often in public records that litigation seems to have been a favorite pastime.

Florence thus developed into a city of many groups which constantly collaborated or competed with each other. People had to keep track of the doings of their fellow citizens as they did business with them. They also had to manage complex logistics, and at the same time, keep an eye on their competitors. Florence's citizens became increasingly used to watching things in several places.

Florentines became increasingly mathematically literate at the same time. They were interested in import and export statistics, populations, prices, and volumes of containers that held goods. The city started to issue the gold florin in the 13th century, which became Europe's most trusted currency. Money, numbers, and commerce grew more prominent in people's thinking, and there was no king to assert his glory over everyone's affairs.

A building boom ensued as commerce increased. A massive ring of walls was erected around the city, and people began its cathedral in 1296. They also built the governors' palace and started to construct Santa Maria Novella and Santa Croce. Paintings from the early 14th century show that buildings already cluttered the entire area within the walls.

Tragically, this crowded city by a river became an ideal breeding ground for contagious diseases, and the bubonic plague carried off as many as half of its inhabitants in the mid 14th century. Florence was spooky after the epidemic subsided. Towering stone houses that were once full of children playing and adults proudly displaying their furniture, paintings, and tapestries were now silent with the sick and mourning. The poet Boccaccio wrote that locals were so used to seeing corpses

that they paid no more attention to a dead person than to a goat's car-
cass. But people remembered the illustrious past and built on it when the
artistic miracles emerged in the early 15th century. They were already
accustomed to managing complex spatial and temporal relationships
and quantifying things, and they were eager to get back to business as
the town grew again.

Florentines thought mathematically as they rebuilt their city. Michael
Baxandall, in *Painting and Experience in Fifteenth-Century Italy*, wrote that
their educations emphasized the mathematics that merchants used.
One of the most commonly studied techniques was gauging (calculating
the volumes of three-dimensional shapes, including barrels and ships'
hulls). This was important to know because containers' sizes weren't
standardized. People needed to calculate the amount of oil or wool that
a barrel could hold when they could only measure its height and its circumference at the middle and ends. Citizens were thereby trained from
childhood to see objects as static, measurable geometric shapes.

Children also learned what was called "the rule of three." Today's
high school students preparing for their SATs know this as the problem:
A is to B as C is to D. People in Florence reduced many things to this
comparison of two entities in terms of geometric proportion, including
the sizes of containers and buildings, the areas of parcels of land, price
discounts, and currency exchanges. The proportioned scenes in paintings were probably influenced by ways in which people were trained to
visualize and think about objects.

People recorded their commercial transactions with equal precision.
Bankers increasingly used double-entry bookkeeping, and merchants
made sure that they kept accurate account books. The ways in which
Florentines represented objects in their art reflected their ways of keeping financial records—both emphasized proportioned relationships.

Florentine society was more than McCarthy's high-strung, quick-
tempered men and Clark's heroic classicists. Industrious merchants
doing their daily business also helped develop three-dimensional perspective. All three mindsets converged and reinforced it.

A fourth group of people, who have often been overlooked, also
influenced the development of Renaissance art and three-dimensional

perspective. St. Francis of Assisi's father, Pietro di Bernardone, was a solid member of the class of proud merchants. He traded silk in the town of Assisi, which still crowns a hill overlooking a verdant Umbrian plain half way between Florence and Rome. He had made trips to France to build his business and hoped that his son would someday take over his legacy and expand it.

At first Francis did what lots of wealthy kids around the end of the 12th century did: he dreamed of being a knight and hung out with fun-loving, party-going youths. But with more inner depth than his pleasure-loving companions and his worldly father had, he became highly conscious of God and Christ. One day while praying in an ancient church, he experienced a vision of Jesus, who told him to repair His house, which had fallen into ruins. Young Francis took that literally and thought Jesus wanted him to repair the old building rather than the entirety of Christendom, which had become worldly and corrupt. His father became infuriated when he learned that Francis had sold some of his goods to pay for the construction, and he publically demanded that he return the money to him.

Francis was sensitive to the world too, but not in his father's way. Instead, he noticed that not everybody was prospering and that many were miserably poor. A large percentage of people in towns had come from the countryside, desperate for food and shelter. Many were exploited as itinerate laborers while others remained unemployed and had to resort to begging. The handicapped, the deformed, and lepers joined them in the town streets, often crowding around churches, hoping for handouts. Francis, preaching in a down-to-earth style, said that God loves everybody and that Christ became human by being born as a naked infant. He quickly attracted a large group of followers, who needed the warmth that they didn't find in their hierarchical society which often showed them more scorn than pity.

His followers grew into one of the 13th century's most influential cultural movements, the Franciscan Order. Its members quickly built churches all over northern Italy, but they were different from Gothic cathedrals. Instead of displaying stained glass and flowery sculptures, they were often large halls that were unembellished. Detractors called them preaching barns. But these open spaces welcomed everybody, making all feel that they were brothers and sisters in Christ. Instead of emphasizing the lines of pillars leading towards the altar, the buildings' interiors were open so that the preacher could view the whole congregation and everyone could see him. Another type of urban space opened up besides the piazzas which also highlighted people's equality.

Florence's Franciscan church, Santa Croce, is about half a mile from the cathedral, in a part of town that was known as a working-class neighborhood (its ornate façade wasn't added until the 19th century). Sitting in the piazza in front of the church gave me a taste of what the area must have been like when the building was new. There were now stone benches that were wide enough for people to sit on both sides, back to back. As I rested on one, a Southeast Asian woman with a large wad of silk scarves wrapped around her forearm walked around the bench, trying to sell them to all of us (I didn't ask where she was from because she seemed too busy to stop and chat, but I thought that she might have come from the Philippines). With all that stuff around her arm, her palm was completely covered with sweat, but she continuously smiled in the hot afternoon sun. Crowds like this were common in front of Franciscan churches during the Middle Ages and the Renaissance. Some folks tried to make a little money, others rested, and more hung around for amusement. Public jousts were regularly held in Santa Croce's piazza. Though St. Francis intensely focused on Christ (he is the first person who is said to have received the stigmata), his churches became places where people could immerse themselves in the secular world as much as the spiritual realm.

Art that the Franciscan Order sponsored also encouraged this worldly focus. People built a two-level basilica in Assisi to honor St. Francis shortly after he died, and many of the 13th and 14th century frescoes on its walls vividly anticipated painting in the Florentine Renaissance. The upper church's nave is lined with scenes from the saint's life, and they were either painted by Giotto or some of his imitators (the identity of the painters has been hotly debated). The image of St. Francis and his father confronting each other is one of the most dramatic urban scenes ever created. The elder man had demanded that Francis return the money after selling his goods or renounce his inheritance. In the painting the young man dramatically renounces all his possessions by taking off his clothes in the middle of town. His naked body is pale and its ribs stick out as much as the muscles. Francis raises his arms and looks up to God's hand, which looms high above, while the bishop drapes a blue robe over his lower body. His father faces him with an enraged expression, and another man grasps his arm before he can punch Francis's pious face with his granite fist. Other people crowd around both father and son so that the space between both geometrically divides the painting as effectively as Piero della Francesca partitioned his works.

Though the father looks brutish, I still feel a bit sorry for him. He toiled for many years, traveling and developing an extensive network of business relationships, hoping that his son would continue his legacy. He must have felt terribly hurt. The painter has sympathized with both men so that the viewer is pulled into the scene. Such an intense public confrontation between father and son is a far cry from Thai culture, but the worldly elder and the idealistic youth expressing irreconcilable differences have comprised gut-wrenching scenes in many Western literary works, movies, TV shows, and popular songs. Nobody ever contrasted both figures better than the painter in this basilica, and the restive crowd of men and two nervous-looking boys add to the drama so that it's as engaging as any scene in today's Times Square.

Another painting glorifies the natural world so well that I find it equally captivating. St. Francis felt that all creatures are brothers and sisters in Christ, and he is still honored as the patron saint of animals. In this scene he preaches to birds. Gracefully shaped doves flock in front of him as readily as his human followers did. A tree with thick, bushy foliage bends towards the holy man as he leans towards the birds. Both figures almost join to provide a protective circle around the doves.

Examining all the images in the basilica gave me one of the most memorable immersions in medieval life I've ever had because the people are realistically portrayed in a variety of scenes that seem to depict the full tapestry of human life as medieval Christians saw it. When I exited the building, a crowd of locals and tourists had gathered in front to enjoy the afternoon sun and each other's company. Many were walking their dogs and a Boxer looked up at me as though he wanted to be petted. I complied and smiled to his owner, who didn't notice me because he was busy eying the women. An elderly man slipped and fell so that his head smacked the ground. He was stunned for a few seconds, but then began to cry like a child. His two middle-aged female companions picked him back up and comforted him. Every large Franciscan church provided a setting for urban scenes that were as lively as the basilica's paintings.

Franciscan piety and art made many of the West's idioms more vivid, including the appreciation of Jesus as a human being, sympathy for the downtrodden, lively urban scenes, and the enjoyment of nature. All these became part of Florence's daily life while its merchants counted and measured, its hot-tempered young men punched and kicked, and its more literate statesmen began to discover cultivated secular living through ancient writings. All together formed a lively, multi-textured urban landscape before the early 15th century artists formalized three-dimensional perspective.

Florence's artistic marvels were also inspired by other cities. The sculptor Nicola Pisano influenced Florentine artists by carving Christ's Passion on the pulpit of Pisa's baptistery around 1260. His figures are massive and stocky rather than enshrouded in long Gothic robes, and they take up most of the framework. Their stateliness makes them resemble images of ancient Roman senators.

Nicola's classicism didn't surprise anyone because he was surrounded by ancient Roman sculpture. Ancient sarcophagi with classical friezes were heaped around the cathedral, which stood in front of the baptistery. Architects had used ancient Roman arches and columns on both buildings. So Nicola was immersed in these images and forms from antiquity when he created works that glorified his city.

Ancient Greco-Roman culture was already in the air when Italian towns grew in the 11th and 12th centuries. Pisa began its cathedral in 1063 and then enlarged it in the 12th century. An inscription from the building says that Pisans had won four naval battles with the Islamic Saracens in Sicily and Sardinia between 1005 and 1034. Another passage states that Pisa took booty after another victory over them in 1064. The city emerged as a commercial empire that would rival Florence and Genoa until the beginning of the 15th century. Thankful for their new wealth and prestige, its people spared no expense to glorify Jesus and the Virgin. They beautified the Holy Family's house, the cathedral, with handsome Romanesque columns and arches. The emerging maritime power thus looked to ancient Rome for fundamental forms to identify itself with and adopted abstract lines and arches as symbols of earthly dominion and divine order.

Figure 18. Pisa's cathedral

As Figure 18 shows, Pisans made these stately forms thinner towards the top, as though the stones rise to dissolve into the heavens. The apex of the roof is crowned with a statue of the Virgin holding the Child—static geometric forms lead to the two great souls who set Pisa on her road to success.

Both Suryavarmans expanded the Khmer Empire when Pisa grew, and they used Indian ideas and images of abundance (Hindu gods, dense vegetal motifs, and complex architectural designs loaded with cosmic symbolism) and shaped them into symmetrical temples to provide overarching models of order. As Italy urbanized again, she harked back to antiquity's simple static forms (the colonnade and the arch), as northern Europe did when Romanesque style spread, and she also rediscovered realistically sculpted bodies of Greek gods and heroes which emphasized mass. The muscles on Michelangelo's *David* grew from many ancient art forms.

In the early 15th century, Italy's geography was likened to a fish's skeleton. The mountains that run north and south comprise its spine, and the ridges that adjoin them and proceed to the coasts are the ribs. The land is thereby sharply divided into small valleys where people in ancient times settled and formed communities. Italy is surrounded by the sea on three sides. As in Greece, the environment is composed of distinct regions separated by clear boundaries. Sea and land, fertile valleys and rocky uplands—domains are clearly distinguished and they are proportionate with each other so that these features have seemed like nature's fundamental order. Ancient Greece and Renaissance Italy usually preferred limits, distinctions, and clear definitions, and they often reduced art and ideas to their most essential forms. The idea that Platonic forms and ratios are divine was a refined expression of those preferences, which had deep roots in geography.

Florence nestles by one of the fish's ribs. Even before ancient Romans colonized the area, tribes decided to leave their more protected hilltops and settle by the Arno River, perhaps to trade. Rome took it over in the first century BCE and built a rectangular military fort which the town expanded from in the Middle Ages. The early Christian buildings that survive also project nature's most essential forms. The first two levels of the baptistery were built in the late 11th and early 12th century, and the abstract rectangles and semicircles separated by black lines that cover its outer walls attest that the focus on static geometric forms long preceded the 15th century. Another one of Florence's most prominent churches since the 11th century, San Miniato al Monte, also has these sharply delineated shapes on its front. Since it overlooks the town from a hillside across the Arno, everyone could gaze towards it as another example of divine order.

So the cultural environment in which three-dimensional perspective emerged was shaped by traditions from antiquity and the Middle Ages, and also by the natural surroundings. The 15th century artists who articulated this dimension had very fertile ground to build on, as the Khmers and Thais did when they formulated their ways of seeing the world.

But what about the cold North? Though northern Europe lacked the Mediterranean's clear sunbathed coasts, it had its own cultures and natural features which converged in ways that helped make three-dimensional perspective pan-European.

Figure 19. San Miniato al Monte, Florence.

When Italian artists were perfecting linear relationships, northern painters advanced realism in their own ways. In the 1430s Jan van Eyck worked in another wealthy city of freedom-loving merchants, Bruges, which is in modern Belgium (Bruges, Ghent, and Ypres became wealthy from the cloth trade around 1100). He began to paint people's features so that warts and wrinkles got as much attention as angelic Italian faces and sun-kissed beefcakes.[8]

His *Adoration of the Lamb* in the Cathedral of St. Bavo in Ghent is a panoramic medieval view of the world with a northern flair. Processions of Old Testament patriarchs and prophets, New Testament figures, popes, bishops, deacons, and virgin martyrs arrive at an altar that's surrounded by angels. A lamb symbolizing Christ stands on it, bleeding into a shiny chalice. Rolling verdant hills and cities with elaborate Gothic towers surround all the people. Van Eyck put everything but an elephant stable into view to stress the theme's universal importance. But to make this all-encompassing landscape real, he showed hundreds of plants and flowers in precise detail. Van Eyck set the standard for northern realism, and many other great Flemish painters quickly followed him, including Petrus Christus, Rogier van der Weyden, Hugo van der Goes, and Dieric Bouts. These northern lights later inspired Rubens and the 17th century Dutch masters.

However, Michelangelo didn't always approve of their work. He said that their paintings only deceive the eye. Instead of portraying higher ideals, like *David's* integration of a noble spirit and a perfect body, they show things in their everyday mundaneness. I've found some of the young women that they painted rather disturbing. Their pretty long blond hair looks like spun gold, but their faces are so pallid and thin that they look sickly or malnourished. They probably did look that way at times because famines and plagues recurred, and medical care was often more harmful than helpful. Why did these painters develop this unsparing realism?

The land around Bruges isn't as picturesque as Italy. It spreads by the sea, around a river that the Rhine flows into. It's flat and often overcast and chilly. People struggled to squeeze livings from its sandy soils, and neighboring countries were often rude. The French ruled the area in the 13th century, and the Spanish took it over in the 16th century. Both taxed its hardworking people and sacked their towns when they rebelled. Why pick on this frugal land?

It was a trading hub between the Rhine, the North Sea, and Paris, and merchants there built international networks. Other states tried to use it as a cash cow, and this encouraged its people to look at the world with a cynical eye.

Nobody had a tougher eye than Reynard the Fox. Flemish people savored stories about his exploits, which were penned by an early 13th century poet named Willem. Historians don't agree about who he was, but his readers enjoyed the fox's quick wit. Reynard lived in a world of bullies. The bears and wolves around him were stronger, but he was cleverer. The king had told Tybert the Cat to bring him to his court because he had stolen many chickens. When he reached Reynard's gate, the fox greeted him, "Good friend! We will go tomorrow. Come and stay with me tonight."

What would they have for dinner? Tybert said, "I'd sure like a nice fat mouse."

"Good cousin! You're in luck! A priest lives near here and his barn is full of mice. I've heard him complain that so many dart around that they'll soon drive him from his house."

Reynard had stolen a rooster from the priest, and he knew that his son had set a trap for him. He led unsuspecting Tybert into it. The priest heard it snap shut, thought it had nabbed the pesky thief, and joyfully bolted out of his cot naked (many people in the medieval West slept in the nude).

He beat the cat with his distaff so savagely that Tybert had to attack him. He bared his teeth and claws, leaped upwards, and ripped off his penis. His horrified wife shrieked that she'd rather lose a whole year's offerings for her soul than her nightly pleasure. Nothing was too sacred for Flemish irreverence towards authority.

Some Italians who visited Flanders in the 16th century wrote that its people lacked style. They worked and drank so hard that their lives alternated between stony sobriety and blind drunkenness. When I explored medieval towns in Belgium in 2010, grey clouds usually covered the sky. Since I always wanted to be sober in order to explore as much as possible, I looked into every one of the many chocolate shops in sight and always carried several pieces with me. I craved something to make me feel warm in the gloomy climate.

But Italian artists learned much from Flemish painters in the 15th century. Oil-based painting was first mastered there and then taken to Italy because it allowed artists to give details sheen to make them stand out. The harsher colors of northern painting (cold blues and reds) were also brought south, and they added drama to many Italian works. Piero della Francesca used them to sharply contrast tones in order to emphasize divine ratios. Italian artists also learned northern techniques for making people's portraits more realistic.

Pan-European trade, Christian traditions, and the ancient Greco-Roman heritage gave both regions many shared meanings, and their ways of looking at the world fused in spite of the cultural gaps. The great Nuremberg painter, Albrecht Durer, spent two years in Venice, and he wrote that Italy had many of the world's most pleasant people, and some of its worst scoundrels. The plain-spoken German wasn't completely at home in a culture that sometimes stressed style over truth. But he brought techniques from its masters north and used them to give medieval visions he had grown up with a scientific realism. Snarling demons look as though they might lunge from the page. The classical heritage from Italy, no-nonsense northern realism, and medieval Christian traditions blended through countless interactions, and three-dimensional perspectives became richer and more widespread.

Italy boasted yet more wonders, and no place has been more wondrous than Venice. Its unique environment (a network of small islands off the coast) makes the linear arrangements of arches on the upper class homes that line its canals seem lilting.

Figure 20. Lines at play, a common Venetian scene.

Ripples in the water, elegant gondolas, slender docking posts, and reflections of light soften the lines. Clouds and fogs rolling in from the sea transform the views quickly. Perspectives often become whimsical in Venice.

These plays of light influenced some of Europe's greatest paintings, and they were different from what Florentines created. Venice's artists often treated color as the most basic element. Florentine painters usually began a picture by drawing and measuring outlines, but Venetians often started with colors. Florentine painting was more inspired by sculpture and abstract geometry. Venetians were trained from birth to appreciate hues and not hold them second to static shapes and proportions.

According to Kenneth Clark, Titian (1488–1576) was one of the three greatest painters of one of the hardest things to paint well, human skin. Rubens and Renoir were the other two, but since Titian lived first, he was the pioneer. He advanced Western artists' ability to realistically portray people and depicted them so well that he sometimes exposed aspects of their personalities that they probably didn't want to be aware of.

One of his subjects was twelve-year-old Ranuccio Farnese. He belonged to an eminent family, which sired a pope (Paul III). Ranuccio became a cardinal when he grew up, largely because of his family's connections. Titian painted him in an expensive crimson doublet, perhaps alluding to his family's ambitions (cardinals wore red), but the boy looks uncomfortable playing dress-up. He glances to the side with a somber expression as though he'd rather be running through an orchard, chasing rabbits with a slingshot.

One of Titian's closest friends was a satirical writer named Pietro Aretino. He was born in Arezzo, where Francesco had painted the scenes of the recovery of the cross in geometrically ordered colors, but Aretino was as far from those frescos' Platonism as a person could be. He left for Rome but his sexually graphic wit angered so many leaders in its high-strung papal politics that he left town, wandered around northern Italy, and ultimately settled in Venice. The pleasure lover found his home.

Aretino was a connoisseur in everything, and he savored love affairs, art, food, and wine. He and Titian became the center of a group of bon vivants who gathered to enjoy and discuss all of life's delights. Venice was a perfect city for pioneering explicit worldliness. Titian painted his companion several times and did him justice. In the most famous portrait, a sparkling crimson robe drapes around a mountain of flesh that had imbibed more calories than Milan's army. A long and bushy beard with glinting grey hairs tumbles to the chest. The large eyes over the hair twinkle, making it clear that he's eager for more wine and flesh. Titian obviously felt affection for him, and he used color to show a man as grounded in the world as Michelangelo's *David* is.[9]

Traditional Thai paintings don't reveal the multi-textured skin tones in Titian's scenes or the sinews of Michelangelo's subjects. They weren't made to make viewers feel that there's a massive body in front of them. Instead, they encourage the eye to mosey in an even flow. Silpa Bhirasri, in *An Appreciation of Sukhothai Art*, wrote that much of the beauty in Thai paintings is in the expressiveness of their lines.

The outlines of human figures often curve in elegant patterns. The eye can glide over them, and it can meander through scenes at a relaxed pace which doesn't stop for long periods to analyze the details of any single object. As in ambles through markets and neighborhoods, viewers can enjoy the multitude of forms and hues without feeling confronted by any single figure.

Venice felt like a different world from the rest of Italy as soon as I arrived at its Santa Lucia train station from Milan in 2008. The aroma of the salty air and the calls of seagulls seemed more ethereal than the solid earth I had become accustomed to in Rome, Florence, the Viscontis' stomping ground, and many smaller towns. I spent the next two weeks exploring almost all of the city's islands, museums, and churches, and I thought I had seen just about everything there until I returned in 2013.

My 2008 trip was in June, and Venice was baking in a heat wave. But the sky clouded up on the third day of my return visit and the city transformed. The church domes and steeples which formerly basked in the golden sunshine were now grey, and they barely stood out from the light grey overcast. The canals, boats, and building fronts were all darker too, and all were enshrouded in mists—the formerly clear outlines had dissolved into an atmosphere of intrigue.

The tide peaked on the next day so that the water was lapping over the pavement. Much of St. Mark's Square was underwater and people had to wear tall plastic boots to wade through it. The boundaries between land and sea had been breached and everything was at the mercy of nature's power.

Figure 21. Outlines in traditional Thai painting are typically elegant.

In the late afternoon the tide receded and the sky cleared halfway. The areas where the sun poked through were luminous pinkish oranges, and they hovered over the churches' domes. The tallest domes seemed close enough to tickle them. The city's charm isn't just in its varied buildings and waterways, but also in the ways the weather makes the views and moods quickly change.

Venice's canals, shifting colors, and playful forms can evoke Thai art, but the city is still Western in culture. The ancient Greco-Roman and Gothic heritages (the city is full of fine Gothic churches and homes), Christian theology, exchanges of artists with Florence and Rome, and the prominence of merchants and money converged to make Venetians see the world in Western terms. Like Florence, she established a currency that became one of Europe's most widely used, the ducat. Physical bodies are still elemental in most Venetian art, but much of it is sprightlier than other cities' paintings. Its engaging colors added liveliness to the West's artistic heritage and thus made its products seem even more real.

While Venetians enjoyed their sensual surroundings, Rome thundered. Pope Julius II had always looked like a man of authority. While young, his large shaved head climaxed his level-gazing eyes and prominent chin. While aging, his long white beard projected the look of a prophet. After his election in 1503, he resolved to give Rome a makeover that would restore its ancient magnificence.

Julius was the pope who called Michelangelo to paint the Sistine Chapel ceiling. These two colossal egos—one over the spirit and one over the artistic world—labored to give Rome monuments that would surpass anything that the ancients had made. They often tangled. The artist preferred to sculpt but had to work on the ceiling for four years, and he wrote about paint dripping into his face and beard. The pope once whacked him with his distaff when he became impatient with the slow progress.

The pope's mind was on bigger projects than the chapel. St. Peter's was a cavernous building that was erected back in the fourth century. Julius II decided to tear it down and build a more splendid monument even though it was considered the holiest church in the world. Only about 50,000 people lived in Rome in 1503 (its population in antiquity had peaked at about one million). Many travelers bemoaned the contrast between the ancient grandeur and what they saw. Buildings were crumbling, cows grazed in the once mighty forum, and prostitutes propositioned people from under ancient arches. The aqueducts that once provided the city with its drinking water had been in disrepair for centuries, and citizens had to drink from the Tiber River, which animal carcasses rotted in. Iron-willed Julius II was determined to bring the center of Christendom up to par with the ancient past, and the expenses of his ambition provoked Martin Luther (another plain-spoken German who was uncomfortable with valuing style over truth) to protests which spearheaded the Protestant Reformation.

Rome gave me a cold feeling when I first got there in 2008 and exited its central train station. Its wide, straight streets lined with large stone and concrete buildings with linear facades made me wonder if Julius II's spirit would belt me for not bowing. Their lines and abstract shapes echoed the ancient Coliseum's grand arches.

But the city quickly grew on me. Sunsets over the Tiber River that made the white dome of St. Peter's shine over it like a star, gelato shops that always carried pistachio and tiramisu flavors, laidback crowds lounging on the Spanish Steps, Gypsy jazz musicians in the Piazza Navona, honey-voiced singers serenading people in sidewalk restaurants, and greenery in parks that allowed breaks from the crowds gave Rome so much variety that I'd choose it if I were to live in Italy. Some of these scene softeners were created in modern times, but the 16th century still saw the vibrant menageries of people, and they added life to the monumental architecture.

Another one of Western history's greatest painters, Raphael (1483–1520), added refinement to the grandeur. He first worked in Florence (after learning his craft in Urbino), where he saw the work of Leonardo and Michelangelo. While there, he collaborated with a painter called Perugino, whose scenes became known for *dolce*, which means both sweetness and lightness. Instead of the commanding bodies of Masaccio, Mantegna, and Michelangelo, many of Perugino's figures have graceful outlines, often in S patterns so that they appear to be dancing. Julius II then recruited Raphael to paint scenes on the walls of his private apartment in the Vatican. Raphael would synthesize Perugino's delicacy with the monumentality he saw in other artists' works into a standard that Western painters have aspired to ever since.

The Sistine Chapel's ceiling hovers so far above the floor that many of Michelangelo's details are invisible to the naked eye, but everything Raphael did would be closely scrutinized. The art historian Ross King wrote that a little boy on the Sistine Chapel's ceiling makes an obscene gesture at an ancient prophetess called the Cumaean Sibyl. He gives her "the fig" by sticking his thumb between his index and middle finger, which many people in Italy then and in modern times considered blatantly disrespectful. The papal court was spreading propaganda about Julius II spearheading a golden age of Christendom, and some of it declared that ancient seers had foretold this. Was the reluctant painter giving his overbearing employer what King said was the equivalent of the middle finger? There's no concrete evidence, but it would have been consistent with the temperamental artist who was quick to complain in blunt terms. He could at least be thankful that he had room to do this—the thumb doesn't stick out, so it's invisible from the floor. But every square inch of Raphael's work would have to please his irritable patron.

Julius II had a knack for choosing the right man for the job, even though Raphael had never painted such large, complex works before. He was only in his twenties when he began working on the pope's library. His most famous scene in it is known as the *School of Athens*, in which exemplary thinkers from the past politely discuss their ideas in a setting that has been one of the West's main ideals of civilization. Plato and Aristotle are the central figures and they impeccably balance each other. Plato points upwards as though he's saying that the locus of reality is in the eternal forms from the spiritual world, and the latter makes a gesture towards the earth because he was more interested in the observable natural world. I had a philosophy professor in college who said that those two men's minds conceived everything that all subsequent Western thinkers pondered. The young Raphael summed them up with exquisite balance, and there are no rude gestures—all people politely discuss their differences.

The thinkers around Plato and Aristotle consult with each other and teach students under a series of arches with coffered ceilings rising over wall niches which hold marble statues. Many historians have said that the architecture resembles today's St. Peter's (though the new building's construction was only just beginning then). Masaccio had painted the Trinity under a coffered Roman arch in Florence's Santa Maria Novella; that was the first painting to integrate a realistically shown body with classical architecture. Raphael made this scene not only more complex, but also more graceful. The word *grazia* was increasingly used in the arts, and Raphael advanced it so much that his name is still associated with it. Everything is proportioned, but not in a way that seems rigid or mechanical. Each figure in the *School of Athens* is individualized. Several teachers are with a small group of students, and all these intimate clusters are distributed under the arches so that the full and empty spaces are balanced.

Raphael might have included Michelangelo in this scene, in the guise of an ancient philosopher called Heraclitus, who was known for being solitary and rough-mannered. Unlike the other dignitaries in the painting, this figure is not dressed in a stately gown, but in a painter's coarse work clothes, and he broods while staring at the floor. Michelangelo was notoriously unkempt, sometimes sleeping in the outfit he painted in, including his boots. Raphael surely admired him if he portrayed him with the West's most distinguished thinkers, but he was able to show his blemishes without compromising the scene's beauty. That's *grazia*— being polite and proportioned, but in a way that seems natural and unaffected.

I find it amazing that this youthful painter perfected this standard under the nose of the thunderous pope. Since this was part of Julius's apartment, he must have frequently inspected the work. If Raphael did depict Michelangelo as the grumpy thinker, the pope might have laughed at this image of the man that he found difficult to manage but too gifted to let go. Unlike that volatile artist, Raphael was charming, popular, well-dressed, and handsome, and he often had a circle of admirers and students around him who later spread his style all over Europe. Rome became the West's leader in developing expressions that mix of grandeur and grace.

Roman artists quickly spearheaded a third way of treating three-dimensional perspective: They rebelled against it. In the 1520s several painters gave scenes extra emotional power by distorting appearances. Bodies were sometimes elongated, colors became more intense and less realistic, faces were contorted, and swirling action filled many scenes. This movement is called mannerism, and Michelangelo painted one of its greatest early works: *The Last Judgment*, which presides on the far end wall of the Sistine Chapel. The damned suffer in hell as twisted bodies clumped together, and their faces are grotesquely distorted into exaggerated grimaces. A skinned man dangles in midair, and art historians have noted that the face looks like Michelangelo's. The artist who had glorified the body now showed its mutability. Scenes like these are supposed to induce what artists have called *stupore*, or awe in the presence of divine truths that overwhelm reason. Raphael also became one of the style's pioneers before his mysterious death at the age of thirty-seven.

So as artists perfected three-dimensional perspective and used it for many types of scenes, others began to deliberately break its rules. As in the Middle Ages, some Westerners tried to put all of nature and humanity under a permanent order based on a few simple principles, and others flouted that system and looked for alternatives. But the latter also reinforced the importance of that order because they made the issue of following formal rules or the imagination central in approaches to art.

Florence's emphasis on mathematics, Venice's sensuality, and Rome's grandeur, grace, and melodrama combined to encourage modern Westerners to emphasize three-dimensional perspective, static geometric forms, and the substantiality of bodies. Many currents converged throughout Europe to encourage the focus on them, including:

- Alberti's mathematical theory,
- Platonism's idealization of static forms and ratios,
- Merchants and bankers accustomed to counting and measuring things,
- Franciscans appreciating nature and seeing dignity in common people,
- Empires overstepping their boundaries, including Milan and Spain,
- Antiquity's literary heritage that glorified cultured secular life,
- Ancient Greek and Roman architecture,
- Ancient Greek and Roman sculpture,
- Greece's and Italy's natural environments,
- Florence's polarized politics,
- Violence behind Florence's tidy lines,
- Venice's sprightliness,
- Northern merchants' concerns with precise details,
- Realistic portraiture,
- Ambitious men in love with grandeur, like Julius II,
- People raising the standards of grace, like Raphael,
- Artists deliberately disobeying conventions and creating works that are abrasively against their precepts.

The three cities combined these in their own ways, and their traditions fused as artists and patrons traveled between them, and as other Italian towns patronized the arts, particularly Milan, Mantua, Urbino, Siena, Perugia, Ferrara, Padua, Verona, Rimini, Bologna, and Naples.

These traditions soon spread beyond Italy. Sadly, the early 16th century was traumatic for her. In 1494 the French king, Charles VIII, invaded and Spain quickly followed suit. Plagued with foreign armies trampling through their farmlands, Italian cities lost much of their proud independence. The most horrifying experience for many was a brutal sack of Rome by the Spaniards in 1527—less than 20 years after mighty Julius II vied with ancient Rome's glory. Some art historians have thought that this influenced the pessimism in Michelangelo's *Last Judgment.*

At the same time, Italy had been losing trade to the Spanish and Portuguese, who had begun to sail across the Atlantic and around the Horn of Africa. They were thereby able to undercut Italian merchants by bringing spices and silks into Europe more cheaply than the land-based networks through the Middle East.

However, Italy's loss was the rest of Europe's gain as her artists packed their bags for Germany, France, England, the Low Countries, Spain, and the eastern Hapsburg Empire. They decorated palaces, churches, and public buildings in the growing states in the north, west, and east and thereby provided visual standards for them as they consolidated.

Ideas and perspectives that Westerners have considered the world's main ordering principles thus converged from an enormous number of currents and places. They spread throughout Europe and were repeatedly reinforced as fundamental.

A. Richard Turner, in *Renaissance Florence,* wrote that three-dimensional perspective didn't become the West's dominant model of reality overnight.[12] The old great chain of being from the Middle Ages remained a powerful concept through the 18th century—most people still thought the universe was hierarchical and that angels and demonic beings influence events in the world. People in the 16th century also still believed in astrology, prophecy, and magic. Locals acting as prophets shared Florence's streets with the bankers and merchants who had studied mathematics, and one of that city's most eminent 15th century intellectuals, Pico della Mirandola, believed in the efficacy of magic. People throughout Europe in the 16th century also believed in witchcraft, demonology, and numerology.

But three-dimensional perspective slowly kept penetrating Western culture, and it did so in new ways. Europeans in the 16th and 17th centuries found it useful as their states expanded and competed with each other. Mapmaking became more advanced in the 16th century, and every major city was drawn so that people could follow its streets and see each building. John Hale, in *The Civilization of Europe in the Renaissance,* said that cartography was almost a craze then. Europe's population grew, literacy increased, governmental bureaucracies expanded, and the largest states began to colonize other continents. The new perspective helped people manage growing amounts of information by allowing things to be more precisely located. The new printing industry allowed maps to be produced and circulated widely.

Globe making grew at the same time. People who could afford one could see all the world's major landmasses and political states reduced to a three-dimensional grid. Fernand Braudel, in *The Perspective of the World,* wrote that the West's economy was becoming more integrated in the 16th century, mingling currencies and goods as trade across borders and between continents increased. Lisa Jardine, in *Worldly Goods; A New History of the Renaissance,* said that books for recording profits and losses and maps of the world which detailed shipping routes and trading relationships were closely associated in that century. The world was becoming more unified by the market as battles between medieval Catholic traditions and new Protestant faiths were shattering people's dreams of Christian unity, and maps helped to bring unity and order to this new world of more trade and less shared faith.

As trade increased, people proudly commissioned artists to display their belongings. Painters used their mastery of realism to show their patrons' glittering jewelry, sparkling coins, glinting mirrors, luscious fabrics, sturdy horses, palatial homes, and expansive gardens. At the same time, landscape painting was becoming an independent genre. From the towering Alps to the flat farmlands around Dutch and Flemish towns, all the natural environments that Europeans knew were increasingly portrayed in three dimensions. More human-made objects and natural landscapes were being depicted in ways that allowed people to analyze, control, and display them.

In the 17th century three-dimensional perspective and modern science helped each other to develop. The coordinates of the X, Y, and Z axes, which today's high school students learn in their first algebra class, began to be used then. Isaac Newton's physics charted motions of objects by plotting the distance they traveled on one axis and the duration of their journeys on another, thereby allowing their future trajectories to be accurately predicted. Newton was also a keen believer in supernatural influences, and he wrote many manuscripts about alchemy, but his scientific work influenced people much more in the 18th century and afterwards.

Ideas of time began to mirror concepts of space. Clocks were installed on many town halls in Italy in the 15th century, and wealthy people began to use portable timekeepers by 1500. Clocks had been used in monasteries and churches to signify the times to pray and hold masses, but people now began to partition time into abstract units and apply them to their daily lives in the material world as business in it became more complex. The expanding governmental bureaucracies increasingly recorded people's births, marriages, and deaths, so it became more common for people to locate the most important events in their lives according the precise times and places in which they occurred. The new views of space and time were beginning to shape people's identities.

Three-dimensional perspective grew in other ways, which were more tangible than abstract mathematics. Language was changing to reflect the emerging way of seeing. For example, people in late 17th century England were increasingly finding the verbiage of Shakespeare's time (around 1600) excessive. They now wanted more precision and clarity and considered the earlier outpourings of words obscure and unwieldy. They used to be good fun. In Shakespeare's *Henry IV, Part I*, the youthful prince is hanging out with a fat old wine-guzzling former knight named Falstaff, and both playfully insult each other. Henry calls his companion, "—this sanguine coward, this bed-presser, this horseback-breaker, this huge hill of flesh—." Falstaff then makes fun of the skinny youth with this exuberant flood of words, "—'sblood, you starveling, you eel-skin, you dried neat's-tongue, you bull's pizzle, you stockfish—o for breath to utter what is like thee!—you tailor's yard, you sheath, you bowcase, you vile standing tuck!" A standing tuck was an upright rapier, and a bull's pizzle was its penis. Falstaff's tongue even outstretched his own girth.

But humor then became more subtle. In 1681 John Dryden lampooned the prolific womanizing of England's current king, Charles II, by saying that he "Scattered his Maker's image through the land." Understatement in a few well-chosen words was replacing the broad caricatures from the beginning of the century, at least among the middle and upper classes who wanted to distinguish themselves from the unlettered.

In Dryden's day the English language was moving away from the variety and license from Shakespeare's time. The Royal Society was established to advance scientific inquiry, and its members wanted sentences to be short and clear. They should detail objects, their qualities, and their locations rather than encourage rhetorical flourishes.

This preference for clarity extended far beyond scientific circles. Newspapers were emerging at the beginning of the 18th century, and people wanted accurate accounts of what was going on around them.

Barbara J. Shapiro, in *A Culture of Fact*, wrote that desires for clear descriptions of details grew in several other fields around that time. As more people were trading and colonizing other lands, travel writing grew and readers wanted to know about other places in a truthful way. People also wanted more focus on facts in history writing and in courtrooms. The novel emerged as a popular literary form then, and readers wanted clear descriptions of characters, places, and events.

Languages changed to accommodate all these demands. In Shakespeare's day people could use words more flexibly. Many were used in several parts of speech. Nouns could become verbs ("Grace me no grace nor uncle me no uncle" is from Shakespeare's *Richard II*), and adjectives could also be used as verbs (a person could *happy* her friend). Verb forms were also flexible. People could choose between multiple forms of the present tense's third-person singular, such as *telleth* and *tells*, and *singeth* and *sings* (the latter *s* ending spread from northern England as more people moved to London in the 16th century; people increasingly discarded the *eth* ending in the early and mid 17th century—it sounded more formal by then and was thus still sometimes used in serious writing). People could also choose between different forms of adjectives, such as *famousest* and *most famous*.

The flexibility of English in Shakespeare's time made it a joy to speak. People could express themselves more spontaneously and exuberantly than predictably—they deeply enjoyed bantering. But by the end of the 17th century, meanings of words and their functions in sentences needed to be stable so that things could be described and located in a world which was increasingly seen as a three-dimensional grid (at least in countries that could take the biggest political and economic initiatives—many people in Ireland, which England ruthlessly suppressed, have been proud of retaining the older flexibility, and I saw them deriving so much joy from speaking when I was there in 1988 that I envied them a bit and felt that the modern world's mechanization has diminished some of our older cultural wealth).

This happened in Italy too, where a dictionary was published to purify language with standardized word meanings. It was also taking place in France. Cardinal Richelieu (1585–1642) established the Academie Francaise to give the French language rules to allow scientists to communicate with each other.

Three-dimensional grids became more prominent in cities so that the eye got the same models of reality that the ear did. Government buildings, upper class homes, and churches in London, Paris, Amsterdam, Vienna, and Prague were designed with colonnades, semicircular arches, and domes, and they became standards of success. A fire wiped out the center of London in 1666. Though this was disastrous at first, people rebuilt their city with stately proportioned buildings, including St. Paul's Cathedral. They provided visual standards as London grew into one of the world's main centers of science, commerce, and enlightenment philosophy.

The 18th and 19th centuries saw more of nature and humanity conceived in terms of three-dimensional perspective. Latitudes and longitudes, amounts of force, economic supply and demand, changes of population, biological processes, and public opinions were increasingly plotted and analyzed on abstract two-and three-dimensional grids.

More and more currents thus kept emerging and reinforcing each other to make three-dimensional perspective dominant in the West. What seems obvious actually isn't so because it comes from an infinitely abundant cultural landscape.[11]

Paris' Louvre gave me a revelation: Some currents that encouraged three-dimensional perspective even flowed into people's stomachs. Its large selection of European ceramics showed a major change in images of well-being around the beginning of the 16th century. Before then much upper class tableware was painted in intricate geometric patterns that reminded me of Islamic designs. But after 1500 more plates, bowls, and drinking cups sported scenes from Biblical narratives and ancient Greek myths, with life-like people in front of buildings with classical columns and porticos. People didn't only admire the new realism in the great artists' works; they brought it into their homes and enjoyed it as they dined, celebrated weddings, and entertained business clients. In innumerable daily interactions, people with money associated classical styles with good living and distinguished themselves from the lower classes who couldn't afford these new fashions. Their appreciations of this type of art were emotional as much as intellectual—they associated it with security and well-being.

I realized that great works of art don't just remain on their pedestals. People imitate them and produce works on tableware, and in parish churches, family Bibles, and portraits they display in their homes. For example, an Italian-American family lived across the street from my family when I was born and they had a daughter my age. She married a policeman who shared her Catholic faith and they had a son. When he was about three, I watched them show him a small painting of an olive-skinned young man with long dark brown hair and ask, "Who is this?" The boy said, "Jesus!" The painting was the type of image that artists made in the Italian Renaissance. His gentle face could have been inspired by Fra Angelico. People surround themselves with imitations of the most influential works of art and associate them with goodness and wellness.

A new way of structuring perceptions and thoughts doesn't just come from a few canonical works of art, but from mutual reinforcement between great opuses and millions of objects people use on a daily basis. Great patronage centers like Florence, Venice, Rome, London, Paris, Antwerp, and Amsterdam flourished, but so did millions of homes, churches, and merchants' shops. In addition, thousands of businesses and government offices that used maps and written records, and thousands of schools that taught modern geography, operated. A shared way of seeing the world becomes dominant when it's reinforced throughout an infinitely creative cultural environment.

The talk show host Johnny Carson used to parody the astrophysicist Carl Sagan by saying "billions and billions." But people can enjoy the world's cultural landscapes and the ideas and art forms that each one treats as fundamental as much as Sagan appreciated the stars. They seem basic because of an astronomical number of experiences that reinforce them as such.

The world's size can open our imaginations into a bottomless well of creativity. It actually rivals anything that astronomers have aimed their telescopes at, and its bigness is within us (in our perspectives and ideas). We can learn to feel wonderment for what we used to consider so obvious that we didn't question it. Instead of mechanically following our conventional perspectives, we can appreciate an infinitely abundant cultural landscape that these conventions emerged in and reflect.

Each culture's bigness is unique, so as we compare more of them, the world's size can keep growing and we can be increasingly free from past conventions and able to enjoy more of it. We will explore more riches in Thailand in the next chapter and compare it with the West's. In Chapter 13, we'll see how comparing cultures can spark a revolution in perspective that can be as monumental as the one that happened in Florence.

CHAPTER 10

GRACE AND SPICE:
MORE ENCHANTMENTS IN THAILAND

A DIFFERENT WAY of perceiving and thinking about the world emerged in Thailand as Europe developed three-dimensional perspective. It has emphasized harmony between a multitude of forms and hues which are too numerous and dynamic to plot on a single grid. It doesn't try to yoke them to one static vantage point or to abstract lines. Instead, each form joins a flow of patterns and colors that's both animated and graceful. This way of seeing reality allows limitless ways to enjoy the moment. You can't fully see a wat or a neighborhood from one point of view. Instead, you wander through them and savor the infinite mixtures of sights and sounds without ever exhausting their varieties of beauty.

However, space in Thai temples isn't random; it does follow an order. The most sacred buildings (the vihara, the stupa, and the monks' ordination hall) rise in the center, and most viharas face east. But this spatial hierarchy is flexible enough to let people meander and enjoy the flows of forms and colors from an endless variety of perspectives. Buildings are lilting rather than densely constructed, and they do not follow lines as rigidly as most Western architecture does. The most important structures rule, but softly. They don't impose on the surroundings.

Wat Hua Khuang, in the northern town Nan, has an assembly hall and stupa whose forms gently taper as they rise. In addition, the grounds contain a library for sacred scriptures, which also becomes more gossamer at higher levels. All the buildings allow each other space, and this gives people room to amble and enjoy them from many places. These structures are centers of perspective in wats because they're the most important constructions and they spread over the middle area, but they permit limitless vantage points. As in Ayutthaya's royal palace, a slow

Figure 22. Wat Hua Khuang, Nan, Thailand.

walk is a common way to appreciate the surroundings. Their forms seem to dance with each other with the grace of a river's flow. The world, with its plethora of life forms, is in balance.

Step inside a vihara and more graceful chemistry takes place. The altar with the main Buddha statue stands at the opposite end, but people's gazes aren't forced towards this figure. Most of the hundreds of wats that I explored in Thailand with an operating meditation hall have several Buddha statues on the altar. There is always a main figure, which is usually the largest and placed in the center, but many other statues surround it. Their sinuous forms and golden surfaces mingled into a slow flow as I strolled around them. Being close together, their forms and glowing hues reflected each other, and the view gently shifted as I moved. It was different every few seconds and always beautiful. The statues didn't stand out as distinct objects that are most fundamentally characterized by abstract lines and points. Instead, they seemed like participants in a genial stream of benevolent energy.[1]

Figure 23. Graceful forms of Buddha statues flowing together in a northern Thai vihara, Nan.

Many other things usually surround the altar. Flowers, incense sticks, banners with brightly painted animals, a pulpit carved in floral patterns, and pictures of the royal family blend with the Buddha statues into a profusion of forms and colors which cannot be reduced to a single vantage point. They make the surroundings appear animated, but their elegance and the slow walking seem to render them kind. They allow an endless variety of perspectives to thrive. All coexist under the Buddha's compassion.

His compassion extends to the people sitting and ambling in the hall. They add to the multitude of slowly moving forms. The whole community seems immersed in his sweet energies.

If you're in a Thai temple, please walk around at a slow pace and then sit for a few minutes. Watch people come and go and enjoy their civility. Stroll a bit more until you find another appealing spot and savor it. Repeat this as long as it makes you happy. For traditional Thais, the world largerly hangs together in this easygoing flow of forms, colors, and people.

These animated and graceful flows of forms and colors also infuse daily life in traditional Thailand, and I was immersed in them in Ayutthaya's night market. We all savored the sundry aromas of food being cooked. The varied impressions that were both scintillating and easygoing reflected the arts that shimmer and sooth. As we all strolled, aromas of spices, vegetables, seafood, and chicken enveloped us. I heard crackling sounds of vegetables being stir-fried and saw shiny silver colors of fish. Fruits came in reds, greens, oranges, yellows, and magentas, and they were often cut into forms that resembled stupas' indentations. I enjoyed all these impressions with the crowd of locals sauntering together. A woman walking in front of me carried her baby so that he peered over her shoulder as two children walked by her side. A teenage boy and girl held hands, and elderly men sat and chatted.

Cuisine, markets, folk arts, sculptures, and domestic architecture have reinforced Thai ways of thinking as much as royal palaces and Buddhist stupas have. So have rivers and rice farming. Even if Buddhism was first adopted by elites and it only slowly penetrated commoners' daily lives, all people still shared experiences in markets, villages surrounded by greenery, river journeys, collective life in and around rice paddies, spirit cults, and religious festivals and processions. Because wats contained the most prominent buildings in most towns and near most villages, everyone saw them on a daily basis. Forms from Buddhist art and rituals meshed with ordinary people's lives, and they all converged into a shared way of seeing the world. As in the West, objects from everyday life fused with great art, and all together made certain perspectives and ideas seem fundamental.

However, many Thai forms also have a dark side because they can suggest danger, as though they embody mysterious powers. The points that project from the corners of roofs, the tops of stupas, and the heads of many Buddha statues are as sharp as daggers. The sheens of gold and bronze plating, colored glass inlay, and brass are pretty, but they blaze under the tropical sun and seem to project energy that can be dangerous if it's disrespected.

Most Thai art isn't serene in the way that a traditional Japanese garden is. Both share a type of perspective that slowly wanders through forms that interplay in ways that cannot be reduced to grids of straight lines. But nothing in a Japanese garden threatens to intrude on anything else because what rules there is pristine politeness. Everything is in its place and entirely tranquil. Thai art's red, silver, and gold hues can seem bombastic to traditional Japanese who prefer the soft and neutral tones that they find in nature. Thailand's tropical exuberance can seem loud to people who like understatement.

Thai forms are lithe, but not like Brazil's bossa nova music. The subtle chord progressions in Antonio Carlos Jobim's songs (such as "The Girl from Ipanema" and "Corcovado") are pure softness. They evoke breezes, the feeling of cool sand over your toes, the rustling of palm fronds, a parrot's plumage, and the swaying of a woman's hips and arms as she walks on the beach without a care in the world. The sharp points and glimmering colors in Thai art suggest a more concentrated energy. Though the forms curve and ripple in long undulating lines which soften animated forces, they can't obliterate them because people often consider nature's powers too strong and prevalent. Instead, they merely try to mute the environment's energies.

I've met a few people who find Thai art somewhat disturbing. I once took friends to a Thai restaurant in California. Their seven-year-old boy, with his fertile imagination, asked if someone would accompany him to the restroom because the wooden carvings on the walls frightened him. He said that they reminded him of monsters. Much Thai art is designed to make people happy, but not usually with the abandon of a Rio carnival. It must be enjoyed in a subdued and respectful way, rather than with a complete lack of reserve. Nobody break dances in a vihara, and everyone must dress modestly.

Thus kids I saw in Thailand were different from ones I met in the streets of Pisa during a parade. One reveler hit me in the head with a balloon shaped like a giant hotdog and smiled. What's adored as harmless fun in Italy would be considered a breach of protocol in Thailand, unless it occurs during a special occasion, like New Year.

No kids ever hit me in Thailand. A typical encounter I had with them happened in the northern town Phrae during the monsoon season in 2012. As I was exploring one of its historic wats, sheets of rain suddenly tumbled down and turned the walkways into rivers. Several children and

I ran for cover under the classroom's overhanging roof. They were spirited enough, constantly chatting and laughing. We said "Hello!" to each other, and they were happy to smile before my camera, but none broke away from the group and ventured towards me. Some of their parents then arrived to drive them home. Others mounted their bikes and waved to me with a smile as they began to speed off. Like many other Thais, they had learned to turn an uncomfortable situation into fun. But at the same time, they remained within their familiar community. They enjoyed the moment, but did so within the limits of their traditional etiquette.

Many Thais have traditionally seen the world as a contrast between the safe zone where they live and the dangerous hinterlands beyond. They have associated the former (called *muang*) with the farming community, the family, and the temple, and they've seen the latter (called *pa thu'an*) as the surrounding forests and mountains. *Pa thu'an* is full of untamed energy, bandits, malevolent spirits, and wild animals.[2] People synthesized this view of the world with Theravada Buddhism and royalty—wats and palaces are in the center of the *muang,* and they radiate their harmonizing energies throughout the community. Art forms in the temple and the palace rule gently, but the meandering they allow must be done with reserve and respect for elites.

I have emphasized the beauty of Thai art so far, but its relaxed flows and rambling perspectives emerged with fears of the unknown and emphases on social hierarchy. The meandering isn't entirely free because it is usually limited by conformity. Thais have typically lived with many rules which have often made them highly aware of proper and improper spatial relationships:

- One of the most common spatial distinctions is between high and low places. A person should not stand above someone who is higher in the social food chain or pass things over his head. Bowing to a Buddha statue or to the king is an expected sign of respect. Young people are supposed to honor elders and to observe the appropriate spatial rules. Hands should be held high when being placed together to greet a social superior, and they should be lower than the eyes when greeting a person at a lower level. The head is the most honored part of the body and the feet have the lowest status, so one should never point his floppy feet at a higher ranking person or touch his head.

- People are also often aware of distinctions between the safe inside and the wild outside. Richard B. Davis, in *Muang Metaphysics*, found many Thais to classify space according to distance from a center of culture and power, and to fear places that are beyond its influence. Along with wats, the *lak muang* (community pillar) is an important ritual center, where people gather to pay homage to a decorated pillar which is seen as the axis of spiritual powers. Bangkok's is across from the royal palace, and the constant flow of people quietly bowing inside the shrine showed me that this tradition thrives even in the big city.

- The four cardinal directions have often been prevalent in Thai culture. Many traditional Thais have associated the west with death and have thus avoided sleeping with their heads in that direction. People have often preferred to point their heads east while sleeping, where the sun rises and where the Buddha faced while meditating and attaining enlightenment.

- Although I've enjoyed meandering through rural neighborhoods, traditional Thais have associated many spatial rules with the home. Davis wrote that the sleeping room for the father and mother is the most sacred area in the house and that there are rules about who may and who may not enter it. There are also many taboos about constructing homes. In traditional communities, people have conducted divination rituals to discern an auspicious place and time to build. Work should begin on certain days and months to encourage health and prosperity. Directions that houses face are also often considered auspicious, and even the building's dimensions sometimes are. And locations of spirits must be respected— many spirits become nasty when humans disrespect their turf.

Some of these rules have slackened in modern times, especially in Bangkok. But almost all Thais live with a strong awareness of boundaries that they shouldn't cross (limits related to the social hierarchy are the most pervasive).

All the same, these spatial limits aren't conceived in terms of an all-encompassing three-dimensional grid as much as space is in the West. These limits are more strictly social—they're often conceived in relation to a social superior or inferior, or as the degree of distance from the central civilizing institutions (including the wat, the palace, and the community pillar), or in relation to aspects of cardinal directions that can help or harm people. They are not as strictly envisioned as a universal and permanent framework that's structured by lines and which is abstracted from the person and community. Thai space is usually more experiential—it's less separate from the self and the community. This allows flexibility. A person walking with a superior through a wat must always be respectfully aware of him. But walking alone or in the company of friends allows more playfulness. Sulamith Heins Potter, in *Family Life in a Northern Thai Village*, wrote that each person experienced the local wat in a different way. Though all acted according to expectations about their social roles (such as the strong father, the grandmother, and the pretty, unmarried young woman), each varied his and her actions and thoughts according to personal inclinations. Thais are more constrained in the presence of an elder or a monk, but the rules loosen when they're out of close proximity. I've found that many Thais' experiences flow between adherence to social rules and whimsical breaches and meanderings. Both go together—the rules give people a sense of stability and the meanderings, *sanuk*, and lithe art forms allow the constraints to be bearable.

Life in Thailand is thus often more of a flow between circumstances that are unpredictable than a line between events that are preplanned. A person can saunter through a wat or a rural neighborhood and then see a monk. Or he can amble through a night market with friends and then encounter his father or boss. In these ways, experiences often alternate between fun and restraint. The world hangs together through congenial flows and through social hierarchy, and the amount of focus on each changes according to the context.

These alternations have a lot of nuances. Though Thais have traditionally thought in terms of contrasts between the cozy inside and the wild outside, these spaces aren't always neatly separated because even the inside can become dangerous. Power is unevenly distributed in the social hierarchy.³ Patron-client relationships are common in many domains, including business, government, the monkhood, voluntary associations, and the family. Thais call this relationship *phuujaj-phuunauauj* (big man-little man). The higher-up is supposed to bestow political connections and financial help, and receive respect and loyalty in return. Both follow social rituals in which compliments and gifts are given, but are they sincere? Can I trust his smiles, soft voice, and acts of kindness, or will he betray me as soon as another big man offers him a better opportunity? Is he gossiping about me behind my back? The pretty surfaces often mask dangers in a society in which people compete for status.

Twenty years ago a friend of mine who was an electrical engineer in one of Detroit's main car companies called me from his home, fuming because his boss had just stolen his patent. Fed up with the car makers' traditions of rewarding those with the most seniority over people who did the best work, he decided to move out to California. He quickly got a job offer and relocated, and he's still doing well. He has a secure position and spare time to indulge his love of buying old cars and fixing them up while listening to old Aerosmith songs. But most people in Thailand haven't had as many alternatives to their current jobs. The economy is smaller and it has largely been run by elite men who enjoy their big man positions. Little men have often had to kiss their boots and vie with each other for the few choice jobs. Social life has thus often consisted of politeness and hidden agendas beneath the surface.

There is also a lot of corruption behind the polite surfaces, partly because of the lack of opportunities to start new ventures. Most industries and markets are smaller in Thailand than in the richest Western countries, and this encourages people to feel that they must milk their positions while they can.

Even popular Buddhist ideas can encourage corruption. Thais represent the Buddha, not as an intense figure like the Christian St. Paul insisting on complete self-surrender, a fanatical old buzzkill like St. Bernard, or Ghiberti's confrontational St. Matthew pointing to the Gospel that he's holding, but as a gently smiling spirit who is tolerant and kind.

So the corruption behind the scenes, anxieties about personal betrayal, and hazards of violence suddenly erupting can encourage fears that danger lurks beneath the smiles, soft voices, and pretty art. These worries also encourage people to long for the gentle beauty that masks the problems. Renaissance Florentines found special meaning in abstract shapes and clear lines, partly because they represented a safe realm above violent politics. In comparison, Thais have traditionally preferred nonconfrontational behavior and smooth flows, partly because they calm energies and spirits that can suddenly become maniacal.

A lot of fighting happens beneath the polite surfaces in Thailand. Cock fights, kick boxing matches surrounded by gamblers, and a high homicide rate attest that the comely stroll through a wat isn't a model for all experiences. The graceful energy flows in temples, viharas, rivers, peaceful villages, and rice fields sometimes explode into violence. Thankfully, I never saw any in Thailand, though I've witnessed several street fights in India. Thais usually make more effort to hide their dirt. But I wasn't looking for any and didn't go to any *muay thai* matches, snookers halls, or sex strips in Patpong or Pattaya. They're easily available for those who want that kind of spice. Thai society has often harmonized prettiness and license by giving both their spaces. The slow flows are necessary for living, but they rule softly enough to allow some disobedience as long as it's not out in the open. Thais expect each other to be comely, but know that boys will be boys (many hold a double standard and expect women to be respectable while the guys are out tomcatting). The graceful abundance in their aesthetics and perspectives allows tolerance of a bit of wildness. When things do get out of hand, most people long for the soft ways. Life has thus often alternated between gentleness and sudden outbursts of mayhem (today's stresses have made returning to the old grace more difficult for many—we'll explore Thailand's recent challenges in Part Three).

Packs of dogs pose real dangers because they roam in many Thai towns, and Ayutthaya had its share. I never saw so many strays in any other country. Thais don't want to put them to sleep because of the Buddhist aversion to taking lives. That's sweet, but some were so mangy and emaciated that it was hard to look at them. Some strays forage in packs and become territorial. One group trapped me in a restaurant one night and I couldn't leave until they decided to move on. That was near Ayutthaya's night market; their sinister silhouettes contrasted with the bazaar's amiable blends of senses.

Dogs also crowd many temples, and I was barked at and sometimes charged in wats in other towns. They always stopped a few inches from me. None tried to bite, but they came close enough to make the experience hair-raising.

But the beauty in Thailand enables people to forget the occasional confrontation. Small altars for offerings and pedestals for Buddha statues project sinuous lines and shimmering golds. Lids of lacquer jars for offerings become progressively narrow and steep in the middle as though they're lotus buds or miniature stupas. Many little things from secular life are pleasing too. Some ceramic bowls include a charming painting of fish in the middle, and other ceramics are in glittering colors that suggest Persian influence (Persian traders and courtiers were prominent in Ayutthaya). Silver bowls and jars glitter like diamonds. Many traditional eating utensils, chairs, and pillows have elegantly flowing designs. I even saw bus stops in several northern towns that were in the shape of a vihara—two wooden benches faced each other, and a steep gabled roof that curved upwards into a point crowned them.

Food presentation is also an art. Thais savor its visual beauty and spicy aromas as well as the tastes—several senses combine pleasing stimuli. Many dishes blend multiple flavors. Bean thread noodles, chopped carrots, a few chopped onions, a little mint, some ginger, fried tofu, a few shrimps, and spices mixed in some of the fare that spoiled me so that when I eat in most Thai restaurants in America, I think, This isn't like Thailand. Every mouthful had a different mixture of flavors, but each was both effervescent and homey.

Senses fuse in many other ways. Sounds often mix several stimuli at the same time. Whether they're the birds and crickets around villages, or the cars, trucks, and tuk tuks in towns and cities, the ear often becomes immersed in a steady hum rather than hearing one noise that stands out. As I walked around many wats, birdsong blended with the art. Sometimes faint sounds of traffic outside the walls wafted in. Monks' chants breezed through the air at other times. Several stimuli often fuse in Thailand, and this encourages people to feel absorbed in the whole environment.

Please spend several days in Ayutthaya if you visit it and enjoy it at a relaxed pace. There is endless wealth in everyday things in Thailand. Savor the surroundings, but don't completely lose your guard. This is the Thai way.

Later in Bangkok, I visited the parents of a restaurant manager that I knew in California. They owned a cheerful white two-story home in a leafy neighborhood across the river, in Thonburi. Both were friendly, but from behind a safe wall of reserve. She had been a teacher and was discussing the English language. "I can understand the English of all Americans except Southerners." I erupted into a mock description of my power tools in an exaggerated Texas drawl and both burst into uproarious laughter. She exclaimed, "You sound like George Bush!" These joyful interruptions of normal composure often delight travelers.

Many fans of Thai art enjoy its humor. A close look at scenes in wats' murals often reveals people flirting, smoking, gambling, and fighting.

These switches between control and exuberance emerge in limitless ways, and the breaches are often utterly charming. When I was in a town near Ayutthaya called Lopburi, I heard driving pop music booming from enormous speakers two blocks away. I dodged the dense traffic and reached the center of activity, which was a large flatbed truck surrounded by a crowd. Middle-aged women and a few children joyfully danced on it. They smiled at me and a young man standing nearby gave me a hug. Buddhist symbols indicated that this was a religious celebration. Religious ceremonies with loud music have become more common in Thailand over the last 40 years, but they're still in the fine tradition of having fun in rituals.

These shifts between reserve and esprit often take place, and you can never come to a full perspective of them. There's always more to enjoy in the conversations, food, art, and temples. I never went to the wilder places because I always found respectable life too interesting to leave.

Lopburi also created graceful art forms that have permeated Thai society since Ayutthaya's prime. The grounds of its Wat Mahathat have rows of thin stupas that surround a main tower. They project 20 to 40 feet upwards, and each is in a different form. Some are crowned by a corrugated bulb that looks like a cucumber, and most are indented in unique patterns in the corners. The central shrine is the tallest and it's covered with dainty stucco carvings. The whole place exuded tenderness as I walked around and enjoyed the forms flowing together. Florence's baptistery would have seemed as mechanical as a military march, but Lopburi reinforced the aesthetics of animated grace.

The more I explored Thai traditions, the more richness I found. I kept seeing shifts between etiquette and spiritedness, and between flowing meanders and fears of unseen dangers. As in the West, the most common forms and styles of art have many levels of meaning.

The enchanting art in Thailand assumed endless varieties, but I had only visited one of its old capitals, and that was the most influenced by Khmer grandeur. Sukhothai was next, and many Thais have seen it as the wellspring of their culture. The site impressed me as much as Angkor Wat did. The next section will show Thai cultural varieties in full bloom. It will also reveal more about how big a culture's landscape is, and how the next revolution in perspective can allow us to revel in this bigness.

PART TWO

THAILAND

SECTION TWO

MORE CULTURAL RICHES
AND A METHOD FOR FINDING
THE WORLD'S
FULL HUMAN WEALTH

CHAPTER 11

THE DAWN OF HAPPINESS: THAI CULTURE'S ORIGINS

THIS SECOND SECTION of Part Two explores the two Thai kingdoms that I enjoyed the most. They showed me that Thai culture is much richer than what I had discovered in Ayutthaya. After we see its full effervescence, we'll detail the method for finding paradise in the world.

I rode through the country's heartland to Sukhothai, which nestles by hills around its northern end. This area is a transition between the flat plains and the northern mountains, and it was thus a meeting place for many different groups of people. The Khmers took it over by the 12th century and built several temples there. In the mid 13th century, two local Tai chieftains spearheaded a war of independence and created the Sukhothai state. Blending cultures and natural landscapes is thus in Sukhothai's DNA.

I booked a bungalow in a compound run by a man and wife with a son who was about six. The husband was Belgian and she was Thai, and both were short and middle-aged. She did most of the talking and he was bashful. She dealt with all the guests and helped them make travel arrangements, and he never spoke unless he was addressed first. I wondered if she was the one who proposed the marriage.

Their place was homey in a Thai way. An open-air restaurant spread by the main entrance. The family and their friends relaxed in a small garden next to the dining area in the evenings, and I often returned there for dinners. Lush vegetation, spry lizards, and swarms of mosquitoes at twilight wrapped us in a profusion of life. This cozy family lived surrounded by nature's power.

The next morning, I hopped on an equally homey bus. The passengers rode on a long, flat bed with a tin roof and a wooden bench along each side. The benches faced each other so that the vehicle was filled with locals in close quarters. My goal was to explore the ancient city center, which was about eight miles to the west. The homes on the roadside were wooden and many were unpainted. Some houses either had no fence or a small one that a six-year-old boy could have jumped over—the locals didn't seem very worried about security. The people in the back with me were as relaxed as the scenery. The folksy ride in the funky bus seemed like an apt procession into Thai cultural origins.

I could see why Thais have honored Sukhothai as their culture's birthplace. The ritual center was full of stupas and temples, and they shared the grounds with canals and ponds, but its buildings were smaller than Ayutthaya's royal meeting halls. Sukhothai encouraged more empathy between all people.

Sukhothai's charm extended beyond its center. Remains of dozens of monasteries dot the land, and the surrounding forested hills shelter several temples. So the valley in its heyday was a green carpet of rice fields bejeweled with shrines and lined with waterways. The place seemed idyllic, and its most honored king, Ramkhamhaeng, wanted us to think so. An inscription from his reign (in the late 13th century) differentiated Thai from Khmer politics by highlighting its softness. The text covers the four long sides of a rectangular stone and it's a masterpiece of real estate salesmanship.

The stele proclaims that people can use Sukhothai's roads without paying burdensome tolls. They can take animals, produce, and precious metals to market without handing anything to the state. Some historians have interpreted this boast as an elbow in the Khmer Empire's ribs.[1] Jayavarman VII had built a network of roads across the state, but people paid to use them by Ramkhamhaeng's time.

The inscription also distinguishes Sukhothai from Angkor by saying that the king is a nice guy. The stone proclaims that anyone can come to the palace, ring a bell, and discuss a problem with him. He doesn't kill or beat captured enemy warriors. Instead, he teaches people about Buddhist merit and dharma. It all sounds too good to be true.

The name *Sukhothai* means *Dawn of Happiness*, and Ramkkhamhaeng's stele states that his people had many reasons for joy. The land was full of mango groves and fields of coconut, jackfruit, tamarind, and areca nuts. Those who cultivated them could keep their harvests. People held religious celebrations and conducted processions while singing, laughing, and playing music.

The inscription describes a month-long festival at the end of the rainy season, called *Kathina*. People brought gifts to monks, carrying heaps of flowers, cushions, pillows, cowries, and areca nuts along paths between rice fields to the monasteries. This is actually a custom throughout Buddhist Southeast Asia, and it's still commonly practiced in Thailand.

However, the stele's authenticity has recently been questioned. Some historians have claimed that it was actually written in the middle of the 19th century. King Mongkut, who reigned from 1851 to 1868, supposedly discovered it when he was still a young monk. After becoming king, he boosted the image of his country and its monarchy by restoring many ancient sites. Over the last 20 years, some historians have claimed that he fabricated the stele as an icon of royal merit.

Doubts have also arisen about the ritual center's authenticity. How much of it is original, and how much was reconstructed in the 19th century? Also, how true were UNESCO-supported restorations in the 1980s?[2] Victor Lieberman said that many historians now feel that most commoners in Sukhothai were more animistic than Buddhist. Some have even said that Ramkhamhaeng might have been a mythical figure rather than a real person.[3]

In spite of the quibbling and the revisionist histories, the inscriptions and the site have symbolized a key ideal for Thais. These have been emotional questions because many Thais have derived a lot of identity from Sukhothai's heritage. Irrespective of the authenticity of the stele and the site, people have felt that their country is grounded in their mixtures of humanity, Buddhist piety, artistic beauty, happiness, and a benevolent king. Many Thais have seen Sukhothai as a model for their society.

A group of schoolchildren who were eleven or twelve years old coyly approached me in tidy pink and brown uniforms in the old ritual center. A tall, thin girl softly said, "Hello, where are you from?" They were ethnically diverse; half were brown-skinned and the others looked Chinese. As I was photographing a 30-foot-tall Buddha statue, a middle-aged man who was accidentally in the shot posed and smiled. Mundane acts of civility like these are repeated over and over in traditional Thai culture, and they blend with monuments' gentle forms. I ultimately saw at least half a dozen groups of school kids exploring the monuments, internalizing their heritage.

The site's showpiece, Wat Mahathat, lifted me into Sukhothai's ideals. Its main stupa strengthened the Thai tradition of combining forms from many cultures and making them more graceful. A tall and narrow central tower with several indentations in each corner soars over the other shrines. The top takes the form of a lotus bud it's round and bulbous at the bottom, and it slowly becomes narrower and steeper until it ends in a long point. Sukhothai also crowned some stupas in key provincial ritual centers with this form. The art historians Carol Stratton and Miriam McNair Scott felt that these lotus blossom towers symbolized political and religious power. If so, royalty and spiritual energies were softened by this delicately curving form from nature.

Eight smaller towers surround the central spire. Four are in the cardinal directions and their style is Khmer, with several relatively flat roofs stacked on top of each other. Niches for Buddha statues indent each tower, and stucco scenes from his life enliven the lowest roof. The other spires rise in the corners. Stratton and McNair Scott thought the Burmese capital, Pagan, influenced their design, and Betty Gosling saw influence from a large state down in the Malay Peninsula and Sumatra called Srivijaya.[4] These towers alternate with the blockier Khmer shrines. When this multicultural mixture of forms was newly constructed, it was covered with cheerful white stucco. All the towers share a platform that's four to five feet high. As people strolled around it in processions, the spires' slowly shifting parallaxes bestowed perspectives that merged in yet another model of animated grace.[5]

These interplays of forms and colors ripple through the rest of the ritual center in a very Thai way. Over 150 shrines surround the central towers. Many are supposed to have housed ashes of Sukkothai royalty.[6] Angkor Wat honored an aloof god and king, but this place felt intimate because it embodied family and the Buddha's compassion. As I walked through the grounds, thousands of forms slowly mixed with the main stupa. There is nothing massive there. Instead, it's the ultimate Thai expression of the benevolent center which allows playful meanderings. There are no large Ayutthayan halls; people just float through the heavens.

And float, and float. The grounds are surrounded by yet more temples, canals, and ponds. I found a wat called Sa Si especially easy on the eye. Its central stupa is in the Sri Lankan bell form, and it sits on an island in a pond. I could see its reflection in the water, and as I strolled around, tree foliage gently fluttered around the stupa, and images of both glimmered in the water. A procession at this wat would have married water, harmonious architectural forms, flickering greenery, and cheerful gilts.

I imagined the processions that the Ramkhamhaeng stele vaunts. The brilliant colors of flowers and saffron gowns and the sounds of singing and musical instruments would have added more vibrancy to the area. According to inscriptions, devotees decorated roads with flowers, flags, and candles as they celebrated the installations of Buddha statues and relics. The drama professor Mattani Mojdara Rutnin (at Bangkok's Thammasat University) said that dance and music developed during Sukhothai's apogee into some of Thailand's most hallowed forms. I wondered, Did any other place on earth create more beauty?

Some historians may think I was idealizing the place. Victor Lieberman wrote that a shrine a little south of Wat Mahathat was dedicated to Sukhothai's guardian spirit and that buffalos were sacrificed there.[7] Betty Gosling said that it was probably the largest building that the locals constructed in the immediate post-Khmer period, but the Buddhist temples and stupas that were built in the 14th century are larger and they surround the older shrine. So despite the persistence of animism, the ethereal interplays of Thai forms quickly became dominant sights in Sukhothai. Some of the animistic rituals were bloody, but they were balanced with refined Buddhist art and beautiful ceremonies. Both traditions fused in this tolerant society.

A local tuk tuk driver motored me around the temples beyond the center. No massive Preah Khans were in sight. All the shrines are smaller, though they still dwarf the older one for the town's guardian spirit. Their medium sizes allow them to mingle with the surrounding forest. Sukhothai's center's harmony reverberates through the whole valley.

It also ripples up the hillsides that rise in the west. On the next day another driver took me to some of their temples. My favorite was Wat

Saphan Hin. I reached it by climbing an ancient stairway of large stone slabs that ascends about 200 feet. I had to watch my step because they're unevenly settled and many are now broken, but their weathered state gave the approach a romantic air.

A 40-foot-tall Buddha statue from the late 13th or early 14th century stands on the top. He wears a gentle smile and holds the palm of his long right hand forward in a position that means "Don't fear." Pillars of a ruined assembly hall surround him. An inscription states that Ramkhamhaeng rode to the wat's area on a white elephant during full moons. When I was there, two women were quietly kneeling in front of the statue. More than 700 years apart, both visits represented the continuity of a tradition that links beauty and piety. The two women lacked their predecessor's mount, but not his grace.

Being in Thailand, this grace was tinged with animism. The Ramkhamhaeng stele honors a local mountain spirit that is the most powerful soul in the land, and it says that the king must give him offerings. If he does, Sukhothai will thrive, but if he doesn't, the guardian will withdraw his protection and the state will be ruined. Though Wat Saphan Hin is pretty, the western hills it resides in were considered the main hangout for spirits. Several other wats rise there as though the kings felt that they needed to keep them mellow.

Sukhothai reminded me of what I explored in Ayutthaya. Perspectives meander and let people enjoy endless ways in which forms and colors blend, but the pleasure is often muted by fear of unseen dangers and respect for the social hierarchy. Both kingdoms concurrently developed aesthetics that are both animated and graceful.

But things weren't always so pretty in Sukhothai in the late 14th and early 15th centuries. Many battles with expanding Ayutthaya and between local lords plagued the kingdom. Ayutthaya forced it to become a vassal in 1378, and it finally annexed it as a province around 1438.[8] But these conflicts further spread Sukhothai art to its southern neighbor, and they might have made Sukhothai's residents look to it for comfort when the wars flared up.

When Europe was beginning to structure its thought around three-dimensional perspective and material bodies, both Thai states created art and rituals that blended profusions of forms and colors into flows that are both lively and congenial. Their creations have mixed Buddhist piety, animism, political authority, fun, and meandering perspectives. If this way of seeing the world was so well-developed in both places, how did it first emerge?

I found the answer even more beautiful than Thailand's art because it shows how fertile a culture's origins and perspectives are. What people assume to be so fundamental that they don't question it can reveal an infinitely rich world that can be an endless wellspring of creativity and a constant source of pleasure.

Thirteenth century Sukhothai mixed Mon-speaking locals and Khmer-speaking overlords (and probably priests and artists) with Tai groups who had been moving into the area. Most historians think the latter originated in southern China. Tais had lived in Guangxi, Guizhou, Yunnan, and Guangdong. Some might have fanned out around 2,000 years ago, when China's Han Dynasty expanded from the north.[9] But many historians see the late first millennium CE as the main period when Tais expanded from the borderlands of southern China and northwestern Vietnam (around Dien Bien Phu), and moved into lands that became modern Thailand and Burma. More came into Thailand during the Mongol expansion in the 13th century.[10]

Ancient Tais organized themselves into several little groups and perhaps small states (some chronicles say that these states existed in Yunnan and northern Thailand in the late first millennium CE, before the Khmers conquered much of the area) rather than a single empire with a bureaucracy to unify it, as China's Han Dynasty did. Tai political systems were more decentralized and personal. Lots of groups formed *muang* systems. The word *Muang* was used for the territory that encompassed a cluster of villages. It also often meant the largest local village, which was the political hub for all the others. But its meaning was personal as well as geographic because the leader of the most prominent family in the most important village often acted as the entire *muang's* headman. Some headmen erected a pillar outside their houses, treating it as the center of supernatural powers, which they probably distributed throughout their territory by conducting rituals. The concept of *muang* thus included a male with enough prestige to attract followers, as well as local spirit cults, the human community, and the land's life-generating power (when towns later grew, it also came to mean a fortified town which was the center of power and civilization).[11] Long before the 13th century, Tais were used to residing in intimate groups that were held together with personal relationships instead of a more abstract and centralized Confucian bureaucracy.

David Wyatt wrote that most ancient Tai households were probably single nuclear families. They grew rice and vegetables, fished in nearby rivers, tended domestic animals, hunted in the surrounding forest, made tools, and wove cloth. One to two dozen households cooperated to harvest rice, coordinate water flows, and repair homes and bridges.

People could shift their loyalties to another strongman if he became more powerful or if their current leader became too demanding. Because populations weren't dense, it was relatively easy to move to another place. Chinese culture was more oriented to a centralized government and settled communities that extended families were rooted in, but Tai ideas that unified the world were more flexible. They reflected a multitude of little communities rather than a huge empire.

Growing rice in small riverine valleys and upland plains, ancient Tais were intimate with nature, and they probably honored spirits of rivers, mountains, rice, trees, the land's power, and ancestors. They generally lived on a small scale and focused on the immediate landscape and personal relationships. Modern Thais' preferences for coziness have ancient roots.

Most historians think Tais spread through Thailand, Laos, eastern Burma, and Assam over several centuries in multiple groups rather than one mass migration. The people who moved into Thailand's central plains encountered the sophisticated Dvaravati civilization.[12]

Dvaravati communities had traded with each other for many centuries, and they used money and made refined art that people still admire. Many of their sculptures of Buddhas, saints, and Hindu gods smile, and dancers' bodies curve almost as gracefully as Angkor Wat's devatas. The art historian Hiram W. Woodward Jr. enjoyed their approachability.[13] Their scale is human-sized rather than monumental, and their faces and forms are usually gentle (though a few statues are of people manhandling prisoners or slaves).

Much of Thailand's architecture that preceded the formation of Thai states in the 13th century was equally graceful. One of my favorite examples is this stupa form that a Mon kingdom in the north called Haripunchai built in several wats (Figure 24).

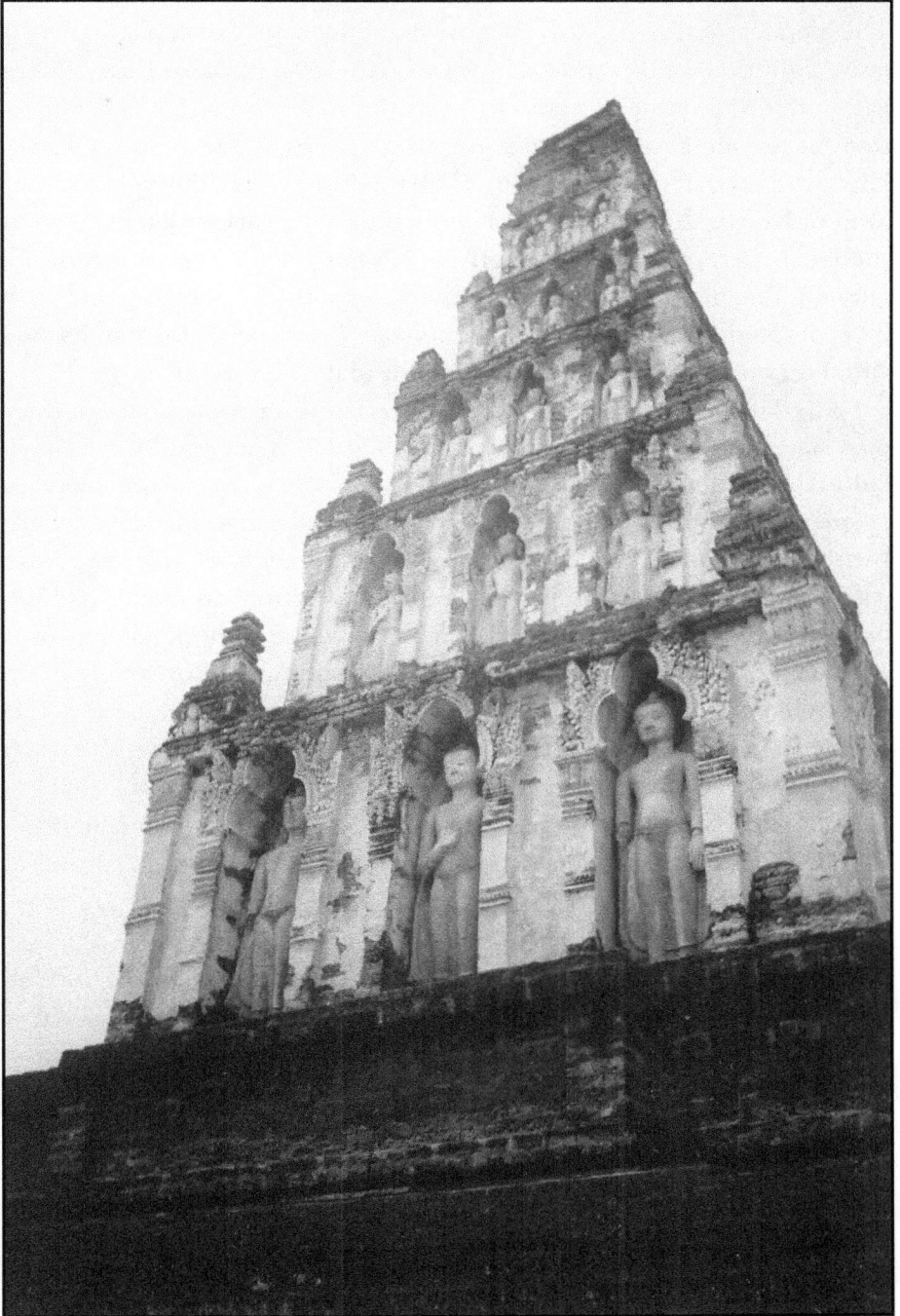

Figure 24. Stupa in Wat Kukut, Lamphun.

The slender outline of this narrow pyramid with five levels makes it more light than bulky, and each side of every level contains three niches with a Buddha statue in a standing position. The five layers of Buddhas thereby calmly bestowed grace on all quarters of the realm. Charles Higham said that most people in Thailand just before 1200 spoke either Mon or Khmer, so the realm was multicultural as Tais settled in.[14] When the locals were ready to throw off the Khmer yoke in the 13th century, enough Tais had moved in to assume the political leadership, but they incorporated Mon art. Sukhothai duplicated this stupa's form in its own ritual center so that it added yet more lilt to its mixture of shrines.

The Thai states (now spelled *Thai* because Tai people now had their own states in what is now modern Thailand) thus emerged when many cultures' art forms were influencing each other and being blended by people who had been used to human-scale environments. Victor Lieberman thought that Tais brought new systems of rice irrigation with them after living in uplands and learning how to create paddies on slopes.[15] The historians Chris Baker and Pasuk Phongpaichit, in *A History of Thailand*, noted that Khmer and Dvaravati cultures were more used to constructing large ponds in flatlands to trap rainfall. Both Tais and Mon–Khmers probably shared their farming expertise with each other, and Tais were inspired by the Dvaravati and Khmer art.

Thai culture's development then became even more enchanting because Sukhothai imbibed art and ideas from several other cultures at the same time:

- Sukhothai adopted Theravada practices from Sri Lanka that followed the Buddha's original teachings about simple living. These traditions avoided the Mahayana speculations that expanded the universe into deities and domains that zoom into outer space and beyond. Thais, accustomed to living in small communities and promoting harmony with local spirits, found Sri Lanka's down-to-earth Theravada more appealing. Sukhothai's early kings imported monks and artists from Sri Lanka as they built shrines and monasteries.
- Sukkhothai also imported monks and artists from towns down on the peninsula, near the border with modern Malaysia. The

peninsula had been an international trading hub for many centuries because water surrounded it on three sides and it was
between India and China. The city Nakhon Si Thammarat was
the peninsula's Theravada spiritual center and it had a close
relationship with Sri Lanka; Sukhothai's king brought one of its
monks to his capital to become its patriarch.

The peninsula already had an ancient cultural heritage.
People had built an empire called Srivijaya in the seventh century (where Malaysia and western Indonesia currently are), and
it remained the main power in the region for the next four centuries.[16] It coexisted with Angkor, but both were different in key
ways. While the latter was centered on rice farming, the Malay
state focused more on the sea. It straddled the straits of Malacca
and controlled trade between India and China, as Malacca
would in the 15th century. Chinese thought its forest products
had medicinal properties, and they traded silks, lacquers, and
ceramics for them. Its main city was near Palembang, in southeastern Sumatra, and it contrasted with Angkor.[17] The historian
John N. Miksic wrote that its people probably built their homes
over water rather than on dry land, and that the city was several
miles long and often only one house wide.[18] A visitor wouldn't
have seen enormous stone temples, but the endless line of stilt
homes bustling with families selling goods must have been pulse-
quickening too.

The Srivijaya Empire declined in the late 11th century, after
a southern Indian state called Chola attacked it to gain more
control of Southeast Asian commerce. Several port towns then
shared the trade in the straits, and they retained Srivijaya's artistic influence. The old empire had fashioned many refined statues of Buddhas and Mahayana deities. Some were slender, with
bodies in soft S curves, and others were decked with thin garlands of jewelry. These elegant images, which contrasted with the
massiveness of many Khmer temples, probably resonated with
the people, who lived by the water, sailed in limber boats, and
valued the physical and mental deftness that ocean-going trade
requires. They probably inspired some of Sukhothai's artists.

I found Srivijaya's environment as appealing as Thailand's when I visited fishing villages in northeastern Malaysia during my 2007 trip. As in Thailand, dense greenery surrounded intimate communities that emphasized politeness, but their environments were different too. The water in the lagoons reflected crowds of boats and palm trees so that the ripples seemed as animated as the fronds blowing in the breezes. Forests of stilts rose from the waters and supported wooden homes and planked walkways. Most Thais were more oriented to land, but those who migrated to or traded with coastal communities still must have related to the combination of animated energy and cozy villages, and to the flowing art forms.

- Burmese connections also grew. Pagan and Sri Lanka had shared Theravada forms of worship since the 11th century. A Mon-speaking society in what is now southeastern Burma also influenced Thai culture. One of its leading monks was brought to Sukhothai because it had become a Theravada stronghold. Both cultures in Burma built stupas in forms that slowly tapered.

- Chinese artisans were moving into Sukhothai, and they influenced Thai ceramics. Chinese artists also added design elements to lacquerware and mother-of-pearl inlay, and their zodiacal animals appear on some Thai artworks. Thais assimilated their images and ideas in their own ways, fusing them with the wealth of other cultures' traditions that they had absorbed.

- Of course Indian influences were pervasive (including Buddhism and Hindu mythology) but many came secondhand from lands other than India. Theravada traditions were brought from Sri Lanka, and much of the Hindu art came from the Khmers. The Indian heritage was thus adopted in a loosser way than it probably would have been if it all had come directly from one Indian state. By assimilating it indirectly from multiple cultures, Thais could more easily synthesize it with their own sensibilities, adopting what they found appealing and ignoring what they didn't.

Contact between Sukhothai and the peninsula, Angkor, Sri Lanka, Burma, indigenous Mon people, India, and the Chinese diaspora was continuous. All these cultures added to Thais' mixtures of ideas, artistic images, and rituals as their own kingdoms emerged. These international connections helped establish Thais' assumptions about the most fundamental forms and ideas.

Art forms and ways of perceiving and thinking that mix grace and animation became prevalent in Thai culture, and have usually remained so, because they converged from an enormous number of places, times, interactions between people, and experiences with the natural environment. People shared ceremonies and pilgrimage sites, traded goods, visited wats, saw graceful shrines and processions of monks, heard the same music, emphasized deference to social superiors, believed in local spirits, and shared the rice growing cycle and the prominence of waterways. All of these converged over time into people's shared experiences, and this provided them with a common field of meanings that has been uniquely Thai.[19]

The West's focus on three-dimensional perspective, abstract linear relationships, and distinct objects and their masses also converged from many political centers and an enormous number of influences. Florence, Rome, Venice, Byzantium, and northern Europe developed these influences together. An untold number of interactions that fleshed them out created the West's fundamental assumptions about how the world coheres. These influences were initially inspired by ancient Greece and Rome, their natural environments, and antiquity's fusion with the Christian Middle Ages—the roots they grew from were already very deep and widespread. Great Renaissance artists later developed them further, and secondary artists spread them even more.

So if you ask what made Thailand Thai, or what made the West Western, your horizon opens into an international tapestry with infinite creativity—with limitless abilities to blend multiple societies and to generate new ideas and works of art. Instead of being bound to one idea, art form, or general perspective and treating it as universal truth which holds all things and experiences to its terms, your view can become liberated so that it widens into the diversity of people's ideas and their interactions with each other and with the environment. This convergence of cultures and nature constitutes assumptions about what ideas and art forms are most fundamental. When you examine your innermost thoughts (the ideas that your culture and personality have used to cohere with), your view can shift from one conventional perspective to a field of multiple cultures and historical periods that you can enjoy for the rest of your life, and which can give you one new perspective of the world after another.

You can see limitless abundance in the ideas and art forms that your culture has treated as fundamental, and in aspects of your daily life, including your cuisine, interpersonal behavior, and objects that you live closely with. They all glimmer when you see them in enough ways. So does the Roman arch. So do the vegetal patterns on Khmer sculpted friezes. So do the muscles on Michelangelo's *David*. And so does every Thai stupa. As you keep studying multiple cultural landscapes and comparing them with each other, your perspective can increasingly shift to this radiance. Everything around you, from high art to everyday objects, can become luminous. It can shine, not only in a way that reflects its own cultural milieu, but all societies around the globe.

Sukhothai's synthesis of cultural patterns created one of Thailand's most admired art forms: the Sukhothai Buddha statue. Gentle curves flow from his crown to his toes. A flame flares from the top of his head in tall, thin swirls. His hair's curls are smaller than most other types of Buddha statues' curls. His face is long and oval, and the small mouth turns slightly upwards into a mellow smile—sacred *sabai*. This gentle vitality extends down his body. Long, sinuous arms swing from his broad shoulders, and the torso tapers into a narrow waist. A long, thin cloth drapes over his left shoulder and curves down his chest. The entire statue flows in a way that's both suave and animated.

People brought the Sukhothai Buddha into their hearts and homes, and spread it all over the country and to overseas Thai communities. I've seen it in many restaurants in America and Europe. Carol Stratton and Miriam McNair Scott saw uniquely Thai aesthetics in it. Sukhothai imported Sri Lankan artists and monks, but most Sri Lankan statues from that time were made of stone while Sukhothai often used bronze. Stone expresses solidity and permanence; bronze looks fluid and energized. Thais polished the bronze to appear even smoother. The sculpture seems to transcend its own material and become a gentle spiritual energy.

Stratton and McNair Scott felt that the poses that the two lands favored also reflect their different cultures. Sri Lankans more often portrayed the Buddha sitting still in meditation. In contrast, Sukhothai artists preferred to show him with his right hand pointing to the ground, in the famous gesture of invoking the earth as a witness. The demon Mara ruled the kingdom of desire and tried to thwart the Buddha's enlightenment—Mara would lose his power if an enlightened being could teach people how to extinguish their cravings. The soon-to-be Buddha countered his assault by pointing to the earth to prove his merit, which he had earned over hundreds of past lives. A goddess called Dharani, who personified the earth, wrung her hair and water from his donations in previous lives gushed out, flooded the ground, and flushed Mara and his soldiers away. He then attained enlightenment and became the Buddha. So this statue represents a pivotal moment, but its energy flows in gentle curves that render it elegant. These serene forms buffer the clash with Mara. The Buddha softly smiles as he has just mastered desire.[20]

Figure 25. Sukhothai-style Buddha, Wat Traimit, Bangkok.

Sukhothai made a type of Buddha statue that is rare in Sri Lanka, called the Walking Buddha. This figure strolls as calmly as an amble around a wat. One of the temples a little south of its capital's ritual center (Wat Chetuphon) has a tall brick structure with a niche that contains a large walking Buddha. The old shrine for the city god, where people sacrificed buffalos, is nearby. The Buddha's gliding steps seem to calm all the spirits in the area.

Sukhothai art permeated homes and hearts in other ways. In the 14th century its capital and a satellite town called Si Satchanalai developed a ceramics industry, and people all over Southeast Asia desired their products. Potters fashioned countless little figures that added cheer to homes. They created many types of miniature bowls and boxes for storing cosmetics, spices, drugs, and accessories for betel chewing. Many mix soft brown and white tones; these neutral colors are in harmony with nature. The minute sizes and gentle hues complemented the browns and beiges of wooden homes and the surrounding greenery.

Potters also made little human and animal figures. The animals might have been offerings to local spirits. Elephants and birds were especially popular, and many of their bodies are so round that they look like toys. The figures' business might have been animistic but their creators added fun to it.

They also made small female human figurines. Many kneel and hold a baby to their breasts. The women smile and the bodies of some are as rotund as the animal figures. They might have been used to encourage fertility for child bearing or crops, but many were decapitated, and some historians have thought that dangers from spirits might have been ritually transferred to them to protect their owners.[21] If so, their smiles made the potential conflict safe.

All these ceramics added suave touches to homes. As families sat on mats and shared Mother Rice's blessings, people imbibed messages that the world hangs together in these gentle forms and colors.

Sukhothai pottery became a major international industry. The Sawankhalok site included about 1,000 kilns over a six-mile stretch along both sides of the Yom River. Ceramics were exported through Ayutthaya to China and much of island Southeast Asia. Ayutthaya and Chiang Mai clashed many times for control of the kilns. Even the political rivalries spread the charming aesthetics throughout the land.

The Belgian man who co-owned the guesthouse I stayed in drove me to a wat that a recently deceased monk had built which showed the old aesthetics in a more humorous way. He told me that the holy man was an alcoholic and that empty beer bottles were found embedded in some of the walls. Little gilded Buddha statues in the Sukhothai style serenely sat on the second-story railings, glittering among the trees' foliage. Pieces of colored glass lodged in the walls added cheerful reds, greens, and blues to the white stucco. Thais' tolerance of contradictions, the continuity of happy art forms, and the abundant greenery merged and encouraged more mellow happiness.

I met several especially delightful people in an old satellite town of Sukhothai's called Kamphaeng Phet. Two grounds with a large cluster of ancient shrines spread within walking distance from each other. After exploring the first, I arrived at an intersection of dirt roads and pondered which one to take. A smiling middle-aged woman immediately asked if I needed help and walked with me to the other location.

The second site sprawls over a wide area so that many visitors rent bikes to tour it. I walked in order to experience the place as people did when it was newly built. Lots of bell-shaped stupas blended with trees, but I couldn't savor this dream world for long because it lacked a restaurant. Because there were just two junk food counters in the area, I bought some potato chips and started munching under a small pavilion to escape the midday sun. In the corner of my eye, I saw a big yellow dog sheepishly trudging over. I wondered how he could feed himself in an area with little food and few tourists. He stopped in front of me and looked up with two of the most plaintive eyes I ever saw.

I gave him the chips, trotted back to the counter, and bought more for him. But given the risk of rabies, I didn't want him to become a companion and start following me. Unable to bring myself to shoe him away, I snuck off immediately after dumping the second bag in front of him. I thus ate little for the energy to walk all day in the heat, but I figured, No worries, I'll pig out back in Sukhothai.

I left the archeological site around four o'clock, in what seemed like enough time to find a tuk tuk to the station for the last bus. I arrived at the main road and walked, and walked, but saw no tuk tuks. I then passed the other ritual center and still didn't see any. I briskly walked along the road that ran through the ancient city wall and into the modern town, but still no tuk tuks. The station was about five miles away and I didn't have enough time or energy to leg it.

I was beginning to feel as desperate as the dog when I reached a large, plain white modern building with a flat roof. I ventured through the parking lot gates to a little guardhouse and asked where I could find a tuk tuk. One of the three men lounging there told me that there were no tuk tuks in Kamphaeng Phet, but one said that he was about to drive home and offered to take me to the station. As we left he told me that he was a policeman—in my haste I had wandered into the local police station. After being conned by the cop in Cambodia, I expected the same request. Feeling like a dolt for impulsively walking into an official place I knew nothing about, I offered him a little money. He refused with a smile and chatted the whole way. He said he was fifty-three and talked about his children. Like many Thais, he looked ten years younger than his age.

So nothing big happened when I was in Sukhothai or Ayutthaya. Much of Thailand's cultural wealth is in the little everyday things. But when you look closely at them, they reveal an environment that never runs out of enchantments. This made my trip to Thailand better and better as it progressed.

We will enter my favorite Thai kingdom in the next chapter. Afterwards, we'll explore the method for finding paradise on earth.

This method will show how to spearhead a revolution in thinking that would be in step with our globalized world. A key aspect of this shift is the ability to venture beyond the ways your culture shapes your thought and perceptions. A real revolution in thought is to master your way of thinking and transcend it to explore other ways, and to synthesize unforeseen views so that you see things in ways you never previously thought possible. A true revolution goes further than expanding from one viewpoint into another and then treating the new view as the only reality. Instead, it expands into one after another and synthesizes them. The world keeps getting bigger and more able to engender creativity and happiness. You become increasingly free and able to find more wonders around you.

Your perspective shifts from a habitual way of seeing to an environment in which you keep finding more beauty, and in which all cultures and people shine on each other so that their beauty is increasingly exposed—in other words, paradise. We can nurture each other and expose each other's wealth until the field of connections we live in becomes pervaded with love.

CHAPTER 12

⌒

NORTHERN THAILAND: FROM HOME COOKING TO INFINITY

THE NEXT PLACE in my Thai journey was my favorite: the fabled Lan Na kingdom. It was the most remote of the three main Thai states before the whole country was unified—it was the farthest north and the most land-locked. Chiang Mai has been its cultural and political capital. Though Lan Na was established in the 13th century, its traditions still thrive.

The ride from Sukhothai made it clear that I was approaching a different world. The scenery suddenly changed from flat rice fields to steep forested mountains which the road nimbly wound between. The anticipation built as I looked up at the slopes covered in dark green. I wondered, What mysteries will I find there?

Few Westerners ventured that far north during Ayutthaya's heyday. People had to trek for many days to get there until a railroad was built in 1921. Thailand's government down in Bangkok finally organized Lan Na as a province in 1932. So its culture had a long time to develop its own architecture, sculpture, festivals, cuisine, music, and mixture of ethnicities.

However, Lan Na is still unmistakably Thai and Southeast Asian. Its people are as fun-loving, animistic, and piously Buddhist as any others in Thailand. Many Western visitors fall in love with Lan Na, and I found it easy to see why.

Chiang Mai is my favorite Thai city. It has about 200,000 residents, and nearly one million call its metropolitan area home. It is large enough to be cosmopolitan, unlike the other Thai towns I had just vis-ited, but it's more relaxed than Bangkok's bump and grind. Part of the old capital now has a college town's atmosphere, since a major university was established there in 1964—several used bookstores and quirky people who frequent them grace the town's center. Many restaurants host live music, and most performers are Thais singing and playing guitars. Chiang Mai puts on lots of festivals and organizes a huge night bazaar near the Ping River. The town swings.

Many tourists and expats visit Chiang Mai, and some old timers complain that they have made it more crowded and commercial, but most visitors cluster in the center of town (where several popular bars operate) and Nimmanhaemin Road (which has recently become a fashional upscale haunt). Many surrounding neighborhoods still feel like a small town, with winding roads and wooden homes surrounded by trees. Everyone can thus enjoy both worlds. Wealthy Bangkok residents on vacations join the fun. So far, modern times have often added to the old patterns of diverse people in a tolerant and eclectic society that allows plenty of room for the unexpected and for people with unusual personalities to live.

I liked Chiang Mai as soon as I saw it. During the drive along the Ping River to my hotel, I surveyed its small crop of mid-rise skyscrapers. The tallest had about 25 floors and most buildings were white, so they didn't overwhelm the rest of the town and they blended with the trees into a soft color scheme. My hotel stood by the riverside and it was the first large modern building I entered after leaving Bangkok's airport. Surprised by its size and glitz, I felt like a country boy when I first walked into the lobby. My room was spacious and modern, but I was reminded that this was Thailand when I left it. I had been playing guitar on my bed and a cleaning woman greeted me in the hall with an ear-to-ear grin. "You play guitar!" The Thai custom of having fun on the job is flourishing in Lan Na.

The old part of Chiang Mai is about half a mile from the river. It's within the remains of an almost square wall that was first built in the 13th century and later reconstructed. The enclosure houses some of Thailand's most beautiful wats, and more temples ornament the land outside the wall.

But since this was my first large Thai town, I was looking forward to some nightlife. A young British man in Sukhothai had told me about a rock guitarist named Took, and my *Lonely Planet* guidebook also raved about him. In the evening I headed for the club where he regularly performed.

Several bars and nightclubs pulsated near the river. A couple of joints hosted classic rock bands. Many of their patrons were forty-something white men in jeans and tank tops, clasping beer mugs and smoking cigarettes. Modern jazz breezed from another place. This was the first jazz band I heard on this trip, and I was impressed by the guitarist's fluid playing—a lot smoother than my jazz fumblings. The whole street had a pleasant vibe, with a mixture of convivial locals and Westerners. One Thai man asked me where I was from and if I needed anything. When I told him that I was just waiting to see a guitarist perform he gave me a hug.

I reached Took's place and sat at a table near the stage. The opening act was a Thai reggae group. The lead singer/guitarist sported dreadlocks that tumbled to his waist. He sang with a smile rather than Bob Marley's pained expressions.

Took and his band then hit the stage. He was tall and thin, with waist-length hair and a mischievous smile that often flashed. He played a lot of blues-based classic rock from the late 60s and early 70s, by Jimi Hendrix, Eric Clapton, and the Allman Brothers, and he unleashed more aggression and improvisation than I found in other Thai rock bands. His old guitar had a clear and biting tone like a Fender Stratocaster copy. His playing was sometimes more showy than musical—he would quickly rub his left hand up and down the strings without fingering any notes. He sounded like a sloppy Stevie Ray Vaughn, but his joy was so infectious that it was hard to be critical. He clinked his little glass of what looked like vodka to the drinks of a couple at a small table next to the stage, strutted over to the rhythm guitarist, and held down the notes on his sacred sword while the rhythm player strummed. It was corny stuff, but he was enjoying himself and relating to his audience so much, and his playing was so energetic, that it was a great show. A young American man said, "He's incredible, isn't he?"

The drummer was in constant motion. Trying to hit all the skins at once, he seemed like a well-behaved Keith Moon.

As in most other bars on that street, the audience was an equal mixture of Thais and Westerners grooving together. The vibe reminded me of popular idealized images of Woodstock that spread from that concert's documentary movie, but on the cozy scale of a Thai village. There were lots of smiles in the audience and on stage, and no scowls.

Lan Na has a colorful history. Its seminal ruler, Mangrai, was born in 1239, and he inherited his father's throne in 1259. Within five years the ambitious youth expanded his state to the south and west. By then he had established Chiang Rai (a town northeast of Chiang Mai, near the borders of modern Burma and Laos) as the political center. It's near the Mekong and thus in a good location for managing trade routes and overseeing subordinate lords' lands. But in the 1290s, Mangrai founded Chiang Mai (which means *New City*) as the capital. He had conquered a legendary Mon-dominated kingdom a little to the south called Hariphunchai (Figure 24), so his new location was in a central place. Chiang Mai was ready for fusing cultures.

The Chiang Mai chronicles tell lively stories about Lan Na's founding. Mangrai was searching for the best site for Chiang Mai and saw a pack of wolves trying to catch two hog-deer (hunting dogs were the aggressors in some versions—monks and court officials wrote several chronicles and stored them in Lan Na's many wats). The deer confronted their attackers and forced them to flee. Mangrai liked their spunk, and local elders confirmed that this was a special place.

The chronicles added Thai touches to Indian concepts of a vast universe. The texts start with a history of a lineage of hundreds of thousands of kings who were connected with the Buddha. For example, there were 276,275 rulers from Mahasamantaraja to Vessantara (the latter was the last of the Buddha's prior incarnations). The chronicles thereby grounded Lan Na's royal line in Indian concepts of time as inconceivably long, and in the Buddha's merit. This encouraged people to honor royalty, but the perspective quickly shifts from the huge Indian panoramas to Lan Na's own kings, and it takes a Thai turn.

In the 14th century an aesthetically ugly merchant named Ngua Hong lived in an important town on the Mekong called Chiang Saen. He and King Kham Fu were close friends and Ngua Hong stayed in the royal palace whenever he visited the capital, and always received full hospitality. A beautiful noble woman and a wife of the king bathed his feet, even though they considered him homely. Then one day the king decided to play a trick on his friend.

King Kham Fu took a shaved monkey, painted skin on him with gum from trees, and stuck white cotton on him to look like body hair. He sealed him in a box and had two court jesters carry it to Ngua Hong with a message that the king is sending him this handsome servant.

Ngua Hong was furious! Beauty meant a lot in Lan Na, so he couldn't stand people making fun of his appearance. He chased the two jokers but they outran him and escaped. Kham Fu knew that his friend was in a huff, so he traveled to Chiang Saen to calm him. When he arrived at his home, one of Ngua Hong's wives greeted him and bathed his feet. The woman was beautiful, and she and the king were both aroused. He signaled his desire to her with his hands, and both bedded together for the night.

Ngua Hong never found this out, but a week later the king went to a river that flows into the Mekong to wash his hair. A water ogress reared up and pulled him down into her lair, and his corpse surfaced seven days later.

This sounds like a folk tale which was incorporated to illustrate Buddhist ethics (control your cravings or else). But the story is told with a sense of fun and a love of beauty that can make people more attached to the world which the faith is supposed to liberate them from. Sure I want to reach nirvana, but can I wait a while and enjoy more of life? It's hard not to think like this in northern Thailand, with its verdant valleys between mountains enshrouded in mists and its mild climate. It brings Indian views of the vast cosmos down to earth and encourages people to relish the world's delights. Count me among the faithful.

Like Sukhothai, Chiang Mai must respect its mountain spirits. Pu Sae and Ya Sae guard the city and roam the slopes of Doi Suthep and Doi Kham. This mountain punctuates the western side of the town. Like Sukhothai's western hills, it was associated with wild energy, and the two spirits and their son were once cannibals. The Buddha traveled through there and the family stalked him, hankering to sink their teeth into his golden skin. He discovered this while meditating and pressed his foot on a boulder. Locals have claimed that the imprint is still visible, so it became a shrine. Awed by his power, the parents and son sat down while he lectured. They gave up cannibalism and the son even became a monk. When they died their souls returned to Doi Suthep.

Once a year locals have sacrificed a water buffalo to satisfy the spirits' appetites. A medium becomes possessed and increasingly uncouth, and begins to chomp on the raw meat and guzzle whiskey. This placates the spirits so that communal harmony is maintained. The occasional breach of order quells potentially dangerous phantoms and renders them friendly.

Lan Na also became a beacon of Buddhist piety. Mangrai and other kings over the next two centuries imported the Theravada faith from Sri Lanka and bejeweled the realm with wats. Lan Na followed it so well that it hosted the Eighth World Buddhist Council in 1477 to purify the Pali Canon (the collection of texts on which the Theravada is based). Golden stupas shone from the hills, forests, and city center. Monks in flowing robes ambled through the winding footpaths and bustling market towns. Many Buddha statues had names and were renowned for certain powers. Some had reputations for bringing rain, and people carried them through towns in processions.

Locals conducted many festivals that were enlivened by northern Thailand's wealth of flowers. Thais, people from Yunnan, Burmese, and native Mon and Lawa people rubbed shoulders in their own costumes. The feasts of colors must have equaled those in wats.

People traveled in caravans through the twisting roads and pathways that crisscrossed the land, and by boats that plied the rivers—they exchanged cultures in many places. Many areas in Lan Na held revolving bazaars and villages took turns hosting markets. Folks shared religious ideas and artistic images in everyday settings, surrounded by playing children, haggling sellers, singing birds, barking dogs, rascally monkeys, waddling ducks, and aromas of food. In thousands of places, the loftiest art mixed with home cooking.

But life in Lan Na wasn't always so idyllic, and the Chiang Mai chronicles detail many wars that it fought. Ayutthaya was expanding northwards, and with more land for growing rice and more commerce from the sea, it was too powerful for the more mountainous northern kingdom to take on toe-to-toe. But Lan Na had a brilliant king, Tilokaracha, who enjoyed a long reign from 1441 to 1487. He brought the realm some military victories and much cultural glory (he was the one who hosted the Buddhist council).

However, Lan Na's fortunes quickly waned in the early 16th century, and it was largely forgotten while Ayutthaya flexed its muscles. Wars with its southern neighbor and the many religious building projects taxed the state's finances. Royal succession disputes added more chaos and the kingdom became vulnerable to invasion. In 1558 the Burmese king Bayinnaung was able to take it without a battle because its funds were drained. The Burmese ruled it for most of the next 200 years.

Lan Na suffered more calamities in the late 18th century. It was trapped between two heavyweight fighters as Ayutthaya and Burma slugged it out. In the 1770s the Thais took Chiang Mai in their quest for independence from the Burmese, but it was so devastated after all the fighting that everyone abandoned it.

Chiang Mai finally began to enjoy a renaissance in the 19th century. People resettled there and it prospered from growing industries, especially logging. Many new wats were built and they now blend with the buildings from Lan Na's heyday. The old traditions of mixing a wealth of cultural and natural forms are blooming again. I met several people in northern Thailand who were proud of this, and they said that they didn't like Bangkok because it's too crowded and corrupt. They considered Lan Na to be the best example of Thai culture.

Several friendly tuk tuk drivers lined the street by my hotel, eager to take passengers to the town's center. Old Chiang Mai is within the city walls. We took one of the main streets, which bisects the city from east to west. It ends at Chiang Mai's most revered wat, Phra Singh, which is one of the best places to discover what makes Lan Na special.

The compound glints with buildings in the region's distinct architecture. As in other Thai temples, the vihara and stupa are central structures, but they have unique features that make the loftiest artistic flights tangible for ordinary people.

One of Lan Na architecture's most famous traits is the vihara roof—it's one of my all-time favorite art forms. It is composed of several levels of gables that sit on top of each other. There are usually three or five sets of them (one in the middle and one or two radiating from each end). The middle stack is the highest and the end ones are the lowest. The whole set cascades like two waterfalls flowing in opposite directions.

Figure 26. Wat Phra That Chae Haeng, Nan.

The bottoms of the lowest stacks are often near the ground, sometimes close enough to be touched. So the loftiest part of the temple comes down to us. The entire roof set flows from the sky like a shower of grace and makes the heavens tangible for common folks.

Figure 27. Wat Phan Tao, Chiang Mai.

The bottom corners of the roofs add zest to the shower. Edges that line the gables at each end of the vihara are shaped like a naga's body. It slithers down from the peak, and its head rears up at the bottom into sharp points at its crest and nose to force evil spirits to back off. A flame shooting from the top of its head makes it appear even more potent.

Intricate wooden carvings in the upper triangle of the gable add even more tang. They're often painted and gilded in bright colors, and they curve in flowing lines and thorny points. Many represent the forest so that vines, flowers, and animals intertwine. On some panels, inlaid colored glass pieces add shimmering reds, greens, and blues. Many locals have believed that evil spirits are ugly and that they flee when they see their own reflections.

So the whole roof balances heaven and earth, as well as grace and energy. It's an irresistible invitation to come inside, and it often made me feel that I was about to get a friendly version of spirituality.

I always enjoyed taking my shoes off, climbing the few steps onto the portico, and feeling its sunbathed warmth on my way to the entrance. The interiors of Lan Na viharas are smaller and more intimate than Ayutthaya's largest. Walls, pillars, and ceilings are often painted in friendly reds, golds, and whites. Stenciled gold leaf patterns often adorn the pillars, and lacquered and carved rosettes often line ceilings. The spiritual realm is made human with cheerful colors and natural forms, and worshipers mingle with them as they walk around and sit on the floor to bow to the altar.

The side walls contain scenes of the Buddha's past lives from Indian tales called *Jatakas*, and Lan Na artists made some of the best of these paintings in Thailand. Most are from the 19th and 20th centuries and were thus created later than the founding of Wat Prah Singh (1345), but people probably painted images of the Buddha during Lan Na's acme too. Today's existing scenes show people how to emulate him and accumulate merit for a better rebirth or nirvana. The story of each incarnation is about a specific virtue. In this way, locals receive models in palpable terms about how to live.

The most popular Jataka in Thailand is about the last incarnation before the life in which Siddhartha became the Buddha. He was then

King Vessantara, who showed generosity by giving all of his possessions away. Thais are taught to be generous from an early age. The five-year-old daughter of a California restaurant owner once came to my table with a carton of ice cream and said, "One ice cream, two spoons!"

Another popular Jataka is of Sama, who exemplified filial piety by risking his life for his parents. Honoring them, especially Mother, strongly resonates in Thai hearts. I discovered this two years before, when my mom had a stroke. I had frequented a nearby Thai restaurant enough to know the servers. One asked, "How are you?" I told her about my mom, and she gushed when she learned that I was taking care of her. She was so effusive that I felt that I had to balance her mushy "Aaawh!" by joking, "I'll get my butt kicked if I don't."

Many Lan Na paintings thus show the Buddha in personal terms. Jataka scenes in the north, and in the rest of Thailand, usually focus on specific episodes. Interactions between people are often more prominent there than they are in Indian and Tibetan portrayals of cosmic realms, which are so vast that they dwarf the viewer and dissolve him into nothingness. Thais more often emphasize daily life in their scenes and thereby give all mentalities a place in spirituality.

Folksy scenes often surround the Buddha's past incarnations. People chat, women smoke, locals trade, children play, couples flirt, musicians perform, and women wash clothes in rivers. These daily events are sometimes as prominent as the holy stories. Locals can shift between revering the great teacher and enjoying everyday life at their own paces.

Lan Na Viharas contain other charms. An ornately carved wooden pulpit for lecturing graces many of them. People sometimes hang long, slim banners with painted scenes of stylized zodiacal animals, stupas, or the Buddha's life from the roof beams. Offerings glimmer around the main statue, amid arrangements of orchids, candles, and incense sticks that mix with all the other happy colors and forms. So Lan Na viharas balance intimacy, good behavior, unearthly elegance, folksy paintings, sensual stimulation, and cordial people kneeling in front of the altar. *Sabai* indeed!

The main Buddha statue faces people as they enter the vihara, and Lan Na developed one of Thailand's most admired types. Its artistry ranks with Sukhothai statues' exquisiteness, and its style spread all over northern Thailand.

The Lan Na-style Buddha is earthier than the Sukhothai Buddha's super-refined forms. Its fleshy face impressed me the most. It's a bit chubby, but not enough to diminish the statue's dignity. Solidity is conveyed by the face's square-like shape. In contrast, the Sukhothai statue's is oval. But the Lan Na-style Buddha's face isn't a perfect square because the lines of the cheeks and under the chin slightly curve and become round in the corners. This seamless integration of a square and round form gives the face both sturdiness and softness. It also has a little round chin that's as dainty as a baby's. This motherly tenderness is balanced by the large masculine hair curls on top of the head (Sukhothai curls are small). I saw this type of face in wats and museums all over Chiang Mai. It attunes heaven and earth as well as vihara roofs do.

The statue's body also harmonizes them. Its chest is broad and the arms are shorter and thicker than the Sukhothai Buddha's. But the arms are rounded and smooth rather than muscled like ancient Greek and Italian Renaissance statues. The body is both strong and soft. The soon-to-be Buddha is calling the earth as a witness (like the Sukhothai statue), so he is in the process of enlightenment, exhibiting both heroically firm will and compassion. This type of Lan Na Buddha statue is called the Phra Singh. *Singh* means *lion* in Thai, but this kingly soul is also a gentle man that people can pray to when they're troubled.

A legend says that monks in Chiang Mai felt that Sukhothai's art had become too unrealistic, so they brought the original Phra Singh statue from Sri Lanka and used it as a model for many others in order to return sculpture to pure forms. Art historians actually don't agree on whether the Phra Singh or Sukhothai type emerged first, but Lan Na artists soon made statues with features of both and then synthesized new styles from them (the most renowned are called Thai Ping and Thai Yuan). Sukhothai artists learned from the north and fashioned Lan Na-style Buddhas in their own workshops. So sculptors during Lan Na's golden age were mixing the most pleasing aspects of both styles and creating new images. People could see thousands of stylistic mixtures from this period as they traveled through the land.

Figure 28. The Phra Singh Buddha, Chiang Mai.

Figure 29. Heaven and earth in balance at Wat Chiang Man, Chiang Mai.

The stupa typically is a wat's tallest structure, so people can see it shining over the other buildings. Lan Na styles have three sections. The first is a high square base with indented corners. This gives shrines solidity that grounds them in spite of their heavenly flights. The central section is a series of increasingly small squares, octagons, and circles. It forms a smooth transition to the highest level, which is a bell shape with a tall conical spire on top. Lan Na stupas blend Sukhothai dreaminess with Planet Earth. Every wat's spire's form is unique, so I saw a new variety every time I explored a temple.

The real magic in Lan Na wats happens when you appreciate all of their features:

- Flowing stacks of vihara roofs,
- Intricate wooden carvings of plants and animals,
- Lively wall paintings of the Buddha's past lives,
- Phra Singh-style Buddha sculptures,
- Stupas that are both solid and soaring,
- Banners and multicolored offerings of flowers,
- Candles and incense sticks,
- Serene orange-robed monks,
- Gentle locals in the act of worshiping,
- Chirping birds and vibrant foliage that mesh wats' art forms with nature's vitality.

They all comprise an environment in which people can enjoy more types of Thai art with endless mixtures of forms and colors that are both fervent and comely. But Lan Na art has many of its own folksy touches. Though I marveled at how vihara roofs seem to come down from the heavens, some locals liken them to a hen spreading her wings to shelter her chicks. Though northern Thai wats can be interpreted in different ways and each temple is unique, one man in an old Lan Na town called Nan told me, "All Lan Na wats are beautiful." As in many other Thai arts, the perspective can meander without coming to a stopping point. And who would want to stop enjoying it? The art in Lan Na wats both expresses mystical forces and accepts us as we are.

I frequented an Indian restaurant that was half a block from my hotel and completely open to the street, and found myself immersed in scenes as savory as the wats' paintings. Towns all over Southeast Asia pulsate with streets with eclectic mixtures of pedestrians, bikes, motor scooters, slinky cats, fruit stands, vegetable sellers, and cute little cars with equally eclectic assortments of parts (though you can add a few luxury cars and SUVs in Chiang Mai). People's identities integrate with surroundings that are both vibrant and calm. Roads in Indian towns are often more intense. They're louder, bumpier, dustier, smellier, and more germ-ridden, but they too feel like a big river of life that you're absorbed in. Roads in Southeast Asian communities are often more soothing, and most restaurants have open fronts which allow their customers to become part of this flow. Lots of Westerners find it addictive and it's still in my system.

People walked off their dinners in the night market. The sidewalks on both sides of the streets were lined with makeshift stalls displaying T-shirts, luggage, jewelry, purses, shoes, CDs, cellphones, chicken satays, and fruit. Tourists have transformed it into rivers of commercialism that sometimes made me think of the cheesy souvenir shops at San Francisco's Fisherman's Wharf, but the warm night air, the crowd's relaxed pace, and the lively medleys of trinkets reminded me that I was in Thailand. Its tolerant mixtures can beautify almost anything.

During a day trip to a historic town called Lamphun my driver asked, "Are you married?"

"No, I'm single."

"That's good! No yap yap yap!"

His response was very Thai. Several people that I later met in Africa and the Middle East expressed puzzlement about my bachelorhood. A few became a bit contentious. A woman in Mauritius declared, "You must get married and bring your wife back to Mauritius!" So when I arrived in Jordan and my driver asked if I'm conjoined, I expected a little tussle. I tried to avoid it by repeating the Thai driver's "No yap yap yap!" to him.

"No son!"

People in Africa, Arabic countries, and Turkey are sometimes more direct than Thais have traditionally been. Family is basic in all the places I visited during this trip. It's central in Thailand too. Many Thais' worst fear is to be alone in the world, open to its dangers and lacking the group's warmth. Being California-born with Irish blood, I'm from cultures that value freedom, individuality, and wide-open horizons. Additionally, as a native of male-and technology-dominated Silicon Valley, I've found it hard to meet women to share cultural flights with—hairy geeks greatly outnumber devatas, and most women who move there focus on technical careers. Many things have thus encouraged me to be happy without a life-long relationship with one person. But most Thais would be uncomfortable with my amount of independence. Yet my driver still complimented my lifestyle. Thai children are taught to be sensitive to others' feelings and to say what they want to hear, even if they don't mean it. This is especially so when they're with social superiors.

A woman in Bangkok also asked me if I'm married. When I said "No," she asked, "Are you gay?" with a laugh like a sparrow's fluttering. "I'm sorry!" she immediately said with a bright smile. I told her that I can travel anywhere in the world, and she responded, "Oh, I know! You like freedom!"

She was from Isaan, which is a region in eastern Thailand. It's poorer than the well-established Chao Phraya basin, and much of its soil is more barren. People move from there to Bangkok in search of menial jobs, and many city folks see them as simpletons, even though many farming communities in ancient times had formed in their homeland. Her spicy response wasn't surprising because some Isaan people are a little less reserved. But her laugh and quick apology were thoroughly charming. After her little breach of protocol, she too affirmed my situation.

Yes, both people can be accused of fawning. I enjoyed the honesty and directness of Africans and Middle Easterners. They told me what they really thought, so we interacted as human beings rather than within constraints of social roles. But Thai thinking tolerates diversity and values politeness so that people traditionally haven't felt a need to confront each other unless social status or economic security is at stake. And both Thais were having fun. My driver often laughed. I fell asleep in the back seat on the way back to Chiang Mai, and when I woke up he said, "You sleep!" and chortled away. No matter how mundane something is, Thais can make it fun.

I hired a tuk tuk driver to take me to another wat, and had a meeting that I didn't bargain for when he told me that its master wanted to see me. He was lounging outside on a plastic chair and told me to sit next to him. Middle-aged, balding, and with a deep, booming voice, he projected the gravity of the school teacher I saw in Ayutthaya's museum. He gave me a handful of Mandarin oranges and began to lecture to me. The gist was, "Be good and enjoy life," which is very Thai. But his talk had an even earthier side which he surely didn't intend to reveal.

He proclaimed, "People should behave with respect. A young lady should not scream, 'Hi Sir!' to a monk." Neither of us had mentioned women and none were present, so I was surprised when he squealed "Hi Sir!" in a loud falsetto voice. His tone sounded frustrated. I had just written a song called "Wat Blues" and emailed the lyrics to a Thai friend back home:

"I live in a wat, and I sit and pray all day,
I live in a wat, and I sit and pray all day,
Oh I sit and pray that a pretty girl come my way.

The master tells me to concentrate; he always tells me what to do,
The master tells me to meditate; he always tells me what to do,
Oh the master is so hard, he must be lonely too."

I had forgotten about the ditty when I returned home, but he brought it up with a chuckle and said that he really liked it. Another man had told me that when he was a boy he noticed monks passing magazine stands gazing at the covers with the sexiest pictures. Maybe the song did reflect reality. I found the master's little display of spirit refreshing after seeing several sullen monks in Cambodia.

However, Buddhist piety assumes many varieties in Lan Na and in the rest of Thailand. A wat called Chedi Luang grandly stands in Chiang Mai's central area. It was built in the 14th or 15th century, and the town's one massive stupa punctuates it. It was 250 feet high until an earthquake crumbled the top 100 feet in 1545. It's still a stunner, though the authenticity of its restoration in the early 1990s is controversial. A base of two large square platforms on top of each other gives it bulk as well as loftiness. This wat is now a modern university that teaches Buddhist scriptures. Other buildings form a large rectangle around the stupa, and a little outdoor café in the middle allows the aspiring monks to refresh themselves. All the students there looked reserved and serious. Their studiousness and the stupa's grandeur provided a dignified setting for learning the Buddha's teachings.

My attraction to Lan Na strengthened when I visited minority groups in the hills. Many non-Thai minorities live in Lan Na, and they offer a treasure-trove of customs. The largest group is the Karen, who probably migrated from southwestern China or southeastern Tibet to Burma and Thailand. Lahu and Akha people live at higher elevations. Hmong people also reside in Thailand; some were already there when King Mangrai ruled, but most came within the last 200 years. Many Hmong are refugees from battles between Burma's government and Shan groups fighting for independence near the Thai border. All these cultures add to Lan Na's diversity of lifestyles—a person can drive from a modern hotel to villages of bamboo homes within an hour.

But many villages are Mc Ethnic. The government sets aside land for minorities to play dress-up while tourists are bused in to snap photos. The visitors are then whisked to an orchid farm and an elephant stable, and then motored back to their hotels in time for the dinner buffet.

Advocates of the system say that refugees are given safe homes for maintaining their traditions. Critics retort that impoverished parents sell their daughters to be manufactured as "long neck" people. They're forced to squeeze brass rings around their necks, which depress the shoulders so that they appear long. This is an old custom among Padaung tribes in Thailand and Burma (they're a subgroup of the Karen). Some reasons that have been cited for it are feelings that it makes women look graceful, associations between their long necks and dragons (which some Padaung venerate), and men's desires to make their women unattractive to other tribes so they won't abduct them. There's no consensus about a single reason, but when a Padaung girl is two to five years old, the first few rings are placed around her neck with a ceremony (some girls wear a single piece, which is coiled around several times). A new circle is added every year until she becomes an adult. But the number of Chiang Mai and Chiang Rai tour operators displaying pictures of smiling teenage girls with a seven-inch stack of dog collars around their throats made it obvious that many are treated like circus animals.

Big companies have bought a lot of land in the north for tourist resorts and large-scale farming. They have taken common woods that locals used to use, and this has left many without enough land to feed themselves. Other minorities have lost their homes through legal manipulations that they don't understand, and some have been forcibly resettled.[1]

I thus felt both excited and nervous. Was I going to have profound cultural experiences or reinforce exploitive systems? I would at least attempt the former. Sadly, I only had one day to visit, but I was alone and would spend all day with them rather than the usual one or two hours that tour groups sell. I carried my guitar for meetings of souls and hoped for the best.

My taxi driver wheeled out of town and up into the hills. He hung a left onto a narrow dirt road that twisted for about a mile, stopped in a small clearing, and pointed to where I should walk.

A path led through thick brush and into a compound of low stilt homes. Each was a typical Karen house, with a bamboo floor, wooden frame, thatched roof, and no outer walls. People cooked and ate in its single spacious area during the day, then unrolled mats in it for the night's sleep. Five middle-aged and elderly women sat on the outer edge of a home. They wore bright red and blue striped sarongs and blue tops, and some of their mouths were red from betel chewing. The whole scene looked picturesque, but I wondered if it was fabricated.

A lot of Karen live between worlds that are hard to integrate. They traditionally stress harmony with spirits, village leaders, and neighbors. Many villages have a person who leads their rituals, and he watches members' behavior to keep it within communal rectitude. Karen strongly disapprove of divorce and adultery. Both require expensive rituals to restore order, and transgressors are sometimes run out of the village because violating marital ties offends ancestral spirits. But the modern world has ruptured this commonly Southeast Asian mixture of coziness and caution. Missionaries converted many Karen to Christianity, and others embraced Buddhism. Since Karen typically live in the lower elevations of uplands (around 2,000 to 3,000 feet), they reside between the Thais on the valley floors and other minority cultures higher up. They thus often serve as go-betweens. Many work in lowland towns and periodically return to their communities. How did this contrast between a conservative culture and recent dislocations affect the people in this village?

The one person who spoke English was in her mid forties. She told me that she had married a Thai man and then divorced him because he drank too much whiskey, and that she didn't have any children. Without a family, she represented her people's traditions to modern tourists and commuted to Chiang Mai for a class on becoming a guide.

The other women were elderly and seemed more settled in traditional life. They were so cheerful that they reminded me of carefree schoolgirls. But an old man who joined them seemed traumatized. He was practically toothless and dark green tattoos covered his chest. He said nothing and his eyes appeared forlorn. I wondered if he had been forcibly uprooted from his world. Did he suffer in Burma? It seemed indelicate to ask.

I started to play guitar for them, mixing mellow jazz and driving rock songs. The guide told me that one liked the soft numbers more and that another enjoyed the rock songs. I said, "I'll play more of both and make everyone happy."

My guide then walked with me to a village of the Lahu people. This ethnic group migrated into Burma and Thailand from southwestern China. Most of them don't form clans; small families are their main social groups. The Lahu honor village and nature spirits and stress communal harmony by giving them offerings to avoid conflicts. They prefer to keep things safe and familiar and avoid wandering far outside their community, where spirits can be more dangerous.

I played guitar for an elderly man and wife, and he dashed into their home and brought out a small mouthorgan. Many people in mainland Southeast Asian hills play them, and they're popular among the Lahu. Some of their priests perform on five-foot-long pipes in ceremonies. We sat shoulder to shoulder and played a few tunes. He then stood up and began to dance in steps that seemed preplanned rather than improvised. Lahu enjoy dancing during their traditional New Year festivals, when people go to nearby villages to share food and dance. This affirms communal harmony. Maybe this man's hoofing brought back happy memories—his mellow smile suggested so.

My guide and I then left the village and headed for "the main attraction." We walked uphill and arrived at a circle of one-room houses on low stilts, with bamboo walls and thatched roofs. About 12 teenage Padaung girls with shiny brass rings around their necks sat under tiny pavilions in front of the houses, dutifully waiting to be photographed. Most were knitting and politely smiling, and two were reading fashion magazines.

One girl was playing a homemade guitar with only four strings and a rough-hewn body. I sat with her and jammed along. Three of them played and all could position their fingers into chords quickly—they had spent time practicing. One smiled when I strummed the same chord at the same time. I then sounded higher notes that harmonized with hers.

The girls only knew a few chords; they had not learned scales or higher notes than ones played near the end of the neck. But as I walked back to the Karen village, high tones rang through the brush. The lack of tempo made me think that one of them was experimenting. It seemed that she hadn't thought of playing anything besides chords and low notes before and that she was discovering a new dimension of music. I enjoyed thinking that I had added something to their lives.

Back in the Karen village, a burly young man with a deep and soft voice said, "We have been hearing your guitar all day. Will you come into our home and play for us? We will cook dinner for you."

It was another typical Karen house, on three-foot stilts, with a bamboo floor, wooden frame, thatched roof, and no walls on three of its sides. I had to get used to the floor's bending as I walked on it, but I soon enjoyed the rhythm because I felt in harmony with nature. The open sides of the house allowed us to see neighbors' homes and the trees that surrounded us. This was one of my deepest impressions from that day— being immersed in nature and the community, with no walls between places. As in perspectives in wats, paintings, and neighborhoods, every-thing mingled in a flow that was both animated and soft. Even the floor rippled like a river. Millennia of living in such surroundings probably encouraged people to develop and emphasize this kind of perspective in their arts.

The elderly Karen women I had met earlier were sitting on the floor knitting, chatting, and giggling. One got sleepy and curled up where she had been working. She woke up about an hour later, picked up the bright red and blue threads, and started to knit again. There was no time clock or factory supervisor—only family and friends. Of course I was only see-ing the happy sides of traditional village life (there were no dangerous animals around), but I longed for more when I got back to town.

Many Thais do too. They created a popular genre of music about a villager moving to Bangkok to find work and missing the country. Since the big city has grown severalfold since 1970, lots of Thais have heart-strings attached to the old farmlands. The dining room of my hotel in Bangkok displayed a large painting that looked just like the view from the inside of the Karen home I was in. I always lingered on it before heading out to the busy streets.

My Karen hosts brought me one of their traditional meals: rice with an assortment of vegetables and sauces to pour over it. They served it on a large banana leaf. I had eaten on them in southern India and always had to make an effort to avoid spilling food on my lap because they were so flimsy. But I enjoyed this timeless village experience because all objects came from nature.

As I was eating, the wife of the Lahu man that played the mouth-organ slowly walked over from their village. Her stiff waddle suggested arthritis. She stood by the edge of the house and watched us for a while, but spoke a different language and thus couldn't communicate with any-one. She left after a few minutes, looking bored. Life seemed good for some of the Karen, but the Lahu woman had fewer people to relate to.

The man who offered me dinner was going to walk to his father's village the next day, and he invited me to join him and sleep there. Alas, I had to fly down to Bangkok two days later, but I was happy to see that he still lived a traditional life, and that he had a direct bearing that exuded peace. My guide then sat down with us and leaned over a worn paperback book to study for her class. She was now wearing jeans and a bright red T-shirt.

So the site was neither idyllic nor sordid. Most people welcomed my extensions beyond tourist-actor roles. They also enjoyed sharing music. Their degrees of happiness and abilities to preserve their pasts seemed to differ, but the communities were clean, pretty, and enveloped in nature. I felt sad for some people, but deep respect for all because of their dignity. It was one of the most moving days of the whole trip.

The day also transformed my perceptions for a while. When I returned to Chiang Mai, the city that I formerly thought swung looked like a giant octopus. Streets with wall-to-wall concrete buildings lining both sides seemed like tentacles spreading all over the land. What I had found humanistic now looked monstrous.

But I'm basically a city boy and I usually adjust to the bustle within a day, especially when it includes Thai food. Chiang Mai is still small enough to quickly become comfortable, and it presents an endless variety of enchantments to speed up the process. More awaited me.

Burma has added even more color to Lan Na. Both cultures' connections go way back. Mangrai visited King Suttasoma's court in Pegu at the end of the 13th century and married his daughter to strengthen their alliance. The two rulers celebrated by feasting with their retainers by the river and staging entertainments for three days and nights.

Though wars between Burmese and Thais ravaged Lan Na from the 16th through the 18th century, Burma's unique traditions have added wealth to the land in modern times. For thousands of years, diverse societies migrated from the north to Burma's riverine plains. Many cultures speaking languages in the Sino-Tibetan family mixed with each other, so the country's cultural landscape was very rich long before Pagan emerged.

I find the ancient Pyu culture especially intriguing because it built a federation of city-states that ruled central Burma for almost 1,000 years before Pagan became a large state in the 11th century. It constructed fortified cities surrounded by thick, high walls lined with bricks (the perimeter of the largest was almost 14 kilometers). Pyu societies also built hydraulic systems and large temples, minted silver coins, and used writing with an alphabet derived from India. Their people were mostly Buddhist, but some worshiped Hindu gods. Burma was prosperous and international long before its most famous empire emerged.

Pagan's King Anawratha then consolidated his kingdom in the 11th century by importing Buddhist monks and artists from Sri Lanka and expanding the state into southern Burma, where Mon cultures predominated. Michael Aung-Thwin, in *Pagan; The Origins of Modern Burma*, wrote that Pagan further synthesized its many cultures during the reign of the next great king, Kyanzittha (r. 1084–1111). Some governing classes were Burmese and he satisfied them by allowing them to retain their prestige. However, many people were Mon and he patronized Mon scholars and artists. Their language was used a lot at his court, and Aung-Thwin said that they became the intellectual elite (Burmese was increasingly used in the royal court in the 13th century).

Kyanzittha also emphasized continuity with the Pyu by linking his own ancestors with their real and mythical ancestors. Aung-Thwin wrote that Pagan wasn't fully Burmese, Mon, or Pyu. Instead, it mixed all into a luscious multicultural landscape. At the same time, Sri Lanka and northeastern India influenced much of Pagan's art and architecture, and people honored local spirits in addition to Shiva and Vishnu.

Almost 3,000 of the brick monuments within Pagan's archeological site still exist, and some historians think that the kingdom built as many as 10,000. The Burmese studies professor Donald M. Stadtner wrote that friends in his archeology department told him that they didn't expect to visit even half of the extant shrines in their lifetimes.

Indian traders settled around the northwestern coast and helped develop Rakhine into a bustling state (it's also called Arakan) before Burma annexed it in the late 18th century. Many Brahmin priests were then brought to the Burmese court, where they acted as ritual specialists, conducting ceremonies for deceased kings and queens and for deities associated with the sun, moon, and planets. Some brought Sanskrit and Indian vernacular texts to the court's library.

Many more Indians came in the 19th century, when England ruled both countries. Because a large percentage of immigrants could read and write, they held government jobs, worked in finance, and ran independent shops. Though Indians enriched the cultural landscape, many Burmese peasants went deeply into debt to the moneylenders, and this made some people resent all Indians. Some historians have considered the government's deportation of its Indian population after World War II a national economic catastrophe. Though the country lost many of its most skilled people, its corrupt rulers didn't have to contend with enterprising and literate people with their own international networks to criticize it.

Lan Na had a stroke of luck when Burmese settled there in the 19th century. The British took large chunks of Burma in three wars, and Burmese laborers and managers moved to Lan Na to find work, especially in logging. Many of them prospered and built wats that sparkle with Burmese features.

Burmese architecture adds more variety to Lan Na. A popular form is a tall, thin, and square stack of roofs. Every roof has a steep gable in the middle of each side and in each corner. Several of these tiers often soar next to each other, and they're often painted gold. The interplay between them creates glitter that can seem a bit loud for northern Thailand. Sukhothai art can seem unreal too, but it's tempered by softly rippling forms. These roofs are flashier.

However, a Burmese vihara that I explored in a historic Lan Na town called Phrae is one of the handsomest buildings I've ever seen. It's entirely built of stately dark wood. Outside, interlocking roofs crowned by stacks of cupolas mix with the trees' foliage. Inside, rows of tall, thin pillars frame worshippers with square spaces that are stately. Large square sections of the surrounding walls are painted reddish brown, and thin gold lines border their edges. The lines balance the sober colors with a little shimmer.

Burmese temples add all the more variety to Lan Na. The more tasteful buildings complement northern Thai art, and the showier ones add sizzle. Lan Na seems to make everything more savory.

So Lan Na's cultural landscape is infinitely creative, as Sukhothai's, Ayutthaya's, Cambodia's, and the West's have been. How do you fathom this limitless abundance? It's basic in people's cultural environments, and developing the ability to appreciate it fully can spark a revolution in perspective that can make the world more enjoyable for all people and foster harmony between all societies. We will learn how in the next chapter, now that we have explored enough material to apply to the method for appreciating our full human wealth.

CHAPTER 13

A METHOD FOR FINDING PARADISE IN THE WORLD

Now THAT WE have explored several places and times, we can detail the method for finding a more rewarding view of the world, which can rival many people's dreams of paradise. Thailand and Cambodia are two societies that are not usually studied outside their national borders, but they're bottomless treasure chests of creativity and beauty. I had already seen the synthesis of Thai cultural patterns in Sukhothai, which combined influences from:

- Angkor,
- Sri Lanka,
- India,
- The lower Thai peninsula and Malay states farther south,
- Pagan,
- Mon societies in Burma,
- The Dvaravati civilization,
- The Chinese diaspora,
- Ancient traditions that Tais had brought when they moved in,
- Rivers that help unify the land's diverse environments and abundant growth,
- The tropical heat and dramatic monsoons,
- Wet rice farming and the communal life that it encourages.

These places and environmental features converged in billions of interpersonal interactions, and they fostered Thai art and ways of thinking about the world (I calculated billions because millions of people communicated with each other dozens of times each day over many centuries). They reinforced each other and engendered a field of meanings that people throughout the land have shared up to today. This field has synthesized:

- The importance of the wat and its vihara in the community,
- Animistic traditions that harmonize a multitude of spirits,
- Aesthetics that mix gracefulness and vibrancy,
- Etiquette alternating with esprit,
- Reverence for the royal court, which is associated with Buddhism and animated power,
- Social hierarchy and following the conventions of one's in-group and superiors,
- Distinctions between the safe inside/*muang* (the family, rice farming, and the temple) and the wild outside/*pa*,
- Desires to hide conflicts over social status beneath pretty surfaces.

Thai culture is actually much richer than what I saw in Sukhothai. Lan Na also synthesized these patterns, and it developed its own varieties and gave them many down-home touches.

Ayutthaya was also central in the emergence of Thai culture. It absorbed the most Khmer influences and added their majesty to it.

The key thing about Thai culture's development and continuity is: These three states emerged together, and they influenced each other. They constantly exchanged monks, artists, political envoys, and goods. Combinations of Sukhothai, Lan Na, and Ayutthayan art and customs pervaded markets, wats, palaces, and homes so much that people from at least the 15th century on imbibed these impressions every day. This shaped their outlooks in ways that have been uniquely Thai ever since.

How can people fathom all these aspects of Thai culture when they're used to categorizing things and seeing them as separate objects? Academic conventions and online search engines encourage people to treat topics in this way. But the entire fusion of natural and cultural landscapes has made Thai society what it is. It has also given the West many of its most enduring and recognizable traits, so we need to be able to conceive cultures in a new way.

Thai culture is both infinite and unified. The ways in which its people have conceived and represented the world comprise an infinitely abundant landscape—its artworks, rituals, economic goods, cuisine, stories, domestic architecture, and combinations of etiquette and esprit can be endlessly varied, as well as mixed with each other in limitless ways. They have regularly been shared between several political centers, and between elite and folk cultures. All these interactions have reinforced a shared way of portraying and thinking about the world that has been unified enough to be distinctly Thai, and to endure throughout Thailand's history until now.[1]

This fusion of infinity and unity of a culture is not conventionally studied, so there is no established concept of it. But it's a key aspect of a culture because it patterns the perceptions, thoughts, art forms, and identities of people who are raised in it. This coalescence of both is a basic aspect of who we are, and a key part of this method for finding paradise in the world. Appreciating it can expand your world into one new vista after another so that your perspectives will become increasingly rewarding.

The unity of Thai culture has allowed limitless scope for creativity. Artworks in the Thai capitals and in satellite towns, villages, and rural wats have assumed endless varieties which are still characteristically Thai. The three great kingdoms consolidated influences from all over Southeast Asia, India, and Sri Lanka into a cultural landscape that has been fruitful enough to allow ever more variations to emerge, and yet be shared within an environment of common meanings and assumptions about the world.

At the same time, the variations have reinforced Thai culture's unity because they have permeated daily life in so many ways (in sculpture, temple architecture, rituals, behavior, cuisine, stories, literature, and common objects like ceramics, furniture, fabrics, and houses) that they have converged into a common field meanings for everyone. Because they're constantly reinforced, people have considered them to be the most basic patterns in the world. What seems obvious actually reflects an inexhaustibly rich cultural landscape.

This means cultures are bigger than ism's. Classicism sees an elite (and usually male) center that generates and spreads the most important traditions. It has proclaimed that Greek men in colonnaded agoras creating geometric forms, discussing abstract philosophic ideas, and fashioning realistic sculpture developed the standard of civilization. But since the 1970s, academia has often shifted towards the opposite idea: Cultures are in flux and pluralistic. The rising number of children of parents from different ethnic backgrounds and the millions of immigrants on every continent are often cited to prove this statement.

But cultural landscapes are richer than a choice between one dominant group of dead guys and a mishmash lacking ideas and perspectives that everyone shares. Elite patronage centers (such as the Thai and Khmer royal courts, Florence's guilds of wealthy merchants, and the Catholic Church) and folk cultures have influenced each other through many media, and this unifies societies enough to allow everyone to share enough of the same mindset to communicate. Royal and village wats resemble each other. Pictures in family Bibles and parish churches are similar in content and form to the Vatican's paintings. All media reinforce a common way of perceiving and thinking. It's common because people share similar perceptions, thoughts, artworks, stories, and expectations of how to behave, and they discuss them multiple times each day. They are thus ingrained in their language and the images they fashion. These similar perceptions, thoughts, and encounters are shared in upper class venues, common people's homes, streets, markets, schools, and houses of worship. At the same time, they're shared within the same natural environment. Since they are experienced in all places people are familiar with, they're constantly reinforced. They thereby seem like the world's most fundamental patterns, which unify it.

At the same time, the abundance of ideas, artworks, interpersonal interactions, and social groups within this unity encourages more variations because the variations can be synthesized in endless ways. It also allows exchanges with other cultures by giving all societies many points of contact. A culture's unity and infinite creativity thus engender each other.

Cambodian culture is also both infinite and unified. Khmer society was usually dominated by one capital, but Khmers synthesized art, ideas, stories, and rituals from multiple Hindu traditions (both Shiva and Vishnu worship) and Buddhist faiths. Their culture was influenced by several states in both India and the rest of Southeast Asia. It mixed art and ideas from all these lands with its own traditions, including ancestral cults, rituals for spirits in nature, and folklore, as well as with its unique natural landscape. This multitude of influences fertilized Khmer art's mixtures of elegance and grandeur. Angkor always had a rich stock of forms and ideas for both types of expressions. New artistic organizations, like Our Strength and Sammaki, which I had the pleasure of encountering in Battambang, promise more creativity in the future.

But Cambodia and Thailand are only two countries in this region. Next door are Burma, Vietnam, Laos, and Malaysia, and each has experienced its own interchanges between political centers, folk cultures, and the natural environment. Farther south is Indonesia, where many states thrived over the centuries. And nearby are two little countries called India and China, which have been in contact with Southeast Asia for more than 2,000 years. So the more I saw on this trip, the richer Southeast Asia appeared to me.

And the richer the whole world became. I kept comparing Southeast Asia with my own cultural origins. The Western tradition also emerged as both infinity and unity. In the ancient Middle East and ancient Greece, ideas, aesthetics, and faiths emerged that have been treated as basic ever since. Monotheistic religions developed in the Middle East, and Greeks created and refined ways to express proportion, distinct entities, abstraction, linear relationships, the human body, and people's portraits. Ancient Romans synthesized all these traditions from both areas and reinforced them as fundamental. They also added the arch and the dome to them. Europeans in the Middle Ages then emphasized Biblical stories and metaphysical ideas (like the great chain of being, which they expressed in Gothic cathedrals) and blended them with ancient Greco-Roman ideas and aesthetics. Fifteenth century Florentines then synthesized these ancient and medieval currents with new techniques for three-dimensional perspective and for representing the body, and many artists added their own styles to them. Together, they fleshed both out and helped to make them seem like basic reality. Venetian, Roman, and northern European artists added their own backgrounds and made the new perspective seem even more real. Like Southeast Asia, the West has combined continuity of ideas and art forms that it has found most meaningful with infinite creativity.

Who are you? Who am I? People harbor heritages of cultures with limitless wealth and creativity. Ideas and perceptions that people have considered most basic have been established as such within a whole culture. They are not isolated things; they're meaningful within this limitlessly abundant whole.

Our cultures are so abundant that they can rival many dreams of paradise because growth is fused with a culture's infinity and unity. New meanings are always possible in a society because:

- Mental horizons can expand in many directions because each culture can interact with several others.
- A culture always has more riches in its own past, which can be discovered as people see it from new perspectives that emerge as times change and as other cultures are explored.
- New artistic styles can emerge, like Picasso's flouting of three-dimensional perspective at the beginning of the 20th century. Also, new combinations of old art forms can be synthesized. This has happened many times in Thailand as people have combined features of different Buddha statues.

So to understand your own thought and identity thoroughly (to understand their full range of meanings), you must reach out to other cultures, as well as explore the heritage and future possibilities of your own. This is a wonderful paradox. The ways in which people unify their perspectives of the world (their perceptual patterns, art forms, and fundamental concepts) encourage them to look beyond those perspectives. And these ways are intertwined with so many pasts and other cultures, and they're intertwined through so many media, that the expansion of mental horizons beyond the current perspective can become at least as basic in our experience as holding them to the same boundaries. Perceptual patterns, common art forms, and fundamental concepts unify our world, but they also encourage us to transcend the ways in which they unify it and to arrive at bigger and more inclusive views of the world. They encourage us to always find more meaning and more wonders around us so that seeing all cultures shine on each other becomes ordinary.

Furthermore, our horizons can grow in infinite possible directions. We can explore many cultures, and we can do so through multiple media. We can also choose many possible sequences of societies and media, and my trip's unusual sequence (Southeast Asia, Africa, and the Middle East) showed me that the possibilities are unlimited. My journey's unconventionality demonstrated to me that we can transcend our current perspectives, not once, but again and again.

Thinking can thereby evolve from strictly apprehending things as they are conventionally defined to expanding into bigger landscapes which include more ideas and mindsets, and which encourage all to enrich each other. The conjoining of unity and infinity encourages limitless growth of horizons into all cultures and temporal periods. Each culture is thus a fusion of unity, infinity, and growth (UIG). Moreover, as you explore one culture, you can increasingly appreciate others. As you do this, you can find that all societies can inspire each other so that the whole world can be shown to be UIG—all of its cultures and people can always highlight and influence each other in more ways. This mutual reflection can become predominant in our perspectives and identities so that they're not confined to conventional borders between societies.

In *The Untethered Soul*, the yoga teacher Michael A. Singer said that the highest state of happiness and creativity that people experience results from how open they are, and he thus recommended a constant state of openness.[2] What we can be open to is actually much bigger than what anyone has realized so far because it can expand in limitless directions as cultures interact more deeply and share more ideas, arts, and experiences. We all have seen only a miniscule fraction of what we can become.

As people learn about more cultures, the unity of their own will become richer because they will have more ideas, artworks, and types of experiences to share with others who live in it. As more people share their new views with each other, the infinity of their own cultures will increase because their societies will become even more creative. As unity and infinity become richer, more growth will happen because people will have more ways to expand their horizons. A self-reinforcing process can thereby emerge in which people deepen their enjoyment of all cultures, and cultures continue to inspire each other. Every artwork, fundamental idea, and person is a threshold to explorations that become ever more blissful.

But what is this bliss? How can we wrap our minds around the idea of an infinite cultural landscape expanding in limitless directions? It can seem more intangible than any pantheon that Mahayana Buddhists dreamed of. Recent studies of peak experiences can connect this idea with the here and now.

The psychologist Abraham Maslow made peak experiences his business, and he explored them in *Toward a Psychology of Being*. Many people today know him for his hierarchy of needs because high school and college freshman marketing classes teach this concept. According to this hierarchy, our physical needs must first be met. We then focus on social needs, such as the approval of others and the feeling of belonging. After they're satisfied we strive for the highest human goals. This high end of the spectrum was Maslow's main interest, and it included being the happiest and most creative that we can be.

Back in the 1930s, Maslow noted that psychology mainly dealt with troubled people and that it usually defined mental health in negative terms—as not being sick. But what about the top 50 percent on the scale of well-being? What about the top one percent? Wouldn't it be better for us to study them and see them as our models?

One trait that Maslow noticed in people in the top percentiles was they had more peak experiences. He saw several aspects of pinnacle experiences:

- A wider range of perceptions and ideas emerge.
- There is a more creative flow of thoughts, which is less bound to social conventions. Many great artists experience this. For example, Picasso painted in several styles throughout his long career. People can liberate themselves from the mechanics of a situation and see wider ranges of connections.
- People feel more deeply integrated with their surroundings and able to find more beauty in them.

- They feel more whole and they don't fight with themselves. Instead of feeling like bundles of drives and social roles pulling in opposite directions, they're spontaneous, joyful, and fully expressive, and they feel that whatever they do is good.

I enjoyed many peak experiences while traveling, in which multiple times and places seemed to fuse. Instead of being bound to one time and culture, I felt that I was in a larger field in which I could see a wider range of ideas and art forms reflect each other.

This first experience occurred when I reached Angkor Wat's upper terrace. After the long procession through the temple, I found people from all over the world in this place which Khmers had envisioned as heaven. The visitors from many cultures, the terrace's refined forms and carvings, the breezes through the window slats, and the chirping of birds and bats merged into a field that both transcended and included all times and places. I felt deeply integrated with all these times and places, and all became integrated in this field which seemed increasingly luminous.

I enjoyed Thailand's sinuous forms in temples, markets, sculptures, and paintings even more than I would have if I had not seen Cambodia first because memories of the more monumental Khmer buildings were still fresh. I also often thought of the West's greater focus on static linear forms and distinct bodies. Since Thais have created congenial streams of many patterns, my memories of other cultures added to the flows I saw and enhanced my experiences. All these cultures seemed to mesh into a larger graceful flow.

When I arrived at the Parthenon in 2008, I stood in front of it and admired its balanced proportions, but I enjoyed them even more when I thought of other cultures' ideas of balance. Thai flows are also balanced, but according to different perceptions, concepts, and shared experiences—they balance grace and animation and thereby tame the environment's energies. Many Khmer temples balance elegance and power. Chinese ideas of yin and yang also express balanced energy flows, but in a different way than Thai flows. They're more symmetrical by moving in circular patterns that repeat.

*Figure 30. Representation of the harmonious universe
in a Daoist temple in Kaifeng, China.*

So the kind of balance that each society has emphasized reflects ideas it has considered most fundamental. When I was in front of the Parthenon, I thought that the idea of balance can now be expanded to our global-ized world as a balance of many cultures' perspectives. No single one dominates the others, and people are free to explore all the different varieties, synthesize them, and appreciate more types of beauty. I thus savored cultures from all over the world as I enjoyed the Parthenon. All mixed into a field that was richer than any single form.

I then went to Italy and when I arrived in Florence from Rome, I sat on the cathedral's front steps, which face the baptistery that Brunelleschi painted to demonstrate three-dimensional perspective. As I thought that it's now possible to expand our views of the world to include all cultures, the baptistery's static shapes and thick lines became less rigid, and they became part of a dialog with other societies' favored patterns, like Thai flows, yin-yang patterns, and India's vast metaphysical landscapes. The baptistery's lines highlighted my memories of these patterns and the cultures that have emphasized them because they contrasted with them. In turn, these other cultures accentuated the West's focus on abstract lines and shapes. The lines and forms seemed to twinkle like stars as they expanded into a larger field in which all cultures illuminated each other.

So, many places expanded from one time and culture. Multiple mindsets, times, and places became interlaced in a bigger field in which everything's meaning deepened. One place after another expanded from mechanics to magic—it became a portal to higher levels of integration in which things became increasingly free from one system of categories, and in which unexpected vistas emerged. Places became increasingly luminous, and as they did, they glimmered together so that the whole world seemed like a field of light and love.

The psychologist Martin Seligman has updated research on the positive psychology that Maslow pioneered. In a book called *Flourish*, he said that he prefers not to use the word *happiness* because it's hard to define and measure. He thus focuses on well-being, and he defined several components of it, which can be measured more accurately in experiments and surveys:

- Positive emotion. I felt many types while exploring different cultures' world-views. Sometimes I felt ecstatic while going beyond one convention after another. Other times, I felt warmth by relating to people with so many different mindsets. My afternoon in Theanly's home in Battambang, when he showed me his paintings, was a good example of this. I also often felt gratitude for the experiences that I had in all countries.
- Engagement. Seligman sees this as being in a flow. The psychologist Mihaly Csikszentmihalyi also considers flow to be central in happiness and well-being. Both see flow as a full involvement with your activity so that your consciousness becomes absorbed in it. I felt this in all the countries I visited. Walking through Khmer and Thai temples immersed me in their cultures, and ultimately that trip became a larger flow that took me around the world.

- Meaning. This is belonging to something larger than yourself. I first felt involved with each culture I visited. The feeling of engagement then expanded to the whole world.
- Fulfilling relationships with others. I enjoyed expanding the types of people I related to. For example, playing guitar allowed me to get closer to people in Thailand's hill tribes.

Entering different cultures also kept expanding the types of happiness I experienced. I learned how the mellowness of the Thai feeling *sabai* is embedded in its culture. I equally enjoyed contemplative moods in Romanesque and Gothic cathedrals. I found that the more open you are to different types of happiness, the more often you can be happy.

Seligman found that curiosity, interest in the world, and tolerance of ambiguity enhance well-being. These are all in line with the constant growth of horizons that comes from exploring other cultures and increasingly appreciating their unity and infinity.

Seligman also wrote that appreciating beauty can increase well-being, and he advocates remembering the times when you've been thrilled by excellence in art, music, movies, science, and mathematics. If you often have these experiences, and if you frequently remember them, you're likely to enjoy more well-being. I found that exploring excellence and beauty in other cultures greatly expands the range of what you can appreciate, and it increases the frequency of these moments.

Seeing our world as a fusion of unity, infinity, and growth enhances many findings about what encourages happiness and well-being. When you see this mixture in the world and in yourself:

- You're constantly open to enjoying more of the world's diversity of cultures,
- You feel related to more types of people,
- You feel engaged with the whole world,
- You have many memories that elicit positive emotions,
- You have a greater diversity of ideas and experiences to enhance your creative flows,
- You enjoy more types of beauty.

More and more places and people can inspire peak experiences and become sources of joy. They make the ways in which you were trained to perceive and think less constricting, and the world around you can expand into limitless enchantments.

But what the heck is infinity? It is a key aspect of our thought and identities, but academia and science have usually shied from it as though it's a flame-spitting demon ready to attack the established order. Thinking must rest on secure foundations so that people can share ideas in ways that are reliable for acquiring more knowledge. Infinity seems dangerous because it's unclear.

But infinity has always been within and around us, and it can inspire us to reach our highest potentials for enjoying the world and being creative. How can we appreciate it in a way that is on speaking terms with conventional knowledge?

This is what the rest of the method allows. Unity, Infinity, and Growth comprise the first half: UIG. Their fusion is the cultural environment in which people live, which patterns our thought, art forms, identities, and behavior. The other half is how we can relate to this field—how we can perceive and think about it so that we can fully appreciate it and optimize it for encouraging more creativity and happiness.

This half also has three aspects. They're three types of perceiving and thinking, and we can alternate them and thereby avoid getting stuck in one of them. This will allow us to keep exploring the integration of Unity, Infinity, and Growth.

The first is looking *At*. This is conventional knowledge—you look *At* something according to the perspectives you're accustomed to. A Westerner can linger over the details of Michelangelo's *David* and examine every limb, muscle, facial feature, and hair curl. He can then walk around and see them from many angles. As a person continues to look *At*, he learns more details according to the network of ideas that his culture most commonly uses.

If you're multicultural (if your parents are from different cultures, or if you have lived in more than one culture, or feel deep affinity with more than one) you probably combine those cultures' ways of thinking.

If so, this is your way of looking *At*—you are following the conventions you're most accustomed to.

Academia usually looks *At* by adhering to its own conventions, and they have become common where the world has modernized. It focuses on facts and techniques for analyzing them, and it's partitioned into different fields, each with its own specialized terms and techniques. But most of these conventions don't encourage people to discuss big ideas like *paradise*. Though it's necessary to keep knowledge communicable within conventions so that everyone can share it and build on it, binding all reality to them narrows our perspectives of the world and of ourselves.

However, we can have the best of both worlds. We can use our conventions and thereby be confident that we're standing on firm ground, and we can also be free enough from them to appreciate other experiences and ways of thinking. We can then return to our conventions, express other cultures in our own society's terms, and see our own backgrounds from new perspectives.

Mihaly Csikszentmihaly wrote that the flows that people he studied experienced were usually directed towards some goal, such as writing a book, conducting a scientific experiment, climbing a mountain, or winning a basketball game. He found that these activities are structured by rules and that people's focuses narrow to performing their current tasks.[3] But he also noted that being in a flow doesn't prevent it from becoming destructive, and he said that developing nuclear weapons and manufacturing nerve gas can also be highly engrossing. I imagine that many Khmer Rouge soldiers were fully absorbed in their killing rampages. Mihaly also noted that a person who has spent years working within the conventions of one field naturally thinks that developments in it are the most important events in the world.[4] He thus recommends constant re-evaluation of what we do, with the most inclusive political criteria we can think of.[5] So being able to see beyond our current way of looking *At* is crucial for maximizing well-being. The wider the range of ideas and experiences we can explore, the more inclusive our evaluations can be.

The second type of perceiving is looking *With*. This is examining your own culture's conventions. As you explore its historical and natural environment, you can appreciate the abundant landscape that your own ways of thinking developed in. As you look *With*, you can see limitless creativity and beauty in the ways in which you have conventionally perceived and thought (looking *At*).

This is similar to forms of meditation in which people examine their own thoughts. In *Vipassana* traditions, they learn to think about why they are thinking certain things and why they're feeling in certain ways. They thereby see themselves more objectively, and they're more able to control negative emotions, like fear and anger. Looking *With* broadens self-examination to the culture that you live in. Westerners can see more ways in which the Italian Renaissance, northern Europe, the medieval heritage, and antiquity converged, and how they have shaped their ideas of the world. As you keep discovering more of the infinite beauty within your own thinking, your emotions can become more positive. You can enjoy the riches in your own perceptions, thoughts, and identity so that what formerly seemed ordinary become sources of awe and wonderment.

The third way of perceiving is looking *Beyond*. By doing this, you appreciate the ways in which people in another culture perceive and think. If you're not Thai you can realize that Thai ways of perceiving and thinking emerged in an infinitely prolific landscape. You can thereby see limitless riches in another society, use them to highlight your own, and then inspire other people in your society to expand their horizons into a wider range of ideas.

So you can approach AWB as a circle:

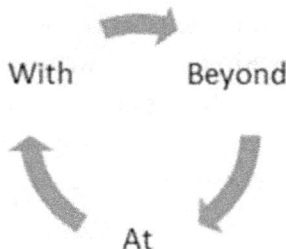

With   Beyond

At

Look *At* anything you find meaningful and view it in the ways in which you're used to perceiving and thinking. You can then study some of your own culture's heritage (looking *With*) and see more riches in your own ways of looking *At*. Then explore another society (looking *Beyond*). You can then look *At* again and see your own culture in new ways. If you keep journeying through this circle, your perceptions and ideas can become more inspiring and enjoyable. Places can become related more on the basis of mutual reflection than rigid boundaries.

You can also journey in the other direction. You can look *At*, then *Beyond*, and then *With*. In other words, you can venture into another culture and then look more deeply into your own history. You can also look *Beyond* multiple times in a succession by exploring several societies, and then delve into your own heritage. The combination of my 2007 round-the-world journey and my 2008 trip through the West's heritage in Greece and Italy followed this pattern. All these types of sequences will keep expanding your horizons as long as you mix looking *At*, *With*, and *Beyond* in some way.

A key thing about this method is: All three components in each half enhance each other as you travel through the circle again and again. Within the Unity/Infinity/Growth half (within a culture's and person's field of connections):

- Unity becomes richer as you compare your culture's shard meanings with other societies' ideas and art forms. You can then see aspects of your culture's unity from more perspectives and share these new views with others in it. The people around you can then incorporate what they just learned and share it with others that they know. In this way, the unity of your culture can become even richer.
- Infinity is exposed in more ways in the world's cultures and people—they all become more creative as people gain new perspectives and apply new ideas to their surroundings.
- Growth of mental horizons and affinities with other cultures happens in more people, and in more directions, as unity becomes richer and as infinity is further exposed. Expansion of horizons can become as constant as any conventional order of meanings.

All three components in the other half of the method also enhance each other. Within At/With/Beyond (the optimal way to perceive this field):

- You can look *At* the world according to your conventions after you've looked *With* or *Beyond* and find more inspiration and beauty in them. I found more meaning in the Parthenon and Renaissance European art because I could compare them with other cultures.
- You gain more ways to look *With.* You can see your own culture from more perspectives as you look *Beyond* and compare it with ideas and art from other societies. I enjoyed seeing how three-dimensional perspective developed in the great 15th century Italian painters' works even more by comparing their world with Thailand, which developed a different way of thinking and perceiving.
- You gain more skills in looking *Beyond.* As you explore more cultures and increase your range of ideas and perceptions, you become more mentally flexible and thus able to appreciate new societies more deeply. You can also mix all these cultures' traditions and ideas in new ways.

Another key aspect of this method is: Both halves (Unity/Infinity/ Growth and At/With/Beyond) enhance each other. As we continue to look *At, With,* and *Beyond,* we will appreciate ever more riches in our field of connections. In turn, we'll further enhance our abilities to combine looking *At, With,* and *Beyond* as we bring other cultures into our flows of ideas and perceptions. This will increase our ability to find and expose yet more aspects of our field of connections. All six of these components thus empower each other—they increase each other's ability to help people find more beauty and radiance in the world and in themselves. They're not abstract variables or static categories which are separate from each other; they work together to make the world ever more fulfilling, and they co-develop further as they do.

So the whole method is:

UIG><AWB

With it, our field of connections and our perspectives of it can continuously enrich each other without a final limit. As this happens, infinity becomes more prevalent in the world, and in our ideas of it.

But what is infinity? This has been an elusive concept, but we can identify three aspects of it here:

1. Infinity is not merely a static quantity. It's not just some ultimate high number, ready to be counted up to. Instead, it expands. As more of infinity is exposed in more people, and in more cultures, each person and each culture can inspire others to become more imaginative and creative. Humanity's field of connections can become increasingly infinite as people and societies enhance each other. Infinity is thus dynamic—it grows, and the more people appreciate and share it, the more it can grow.

    Furthermore, the dimensions in which infinity grows can multiply without a final limit. This happens as more cultures are compared and then combined in new ways, and as more people expose more of each other's inner wealth (their cultural heritages, personalities, and imaginations).

2. Infinity is not confined to one meaning. Instead, it's limitless in many ways. A lot of modern studies of infinity have been based on the work of the mathematician George Cantor (1845–1918). He analyzed sets of objects and said that a set is infinite if its members can be put in a one-to-one correspondence with the natural numbers, which progress in this series: 0, 1, 2, 3 . . . to infinity.[6] This kind of set can be counted one-by-one without a final limit. One-to-one correspondence with numbers in an endless series has been one of the most common concepts of infinity in the modern West, but it's inadequate for understanding the world's cultures, our own identities, and our potential for creativity and happiness.

    For instance, a culture regularly interacts with several others. It influences them,   and it's influenced by them. Their relationships are not strictly one-to-one, but multidimensional, and these cultures change as they interact. They don't become completely different (they retain many of their most common traditions), but because they have assimilated new ideas and art forms, they're not exactly the same. Cultures are richer and more multifaceted than simple objects that can be fully understood by being counted.

Artworks are not just separate objects to be counted either. A whole cultural environment shaped a work of art. This is why a Thai temple is the way it is, and why an Italian Renaissance painting has its own features. Furthermore, they're interlaced so that each artwork is influenced by several others. Attempting to count artworks one-by-one won't fully grasp them. It's the multi-dimensional interlacing that gives them many of their meanings and their most recognizable characteristics.

People are also not strictly abstract objects which can be counted one-by-one. Each person grew up in a culture, or in a fusion of cultures, and each human being has a personality, an identity, an imagination, integrating ideas, aesthetical pref-erences, emotional patterns, interpersonal relationships, and a natural environment. We all have many facets, and we're con-nected with each other through all of them.

So a culture, an artwork, and a person is more than just a countable object. Each is interwoven with many others of its kind (cultures influence each other, and so do artworks and people). Furthermore, a culture, an artwork, and a person are interwoven with each other. Their relationships are thus multidimensional—they're related to several others, and they all affect each other.

The web of connections that all three share can be seen as infinite in many ways, and different cultures and people have emphasized different aspects of infinity:

- It can be somewhat conceived as a set of countable objects, as modern mathematical conventions have treated it.
- It can also be unbounded love for all beings. Mystics and saints have stressed this inner dimension of infinity. The 16th century Spanish Saint Teresa of Avila and the 16th century Hindu mystic Mira Bai wrote of limitless love for divinity. They didn't experience it by counting, but

by feeling enraptured. This type of infinity is more connected with the heart than the head.

- Unbounded creativity—the ability to synthesize ideas and art in new and unforeseen ways. The psychologist and anthropologist Gregory Bateson said that cultural patterns can emerge from a field that's more chaotic than settled into countable objects, and that this makes creativity unpredictable. People cannot line up all the possible outcomes beforehand and count them because unforeseen patterns can emerge.[7]

- Sheer exuberance. The focus is not on one object; instead the person is immersed in a surge of things and forms. She doesn't experience this surge by counting everything in it, but by experiencing it as a whole and reveling in its vitality. Khmer temples and sculpted vegetal motifs have expressed this. Some types of African, Latin American, and hip hop dance embody nature's vitality by allowing each dancer to improvise movements instead of being confined to pre-established steps. All performers can intermix in an exuberant whirl of patterns that cannot be predicted or reduced to one form.

- Concepts of divinity. The German theologian Friedrich Schleiermacher (1768–1834) and the Danish philosopher Soren Kierkegaard (1813–1855) felt that a key aspect of human existence is the idea of divinity which is infinitely greater than us. Kierkegaard felt that this divinity cannot be approached analytically, but with a total leap of faith.

    The Jewish mystical tradition, the Kabbalah, grounds the universe in God's infinity, which is called *Ein-Sof.* All the things we see in the world came from it.

- Human relationships. A meeting between two people is infinite possibility because we reflect our whole cultures and personalities. Many Jewish traditions emphasize ethical relationships over treating other people as objects to be counted. Martin Buber said that the latter approach treats another person as an *it*. He felt that reality is more fundamentally *I and Thou*—we are human by interacting as people and respecting each other's needs and views. Because each person's needs and views are different, a meeting of two people requires both to expand their horizons.

Human relationships can change in ways that are open-ended. The Talmud is an ancient Jewish tradition of discussions about how people can live in accordance with God and follow ethical obligations to Him and to each other, and it was first compiled around the time that Christianity was emerging. Recently dialogs have been added to it about how ethics and divine laws apply to the internet. Human life thus changes, and new situations can always arise which require innovative thought about ethics.

- Indian ideas of a vast cosmos. This universe is more subtle than something that can be measured in just three dimensions, along the X, Y, and Z axes. More than 2,500 years ago, composers of the *Upanisads* said that the universe's essence is in a tiny space within the heart, called the *hridaya akasha*. An adept yogi can meditate on it and feel that he's unified with all creation. Ancient Indians imagined an image of this unity. The chief god in the *Rg Veda*, Indra, has a web of jewels. Each jewel reflects every other, and each contains reflections of all the others. I've often thought that this is an excellent way to envision the world's cultures.

So infinity has been seen in many ways besides objects that can be counted one-by-one. These ways have come from the varieties of people's experiences, and experiences are influenced by the culture and natural environment they emerge in. Any one-sided definition of infinity is only partial. It leaves out most types of human experiences. A richer way of seeing it is necessary in order to fully relate it to our field of connections and ourselves.

This list isn't comprehensive; people in other cultures have seen infinity in yet other ways.[8] The idea of infinity can expand from one variable to as many as we have the ability to imagine, and this ability can increase as we have more types of experiences and appreciate more cultures.

3.   Infinity isn't just an abstraction. People can become it to an ever greater extent. You can do this by opening yourself to more ways of appreciating the world, by enlarging your imagination, by relating to more types of people, and by having new types of experiences. As you do, and as you share your discoveries with others, you can help them become more infinite. Each person can then become a force for extending infinity even more—each can inspire more people, and the six aspects of UIG><AWB will further enhance each other.

Infinity can thereby grow in all aspects that cultures imagine. This ever-increasing growth of infinity can become fundamental in our identities and in our perspectives.

Infinity can thus evolve. It can grow in more people and in more directions. It can also assume more varieties. As people increasingly become it, they can help it to grow even more. Our perspectives and our identities can expand from one culture's lens to this ever-growing enrichment of more people and societies, in more directions and variations, as these expansions become more common.

However, infinite possibility can seem paralyzing. Where in the world do you start? What direction do you take? What goal do you set, and how do you monitor your progress towards it? How do you know if you're deviating from it? People usually need limits to focus on in order to get things done. In addition, no matter how many other cultures we explore, we need to communicate our findings in at least one society's terms if we want to do anything creative. There is a big difference between creativity and just having ideas—we need to share ideas with others and turn them into methods, products, services, and works of art that other people can use.

Looking *At*, *With*, and *Beyond* in a circle always allows you to work with a structure. You can begin with the limits that your own culture has emphasized. You can then look *With* and develop a deeper appreciation of those limits by more fully understanding the traditions that have focused on them. You can then look *Beyond* and see limits that another culture has ordered itself with, such as the symmetry of Angkor's temples, which structured exuberant Khmer motifs. You can then look *Beyond* again and appreciate limits that another culture has made fundamental, like the decorum in traditional Thai etiquette and the usual avoidance of grandiose monuments in Thai architecture. Then you can appreciate your own culture's conventions from more perspectives. When you explore several cultures' favored limits back to back, your perspective can expand beyond one system of limits and into a field in which each culture reflects the others.

A culture's emphasis on certain limits also reflects its own infinitely creative history. The more varieties of limits you explore and compare, the more your perspective can expand to this multidimensional and infinitely creative inter-reflection. You're always within limits, but your horizons are not bound to any single one forever. Instead, you can see an enlarging variety of limits, be increasingly free from each one, and appreciate the infinitely creative cultures that have emphasized each.

Looking *At*, *With*, and *Beyond* allows you to work with limits in a way that helps you appreciate infinity to an ever greater extent. You can always have a structure, but you can also see infinity in the cultural environment in which it has been emphasized, and you can expand your horizons beyond it and appreciate other types of limits and the infinite landscapes they reflect. You can be grounded in limits, but you can also use them as portals to new perspectives that keep enlarging your appreciation of Unity/Infinity/Growth.

However, many psychologists and anthropologists have said that most people prefer their own cultures and that they feel uncomfortable when they're outside of them for a long time.[9] Gregory Bateson, in *Mind and Nature*, saw similarities between cultures and biology. A society and an organism need internal coherence to maintain themselves (an organism can only live on certain types of food, have a certain metabolism, and maintain a certain body temperature). We have just seen that the dominant perspectives that people in a culture share are dominant because they're reinforced by an astronomical number of experiences. The very multitude of experiences that reinforce a culture's worldview thus encourages conservatism so that looking *Beyond* often feels threatening.

Combining looking *At, With,* and *Beyond* is an optimal solution to this problem because it encourages people to realize that there isn't a stark difference between their conventions and novelty. Instead, all three types of perceiving enhance each other. Looking *With* and looking *Beyond* add more richness to looking *At*; they don't replace it. They add perspectives that show more riches in conventions—they reveal more historical depth, more beauty, and more bridges to other cultures.

You don't need to time looking *At, With,* and *Beyond* with a stopwatch (though you can if you're most comfortable with that approach). I never do them in that way; I like to allow enough time to savor each experience for as long as I want, and that often varies. Sometimes I favor a certain way of perceiving on a certain day. But I alternate them often enough to avoid getting stuck in one. The key thing is to alternate so that your perspective always expands and becomes more inclusive.

However, most fields of knowledge are highly specialized today, and the time required for keeping up with developments in one field makes it hard to take time to look *With* and *Beyond*. But if you do at least a little of both each day so that they become ingrained in your routine, you can increasingly appreciate the Unity/Infinity/Growth that each culture's way of looking *At* emerged within, and this will give you more perspectives to apply to your field. The manual at the end of this book details ways to mix all three types of perceiving.

Any culture can initiate a shift in perspective to UIG><AWB. Thailand's and Cambodia's heritages of irreducible variety can encourage ways to express our world's diversity. Indians can use their traditions of imagining a vast universe to inspire bigger views of the world's

tapestry of cultures. Each society can develop its own style of looking *At,
With,* and *Beyond* and thereby enhance UIG all the more.

America has tremendous potential for leading this revolution in
perspective, since people from cultures all over the world live here. If
enough people discover the depths of their human wealth and share
it, we can lead the world in developing perspectives that are richer and
more creative. A lot of Americans currently feel straightjacketed as economic demands have become increasingly pressing. Hedrick Smith (in
Who Stole the American Dream?) and Joseph Stieglitz (in several recent
books) have detailed the rise of inequality in this country over the last
35 years, which is now so great that 1% of its people own 40% of the
wealth. But money is only one dimension of our founding fathers' vision
of maximizing life, liberty, and the pursuit of happiness. Yet financial
worries have been pressuring people into narrowing their focus to this
dimension, and this greatly diminishes the dream. Looking *At, With,*
and *Beyond* can enable us to develop the other dimensions so that all can
grow equally.

It can also help us to extend the freedom which Americans are proud
of. Freedom within habits of perceiving and thinking isn't the highest
freedom that people can attain. When we liberate ourselves from depen-
dence on looking *At* according to one convention, we can explore a field
of connections that's infinitely larger, as well as advance America's heritage of exploring new frontiers and innovating.

Each culture has enough wealth in its past to pioneer a new way of
viewing the world. It's win-win because everybody exposes more wealth
in more people, and each culture enhances itself and the rest of the
world at the same time. More creativity surges in more people, and they
can help others to boost their own. A limitless number of infinities
can keep nurturing each other. As this happens, infinity can grow and
become more prevalent in our views of the world.

As this happens, love can become an increasingly fundamental
aspect of thinking. People can always see more potential in each other
and become more able to help it grow. In the West thought has usually
been seen as defining and analyzing things. But we can also see more
in things, and as we learn about other cultures' perspectives and ideas,

the *more* can increase so much that we can see the essence of a person, an idea, an artwork, and a culture as more than what she/it is currently defined as. Her/its essence is to keep growing richer in multiple dimensions and increasingly able to enrich others.

Unity, Infinity, and Growth are interwoven through so many places, temporal periods, artworks, human interactions, and varieties of experience that there are limitless ways in which we can become more. The next major expansion of perspective can shift from "It is" to "It's more." If we balance looking *At, With,* and *Beyond,* all components of UIG><AWB will enhance each other so that *more* can become increasingly prominent in our world and in ourselves.

Since people have usually looked *At* so far, saying that the essence of a person, an idea, an artwork, or a culture is to become more than what she/it is can seem like a paradox: Something is what it is by being more than what it is. But the ability of the components of UIG><AWB to enhance each other without an ultimate stopping point allows *more* aspcts to grow and be exposed in limitless ways. This ability opens the field of possibilities to so much more than what each thing is currently seen as that new perspectives can emerge on a regular basis. Seeing *more* can thus become a regular experience.

The limitlessness of the possibilities to see *more* in things means the perspective can shift from a focus on conventional definitions to the experience of widening the perspective. This can seem like another paradox: A perspective is not just of a thing or a situation; it's also its own widening beyond that view of it. But as U, I, G, A, W, and B keep enhancing each other, new ways of envisioning and connecting things, and new ways of seeing potential in people and cultures, keep opening up. Thinking can become like flying around the world rather than adhering to one established footpath. The joy of flying and seeing the world as an infinite field growing richer and more loving can become increasingly central in our experience.

Both apparent paradoxes (an entity is more than what it is, and a perspective widens beyond its current horizons) complement each other. As U, I, G, A, W, and B keep enhancing each other, continuing enrichment of everything can become our basic reality. The chapter on the Italian Renaissance explained that we can see the world become bigger and bigger. This growth can actually happen in ever more people, cultures, directions, and combinations. As it does, giving and mutual growth can become increasingly central in our views of the world. We'll explore what this reality can be like more deeply in Part Three.

I wonder if UIG><AWB is in the architecture of paradise because it encourages perspectives and love to advance in limitless directions so that all societies are part of an ever-enlarging field of love. Whether it is or if I'm dreaming, it's at least an optimal general framework for envisioning our globalized world. It lets each culture be itself because it doesn't impose any other's favorite conventions on it, and it encourages all societies and people to keep appreciating each other more deeply, and to keep nurturing each other. If it is not the architecture of paradise, it's an excellent general orientation for a global civilization that can rival people's dreams of paradise.

But first, some nasty stuff. How does this ever-enlarging world full of love mesh with today's power politics, financial difficulties, and ecological perils? Huge gaps between rich and poor fester all over the globe. Political corruption reeks, not only in all the Third World countries I visited, but in the good old USA. The year after I returned home from my blissful 2007 trip, the global banking system nearly crashed, I lost 25 percent of my net worth, and most Wall Street tycoons who developed its crooked policies kept doing business as usual and grew even richer. Some economists worry about a future global financial crisis that will be even more traumatic because many governments are now carrying too much debt to be able to alleviate it. Thai politics became increasingly violent and resulted in a military coup. The political situation in many Middle Eastern countries became more bloody and oppressive. The ancient Sanskrit term *matsya nyaya* (the law of the fish—the big ones eat the small) is evident all over the world. How can you expose infinite paradise in the world when many of the people who run the political system you live in behave like sharks?

After Chiang Mai, I explored the concrete dragon called Bangkok. The sequence seemed apt to me because after musing over old temples and celestial palaces, I explored the city's simmering streets. They gave me insights for implementing this method in the real world.

PART TWO

THAILAND

SECTION THREE

HIDDEN RICHES
IN THE MODERN WORLD

CHAPTER 14

BETWEEN BAMBOO AND CONCRETE: BANGKOK

THE JET WHISKED me from Chiang Mai's comfy valley to Bangkok's ocean-sized sprawl. At the airport I hoisted my bags into a taxi and was off into the steamy traffic.

My hotel was in a lively neighborhood two miles north of the Grand Palace. The district, which is called Banglamphu, became urbanized in the late 19th century as Bangkok grew beyond its center. Today it's popular with backpacking tourists, who cram its streets along with the locals. My hotel stood next to a canal, but the waterway didn't look like an old picture of smiling people on longboats in front of snug stilt homes any more than chugging a six pack in a biker bar resembles Christmas dinner at Mom's house. Concrete buildings pressed against each other on both sides. Some stuck out so that the line on the opposite side from me looked like the front row of a crowd of giants about to plunge into the water from the pressure of the bodies behind them.

But despite the congestion, I still found Bangkok uniquely Thai. Though many Thais say it lacks the warmth and etiquette they're used to in the country, I still found many of its residents as soft-spoken and gracious as the people I had encountered in small towns. My taxi driver had trouble finding my hotel, and locals gave directions with the traditional smile and unassuming voice. Bangkok's politics often reek like the sewers, but the people I met maintained their polite traditions, and they made Bangkok a pleasant place to stay. If I were to live in Thailand I'd choose Chiang Mai, but I would be happy in the capital for a long time. Many Western visitors are.

The courteous locals turned out to be the answer to the question about finding my way around Bangkok, which I asked when I first landed there from Siem Reap. Its endless tangle of serpentine streets seemed intimidating and impossible to grasp in one overarching view, but residents who were happy to help made meandering through the city enjoyable for me.

I promised you dirt in this section, so you'll get it. Considering the violence that broke out in 2010 and 2013, there's plenty to shovel around. But only focusing on the recent negative politics would give you an inaccurate picture of Thailand and Bangkok. The capital is full of both grace and grime, and this combination makes it seem mysterious to many visitors. We'll explore both sides of this city to attain a more complete view of it.

Many currents fostered continuity of the old grace in modern times. They had already permeated so much art, religion, and behavior in Thailand before Bangkok was established that they structured people's experiences. Thai traditions then developed fascinating new aspects as the city grew. We will examine how many old ways have thrived and assumed new varieties in this chapter, and then delve into today's problems in the next. A broader view of modern Thailand will encourage insights about how to begin to implement the method for finding paradise in the world.

The horrors of the sack of Ayutthaya in 1767 made the old traditions seem like a lost haven. The siege dragged on for more than a year and ended in Burma's ruthless destruction of the city. The dreamscape of golden spires collapsed into heaps of burnt bricks.

Siam was orphaned—she had no king, court, or capital. The sudden scarcity of food split up families. Many monks were unable to eat and had to disrobe and find employment in the lay world. People even ransacked wats' libraries for cloth that had protected the hallowed scriptures.

Survivors longed for their traditions. Life without them was so stressful that old contrasts between the safety of communal life and the wild outside were reinforced. Thais would soon have a new king to restore order by invoking their heritage, but they would first suffer another ordeal.

A charismatic military leader named Taksin drove out the Burmese, who had gotten into a war with China which they had to divert resources to. He also moved the capital south, to the other side of the river from where modern Bangkok would soon rise. This area was closer to the sea and thus to international trade routes. Thais could more easily buy arms and escape if the Burmese invaded again.

Taksin is a complex figure for Thais. They admire him as a great general, but after taking the throne, he believed that he was a divinity. He forced monks to worship him and demoted those who refused. Taksin had hundreds flogged and cast into hard labor. French missionaries wrote that he spent his time praying and fasting in order to be able to fly. His conduct was especially disturbing to Thais because many believed that the impiety of Ayutthaya's elites had brought the old kingdom down.

The historian David Wyatt thought Taksin's elevation of himself and his harshness with dissenters might have stemmed from his own insecurity. His parents were not from high society and his father was Chinese.[1] Merchants from China had prospered and gained political clout in the 18th century. The grand old families who ran Ayutthaya's politics probably looked down on Taksin, and they might have fabricated some of the stories about his self-glorification. He was a tremendous general, but while on the throne, he and the noble families who led society lacked empathy with each other. Thais needed a ruler who embodied the best aspects of their past but got one who represented a world out of joint.

The people rebelled against the tax farmer of Ayutthaya for being especially rapacious. Because Taksin had appointed him, locals associated them with each other. The officer that the court sent to quell the uprising joined it and called for Taksin's overthrow. The rebellion met little resistance, the old nobles spearheaded a palace coup, and the great fighter who saved Siam during its darkest hour was executed.

Thais then erected one of their country's greatest pillars. They invited a man who had distinguished himself on the battlefield to be the king. Chaophraya Chakri reigned from 1782 to 1809 as Rama I, and he was the first in the Chakri Dynasty. Recently deceased King Bhumibol continued the line as Rama IX.

The new king immediately started to rebuild his country. After only one month on the throne, he moved the capital across the river to its current location on the east bank. Burma also had a new monarch and seemed ready to pounce again—the east side was easier to defend. It would launch another invasion in 1785, which the Thais rebuffed. The Chakri Dynasty's prestige grew.

Rama knew that the old traditions were political unifiers. He thus continued associations between the monarch and Vishnu (the universe's preserver), which Angkor Wat's builder and Ayutthaya's kings had projected. Since the mythological Rama was an incarnation of Vishnu, the king wrote a Thai version of the *Ramayana* and organized performances of it. The palace sponsored troupes of dancers who dramatized it.

Rama also quickly strengthened the monkhood and ensured that the most pious and educated led its hierarchy. He built several monasteries in Bangkok and brought hundreds of old Buddha statues to them from Ayutthaya and Sukhothai. Because many animistic cults and rituals had grown into Buddhist practices during Ayutthaya's history, Rama sponsored a grand council to establish a definitive corpus of Buddhist scriptures. He also had several Theravada works translated into Thai from Pali. For the lay world, he revived state ceremonies from Ayutthaya. The new monarch tried to revitalize the past and purify it from the decadence which he felt had weakened Ayutthaya.

Bangkok's three central building complexes brilliantly reinforced Thai traditions as the new city developed. One is the Grand Palace, which stands next to the river and projects a shimmering skyline of golden spires. The second, Wat Pho (it's more formally known as Wat Phra Chetuphon), spreads out immediately south of the palace so that it continues the ethereal forms. Wat Arun is the third, and it rises directly across the river. It's dominated by a lofty stupa which begins as a broad base and steadily becomes narrower until it seems to dissolve into the heavens. In the midst of today's smoldering traffic and concrete sprawl, this structure radiates enduring grace.

These three monuments have provided exemplary forms in the city's heart. Rising within sight of each other, their towers flow together as people walk, boat, and drive by. Their lilting and glowing interplays straddle the river as it carries elegant longboats. So here is the old infinitely varied flow of graceful shrines, slow processions, and water from Ayutthaya, Sukhothai, and Lan Na. As in older Thai art, perspectives meander through slowly moving forms and images. Streets are often smoggy, congested, and loud, but this core of sacred buildings opens views into enchanted landscapes.

I stepped into a boat to cross the river for a closer look at Wat Arun. Many long and narrow vessels taxied between both sides and between ports on the east bank. For a humongous city bisected by a river, Bangkok has few bridges—Thais still seem psychically connected to boats on waterways. Four monks in orange robes boarded and sat next to me. Their repose and rippling gowns blended with the breezes and gentle water as we slowly approached the wat.

Wat Arun presides by the dock. This masterpiece soars over 200 feet, and it's surfaced with white stucco and covered with pieces of broken porcelain shaped as flowers with sinuous lines and long points. They add speckles of bright red, yellow, and green to its surface. Four smaller spires surround the central tower, and the contrasting heights make it appear even taller and broader. Wat Arun is both otherworldly and monumental, and since it balances heaven and earth while rising from the rippling waters, it integrates all domains. Many Bangkok residents consider it their favorite temple in the city.

Back on the other side of the river, I headed for the palace. Amulet sellers spread their wares on tables and mats over long stretches of sidewalk that run north from the palace. Locals wear them on chains for good luck, and the assortment I saw was huge. Buddha statues, Hindu gods, phalluses, and portraits of the king and holy men flickered together as spritely as Wat Arun's porcelain. Customers often choose a certain amulet for a specific need. Some buy the phalluses for fertility, and many of these charms bear inscriptions that are supposed to increase their potency. Amulet shoppers clogged the sidewalks into gridlock, showing that animistic beliefs are alive and well in the modern city.

A plain white wall encloses the palace and conceals splendors that people could never imagine from the street. The first courtyard that visitors enter is a large rectangular open space. On the left is the entrance to Wat Phra Kaew, which houses the hall of the Emerald Buddha, Thailand's most revered statue.

A large cloister with a mural of the *Ramayana* surrounds the hall. Its scenes of court life are so numerous that I felt that the Chakri Dynasty was making a political statement. Kings sit in front of gilded halls and pavilions with steep gabled roofs, and courtiers kneel before them in sparkling golden gowns. These elegant gatherings seem like the height of civilization. They dramatically contrast with battle scenes, giant monsters, and animated natural landscapes. The new monarchy seems to have been distinguishing its own goodness from dangers outside of its embrace. This courtly refinement was the standard that would safeguard the new country.

A few scenes lighten the seriousness with images from ordinary life. Women bathe, a boy rides a water buffalo's back, and a deer drinks from a pond covered with lily pads. Like the Buddha, the royal court rules gently.

Several young artists were restoring the walls' original sheen, and they treated the murals with reverence. They all meticulously followed the intricate old lines and remained silent in the midst of their sacred heritage.

Thais especially venerate the Emerald Buddha. King Rama I installed it in Bangkok in his drive to restore traditions, and it is supposed to have magical powers that protect the country.

I found the Emerald Buddha hard to see. It's a little over two feet tall but it sits on a lofty gilded throne in a long hall. Far more noticeable than the Buddha's features was the dense crowd of Thais paying homage. They quietly lined both sides of the hall and slowly proceeded through, perhaps hoping to receive some of the statue's grace. It is clothed in an outfit that matches each of the three seasons (hot, cool, and wet), and the king and his family have changed it in solemn ceremonies—only they can touch this statue.

The Emerald Buddha has a legendary past. It was sculpted from jade or jasper quartzite in the earthy Lan Na style and discovered in a wat up in Chiang Rai in 1434 when lightning struck a stupa that encased it. People thought it had miraculous powers, and they took it to a succession of northern Thai temples until the Laotian king Setthathirat carried it to his kingdom in the 16th century. It remained in Laos until the Thais conquered much of it during Taksin's campaigns, and they brought it back to their own realm. This story and tales of other Buddha statues' journeys to different temples have circulated in Thailand, helping to ingrain these sculptures into people's traditional ideas of geography. Many of the most revered statues have been copied several times, and the power of the original has been ritually transmitted into the newer statues, which were set up in other temples. The wat that housed the Emerald Buddha in Chiang Rai now has a copy which locals honor. When I visited it in 2012, it was housed in its own building, presiding in a tall pavilion on a high platform, and both were decorated with gold filigree to maximize the statue's dignity. Eminent Buddha statues form a field of grace, and their benevolent energies help keep the kingdom in order.

The Emerald Buddha is thus associated with many concepts that have been dear to Thais. They include etiquette, ritual, the Buddha's compassion, and the political center as a space that radiates positive energies. Rama I linked royalty with these ideas by installing the statue at the palace and enacting ceremonies to care for it. He masterfully combined many ideas from the past with the new monarchy and city.

Thailand's heritage glows as much at Wat Pho. In the early 19th century, King Rama III spread time-honored Thai knowledge by establishing this wat as a key center of education in religion, astrology, traditional medicine, and literature. People who went there found a wealth of old Thai art forms as examples of what harmonizes the world. Four tall and narrow stupas punctuate it, and each honors one of the first Chakri kings. The spires flicker with inlay and a different color dominates each one (blue, red, yellow, and silver). About 70 smaller stupas which house the ashes of other royals surround them. This group grounds the Chakri line in the old forms of narrow and sinuous towers that seem to dance as you walk around them. But one of Wat Pho's forms especially stands out.

A sleeping Buddha that is 150 feet long and 50 feet high resides in one of Wat Pho's halls. This is one of the most popular Buddha postures in Thailand. Wat Pho's statue is one of the smoothest-looking monuments

I've ever seen. Although it's enormous, the lines delicately curve and the gold leaf that covers it makes them appear as soft as silk.

The soles of the statue's feet contain a treasured art form in Thailand. Legend says that the Buddha traveled to Sri Lanka and left his footprint on a mountain called Adam's Peak to show that the island is important for spreading his teachings. Ancient Indians fashioned the Buddha's footprint, which often symbolized him before they began to depict his images about 2,000 years ago. Thais later added their own aesthetics to this art form. The footprints in Wat Pho are full of mother-of-pearl inlay, which shines silver, rose, and light green hues against a black background. The designs include gossamer images of trees, plants, birds, Mt. Meru, Indra's palace, and intricate temples. Thais circulated stories about the Buddha wandering through their land, leaving his footprint in different places, and they produced it in wats where they thought he had taught. These artworks thus unify the country in a geography of benevolence, as the Emerald Buddha does.

Bangkok's first kings used several ideas to restore the past as people recovered from the Burmese invasion. Statues, footprints of the Buddha, wats, the royal court, paintings and performances of the *Ramayana*, rivers, and old aesthetics centered on gentle and animated flows reinforced Thailand's ancient heritage. The city sometimes boils and festers, but people are still often reminded of their traditions.

But Bangkok quickly developed another personality. The town beyond the three sacred building complexes grew from a network of forested canals into a modern metropolis. Floating wooden houses and shops were the most common sights in the early 19th century. Travelers wrote of long lines of them on each side of the waterways, which thousands of little boats plied. Temples' spires and the palace rose behind them. Southeast Asians, Chinese, and Westerners rubbed elbows, and bands of musicians pierced the languid air with xylophones and flutes. But these Ayutthayan scenes transformed within 50 years of the city's founding.

The historian Nidhi Eoseewong noted that Bangkok quickly developed a different atmosphere than Ayutthaya's because it became less dominated by the palace and more by commoners. Residents ignored the old social hierarchy from Ayutthaya which had regulated each class's behavior and attire, and common businesspeople built wats and large homes. An increasing number of Chinese moved into the city and formed large commercial networks that traded rice, sugar, cotton, and wood. Money was used much more than it had been in Ayutthaya. Bangkok was becoming more secular and complex.

Eoseewong and David Wyatt noted that literature began to reflect this more commercial world. Ayutthaya's texts focused more on divinities and the royal court, and people had often enacted them in ceremonies. Eoseewong wrote that stories in Bangkok were not as strictly bound to ritualized performances; they were more often privately read. People now enjoyed books in worldly settings as consumer products. Writers often used simpler verse forms that were easier to read, and scenes in literature became more realistic. Cities were depicted in more detail for the sake of enjoyment. Texts were becoming more focused on this world than the supernatural.

Performing arts beyond the palace also grew and they enlivened the streets. Bangkok's zesty night life emerged. Drunks staggered by canals, prostitutes accosted people from boats, and many Chinese men set up gambling houses.

At the same time, some painters learned about Western art and adapted features of three-dimensional perspective. They didn't completely reduce scenes to it because the foreign influences were mixed with traditional graceful lines and meanderings. Like Florence in the 15th century, Bangkok did more business, used more money, and organized more complex commerce than before. However, Florence inherited the ancient Greco-Roman heritage and Christianity, and it was in contact with towns all over Europe which reinforced the ideas and aesthetics from both. It was also in a different natural environment. Thais had their own rich ancient and medieval past, as well as their own natural landscape, and they synthesized what they learned from the West with them. But the newly imported techniques still allowed more analytical arrangements of details. The old elegance was mixing with business people's worldly interests.

Figure 31. Traditional meanderings and modern lines in a 19th century Thai painting. Though lines dominate the scene, people's sizes vary, groups are non-linearly related, and buildings' lines aren't integrated into one three-dimensional perspective. The viewer can still meander.

So Bangkok's spiritual art soon shared space with sensual pop culture, a heady business world, and modern boulevards. Sadly, new experiences also included cholera epidemics and canals stinking with pollution. Many Westerners then and now have felt that the city mixes incongruent realities. Transcendental art alternates with tawdry surroundings.

Wanting to see how average Bangkok residents spent their Friday nights, I headed for one of the most popular shopping districts in the city's center. Siam Square and a hulking multi-story mall called MBK sprawl next to each other. Both mix commercial bustle and traditional aesthetics. MBK is endlessly long, with what seemed to be as many little shops as stars in the sky. A walk through its aisles immersed me in an endlessly varied mixture of colors and forms. Stores displayed T-shirts, sunglasses, cellphones, shoes, handbags, suitcases, backpacks, belts,

Buddha statues, dolls, teapots, and jewelry. Neon lights and advertising signs flickered overhead. No single thing stood out because all objects mingled in a flow of shimmering colors. The aisles teemed with people slowly strolling together in the same relaxed flows I saw in wats and night markets. Groups of friends ambled shoulder to shoulder and young couples held hands. These well-behaved people meandered in cozy clusters, savoring the endless variety of cheerful hues and forms. *Sabai* still lives.

Even Thailand's more unseemly pop culture often reflects her ancient traditions. Tattoos, lady-boys, massage parlors, snookers halls, brightly painted trucks, garish movie posters, soap operas with women fighting like alley cats, kick boxing ads, and glib pop music often blend into the energetic and tolerant flows of forms and colors. The old animated streams can embrace anything that new generations concoct.

The stellar reigns of King Mongkut (Rama IV; r. 1851–1868) and his son Chulalongkorn (Rama V; r. 1868–1910) mixed traditions and modernity in new ways. They helped modernize the country and preserve its customs while European states threatened to take it over. Their brilliant strategies allowed Siam to prosper during those trying times (the country was called Siam before its name was changed to Thailand in 1939). Both people were fascinating mixtures of the old and the new.

Bangkok was bustling with merchants and glimmering with art, but Western canons were casting long shadows. To Siam's west, England was biting off large chunks of Burma. In 1852 it took over its southern region after the second Anglo-Burmese War, which erupted from quarrels over the liberties of British merchants. In 1855 England pressured Siam to accept the Bowring Treaty, which compelled it to lower tariffs and allow British traders to live there with extraterritorial privileges. Siam quickly negotiated similar treaties with the United States, France, and several other countries to avoid domination by England. Though never outright colonized, it lost some of its independence by having to grant foreign countries advantageous trading terms while giving their subjects legal protection when they got into civil and criminal cases.

France brewed equally menacing storms in the east. Cambodia's Prince Norodom signed a treaty with France in 1863 that allowed it to

control his country's foreign relations in return for its protection against
Siam and Vietnam. Siam's next door neighbors were falling under the
tiger powers of Western guns and modern finance.

England and France then assumed firmer control in the region. In
1885 the third Anglo-Burmese War broke out and it ended in a complete takeover of Burma. France had been utterly humiliated in a war
with Prussia in 1870–71 and was eager to recover her pride and to check
England's gains in Asia. In 1893 her gunboats steamed up the Chao
Phraya River and threatened to attack Bangkok.[2] She forced Siam to
accept an even harsher agreement than the Bowring Treaty and took a
lot of eastern land, including what later became modern Laos.

Squeezed between these two giants, both Thai kings realized
that they had to modernize the country so it would be too strong and
respectable for any nation to invade. Father and son would steer Siam
through turbulent waters in ways that mixed traditional and modern
perspectives.

Mongkut fused the old and new even before becoming the king.
He lived in a monastery and studied religious texts with an unusually
critical eye. He rejected old ideas of the supernatural and didn't believe
in heaven and hell. He also studied Latin, English, mathematics, and
astronomy, and spent a great deal of time with Christian missionaries.
Mongkut remained keenly interested in science and technology throughout his reign. He peppered Western technologists with questions and
collected clocks and scientific instruments.

Mongkut accepted the West's discovery that the earth is round and
denounced traditional Buddhist beliefs in a world centered on Mt. Meru.
Many nobles and monks held onto those old ideas, but when Mongkut
became the king, advocates of modern science had much more clout
by being associated with royalty's prestige. People thus increasingly
accepted the new perspectives.

He also brought the palace to the people by posing for photographs
in slick uniforms. The king made himself more visible to the public than
any previous Chakri ruler had.

But Mongkut still bolstered Thai traditions. He reinstated royal rituals from the Ayutthaya period and restored many archeological sites,
including Sukhothai—he is credited with finding (or fabricating) the

Ramkhamhaeng stele. He also outlined a more detailed hierarchy of the royal family to elevate the monarchy's prestige.

Both scholarly and hands-on until the end of his life, Mongkut sailed to the mouth of the Chao Phraya River to observe an eclipse, contracted malaria, and passed away. He had opened doors to the modern world and vistas of the past while protecting the country from Western imperialism. His son's reign would be equally brilliant.

While Bangkok kept growing, two hallowed wats were built a couple of miles from the palace/Wat Pho/Wat Arun area, and they strengthened roots from the past. An artificial hill called the Golden Mount thrusts upwards in Wat Saket. The hill began life as an enormous stupa that Rama III tried to build, but the marshy soil gave way under the weight. Mongkut and Chulalongkorn reinforced the mound and a gilded temple was erected on it. The city's flatness allowed it to stand out like a beacon.

Steps curve around the hill, and the temple on the summit is capped with a tapering spire that soars above the town. The building is gold and white, and it glared enough under the sun to make me wish I had sunglasses. I felt like I was immersed in a fusion of purity and blazing energy when I reached the top.

After descending the stairs around the other side of the hill, I found more entrancing scenery. I ended up in front of a group of small rectangular buildings with white walls and red and gold gabled roofs. Was it a San Francisco 49ers' spiritual retreat? It was actually part of Wat Saket. Many trees provided shade and soft greens to balance the bright hues. Small boat-shaped libraries on stilts rose between some of the dorms.

But the wat's calmness is interrupted in November by a huge fair with musical performances and food to honor relics of the Buddha. People decorate the mount with colored lights and conduct processions to the summit.

This cheer allows visitors to forget that Wat Saket used to be associated with death. Forbidden to cremate bodies within the city walls, people brought them to this temple. So many corpses piled up during cholera outbreaks that there wasn't room to bury all of them. Dogs chomped on bones while vultures perched in the trees. Nineteenth century Western visitors found the wat spooky, but Thais later beautified the mount's ascent with gardens and added the November festivities.

The second wat also mixes majesty and whimsy. Rama I founded it and it's called Wat Suthat. Its buildings are regal. Tall white pillars surround the main hall, which is topped by steep roofs that are stacked on each other. Their red and green colors stand out from the columns. They are so much higher than Lan Na wats' roofs that only spirits seem able to touch them.

Priests conduct sacred royal rituals at Wat Suthat. People have associated the temple with Indra's palace because he is supposed to bring rain. Brahman priests who perform the Royal Plowing Ceremony, which initiates Thailand's rice growing season, are based there. This ritual associates royal merit with crop fertility.

I also found a lot of lightheartedness in the wat. Thin Chinese pagodas 15 to 20 feet high surrounded the hall, and they slowly glissaded with its columns and roofs as I walked around. Two cheerful male groundskeepers said, "Hello!" and one drank from what looked like a beer bottle.

Both wats balance sacred power and meandering perspectives, and the stupa on the Golden Mount makes this area beam for many miles. Both places reinforced Thai traditions in the increasingly fast-paced modern world.

As Bangkok grew, trains, electric street lights, paved roads, wide boulevards, and modern government buildings in Western architectural styles mingled with the temples and waterways. All of these features have made the cityscape irreducible so that it can't be conceived as one system of forms. A meandering perspective is often truer to it than a modern map is. I rode in many tuk tuks through crowded old neighborhoods in the town's central districts and passed motorcycle part shops, fish markets, street food sellers, jewelry stores, pharmacies, clothing marts, and shops selling candles, incense, and banners to offer in temples. Zoning laws seemed non-existent. Motorcycles and people clogged the sidewalks. Suddenly a temple with a golden spire and a multi-gabled vihara would appear. Grunge and charm often alternated.

Many Thais honor Chulalongkorn more than any other king. I've seen his pictures on shelves and altars in hundreds of wats and businesses, and in Bangkok's amulet market. His photo also presides in many restaurants in America as though he looks after the owners like a grandfather's spirit.

Thais have found stability in him in the midst of recent political frays, uncertain economics, and dislocations from the countryside. His face looks both strong and kindly. His drooping moustache suggests masculine vigor, but his eyes often exude warmth.

Chulalongkorn showed signs of being a great king soon after inheriting the throne at the age of fifteen. His father had prepared him to rule by giving him both a modern Western and a traditional Thai education. The new monarch traveled to Singapore, Java, Malaysia, Burma, and India to observe modern political trends to bring home, and to bolster his image as the country's figurehead. He sent 20 people from the royal court to Singapore for educations and sponsored translations of constitutions from several European nations. A wave of reforms to modernize the country followed.

Chulalongkorn centralized state finances, updated education, abolished slavery, and traveled to Europe to observe how Western countries were governed. He also encouraged people to settle in the hinterlands, clear the jungles, and plant rice. Siam became a rice exporter, selling much of its crop to India and China. More land assumed the settled appearance that I first saw from my airplane window.

The king organized the country into provinces, sent officials to govern them, and paid them from Bangkok. Many provincial nobles formerly relied on revenues from their own lands, but Chulalongkorn transformed them from proud medieval lords into the state's subjects. He established a royal auditing office to reform the monarchy's finances, and created accounting and bookkeeping jobs.

New railroads connected the main towns with Bangkok, and mapmakers used techniques they had learned from the West to precisely arrange cities and towns according to latitudes and longitudes. A more modern and analytical view of the world was now growing alongside the older geographies centered on wats, Buddha statues, and palaces.

In the late 1880s Chulalongkorn said that school textbooks were useless because they taught kids about kings and battles rather than modern science. He implemented a new curriculum in 1892, which included the updated ideas of geography. More Thais were assimilating Western concepts of the world as a map of linear coordinates. Before then, borderlands were often vaguely conceived as forests and mountains between villages, and many people living in those areas had submitted to multiple lords. They were willing to pay tribute to anyone who could protect them, and they yielded to several sovereigns to hedge their bets for security. Traditional Thai politics often treated space as ordered by royal and provincial courts and temples, whose power (material and spiritual) radiated throughout the land and became less effective as the distance from the center increased. The borders between these spaces were fuzzy, but modern maps now treated them as abstract lines. Students were learning to sharply divide domains and precisely analyze them as people in other modernizing countries have.[3]

Chulalongkorn projected his image even more than his father had displayed his own. He was photographed and painted more, and he let his face be reproduced on coins, stamps, and postcards. Later in life he enjoyed motoring around Bangkok in a car. It was thus increasingly possible to see him as a real person rather than an aloof king from the Ayutthayan past. Chulalongkorn even abolished the custom of prostrating in the king's presence. People were astounded; even today many Thais feel uncomfortable standing before their king. But he wanted people to realize that he was a human being.

Many of the old landed families resisted these rapid changes. Some of the great lines from Ayutthaya still held court positions and enjoyed privileges in trading and administration. They were so ardent and numerous that Chulalongkorn couldn't immediately challenge them. Instead, he sent many children in his extended family to modern schools and then gave them high positions in the government, hoping that the new generation would cooperate with him as the old guard died out.

His extended family was enormous. He had dozens of consorts and sired nearly 100 children. Many Thais admired his fertility and some associated it with their country's strength. The great reformer had a sensuous side and he composed romantic poems for many in his harem.

Chulalongkorn brought this mixture of tradition, pleasure, and elegance to the arts. He wrote plays, including one about a love triangle between three forest dwellers in the south. Most Thais saw this type of character as the antithesis of courtly and urban refinement, but the king portrayed his with enough tenderness to make people sympathize with them.

He created more fun mixtures of old and new by adding more ceremonies to the ritual calendar. The Royal Tonsure Ceremony, the Investiture of the Crown Prince, the Centennial Celebration of the City of Ratanakosin, and royal cremations were conducted with full pomp. Floats with multi-tiered roofs that stood for the different heavens in Buddhist and Hindu mythology rolled between rows of spectators. Golden royal barges over 100 feet long glided between the Grand Palace, Wat Pho, and Wat Arun.

These ceremonies had many meanings. Chulalongkorn followed King Rama I by strengthening the sacred past. Nostalgia also encouraged them because people craved stability in the uncertain modern world. The historian Maurizio Peleggi noted that Western monarchies did the same thing then. Europeans in the last 30 years of the 19th century saw increasing industrialization, nationalism, and military build-up that would make hamburger out of millions of youths in World War I. Royals tried to ignore the impending carnage by playing dress-up. The 60th anniversary of Queen Victoria's reign was one of the most famous high class ceremonies, with dignitaries from all over the British Empire parading through London.

Peleggi also noted that Chulalongkorn was showing Western nations that Siam deserved respect. Its people could stage equally magnificent shows and follow Victorian manners while wearing dapper suits. But most spectators probably focused more on the fun.

After outlasting the old noble families, Chulalongkorn was confronted by the young generation that he had helped modernize. They had studied Western constitutions and legal theories, and some youths now questioned his authority. Eleven of them sent him a petition that criticized him for holding onto and mixing executive, legislative, and judicial powers. They said that he should share his authority with a prime minister, a cabinet, and a parliament so that Westerners would respect their country.[4]

Chulalongkorn replied wisely: The argument may be right in theory, but the people are not yet ready to govern themselves. Siam lacks educated and loyal people to implement the reforms. Older officials are incompetent and only care about their vested interests, and the young are too inexperienced to carry out the tasks. Chulalongkorn ushered his country into the modern world with sensitivity that China's Mao lacked when he spearheaded the Great Leap Forward, which resulted in millions of deaths.

More wats were constructed in Bangkok as the king worked to modernize the country, including one of my favorites, Wat Benchamabophit. There already was a temple there, but people built a new vihara and several other structures. The vihara has a few Western features—it's made of white Carrara marble and has stained glass windows. But these blend with Thai aesthetics. The windows are full of paintings of leaves in traditional Thai flame patterns, with flowing lines that end in sharp points. The vihara is in a cruciform pattern and it's crowned by a shimmering red and gold roof that rises in tiered gables on all four sides towards the center. Fifty-three Buddha statues in various Thai styles, including Lan Na and Sukhothai, line a covered promenade around a courtyard next to the vihara.

Though people in the late 19th century constructed several buildings in Bangkok with Western colonnades, they didn't dominate the scenery. Instead, they mixed with traditional Thai temples so that the cityscape remained a flow of many forms that people could meander around. Though this mélange became more international, it was still very Thai.

Graceful aesthetics still pervaded the big city as the 20th century roared in. Bangkok's endless waves of concrete and stop-and-go traffic jams have been beautified with shining wats, little spirit houses, monks in flowing saffron robes, and pictures of kings and honored clerics. These art forms developed from the rich art of Sukhothai, Lan Na, and Ayutthaya, and from ancient patterns of cooperative agricultural life in intimate communities. Some of Bangkok's nightlife sizzles, but within this larger environment which has many ancient roots.

Thai culture thus endured through the 20th century while modern problems mounted. Ecological destruction, rampant corruption, frequent changes of political regime, steroidal urban growth, congested slums, the drug trade, prostitution, child labor, AIDS, and the bloody attempts in the largely Islamic southernmost provinces to break away have combined to make people wonder if their country can maintain its stability. Desires for peace have usually mitigated violence, but the political situation recently became more contentious.

Bangkok has a vibrant modern art scene that blends old grace and modern problems, and it has thrived for almost 100 years. This isn't surprising, given Thais' openness to Western influence, but their modern art is distinctly Thai. A museum curator gave me a list of exhibitions around town and I visited four of them. I found that artists have creatively expressed tensions between traditions and modern life.

I thought that the best art was at Silpakorn University. An Italian sculptor named Corrado Feroci founded this school and Thais still honor him for promoting their art. Chulalongkorn's son and successor, King Vajiravudh, invited him to Bangkok in 1923 to design and build monuments to Thai history. Feroci was so enchanted by his new country's art and people that he changed his name to Silpa Bhirasri and convinced the government to finance his school, where he taught for many years. Its location across the street from the Grand Palace bespeaks its prestige.

I thought the students were receiving good training. The paintings and sculptures on display were in many styles, and most balanced colors and forms well. A lot of the schooling was Western, but most students were mixing their own traditions with the foreign inspirations. Many employed old sinuous and animated forms in dialogs with modern life.

Some paintings were impressionistic, but in Thai styles. One was of a temple with a stack of gabled roofs. I enjoyed the combination—impressionism's momentary flickers of light mixed with a wat's animated colors and lilting forms.

Other artists fused Thai and modern Western styles in edgy ways. The main exhibition hall featured a painter named Santi Thongsuk. He created several images of Buddhist monks meditating in rows. Their shaven heads, delicate facial features, and flowing gowns had the expected grace, but there were no cheerful saffron hues. Many canvasses violently contrasted sinister dark greys with bright lights flashing overhead. In one picture, fighter jets with huge missiles drooping from their wings roared low enough to decapitate anyone who stood up.

Montien Boonma fashioned an 88-inch-high stupa form from various modern construction materials found in Bangkok, including cement, steel bars, and plastic sockets. He thereby mixed a hallowed shape with urban blight.

One of Thailand's most famous painters (and poets), Angkarn Kalayaanapongse, more strictly focused on Thai patterns. He employed traditional flame motifs that rise in curvy lines that end in sharp points to depict rice stalks and bamboo shoots. Angkarn thereby portrayed the energy that infuses the plants that sustain people.

Artists incorporate pretty traditions to express modern troubles without being entirely confrontational or despairing. They can use a rich stock of images from their past to buffer the increasing incongruities between traditions and modernity. But the modern world is permeating life in Thailand more and more, and it's creating so many disjunctions from the past that many journalists have wondered if the country will remain peaceful and stable. Bangkok exploded into an all-out battle between the army and the people in 2010, and more violence broke out in 2013 and 2014. We'll explore Thailand's current troubles in the next chapter and see how the method for finding paradise can help to overcome them, as well as other nations' political problems.

CHAPTER 15

A NEW DAWNING OF GRACE: HOW TO SEE BEYOND THAILAND'S AND THE REST OF THE WORLD'S CURRENT PROBLEMS AND DISCOVER HUMANITY'S FULL WEALTH

IN THE 1970s, the writer Suchit Wongthed penned a story that portrayed Thailand as a place that many people wanted to leave. Thai college students studying in America complained about their country during a party, and several wanted to work in the U.S. and make money to buy a house and car. They felt that success in Thailand comes down to the people that one knows, and they didn't look forward to giving up their freedom and returning to familial and class obligations, and to a culture in which folks are afraid to take risks. Instead of investing in new businesses and industries, people showed off their wealth and jockeyed for positions within the established political order.

Suchit wrote an even more disturbing story about a former monk who had lost his faith in Buddhism because the world no longer conformed to its world-view. He felt that the universe is no longer moral and that money and power are the main values. People get away with doing anything in order to acquire them.

A lot of modern Thai literature is critical and sometimes harshly realistic, which is a far cry from Ayutthaya's elegant court performances. Most countries' modern literature is socially realistic and critical, but these traits have been the opposites of many traditional Thai values. Another writer, Anud Aaphaaphirom, compared the *phuujaj* (big man) to a toad. Some Thais consider this creature especially revolting because it's unusually ugly and it can cause skin infections—it seems fiendish in a society that values pretty surfaces. But Anud said that big men are worse because they're arrogant and they suppress others. He vowed to vanquish them and create a new society without them.

Thailand's writing community is small, but the whole country has embraced television. The most noticeable things I saw in a soap opera were women yelling at each other in shrill voices that reminded me of screeching monkeys. Modern media often encourage loudness and Thais have always enjoyed temporary breaches of etiquette; the media let them indulge in them without threatening the status quo. But these portrayals are now prevalent and abrasive enough to show that Thais are aware of deep problems that plague their society.

Thais revere their recently departed king, Bhumibol, and see him as a sacred figure who towered above the tumult and protected his people. Occupying the throne from 1946 to 2016, he was the world's longest-reigning monarch and longest-serving head of state. The politics after Chulalongkorn's reign have encouraged Thais to see him as a central figure in their society's order.

Chulalongkorn's successor, Vajiravudh, spent money as prolifically as fish lay eggs. Like Chulalongkorn, he wrote plays but lavished more on performing arts and courtly fineries while most Thais still farmed to survive. The new generation of political leaders, exposed to ideas of accountable government, found his opulence at the country's expense abhorrent. Many had come from Bangkok's new middle class of lawyers, teachers, journalists, and civil servants, and they increasingly saw the monarchy as outdated, but the king refused people's requests for reforms. So in 1927 a group of young Thai men in Paris planned a revolution.

This group grew into the People's Party, and in 1932 it captured the leader of the royal palace guard, arrested about 40 royal family members, and announced the end of the monarchy's authority. King Prajadhipok (Vajiravudh's successor) graciously didn't resist in order to avoid bloody civil unrest. A constitution was established, and in 1935 the king abdicated.

But the political waters remained stormy. First the Great Depression ravaged the economy. Then World War II broke out and Thailand was caught between Japan and the Allies. The government played it safe by first allying the country with Japan, since it invaded Southeast Asia and became its dominant power by 1941. But Thailand backed away from Japan three years later, when the Allies' victory seemed inevitable. Thailand escaped the devastating battles that Burma suffered, but the powers of both sides to overwhelm it resembled England's and France's in the previous century. Both were too strong to confront directly and this made Thais feel that their security was fragile.

The government decided to bring the monarchy back home after the war. Bhumibol's older brother, Ananda Mahidol, was in line for the throne, but in 1946 he was shot point-blank in the head while in bed at the palace. The murder horrified Thais and it remains unsolved.

Corruption has compounded the modern upheavals. Since 1932 Thailand has changed its constitution about every four years on average. Officials and rich businessmen scratching each other's backs have often dominated politics. The government of Chatichai Choonhavan, who was the prime minister in the late 1980s, was so corrupt that it was called "the buffet cabinet." Politicians and businessmen have typically formed cohorts that vie with each other until the military overthrows the government in the name of stabilizing the country.

Several factors thus added up to a dramatic contrast with idealized images of Chulalongkorn. Impersonal forces of the 20th century that seemed too big to contend with, rampant political misconduct, and stresses of modern life have made Thais long for safety. The idea of a stable royal line from him to Bhumibol has helped people feel secure.

Bhumibol mixed Eastern and Western roots as deftly as his two great predecessors did. He was born in Massachusetts in 1927—his father studied medicine at Harvard so he could bring the most advanced treatments back to his own country. The family soon moved to Thailand and the father tragically died. His widow and her sons then relocated to Switzerland, and Bhumibol seemed on his way to becoming a stylish European. He spoke French, admired fast cars, enjoyed photography and abstract modern painting, and became an accomplished jazz saxophonist.

After his brother's death, Bhumibol took on the colossal burden of being Thailand's figurehead with tireless dedication. He studied

Buddhism and intricate royal rituals in Bangkok's Wat Bowonniwet and is supposed to have learned esoteric ideas about how the king reaches spiritual perfection.

But he still kept ties with Western culture and remained a keen sax blower. He hosted jam sessions at the palace, and musicians visiting Thailand received invitations to join him. Benny Goodman performed with him and Bhumibol was dubbed "The King of Jazz." Bhumibol met another king, Elvis, while visiting America and touring Paramount Studios as *GI Blues* was being made.

In the late 1950s Bhumibol and Prime Minister Sarit Thanarat collaborated to make the young king's image central in modern Thai society. They added even more rituals to the calendar. Anniversaries and birthdays became reasons for spectacular parades and were broadcasted to radios and TVs all over the country.

In the 1960s Bhumibol became even more visible with projects for the ecology and charity work for disadvantaged farmers. He kept a breakneck schedule of travels throughout the country while performing his political functions and rituals in Bangkok. His image often helped people forget that politics during that decade were dominated by an oligarchy of corrupt businessmen and high-ranking military officers.

Thais admire his labors and consider him a model of Buddhist merit. They speak of him with deep reverence. Though he turned eighty in 2007, one man I met in Bangkok then told me that the king is handsome. Most people only say positive things about him and associate everything good with him as though he's a battery of blessings. Maybe he is because Thailand has changed governments like shoes, but with much less bloodshed than Cambodia and Burma have suffered in recent years.

But people all over the country are concerned about what will happen now that Bhumibol has passed away. If Thais have depended on his persona for domestic peace, will their society become unstable?

Thailand's lèse-majesté laws have often been criticized for being the world's harshest. Internet surveillance, website blocking, and summonses to police stations for interrogations have become commonplace.[1] People are touchy about royalty's image, and some journalists have worried that without a revered leader as an icon of merit and stability, who has occupied the throne for several decades, the country will either be vulnerable to the worst violence since the Burmese sacked Ayutthaya, or straitjacketed under an authoritarian regime that will suppress criticism.

Shortly after my blissful 2007 trip, Thailand became more violent and politically volatile. Politics had already polarized around the man who was the prime minister from 2001 to 2006, Thaksin Shinawatra. He was a billionaire-owner of a telecommunications company and a former police officer, and his personal style was brasher than what most Thais were accustomed to. But he was also a populist, with the slogan "Thais love Thais" and an image of an underprivileged boy who later succeeded on his own terms. Many of the rural poor have supported him because he worked to lessen their plight, but urban middle classes found him corrupt and authoritarian, accusing him of lining his own pockets with business concessions he granted and suppressing dissent. Many of his critics thought he used arbitrary and excessive force against Muslim rebels in the south and against the drug trade (though the use of a powerful stimulant called Ya Ba had become a national problem, with more than one million users, many people were hastily identified as traders and shot to death in the streets without due legal process). The conflict between Thaksin's supporters (red shirts) and opponents (yellow shirts) has been unprecedented. Millions of ordinary Thais outside of politics and the military have been at loggerheads, and many have used force against each other.

In 2006 the military ousted Thaksin after large groups of street demonstrators complained about corruption and abuses of power, and he went into exile in Dubai. Several prime ministers have come and gone since then. In 2008 yellow shirts seized Bangkok's main airport and held it for several days to force the government to resign, stranding about 300,000 travelers.

The worst violence exploded in March–May 2010. Thousands of red shirts occupied one of Bangkok's largest parks and one of its main retail districts and tried to advance on Silom Road, where several major banks operate. The military rolled in with tanks, assault rifles, and firehoses, and both groups quickly began to shoot at each other. People disagree about who started the battle (the media also polarized into these two factions and they often told conflicting stories) but about 90 people died during the riots, and roughly 1,800 were hurt, including journalists from overseas.[2] Most casualties were among the red shirts. The army broke up their demonstrations but many outraged red shirts set fires in Bangkok's center, and some torched a large shopping mall. Black smoke flared around the formerly cheerful white skyscrapers. The city that I had found gracious became a war zone.

Bangkok was peaceful when I returned in 2012, but I wondered whether that was a return to normality or a calm between storms. Thaksin's sister, Yingluck, was recently elected as the prime minister by his supporters, and she emphasized compromise with a pretty smile. But yellow shirts suspected that her brother was directing her from overseas. They sprang into action in late 2013 when she tried to allow him back into the country, forcing their way into government office compounds. They battled police in the streets and more than 400 casualties resulted.

After this fighting, an ardent Yingluck foe and former deputy prime minister named Suthep led the demonstrators and insisted that she step down without holding a re-election. Her supporters contended that this was because she would have won, since red shirts still backed her and they held the majority in Thailand, especially in the north. Suthep, known for being fiery, called her shameless and vowed to condemn her every day. This harsh language and unwillingness to compromise is a far cry from the traditional etiquette, but they became more common in the last decade.

In May 2014 a judicial coup removed Yingluck from office. Suthep tried to form a "people's council" to appoint a new prime minister. That would have been outside of the democratic process of holding a nationwide election, but he felt that it was the most effective way to rid the government of her brother's influence. Red shirts camped in Bangkok's suburbs, threatening to move into the city to defend democracy if any more steps were taken against the government.[3]

The military then spearheaded a coup and detained hundreds of politicians, journalists, and activists that its leaders considered suspicious. The violence has eased since then and the junta staged a happiness campaign, with street festivals, free haircuts and hot meals, a petting zoo with ponies, and a dance show with women in miniskirts. But it became a criminal offense to criticize the junta. Because it has made the revival of Thailand's economy a top priority, it needs an air of legitimacy to attract foreign investment and encourage domestic confidence. But *The Economist* (August 9, 2014) noted that institutions that fuel economic growth are eroding, including the rule of law. Though the junta is trying to restore peace and prosperity, many journalists feel that Thailand's political situation remains tense and uncertain. A Chiang Mai-based associate of mine said that the night spots he goes to are less festive than they were when I enjoyed them.

These polarized viewpoints and divisive politics didn't suddenly rush in like a monsoonal storm. Several political analysts have noted that Thai society has had structural problems that will worsen if people keep ignoring them. Many Thais look back to the years from 1985 to 1997 as the good old days. The economy was growing at a dazzling pace and most people seemed to benefit to some extent. Since then, growth has been more unevenly distributed and gaps between the wealthy and poor have increased.[5] However, this problem didn't suddenly emerge; things weren't as rosy as they seemed back then.

The 1997 economic crisis in Southeast Asia hit Thailand especially hard because its economy was already shakier than most people had realized. Its currency, the baht, nosedived; national reserves fell from $38 billion to $2.8 billion; the banking system collapsed; and the IMF and foreign banks took over a lot of the country's finances.[6] Before 1997 many business leaders constructed a multitude of upscale hotels and resorts instead of improving the education system, developing original high-tech products, and diversifying the economy with new industries. The assets that they did build were often prestige items, which didn't make the entire economy more robust by benefitting a large percentage of people outside of their narrow circles.

At the same time, Thailand's loosely regulated financial industry allowed easy credit that seduced people into investing in more unproductive assets.[7] From 1990 to 1996, Bangkok's stock market's index soared from 600 to over 1,400, and some of the new funds were invested in more real estate so that multiple inflated markets were feeding each other.

Foreign investors eagerly joined the banquet, throwing yet more money into an unsound economic system and further inflating the growing credit bubble. They then quickly pulled out when they noticed growing local instability and found more attractive prospects in other countries. This encouraged the prices of assets that had been inflated by the supercharged speculations to suddenly plummet so that many people and businesses defaulted on their debts.

Thailand's economy lacked original high-tech products that could compete in global markets. Many people then and now have held relatively unskilled positions in manufacturing and in service industries like retail, hospitality, and travel, which the spiffy new buildings house. Most of the banks and travel agencies I entered employed more workers at the counters than they seemed to need. I enjoyed the prompt and courteous service, but I wondered what everybody did all day.

New cash crops and machines that were introduced in the 1960s had created a divide between farmers wealthy enough to mechanize and poor peasants who couldn't. The rising costs of agricultural inputs and the often widely fluctuating prices of commodities in global markets forced a lot of small-time farmers into debt. Many of the later migrated to Bangkok. They increased Thailand's large unskilled labor pool, which became increasingly vulnerable to the ups and downs of an economy that's not diverse.

The mechanized factories that many had to labor in were a world away from the pretty rice fields they had grown up around and the relaxed meanders in wats and rural neighborhoods. Thais have traditionally enjoyed *sanuk* for its lightheartedness and lack of regimentation. But the journalist Sanitsuda Ekachai, in *Behind the Smile: Voices of Thailand*, described factory workers taking amphetamines for stamina during the day and then drinking alcohol at bedtime to calm their systems so they could fall asleep.[8]

As gaps between haves and have-nots widened, and as the internet allowed images and criticism to spread like wildfire, Thailand became edgier, with more polarized political viewpoints and hot-headed rhetoric. Michael J. Montesano, in *Legitimacy Crisis in Thailand*, wrote that the red shirt movement is bigger than Thaksin because it grew from disenfranchised people's grievances. He said that the disparity between rich and poor has become so acute that the country will need to reconceive its modern history in more egalitarian and less elitist terms in order to remain stable.[9] Such a big reconceptualization is a far cry from traditions that emphasize meandering perspectives, social hierarchy, and not questioning the order of things.

Modern Thailand's deadliest problem to date has been the rebellion in the deep south, where provinces have Islamic majorities that are ethnically Malay. They don't identify with Buddhism or Thai culture, and they have often felt like second-class citizens.

The rebellion has roots in an 1897 agreement with England. Thais still feared an invasion by Western countries, but Chulalongkorn had an ace up his sleeve. He could build a canal across the narrowest part of the lower peninsula and bite a big chunk out of British revenue—with the world's largest navy, England conducted a lot of shipping in the region. Both nations cut a deal. If Thailand would agree to avoid digging the canal, Britain wouldn't invade.[10] Both countries sat at the bargaining table and decided where the borders between Thailand and British possessions would be. But nobody bothered to ask the Islamic sultanates in the area how they felt, even though some of them had proud histories that went back to Malacca's time.

Some of the sultanates had submitted to Ayutthaya at times, but they still retained their own identities and enjoyed a lot of autonomy. They often only needed to send Ayutthaya tribute and respect its courtly protocols when their envoys met. They were largely left alone to govern themselves. But after their region officially became part of Thailand in 1909, politicians were sent from Bangkok to control them and most weren't Muslims. Locals have often felt politically disenfranchised ever since.

Separatist groups became increasingly violent in the 1970s. According to Duncan McCargo, in *Tearing Apart the Land; Islam and Legitimacy in Southern Thailand*, as many as 1,000 insurgents were staging attacks in the south by 1980, and some began to detonate bombs in Bangkok.

In the 1980s Prime Minister Prem Tinsulanonda's government was able to mute the unrest by giving the region political privileges and funds for development. But Thaksin couldn't have been more insensitive when he assumed leadership in 2001. The ex-policeman and hard-driving tycoon dissolved many of Prem's arrangements and

put the widely disliked police force in charge of security. Feeling disenfranchised again, separatists stepped up attacks on security posts.
Thaksin's administration simplistically branded the insurgents as
hooligans and returned the brutality. In 2004 seventy-eight unarmed
protestors caught in a mass arrest died in military custody, reportedly
from suffocation.

I saw the region during a day trip from the northeastern Malaysian
city Kota Bharu to the border. I walked along the river and gazed
across to the small town on the Thai side. The golden dome of a
mosque shone over the surrounding light-colored buildings and the
densely packed palm trees. On the way back to Kota Bharu, I passed
a couple of Thai-style wats, whose viharas glimmered among the surrounding greenery. The peninsula has been ethnically diverse and
physically beautiful throughout its history. I then stopped to explore
a traditional fishing village. All the residents were elders and children
because the area was economically depressed—the younger adults had
left to find work in cities. Some of the kids were shy, but many of the
older people smiled as we passed each other. But today's hardened
political divisions make it more difficult to appreciate the traditional
Malay and Thai etiquette, the rich cultural blends, and the natural
environment's lushness.

Many people along Thailand's southern coasts have made their
livings by fishing from little boats, but modern trawlers owned by big
companies have often scooped out most of the catch. Unable to afford
their powerful motors and vast nets, the locals can't compete and are
often left with scraps. Many have left their traditional ways of life and
now either labor for the big fishing firms or the tourism industry. The
ranks of uprooted men prone to violence have thus increased. Feeling
religiously persecuted and lacking political autonomy and economic
prospects, separatists have exploded car bombs and shot soldiers, government officials, construction workers, and ordinary Thais. More than
5,000 people have died, and military checkpoints have become a fact of
life in many areas.[11]

So several problems require Thai society to reconceive itself, but a
lot of the values and aesthetics that have held it together discourage

objective criticism. People have often enjoyed the moment, fashioned beautiful art, conducted vibrant rituals, and avoided confronting issues directly. These traditions have reinforced attitudes that it is not proper to question the social hierarchy, which is supposed to safeguard the order of things. Children have been taught to politely follow their superiors.

However, today's breakneck pace often strains the graceful aesthetics and behavioral norms that have helped keep the country peaceful. How can people find time to linger over the sweet sights and sounds in wats? Older models of reality, like the rice growing cycle, the rippling river, the religious procession, and the meandering perspectives in paintings, seem too slow to be in step with the digital world. When I returned in 2012, I often felt like I was shifting between two incongruent worlds. I enjoyed the wats, markets, museums, and neighborhood strolls as much as before, but in the evenings I felt pressured to return to the pace of today's digital world. I had to log on in time to keep up with emails and my social media contacts. I often felt out of synch with the traditions I had savored spontaneously in 2007.

Some Thais have become more willing to be rude. A young German woman I met in 2012 was upset because a woman in Chiang Mai had curtly told her, "It's not my job!" when she asked for help. I felt sorry for her when she later checked out of our guesthouse and a middle-aged male tuk tuk driver refused to lower the price for taking her to the bus station by barking, "You will pay me 200 baht or you will wait here all day!"

I got a few grouchy receptions too. When a female tuk tuk driver in Chiang Mai insisted on an unusually high price, I walked away and began bargaining with another driver. She trotted over and started screeching at him, and I had to dart out of her sight to find another driver.

Political corruption and economic inequality have plagued all the other Southeast Asian countries that I've raved about. Joe Studwell, in *Asian Godfathers,* wrote that tightly knit groups of leading politicians and businessmen have often siphoned the area's resources and retarded sustainable economic progress. They maintain the political status quo and force most people to labor for subsistence wages. In these systems, the government gives a small circle of families monopolistic concessions.

These groups form cartels and enjoy protected markets, and thus feel no pressure to develop technological knowhow or original products that can compete with goods from the West and Northeast Asia. Japan and Korea have produced and exported high-tech products that have challenged Western companies at their own games. But most of Southeast Asia has been stuck in low-cost manufacturing of products that other countries design, and in the extraction of raw materials and agricultural products such as oil, lumber, rubber, tin, rice, sugar, and palm oil. Information workers have recently increased in Vietnam, the Philippines, Indonesia, and Malaysia, but many work for low wages, and all these nations still have large gaps between the wealthy and the poor.

These systems are deeply rooted. The region has always had abundant raw materials and, with the exceptions of northeastern Vietnam, southeastern Bali, ancient Angkor, modern Java, and modern cities, low population densities. European colonizers scooped up the area's natural resources when they moved in. The quick spreading of railroads and steamships in the late 19th century allowed commodities to be sent all over the world with an unprecedented ease as the global economy was becoming more industrial and integrated. Southeast Asia's political leaders could lounge on their verandas, sipping the finest cognac while the land's materials were extracted. When the colonial rulers departed in the 20th century, many new governments maintained the same systems that exploited the land and funneled most of the wealth to a small percentage of people.

Many Thais have proudly said that their country was never colonized, but Studwell noted that it has been saddled with a similar system of elites hogging most of the wealth and road-blocking opportunities for most others. S. J. Tambiah, in *World Conqueror & World Renouncer,* wrote that Thailand's economy has resembled colonial economies by being poor in industrial development while dominated by raw materials (tin) and agricultural products (rice and teak). The young generation that overthrew the monarchy in 1932 wanted to end royal extravagance at the people's expense, but the country since then has been dominated by high-ranking civilian bureaucrats, military officers, and businessmen enjoying many of the same old privileges and guarding their vested interests like watchdogs.[12]

One could counter that many Thais in the 1980s and 90s entered the middle class and enjoyed cars, air-conditioned homes, TVs, pop culture, computers, and cellphones. Teeming malls like MBK and Paragon are supposedly proof of this. But this wealth spread very unevenly. Northeastern Thailand is full of impoverished villagers, dispossessed Muslims in the south seethe, and Bangkok's slums sprawl over more space than the shopping centers.

I found myself wandering through a Bangkok slum while looking for an out-of-the-way wat. The planked walkways over the swampy ground wound between mazes of unpainted wooden homes. Boys played a ball-game on one of the narrow passages because there was no open space nearby except a military base. I never found the wat because the neighborhood was too large and haphazard and I decided to turn back before getting hopelessly lost just before sunset. The people showed the same quietude that I had seen in many other Thais, and I wondered if they were fatalistic about being unable to change the system. Sadly, many of the country's drug addicts come from places like this—they feel that they have no other way to escape the discomforts and boredom. Traditional *sanuk* for them can only be chemically induced.

The roots of these systems which greatly privilege the few were deep even before Europeans came. Angkor's economy was based on agriculture, and it was ruled by an upper class that controlled most of the land's products, widely used slave labor, and projected a sacred mystique. I've idealized Thai art, but Ayutthaya fought 70 wars. Sukhothai had many conflicts with Ayutthaya, and in the second half of its history before the latter conquered it, its own lords often fought each other. The Chiang Mai chronicles describe one war after another that broke out in Lan Na. Thai people imbibed graceful aesthetics, but their rulers behaved as fiercely for their own status as any other culture's leaders. Malacca's sultans shoveled in profits from the foreigners that they let trade on their land. People in all levels of these cultures held assumptions that society is hierarchical and that it's natural for the biggest fish to enjoy the most food.

Southeast Asian commerce flourished back in the 16th century. The historian Anthony Reid noted that cities grew there and that cosmopolitan merchants lined ports with vessels filled with goods from all over the known world. Europe, the Middle East, India, China, and Japan wanted their spices and exotic forest products.

But several Southeast Asian kings increased their authority by claiming ownership of all land and confiscating inheritances when nobles died.[13] Ayutthaya's Prasat Thong (r. 1629–1656), who had piously built that wat by the riverside where his mother had lived (Wat Chai Watthanaram—I compared its graceful silhouette with Angkor Wat's outline), did this too. All these rulers disallowed what developed in England and America in the 17th and 18th centuries: private property law; separate executive, legislative, and judicial bodies in government; and parliaments and houses of representatives that included merchants who were independent from royalty and the clergy. Southeast Asian kings thus retarded the development of a strong class of traders with their own rights, who were free and wealthy enough to take major economic initiatives.

In the 17th century several body blows hit Southeast Asia's economy:

- The Dutch East India Company muscled its way into the region. Locals were formerly able to sell their spices at high prices because they were at the eastern end of a long international chain of middlemen, and several nations competed for their products. But the Dutch now took over the whole supply chain and dictated the prices they paid—dirt-cheap.

  The ruthlessness of the Dutch has disgusted many historians. A prosperous local confederation of spice-producing islands east of Java called Banda tried to resist their attempts to bribe it into granting monopolistic concessions. The Dutch captured it, put all 45 of its ruling merchants to death, and transported 800 locals to Batavia (today's Jakarta) as slaves.[14] Holland took over several other states with equally appalling tactics by 1700 and controlled Southeast Asia's trade so thoroughly that many local entrepreneurs were wiped out.

- The climate cooled and several droughts beset the region. Harvests were thus often diminished.[15]

- The amount of silver and gold which lubricated trade decreased in Asia in the late 17th century. Much of the silver in Asia was distributed from Japan, but in the 1630s its government became isolationistic, expelled foreigners, and forbade Japanese from sailing abroad. It only allowed the Dutch and Chinese to trade in Japan (only from Nagasaki).[16] Much of the silver that China had imported from Japan and South America first passed through Southeast Asian ports, but it suffered a tumultuous dynastic change in 1644, and the new Qing Dynasty was more interested in consolidating its hold over the vast mainland than trading with the outside world.

All three of these setbacks combined with the governmental suppression to make trade so difficult that fewer Southeast Asians had the resources or motivation to invest in roads, ships, machinery, and new farming techniques when people in England were doing all of these and turning their commonwealth into the world's largest economy. Because traditional farming seemed safer than commerce, many people retreated inland and put their savings into jewelry and textiles, which they could use as display items and then hide when greedy tax collectors came around. This was a monumental shift after the increase of trade in Southeast Asia from the 14th century through the 16th, which had encouraged the growth of Ayutthaya, Malacca, Hanoi, and Phnom Penh. Europeans now directed much of the region's economy, and its own people focused more on upholding the social hierarchy, with its ceremonies and etiquette.

Studwell noted that today's tycoons maintain mystiques by making deals behind closed doors and avoiding the public scrutiny that American and British accounting systems insist upon. The gleaming skyscrapers, upscale shopping malls, glamorous resorts, and sprawling villas that they build instill awe in those who can't afford them. According to Studwell, the boys on top revel in erotic massages, gourmet food, top-brand liquor, swanky nightclubs, golf courses, five-star hotels, gambling casinos, and luxury cars with tinted windows while people without political connections sweat in the tropical heat and earn only enough to get by (in millions of cases, under two dollars per day). The elites are embracing old values that have been common in Southeast Asia, such as the pursuit of personal status and the projection of high social rank.

Yes, traditional Thai culture is infinitely rich, but non-confrontational behavior and political authorities with mystiques have reinforced each other for centuries. Many leaders in Thailand and neighboring states have exploited people by assuming that they're too meek to challenge them. Congeniality and oppression have often worked together so that many downtrodden have concluded, "I will stay in my small world and make it pretty and fun because it's my safest option in life. A little fish that becomes visible will be eaten by a big fish."

However, the violence in Bangkok shows that some are now willing to become more confrontational. I always found the city peaceful, and its residents often charmed me as much as people in small towns did. Many still took pride in their etiquette. I never experienced some of the incidents that I did when I returned to Italy in 2013. Twice while jogging through Florence, a man driving a van almost ploughed into me. In each case, I whacked the side of the vehicle as hard as I could with my right palm, but neither guy seemed to care about the loud thud—both just kept going. One time in a restaurant, I requested parmesan cheese for my pasta and the elderly man who ran the place suddenly became testy. "This is fresh-made pasta! You don't need cheese. There's enough fat in the pasta already!" It actually tasted exactly like frozen packaged pasta from a supermarket, but I was in a hurry to explore more of Florence's heritage and didn't argue about what seemed trifling. I knew that times were hard for many Italians after Silvio Berlusconi had let their economy stagnate. People in Southeast Asia don't show anger as readily, and the rudeness I experienced in Thailand was much rarer, but more people than before have expressed frustration with the political system.

Because Thai society has traditionally been integrated with combinations of etiquette and social hierarchy, its people are not as used to public debate as Westerners are. The country wasn't politically unified until Chulalongkorn's reign, so abstract democratic institutions like constitutions and the rule of law aren't as deeply woven into society as the old unifiers are. Personal relationships, mutual obligations, rituals, and graceful aesthetics have been used for social cohesion.[17] But today, the speed of the information economy, the wide gaps between rich and poor, the congestion in Bangkok, political corruption, and the abrasiveness of modern media are combining to make the old meandering perspectives distant memories for many. Traditional geographic landmarks, like wats and Buddha statues and footprints, are best appreciated at a relaxed pace, but this is increasingly difficult today. As society becomes more fast-paced and stressful, traditions that can restrain groups from taking polarized stances and lashing out at each other weaken.

Many schools in Southeast Asia teach little about pan-regional cultural currents. They often focus on rote memorization and etiquette, thereby training students to serve the social hierarchy and making them believe that this is all they can aspire for. They don't fully encourage budding minds to appreciate the world's bigness, or even common cultural wealth that Southeast Asian countries share. Thongchai Winichakul, in *Siam Mapped*, wrote that many Thais feel disdain for those in neighboring countries, and that a poll showed that Cambodia, Laos, and Vietnam are at the top of the list of nations they dislike the most.[18] A Laotian told me, "I don't like Thais." I asked why and he said, "Because they're phony and they look down on Laotians. They're nice to you because you're Caucasian." A Cambodian man once told me, "We're okay with Thais, but we hate Vietnamese." Most Southeast Asian societies have discriminated against their Chinese populations and other minorities.

People in all societies need a way of seeing the world which can lessen oppression and widen definitions of humanity beyond categories in social hierarchies. Otherwise, the infinite creativity in a cultural landscape can become a strong self-justifying force for those on top. They can continue to invoke their rich heritages to say that their abuses are part of the fundamental order of things. India's caste system thrived on this kind of thinking for more than 2,000 years, and Indians, Chinese, and Muslims have suppressed women in this way. Subjugated people have become categorized into the lower levels in the social food chain, and the very abundance in a cultural landscape can make this seem like sacred truth because it's constantly reinforced.

Looking *At*, *With*, and *Beyond* can overcome the abusive aspects of traditions and strengthen societies' abilities to help all people improve their well-being. The more people experience this way of thinking, the more deeply they can realize that there is infinite wealth in everyone, and this will encourage them to develop respect for and empathy with all human beings. Studying cultures around the world can expand people's perspectives from one order of things to a field of limitless creativity which everyone can enhance and savor. Mutual nourishment can become at least as prominent in people's views of the world as monetary values and social distinctions. Political leaders can conclude that there is so much cultural wealth to share that they don't need to spend all their time trying to stuff the world into their bank accounts to be happy. Money and status are parts of a bigger field of connections that has many other dimensions.

This field will become increasingly evident as people learn how much cultural wealth and creative potential all human beings harbor. As all six components of UIG><AWB keep enhancing each other, people can increasingly realize that most of our wealth is in our cultural landscapes. Moreover, it keeps growing, and it does so in more people and more directions.

Sadly, most people haven't yet been educated about this much growth in so many directions. In *Saving Higher Education in the Age of Money*, James Engell and Anthony Dangerfield wrote that money shapes higher education more than it ever has during its history. It determines what fields in universities expand and which ones shrink. It also dictates what research is done, since corporations often fund projects. Both authors feel that higher education has traditionally had multiple goals, including economic, intellectual, ethical, and civic, and they lament that universities are now often only evaluated by how much money their alumni earn.

Martin Seligman wrote that people's behavioral choices are greatly influenced by what they care about. He feels that this should expand from a strict focus on material wealth to everyone's well-being. But since many schools teach youths that life is mainly about obtaining the former, this focus has become self-perpetuating.

Economic forces have been strengthening this focus. Niall Ferguson, in *The Ascent of Money*, wrote that the measured physical output of the whole world in 2006 was worth $48.6 trillion. Yet the market capitalization of all of the world's stock markets was $50.6 trillion (4 percent higher). All domestic and international bonds were valuated at $67.9 trillion (40 percent higher). Ferguson concluded that Planet Finance is now bigger than Planet Earth.[19]

But if people realize how much U, I, G, A, W, and B can enhance each other, and that this can happen without a final limit, thinking can become more based on mutual enhancement than dollar values and inflexible social categories. People, artworks, ideas, and objects from daily life always have more facets than their current conventional definitions highlight. This *more* can become increasingly central in thinking if people appreciate how rich a cultural landscape is, and if they realize that its riches are ingrained in the ways they perceive, think, appreciate art, and derive their own identities. Then as ideas, art, and customs are increasingly used as bridges to other cultures, the *more* in everything can expand exponentially. Paradoxically, the ability to become more than what we are increasingly becomes what we are—our essence is the ability to expand beyond our current horizons and identities and to become ever more infinite.

We can grow so far beyond them that any single dimension or system of valuation, including the financial system and the social hierarchy, can be seen as only one part of us. If more people find enchantment (rather than only status and monetary values) in everyone, Southeast Asia's political and business leaders can become more inclined to foster equitable economic systems in which all can earn livings and still have time to develop their creative potentials. This will enable them to add even more to their own cultural landscapes.

Am I only dreaming? Southeast Asia's infinite cultural wealth already exists in the artworks and customs, and in the natural landscapes that they reflect. The region's future will depend on how deeply people appreciate them, and how much they fuse the refinement, vibrancy, and beauty of their traditions with today's world. It will also depend on how widely and frequently people share their appreciations with others so that this wealth will become increasingly visible in the media.

Bangkok was peaceful when I returned in 2012. Since my hotel was on Silom Road, I routinely walked through the formerly embattled commercial area and park. The malls I had visited in 2007 were still feasts of colors packed with pretty women eager to be seen, guys in T-shirts, blond European tourists taking photos, Indian men negotiating deals, and quiet orange-robed monks. Rows of street food sellers in an outdoor market one block from my hotel filled the area with effervescent aromas of fish cakes, bean noodles, chicken satays, and stir-fried vegetables. I ate there almost every morning and evening, joining the locals at long communal tables and savoring the mixtures of scents, tastes, sights, and sounds as much as I had enjoyed the roadside dining in 2007. I never saw a sign of the 2010 battle. Was the relaxed environment an uneasy tension beneath the surface? I imagine that it was for many, but everyone wanted peace. People were eager to return to the zone of safety and have fun.

Though I witnessed some rudeness on this trip, I found much more graciousness. I didn't explore Chinatown in 2007, so it was at the top of my list of places to see in Bangkok. I had read about its crowds, but they were even more sardine-canned than I expected. Sometimes traffic came to a dead halt as trucks, bikes, men hauling packages on dollies, and women shopping for food tried to squeeze into the same space at the same time. I was the only one who became impatient, and I darted through an 18-inch opening between two stopped trucks. Everyone else was content to wait until the street cleared, even though it seemed that that wouldn't happen until the Buddha's next incarnation.

I had just arrived from Sukhothai the previous day. In my enthusiasm for taking pictures of its old temples that were off the beaten path, I had trampled through tall grasses with foxtails covered with protective oil, and rashes had broken out on my legs. Bangkok's heat made my allergic reaction progressively worse in the afternoon. The walkways in Chinatown's outdoor food market were as crowded as the streets, but I found a place to sit and pour a bottle of cold mineral water on my legs to relieve the itching. An old man watched me, quickly left, returned with a large bag of crushed ice, and handed it to me. He then offered me a plate of rice cakes.

Wat Traimit rises on the edge of Chinatown and it houses Thailand's largest Buddha statue made from solid gold (Figure 25). Impeccably fashioned in Sukhothai's style, it provides people with a model of time-less serenity, and worshipers took up all the floor space in front of it when I was there.

Yes, Thai society has many tensions, and some journalists think it needs to reconceive itself in order to be politically stable and prosper-ous, but its old cultural wealth still remains. Appreciating it fully will add insights to people's new conceptions. They can balance looking *At, With,* and *Beyond* so that their horizons will keep expanding as they reconceive. Thais can look *With* and realize that their heritage of creating balanced flows of many forms and mindsets can provide models for arbitrating today's challenges. Then after finding inspiration in their own wats, sculptures, and paintings, they can look *Beyond* and appreciate other Southeast Asian cultures, as well as China, India, the West, the Middle East, Africa, and Latin America. They can add their discoveries of all these places to their traditional sense of graceful, abundant flows so that they will see all the world's societies and people in this way.

If political and business leaders appreciate the magnitude of UIG (if they see how much wealth there is in people's field of connections, and how much potential each person has to add to it), they will be more inspired to invest in schools, public libraries, museums, job training centers, and artistic organizations so that everybody in their society can enhance it. Because a cultural landscape is infinitely creative, the high of exploring it never wears off. The experience gets better and better as you find more meanings in everything around you. More people can add to the growth of UIG, and its ever-accumulating wealth can outshine one-dimensional focuses on monetary values to an increasing extent.

Money did finance a lot of great art. People used it to build Gothic cathedrals in the Middle Ages, and rich merchants and bankers in Renaissance Florence, Venice, Rome, and Flanders commissioned great artists. But many other types of experiences converged with finance to inspire artists and patrons. The Christian faith was also central, and its Biblical stories provided content for most art into the 16th century. These cultures also had the West's ancient classical heritage to derive many of their most common forms from; this has made Western art distinct from Thailand's, Cambodia's, India's, and all other cultures' art. Medieval and Renaissance Westerners were also intimately connected with the natural landscape in those days before flashing computer and smartphone screens and bedazzling pop stars became centers of many people's attention. The art that has been the most influential in the West was created in societies with many dimensions and infinite facets. Thais and Khmers usually didn't use money when they created their most influential art.

Money has been one aspect of people's field of connections (UIG), but as Niall Ferguson noted, it has become increasing predominant so that it now seems like the main aspect to many, especially in the last 20 years as the aggregate value of stocks, bonds, and derivatives has rocketed above the aggregate value of physical goods. During the Renaissance, money allowed new avenues of creativity and freedom to develop by enabling people to make and trade more goods, but its use has now grown beyond its traditional definition as a medium of exchange for goods—the recent inversion of relative value can make money seem like the basis of reality, and universities and corporate-controlled media often encourage this assumption. The finance industry has acquired more power to strictly define us in terms of the finite quantities it focuses on. We can now take our full humanity back and look *At, With,* and *Beyond* as we reconceive it so that all aspects of UIG can grow and shine on each other. Mutual enrichment of all aspects of being human can then become a predominant idea of ourselves and the world. The more this mutual enrichment is appreciated, the more it can grow and the more we can see beyond monetary values and enjoy all aspects of our humanity. The manual at the end of this book details how we can establish mutual enrichment as a primary idea in our society.

Looking only *At* can bind people to one past, which can then become rigid and used for oppression. When this happens, the system of conventions, including economic exchange values and the established social hierarchy, is easily seen as *the* way things are and the basis of all meanings. But looking *With* opens the perspective into multiple pasts, which can then enhance the present. Ancient Tai rice farming communities, the three biggest pre-modern Thai states, and early Bangkok fertilized Thailand's present by influencing people's artworks, identities, perceptions, ideas, and religious traditions. Western culture has been shaped by its ancient, medieval, Renaissance, and modern periods, and by multiple cultural centers, such as Athens, Rome, the Holy Land, Florence, London, Paris, Amsterdam, Vienna, and New York. All pasts are integrated with the present in UIG. Multidimensional reflections between all periods can strengthen its Unity by adding more perspectives and ideas to it, which can be synthesized into new vistas.

The more a person studies his own culture's many pasts, the more he can be free from one time and one system of values, and use all periods and all ideas from them as his creative fodder. His perspective can shift from *The Past*, which can be used to oppress people, to an infinitely abundant present that all pasts have fertilized, in which all human beings have limitless potential for creativity and joy.

People's perspectives can thereby expand from one-dimensional views of time. They don't have to see time as a line that extends to the future and inescapably determines it, or as a circle that keeps repeating and thereby binding people to fate. Instead, people can choose ideas and perspectives from multiple periods and use all to fertilize their imaginations for envisioning and creating a better future. They can then look *Beyond* and combine aspects of other cultures' heritages in their perspectives. As more of this happens, all societies can increasingly shine on each other.

Thais have striven for this shining without usually realizing it. All their tapering pagodas rise to celestial domains that are not bound to static definitions, and they glitter in all directions. Ayutthaya built at least 300 in its cityscape. They soared over the tree tops and became models for how people can perceive and relate to each other. Thais can now realize this ideal by appreciating their own heritage more deeply and enjoying other cultures. They have lamented the 1767 sack of their mighty city, but now its luminous skyline can become predominant in people's perspectives and ideals, and it can be extended to all cultures and people. The full wealth in each culture and person is like the upper part of a stupa by being able to shine in limitless directions. All stupas can shimmer together. If more political and business leaders see that there is infinite wealth and creative potential in each culture and person, they will realize that they've been vying for fishbowls in the ocean. We'll find out how big our ocean is in Part Three.

PART THREE

THE HEAVENS IN YOUR HOME

CHAPTER 16

⌒

THE WORLD IN A PLACE:
A GEOGRAPHY OF HUMAN WEALTH

IN THIS FINAL part of the book, we will ask how big our world really is and how much it can be like paradise, which everyone can enjoy. This chapter will expand the perspective through more of Southeast Asia so that we'll see how much variety and beauty exist in just one region, and what this means for all the world's societies. The last chapter ended by enlarging the perspective of time from one past to multiple pasts which can fertilize an infinitely abundant present. We'll now expand the view of space and see that UIG is integrated through all places as well as all times.

We have seen how rich Cambodian and Thai cultures are, and we've explored a little of India's vast heritage which they have synthesized with their own. We will now take a brief journey through three other countries that comprise Southeast Asia's cultural environment. We'll find that the more you delve into a place, the more you can see other places reflected in it. Making this ever more central in our perspectives of the world can lessen the one-dimensional focus on money and status that we saw in the last chapter because people can increasingly realize that multidimensional interconnectedness and boundless creativity are basic in our cultures and identities.

After this chapter shows that every space is infinitely abundant, the conclusion will reveal how much abundance there is in the whole world and within us. The manual will then detail how you can bring the highest reaches of humanity's creative potential into your life.

LAOS'S MAJESTIC MOUNTAINS AND VARIED PEOPLE

Thailand's northeastern neighbor, Laos, stretches along the Mekong, up north to the Chinese border, and south to Cambodia. Many people passed through its steep valleys while migrating from southern China and northwestern Vietnam to Thailand over the centuries. It's a challenging place to travel through, even on a bus. I found this out during a 12-hour ride from Vientiane to Luang Prabang when an old woman next to me tired out and leaned her head on my shoulder, and a boy in the seat behind me vomited into a bag.

Laos's natural barriers allowed the people who stayed to develop diverse traditions. Today they're known for emphasizing fun as much as Thais do. I discovered this in a more pleasant experience than the bus ride.

I explored a village in the mountains near Luang Prabang, saw a crowd in front of the local school, and ventured towards it. Within seconds a thirty-something man invited me to join them. They were celebrating a local's birthday, and my host offered me a seat by the DJ and poured a generous amount of Beer Lao for me. His friends then asked me to join the dancing. They all formed a circle and moved their arms and hands in graceful sinuous patterns that reminded me of Thai art forms. So did the music's tempo. It wasn't fast or slow. Instead, it flowed at an even pace that allowed everyone to easily move in synch with each other.

I needed to move on because my driver was waiting for me, and I still wanted to hike to the top of the hill that the village hugged and explore the wat. When I arrived a group of five novice monks invited me to sit with them as quickly as the revelers did. They then asked me to play the guitar I was carrying. I felt a bit uncomfortable about having a beer-buzz in a wat, and I hoped my companions couldn't smell the spuds. But I quickly stopped thinking of contradictions because both venues had the same atmosphere. They were full of friendly people eager for a good time and ready to invite a stranger to join them.

Laos shares more cultural traits with Thailand than with any other country. Luang Prabang, Laos's former political center, nestles in the Mekong valley, and it paid tribute to Sukhothai in the late 13th century. Then in 1353, a Lao warlord named Fa Ngum consolidated several *muangs* into the kingdom of Lan Xang (this name meant *One Million Elephants*, which was probably an exaggerated boast about its military might). He and his father had been exiled in Angkor because the latter had seduced one of his own father's wives. When Fa Ngum grew up, he married one of the daughters of the Khmer king and then marched north towards Luang Prabang. He arrived at Vientiane first and conquered it, and then reached Luang Prabang and established it as his capital.

Lan Xang and the growing Thai states exchanged many goods and art forms with each other, and the Sukhothai-style Buddha became the most influential type of Buddha statue in Luang Prabang. People built so many wats there over the next 400 years that it's called the city of temples. Several have Lan Na features, including cascading roofs with animated painting and glass inlay in the upper triangle under the gables. Because the Lao comprise one of the Tai ethnic groups, they understood languages in the two emerging northern Thai kingdoms more easily than Khmer.

Many fans of Laotian art say that Luang Prabang's Wat Xieng Thong is the most beautiful temple in the country. King Setthathirat built it in 1559. His father, King Phothisarat, had made Lan Xang's Buddhism more orthodox by suppressing local spirit cults and building monasteries, and he linked the newly regimented faith with his court's rituals. Many Southeast Asian monarchs fused religious and royal institutions more closely in the 16th century to consolidate their holdings. But Phothisarat and his son knew that their people's folklore was so rich that they had to compromise with them. Ideas emerged that are characteristically Lao.

Wat Xieng Thong and the royal palace preside by the Mekong, so the kings' most prestigious landmarks were embedded in the natural surroundings, where lore about nagas flourished. The Laotian historians Mayoury and Pheuiphanh Ngaosrivathana, in *The Enduring Sacred Landscape of the Naga*, wrote that locals saw Luang Prabang as a naga's body. Its head is in the south, where Wat Xieng Thong rises. Its belly is the most auspicious place to trade, and the palace stands there. Some people believed that those living at the head and tail can never prosper as much as residents in the stomach. Fifteen nagas protect Luang Prabang, and each is associated with a certain region. Naga lore literally shaped Laotians' ideas of the world.

People believed that kings needed to organize boat races to honor the nagas if they wanted them to be nice to them. The serpents got their respect and the people had fun watching the sport.

In the 1560s, Setthathirat responded to an impending Burmese invasion of Thailand by relocating the capital south to Vientiane. That was a convenient move because it had more flat lands for rice growing, and it was easier for traders to reach from Ayutthaya, Cambodia, and Vietnam. But Luang Prabang still retained its cultural importance. Vientiane also spreads along the Mekong, and its people also believed that a different naga protected each section of the city.

Sulinya Vongse became the king from 1637 to 1694, and many historians feel that his reign was Laos's apogee. Burmese and Thai forces had bashed each other enough to need a break. They now concentrated on their own domains and Laos enjoyed a period of peace. Vientiane became a famous center of Buddhist learning which attracted students from Cambodia, Thailand, and Burma. Western travelers were also impressed by what they saw. In the mid 17th century, an Italian Jesuit named Giovanni-Maria Leria wrote that the royal palace was so big that people could think that it was a whole town. More servants than visitors could count lived within its symmetrical enclosure. A magnificent gateway fronted the king's apartment, which consisted of a great hall and many splendid rooms. Their interiors and exteriors were covered with gilded bas reliefs. The king's home rivaled the older palace at Angkor.

The city also offers many little enchantments, including Buddha statues, small shrines, and ordinary wats (temples not built by the king). They synthesized different cultures' forms.

Figure 32. Floral patterns and nagas in a traditional Khmer style, Vientiane, Laos.

The shrine in Figure 32 is Khmer-influenced, and the ones in Figure 33 are crowned with Burmese-style gables.

Figure 33. Burmese-style gables, Vientiane.

The stupa in Figure 34 is in a Laotian style.

Figure 34. The slowly curving upper section is common on Laotian stupas, Vientiane.

Figure 35. A Laotian-style Buddha at Wat Visoun, Luang Prabang.

So is this Buddha (in Luang Prabang). His gracefully arching eyebrows and somewhat oval face were probably influenced by the Sukhothai Buddha statue, but the combination of long ears, big nose, and wide, fleshy crown is Laotian. Like many Laotian Buddha statues, it has a quirkiness that makes it resemble folk art. This Buddha seems like someone that ordinary people can relate to.

Two traumas then bracketed the 19th century and people lost faith in the nagas' protection. After Sulinya Vongse passed away, Laos split into factional courts. Landlocked and politically divided, she was too weak to defend herself against Thailand and Vietnam as they expanded. Thailand's new Chakri Dynasty annexed much of Laos, and in the 1820s, its armies sacked Vientiane so savagely for staging a revolt that it was abandoned. Then in the 1880s, thugs from Yunnan escaping China's Taiping Rebellion banded together and terrorized every place they could. They partnered with the chief of Lai (an ethnically Tai principality northeast of Luang Prabang), and both sacked Luang Prabang, murdering many ritual performers. Fourteen royal rites subsequently vanished.

But Laotians held so many folk traditions that other ideas replaced naga lore. Some believed that two spirits, a male named Pu Nyoeu and a female called Nya Nyoeu, created the Lao and their land. A roughly fifty-year-old Lao woman told me that people thought of them as grandparents when she was a girl in Vientiane. They poured liquor into the Mekong and offered betel and chicken to them. The old folks had a good time in the afterlife, the living got protection, and everybody had fun.[1]

The Marxist government assumed control in 1975 and tried to suppress the old ways, but the country pulsates with so many of them that they resurface in one form or another. A Laotian friend told me that some older people in Vientiane believe that nagas launch a rocket from their underwater kingdom every year. Some claim to have seen it shooting from the river at night. Locals have traditionally gathered by the shore to play music, drum, and dance in order to coax the serpents to join their celebration and fire the missile. Some have believed that this encourages rain to come and that it improves crop growth.

The stories that integrate Laos's mountainous land have had sticking power because they allow room for fun and family. They're so flexible and diverse that more varieties can emerge when people suffer and lose faith in one custom. Laotians' unifying myths don't conform to one system. Their plentitude reflects the land's forms. So does Laos's cultural variety. Many non-Tai minorities live in Laos, and they make up a higher percentage of the population than in Thailand.

Like Thailand, Laos had a well-regarded king in the late 20th century. But the Marxists carted him to a prison camp shortly after they took over, and he soon died in mysterious circumstances. The government has oppressed the people ever since. Since the country has no access to the sea and domestic transportation is time-consuming, a regime more committed to its own power than the people's economic prospects is the last thing they need.

But Laos's government opened the country up to tourism in the 1980s, and it began to allow some private business initiatives. Its most prominent political figure then, Kaysone Phomvihane, encouraged foreign investment and joint ventures. Its economy is growing, though it is still one of the world's poorest. The young generation is eager for more pop culture and cares less about the old ways that elders reminisce about. I saw a few videos of rock bands with blazing lead guitarists who could hold their own in American metal bands. But whatever the age group, people love fun and are eager to move beyond the turmoil that their lively land has suffered for the last 250 years. India's heritage, Tai traditions, and Laos's mountainous environment fused into a cultural landscape that's both unique and Southeast Asian. I'll always fondly remember the Laotians' warmth and their land's beauty.

VIETNAM'S ENTRANCING BEAUTY AND IRREDUCIBLE DIVERSITY

I explored Vietnam during my 2012 return trip and saw yet another infinitely rich culture with its own patterns, which is nevertheless still Southeast Asian. Its land is drop-dead gorgeous. Majestic mountains, thick jungles, swaying rice fields, and sparkling beaches add up to one of the most beautiful countries I've ever seen.

However, Vietnam's land has been particularly hard to unify. It curves in an S form, with a long coast and two broad, flat plains that nourish each end: the Red River up north, and the land around Ho Chi Minh City in the south. Some locals have likened Vietnam to a carrying pole with a basket on each end.

My visit didn't go well at first. A taxi driver cheated me out of about 50 dollars as soon as my bus arrived in Ho Chi Minh City from Phnom Penh. My guard was completely down because the previous four months in Southeast Asia and China had gone smoothly. Nobody tried to rip me off in the streets, and many people stopped and offered me rides for free. But the woman who checked me into my hotel in Ho Chi Minh City warned that the town is full of taxi scams and pickpockets. She told me that I should always be on guard. Still angry about being robbed, I thought, "I'll just explore the historic sites and museums, and come back to my room to write. Screw the people here."

But I quickly found Vietnam so rewarding that I long to go back. While passing a little temple, I noticed a crowd of people and a priest with a long white beard conducting a service. I popped inside and took a few pictures. On the way out a young man invited me to sit with him at a table by the sidewalk. He told me that they were conducting a funeral for his uncle and that everyone inside was a family member. I felt like a heel with a six-foot strip of toilet paper stuck to it for taking pictures of them, but nobody appeared offended.

My host poured me a glass of tea, and several people soon arrived and sat with us. I had read that weddings and funerals are pivotal events in Vietnam. Large groups of family and friends gather to share these transitional moments. Being surrounded by other people is an important aspect of life in Vietnam.

Inviting many guests to a funeral encourages positive relationships with the spirit world. In traditional Vietnam, a sloppy ceremony can dissatisfy the spirit, who can then haunt the living. A big send-off is also a political statement for the living because it shows that the departed was important in life. To cheer up my host I said, "It looks like your uncle was highly respected." But what happened next made me feel that I was also invited for personal reasons.

Upon noticing that all the guests entered the temple and offered money, I asked the man who invited me if I should too and he said, "What you like." I entered and kneeled in front of the altar. The priest gave me three incense sticks, and I bowed three times while holding them. I placed about a dollar in Vietnamese money on a metal tray, put the palms of my hands together, and looked into the eyes of every one of the seven or eight people in the room. Everyone's face lit up, including the priest's. I was impressed that this family brought me deeply into their lives, especially since I had just come off the street. I enjoyed repaying them during such a difficult time.

Sharing intimate moments with lots of people is a common Vietnamese cultural trait. History has taught them that safety and fun are in numbers.

Many people that I met in Vietnam freely mixed business and personal matters. I moseyed through Hoi An's central bazaar, which crowded a large pavilion. Most of the sellers were middle-aged women hawking fruit, spices, nuts, vegetables, CDs, silverware, pots and pans, shoes, and anything else that a person can stuff into a handbag. One sat me down on a low wooden stool, and three more came over and surrounded me. They asked if I'm single and tried to set me up with a friend. I don't mix love and business because my parents were poor when they met and they had a great marriage until my father passed away. But many visitors in Vietnam have noted people's love of business and quickness to look for a deal. Both instincts—business and intimacy—have ancient roots.

A vibrant culture called Dong Son united the Red and Ma River areas by the middle of the first millennium BCE. Its proud lords maintained showy court lives to awe their followers and foster prosperous relationships between rice growers on the plains and diverse groups in the hills. They made huge bronze drums with carvings of boats, warriors, dancers, musicians, birds, deer, crocodiles, and frogs. The historian Keith Taylor said that lords carried these drums in boats to announce their presence and summon people to give them tribute. Others have felt that priests might have used them to communicate with ancestors and nature spirits. It's possible that these mighty drums had more than one use because many were made, and they were traded among cultures from southwestern China to Indonesia.

But the Dong Son culture had to cope with a severe challenge because some of its prized rice fields were in a key lowland corridor between Tibetan highlands and the sea. People thus had to battle several invaders. Many axes, daggers, swords, arrowheads, and javelin points have been found at their gravesites.

Northern Vietnamese plains close to the sea were swampy. The Dong Son culture cleared marshes and constructed irrigation systems to extend farmlands for growing rice. This was backbreaking work, and the hard-won land was prone to floods.

People in the Dong Son culture thus needed a lot of discipline to flourish, but they forged a civilization that lasted for 400–500 years. They learned the importance of sticking closely together, working hard, and having fun whenever possible. This robust society thrived until China's expanding Qin and Han dynasties sent hundreds of thousands of troops to conquer it. The Chinese turned it into a province in 111 BCE. Locals launched rebellions, but the Chinese conquered the land for the long-run in the mid first century CE.[2]

China ruled Vietnam for more than 1,000 years, and this has made the country unique. Chinese culture wielded much more influence there than anywhere else in Southeast Asia. Confucian temples and architecture with stately halls in the middle of rectangular courtyards preside in old cities. The government that bullied Cambodia in the 19th century built a royal palace in Hue that was modeled on Beijing's Forbidden City.

Vietnamese officials looked down on Cambodians for lacking Confucian literature and for being bare-chested in public, and they tried to impose Confucian customs on them. Cambodians, entrenched in their own culture, rebelled and Vietnamese concluded that they were ungovernable.

I visited Hue's palace and saw several long halls on stone platforms with wide stairways. This arrangement was adopted from imperial Chinese architecture, and it was ideal for formal processions. Carvings of lions formed the banisters on some platforms. Inside, pillars stood in several precise rows, and an altar or a wide throne occupied the middle. A rectangular wall surrounded many of these structures so that the palace was partitioned into several compounds, each with a regal hall or a large residence in its center. Everyone who lived there was in his and her place, and interactions between people were formal and ritualized.

Vietnamese celebrate Tet (New Year) when Chinese New Year occurs. Like traditional Chinese on this auspicious day, many Vietnamese clean their homes, buy new decorations for their ancestral altars, burn votive paper money, give presents to children, and invite departed ancestors to share their food and good cheer. They offer their past relatives wine, tea, candied fruits and nuts, cigarettes, and flowers, and ask them for protection and prosperity in the coming year. Many people also give offerings to the kitchen gods, which protect the home and ensure that the family behaves well. Many Vietnamese see China as their ancient enemy, but they share many cultural traits with it.

In Hoi An, an elderly gentleman invited me into his home. A wall niche graced his parlor with pictures of his parents and his stunningly pretty sister, who had died during the Vietnam War when she was a nurse. He told me that he visits his parents' grave every two weeks. Many Chinese temples and traditional houses also contain altars for honoring past family members. People in both lands have felt that departed relatives are near to them.

The historian Milton Osborne wrote that Vietnamese ideas of geography were influenced by Confucian bureaucratic traditions and that they thus differed from other Southeast Asian cultures' views. While the latter were oriented to ritual centers whose political and metaphysical influences radiated outwards in a circle and became weaker with increasing distance so that the borders between different centers were fuzzy, Vietnamese inherited Chinese ideas of provinces with defined borders. Officials administered these provinces with voluminous written records.[3]

However, Vietnam added its own style to Chinese culture, and it often made the imports more soothing. The buildings in Hue's palace are not as tall as the Forbidden City's grand halls. They don't dominate their surroundings; instead they blend with the surrounding foliage so that culture and nature are harmonized.

Many temples that I saw in Vietnam are Chinese in form, with rectangular courtyards, stately halls, and elegant pagodas, but their color schemes include tones that are both soft and cheerful. I found their pale yellows and blues easier on the eye than China's commanding reds. The Long Tuyen Pagoda is about one mile from Hoi An's center. Most tourists stay in town though this temple is close enough to visit after a quick jog. I went there because it's conveniently located, yet still off the beaten path. I didn't expect much from it, but I immediately found myself in an enchanted world.

The grounds contained several thin multi-story pagodas that were influenced by Chinese architecture, but their mellow hues made them look more softhearted than monumental. Their slender shapes were surrounded by Vietnam's abundant foliage so that a wealth of forms and colors seemed to play with each other.

A high stack of brightly painted lotus forms sprouted up from the middle of the main building. The lotus symbolizes purity in Buddhist traditions because it emerges from the bottoms of ponds and blooms on their surfaces—its blossoms are unsullied by the surroundings. The lotus thus symbolizes the soul's transformation to a spiritual existence that's free from the worldly muck we all live in. The Long Tuyen Pagoda houses many locals' departed relatives, so these flowers symbolize people's hopes about the afterlife. But the lilting interplays of forms and happy colors stress the beauty of this world as much as liberation from it. I met a group of three jovial middle-aged women relaxing on the steps of one of the building's sides, and they seemed in no hurry to leave.

Figure 36. Art and nature play together at the Long Tuyen Pagoda, Hoi An, Vietnam.

Vietnam imported Mahayana traditions from China rather than the Theravada from Cambodia, Laos, and Thailand, but it added its own heritage to them. A statue of Quan Am, who is better known by the Chinese name Quan Yin, fronted many temples that I saw in Vietnam. She represents the Buddha's compassion. This deity doesn't need to be in a woman's form because it can assume any identity to embody the Buddha's kindness. Ancient Indians called it Avalokitesvara and Lokesvara (the Khmer king Jayavarman VII associated his father with him when he built Preah Khan). When the Chinese imported Buddhism to their own land, they conflated this deity with Daoist immortals associated with the west, imagined her as a woman who takes departing souls to paradise, and called her Quan Yin. Both Chinese and Vietnamese turned her into a model of feminine grace and motherly love, as many Westerners have done with Mother Mary. To represent her, Vietnamese made some of the most enjoyable images of female personalities I have ever seen.

Figure 37. An idealized face of Quan Am, Hoi An.

The face in Figure 37 is as idealized as a classical Greek statue, and the person in Figure 38 is as kindly as a mother.

Figure 38. Quan Am represented as a mother caring for her children, Hoi An.

If I see either one when I leave this world, I'll know that I'm in good hands.

Figure 39. Quan Am taming the world's profusion of energies and forms, Hoi An.

Figure 39 is a view of the first Quan Am statue from a distance. I saw this type of sight in many Vietnamese temples—nature's profuse growth intertwines with the gentle colors and forms of the buildings. Quan Am fits in perfectly. Though she rises from a lotus to take souls to paradise, she fuses with her environment into an affirmation of this world which renders it gentle.

After liberation from China, Vietnam's Ly Dynasty (1009–1225) and Tran Dynasty (1225–1400) organized Confucian bureaucracies to unify themselves, but they combined the Chinese traditions with local spirit cults, the abundant natural environment, and looser political structures which allowed women more independence. These dynasties created some of the most pleasing ceramics in the world, with soft yellows and browns that are as soothing as Sukhothai's pottery.

But the Vietnamese were on a collision course with the Chams, who lived along the central and southern coast. The Tran Dynasty's population grew beyond the northern plains' ability to feed it and this pressured people to migrate southwards. The Chams had already ruled central Vietnam for more than 500 years, and their society and land were very different from northern Vietnam's. A major clash of cultures was about to ensue.

The Chams built a civilization that lasted longer than ancient Rome and created some of the finest art in Asian history. I got hooked on Cham art when I saw a drawing of an ancient temple 25 years ago, so the Cham legacy was high on my list of subjects to explore in Vietnam.

These people were more oriented to ocean-going trade than inland empires based on rice growing because their thin land between the two baskets lacked a large plain like the Red River's. They weren't able to build enormous rice surpluses and sustain a lot of people in one location.

The Truong Son Mountains divided their territory with many fast-flowing rivers. The Chams thus organized into a north-to-south chain of states, and each consolidated people from the sea to the mountains in the west. The ocean-trading people and mountain-dwelling tribes within each state lived differently. The hill people relied more on hunting and slash-and-burn farming than the coastal dwellers did. With this type of agriculture, people set the surrounding plants on fire so that the resulting ash is temporarily more fertile for planting crops. They then move to a new area and repeat the same process while the old land replenishes itself. This method of agriculture cannot feed as many people, but it doesn't require the large coordinated labor force that wet rice farming needs. Hill people's populations were thus less dense and more mobile. Since the lowlanders traded with them for their forest products, the Cham realms integrated many ethnic groups.

Instead of being mainly influenced by China, the Chams imported Hinduism and Buddhism from India.[4] Having immigrated to Vietnam from Borneo or the Malay Peninsula, they had less contact with China than the Vietnamese did.[5] They first established themselves around the mouths of rivers and grew rice on their narrow strips of land, and then built fortified settlements upriver, where soil was more fertile than the sandier lowlands. By the middle of the first millennium CE, the ruling families around each river formed alliances with each other, and their society became a major player in Southeast Asia's economy and politics. They assimilated some of India's heritage and used its alphabets, calendars, astronomy, and religious art and rituals to further organize themselves. But they mixed their own traditions with Indian culture. They made nothing huge, like Angkor Wat. Instead, Cham temples and sculptures are small and exquisitely proportioned, as though merchants in a land with less area for marshaling people to build enormous monuments learned to unify their world with more taste than wow factor.

By the ninth century the Chams regularly traded with states down in Java. The maritime empire of Srivijaya that dominated the Malay Peninsula, Sumatra, and most of Java fashioned refined sculptures with delicate facial features and elegant jewelry. Kingdoms in eastern Java did too, and they became central in the spice trade by sending rice and Indian cloth to islands farther east for their cloves and nutmeg. To the west, the Dvaravati civilization, with its own graceful art, was flourishing. The Chams were thus frequently in touch with many other Southeast Asian cultures that shared preferences for elegance instead of grandeur.

But the Cham population was too small to compete with the expanding Vietnamese, who conquered the most prestigious Cham capital, Vijaya, in 1471.[6] The Chams entered a long period of political and economic decline as the Vietnamese kept coming, and many lost their land to the new settlers. Vietnamese began to deal directly with people in the highlands for their forest products, and they ultimately took over most of the trade and further marginalized the Chams. In the 1830s Champa ceased to exist as a state. Its descendants still live in southwestern Vietnam and across the border in Cambodia. They're ethnic minorities in both countries. Many embraced Islam after Vijaya fell and they still follow the faith, which teaches that all are equal under God—they now turn to the spiritual realm for an equitable universe.

Several other ethnic minorities have lived in Vietnam's mountains, and many have moved into the lowland cities in search of work. So in Vietnam, many types of people have shared a land that's hard to politically unify to begin with. Thais have integrated their cultural and natural diversity with a network of ideas and experiences that have blended Theravada Buddhism, the royal court, animism, wet rice farming, the river, social hierarchy, and art with sinuous lines. But Vietnam has been harder to unify with one complex of ideas and experiences.

A middle-aged Vietnamese woman told me that she thought this is why melancholy themes have sometimes been prominent in her culture. The most famous Vietnamese text, *The Tale of Kieu*, was written by Nguyen Du (1766–1820). He lived during turbulent times. The Trinh lords in the north and the Nguyen lords in the south were battling each other for control of the Le dynasty, which nominally ruled both. The people suffered so much hardship from the fighting that Tay Son rebels overthrew the dynasty. Nguyen Du sympathized with the old Confucian virtues that he saw crumbling around him. His tale is about a well-born, beautiful, and artistic young woman who was forced to become a prostitute. It's very refined, with many allusions to earlier texts (a Chinese literary tradition), but it's so sad that I find it hard to read. It begins by saying that life has ups and downs and that fate will ultimately thwart a person's talents.

All the same, the country bustles with eclectic mixtures of cultures. The Cao Dai religion fuses ideas from Buddhism, Confucianism,

Hinduism, and Christianity. In 1920 a provincial governor named Ngo Van Chieu (also called Ngo Minh Chieu) intuited that all the world's religions emerged from the same source and that they should appreciate their common wellspring. Cao Dai followers believe that he received this message from the Supreme Being (*Cao Dai* means *heavenly abode*, which is the symbolic name for the Supreme Being). About a week later, Chieu was resting in a hammock and a huge eye emerged in front of him, shining like the sun, with a halo around it. He became convinced that this was the way God wanted to be symbolized because it stood for the all-seeing power of universal consciousness and global harmony.

Some historians have seen the Cao Dai faith as a reaction to French colonialism because some of its adherents were patriots who tried to free Vietnam. The French suppressed it and exiled some of its leaders to Madagascar. But Cao Dai encourages love and justice because it claims that all beings came from the same source. Its followers believe that the Supreme Being taught the Buddha, Jesus, and Mohammed. Though each religion's believers have their own ways of approaching spirituality, the Vietnamese faith tries to promote harmony between all belief systems. It's much more than a reaction to political suppression because it stresses harmonizing a multitude of mindsets. Because this is an ancient tradition throughout Southeast Asia, Cao Dai is well-rooted in its soil.

The Cao Dai religion was formally founded in 1926, and a governing body formed that resembled the Catholic Church's, with a hierarchy of priests, higher officials responsible for districts (like bishops and cardinals), and one person at the top (called Giao Tong).

The faith also incorporated ideas from China. According to Hum Dac Bui, in *Cao Dai; Faith of Unity*, Caodaists traditionally bring their hands together so that the left represents yang (the active energies in nature) and the right hand is yin (the receptive patterns in the universe). The end of the left thumb touches the base of the left ring finger, and the other fingers wrap around the thumb. The right hand then wraps around the left hand so that the tip of the right thumb touches the base of the left index finger. Both hands thereby join into a microcosm of the Daoist universe in which all energies circulate smoothly. Worshipers embody cosmic harmony, and they proceed through a series of salutations to the altar and each other.

However, Cao Dai is more than a ritual because it also has esoteric traditions. Its followers believe that highly evolved spirits remain in touch with humanity after passing away. A Cao Dai temple that I visited in Ho Chi Minh City housed several altars, and they included photographs of many of the faith's founding fathers.

The Cao Dai community of spirits is eclectic. The 19th century French poet Victor Hugo is one of the most highly honored, and he occupied the middle of a picture in a temple that I visited in Hoi An. On the left was Sun Yat Sen, the leader of the 1911 Chinese revolution which ended the last imperial dynasty. A revered Vietnamese poet from the 16th century, Nguyen Binh Khiem (he is also called Trang Trinh) graced the right. All three were signing an alliance between God and humanity.

Cao Dai also honors feminine principles in nature and often identifies them with yin. The Ho Chi Minh City temple housed a shrine for Quan Am, who was embodied in yet another gentle female statue.

Although the Cao Dai faith has prescribed rituals, temples in which everyone gathers, and a centralized hierarchy, it's flexible. Believers can be herd-like and perform the same rituals in comfy crowds, or they can meditate and commune with spirits. They can also worship a compassionate goddess. Though the faith teaches that there is one Supreme Being and that the world is unified in it, it allows room for many ways of worshiping as long as they encourage love and justice for all beings. Like many Southeast Asian religious traditions, it allows diversity and enables all people to live in harmony with each other.

My experiences in the Cao Dai temples in Ho Chi Minh City, Hoi An, and Danang reflected these values. In the first temple I visited, a young woman showed me around, pointed out all the shrines, and encouraged me to try their vegetarian restaurant for dinner. The temples in the other two towns were empty, but the buildings were open to anyone who wanted to explore them. This atmosphere of trust encouraged me to linger in them. I stayed so long in the one in Danang that a rainstorm trapped me inside, and this gave me even more pleasure. I sat on the veranda and watched the wealth of palm trees, shrubs, and flowers fuse with the Chinese, Indian, and Southeast Asian architectural forms. This harmonious mixture received the life-giving rains as though the Supreme Being and Quan Am were bestowing grace on the world.

I've found Vietnam's fashions as entrancing as its fine art. At first I enjoyed looking at the women, but I found the artistry of their clothing equally pleasant. Flowing Chinese silk gowns sometimes blend with natural features such as flowers and bamboo. Mandarin elegance is made tender. Fashion mixes images as softly as colors fuse in temples and ceramics.

Vietnamese wear modern Western fashions well too. A Vietnamese-American Facebook friend of mine posted pictures of her father on her wall to honor him on his 75th birthday. Someone complimented his attire and said that he'd be at home in a Parisian café. Hanoi became one of Southeast Asia's largest cities in the 15th century, and Hoi An emerged as a major international trading mecca. Then in the early 20th century, French fashions mixed with the region's ancient natural and cultural beauty. Vietnamese can compete with anyone in urbane style.

I entered a bookstore in Hoi An and the owner immediately asked me if I was looking for anything. When I said that I was interested in Vietnamese culture, she showed me a shelf of books about the Vietnam War. I said, "I'm interested in Vietnamese culture, not the war."

"But everybody only cares about the war," she replied.

Cultural knowledge could have prevented America from stumbling into the war in the first place. Robert McNamara, the U.S. secretary of defense from 1961 to 1968, thought that bombing the country would break the people's will. But their more-than 1,000-year history of conflicts with Chinese invaders, and the earlier Dong Son culture's need to defend itself, gave them plenty of models of iron-hard resistance.

But beneath the shallow perspectives that many people currently hold, the Vietnamese have a more-than 2,000-year history of creating some of the most beautiful artistic fusions I've ever seen. They mix with the stunning natural landscape into one of the world's most enjoyable places. Larger nations and local corrupt politicians have tried to monopolize it, and they've given people reasons for expressing sad themes. But Vietnamese still create as much beautiful art as before, and they love fun, business, and deep interpersonal relationships. They are eager to forget past tragedies and combine the best from their traditions with the modern world.

Vietnam is unusual among Southeast Asian countries by being much more influenced by China than India, but it exemplifies this region as well as any other does. It shares a wealth of similarities with many other Southeast Asian societies, including a bountiful natural landscape, tropical heat, monsoons, wet rice farming, Buddhism's heritage, eclectic cultural blends, animism, the closeness of spirits to the living, relatively high amounts of female autonomy, betel chewing, tattooing, tolerance of diversity, love of fun, cuisine that mixes many ingredients and flavors (which is often based on rice), and beautiful art forms that soften nature's power. Victor Lieberman noted that Vietnam and other Southeast Asian countries have also shared many of the same historical cycles of prosperity and hard times.[7] It is unique, yet it's also a variety of Southeast Asia's larger cultural milieu. It enriches the Unity/Infinity/Growth of this region, and it's fertilized by it.

THE WORLDWIDE MALAYS

Then there's the Malay world—actually many Malay worlds. Their ancestors migrated through much of Southeast Asia in a long series of movements, which began from southern China to Taiwan 5,000–6,000 years ago, when rice growing communities were spreading farther beyond the Yangtze River.[8] Between 3,500 and 4,500 years ago, they sailed all the way to Melanesia and established communities there. A reconstructed Proto-Austronesian vocabulary indicates people who grew rice and millet; raised pigs, dogs, and maybe chickens; decorated themselves with tattoos; and used canoes, bows, and arrows. By 2000 BCE many built timber houses on stilts, made pottery, attached sails and outriggers to canoes, chewed betel, and used looms for weaving. Their descendants transplanted their lifestyles to islands from Madagascar to the eastern Pacific.[9] They spread over half the earth's circumference and became the world's most widespread ethno-linguistic population before modern Europeans colonized much of the world. Today they number around 350 million.

Most Malay speakers today live in Indonesia and Malaysia. Their culture is less centralized than the Thai and Khmer worlds. Like the Chams, Malays have lacked long rivers and large plains to unify their lands, so many states have coexisted—pluralism is strong in Malay societies.

These states have usually been hierarchical, with elite families at the top projecting magical auras with flamboyant clothing and ceremonies.

Malays had a special language for speaking to and about royalty. Sultans didn't eat (*makan*) like regular folks do; they feasted (*santap*). Only royalty could wear gold and yellow clothing, and rulers traveled under a white umbrella. The aristocracy also donned gold jewelry and kings sported a belt buckle covered with precious gems. High-ranking men traditionally swaggered with a kris (a small ornately carved dagger), and each kris is supposed to contain spiritual power which must be respected. Many are in the form of a blade that is crooked, as though it embodies the animated forces that its owner claimed to control.

Since Malays settled on many islands, the sea became prominent in their views of the world. When Indian traders arrived and brought their Hindu faiths, Malays adapted their *Ramayana* and shadow puppetry, but they developed their own versions. According to Professor Singaravelu Sachithanantham, in *The Ramayana Tradition in Southeast Asia*, Malay elites focused on themes in the epic that fit their own ideals, including contests of military and athletic prowess, unswerving loyalty to the king, righteous warfare, and fidelity in the family. Malay versions also include tales about seafaring that the Indian texts don't contain.[10]

The Malay chronicles were written by court historians in the 17th century from earlier stories from Malacca's apogee in the 15th century, and they describe many political envoys sailing to other royal courts in ravishing terms. A fleet leaving Palembang contained so many vessels that they almost filled the sea. Their varied prows were too numerous to count. The masts looked like a forest and the standards seemed like floating clouds. They all sailed south for six days and nights until they reached a place called Tanjongpura, whose king and 1,000 of his ministers took them to his throne hall. Many tales in the chronicles alternate between sea voyages and royal pomp.

Like many other seagoing people, Malays have stressed limberness and emotional control. Two of the most popular traditional Malay contests are kite flying and top spinning, and both test these skills. In the latter, tops are tethered to a rope and men launch theirs at others (which are already in motion) to knock them over. Locals in a town in northeastern Malaysia called Kota Bharu invited me to one of these matches. My hosts let me try—over, and over, and over. They remained polite, but if there's a Malay word for *uncoordinated wimp*, they must have been thinking of it.

A traditional Malay art form called *silat* emphasizes control and agility by combining dance and martial arts. Its footwork is likened to the movements of tigers, monkeys, snakes, birds, and crocodiles. I watched two men practice and they blended grace and force like this combination of animals does. Musicians often accompany performers, and a drummer and a player of a loud reed instrument with a deep tone backed up the two men. Both dancers began slowly, with stylized hand and foot movements that reminded me of Thai court dances. But the tempo slowly increased and they became more aggressive until the beat was manic and one threw the other to the ground. Because *silat* fuses elegance and power, it has had many meanings in Malay society, and people have performed different forms of it at functions that include royal ceremonies, receptions for special guests in villages, and even weddings. It's yet another Southeast Asian art form that incorporates nature's power and tames it so that the community is strengthened.[11]

Malacca was founded on the peninsula's southwestern coast at the beginning of the 15th century and quickly became Southeast Asia's main commercial hub. The Chinese learned about its rise and granted it a monopoly of their goods in the region, and this attracted even more international traders. Malacca dominated trade in the straits until the Portuguese conquered it in 1511, and it glittered as much as Ayutthaya did. Merchants from China, India, the Middle East, East Africa, Japan, and other Southeast Asian states unloaded their ships at its warehouses and then waited for the next monsoon to return home. In addition to buying each other's goods, they acquired products from the interior forests, including rattan, canes, gums, and resins. Malacca's rulers provided standardized weights and measures, taxed the trade, and enjoyed sumptuous lives.

The Malay chronicles give glimpses of mindsets in this lively state. Their most famous story is of a courtier called Hang Tuah. Malays gave the title *Hang* to a great warrior, and he was the best. People all over the known world admired him, and they thought it was impossible to defeat him because of his bravery and magic kris.

The sultan, Mansur Shah, valued him so highly that he let him move through the royal palace as though it had no doors, but one of the state's senior ministers became jealous of his prestige and accused him of sleeping with one of the sultan's concubines. Enraged, Mansur Shah ordered a minister to put him to death.

Fortunately, the minister realized that Hang Tuah's guilt wasn't established and that he was too valuable to the state to be hastily killed. He thus hid him in a village (in another version, he hid him in the mountains) and told the sultan that he was dead.

Hang Casturi had been a close friend of Hang Tuah's since childhood. When they were about ten, they attacked pirates off the coast and defeated them. The sultan gave him Hang Tuah's old position at court, but the honor soon went to Hang Casturi's head. He took liberties with one of the concubines, locked all the palace's doors, and spread the brass platters and basins over the floor so that nobody could ram his spear at him through the bamboo. Now completely drunk with power, he slew his lover with his own kris and stripped her.

The sultan ordered his warriors to attack, but no one dared because of Hang Casturi's might. The minister who was hiding Hang Tuah realized that the time was ripe for telling the sultan that their greatest hero was still alive. Mansur Shah and Hang Tuah met and reconciled in a solemn ceremony.

Hang Tuah marched to the palace and both men insulted each other's honor. Figuring that they were an even match, Hang Casturi let him into the palace and the ensuing fight is one of Malay literature's most famous episodes. Both clashed for a long time in the stately wooden halls, trying to plunge their daggers into each other. Hang Casturi let Hang Tuah free his kris after he accidentally stuck it into a wall and asked, "Is it manly to kill an unarmed opponent?" But Hang Tuah didn't return the favor when Casturi's kris got lodged in a door, and he stabbed him in the heart all the way through the back. Hang Casturi asked him how a real man can be so dishonorable, and Tuah coldly replied, "What use is honesty to a wicked man like you?" He stabbed him again, killing him instantly.[12]

This tale has resonated with Malays because it highlights conflicting values in their society. Was Hang Tuah right or mean-spirited to slay his friend, particularly in a disrespectful way? Because Malays value loyalty to superiors, many have felt that Hang Tuah did the right thing because he was serving the sultan. But bonds between friends are also core Malay values. Malays stress collective life, and their *adat* law has focused on village traditions of cooperation. It has often emphasized reparation over punishment, so a murderer often became the bonded servant of his victim's family instead of being incarcerated. He could thus help the grieving relatives and remain an asset to his community. The friendship between Tuah and Casturi since childhood represents this close communal life in which people take care of each other. But societies that make livings from the sea often need to be competitive and sometimes must place martial values above friendship. Like Homer's *Iliad*, the Malay chronicles deal with tensions between cooperation and violent conflict, and they bring them to life with royal pageantry, heroic warriors, engrossing battles, and enchanted natural surroundings. The chronicles portray a vigorous society before the Portuguese colonized it.

The growth of Islam in Southeast Asia has always intrigued me. The faith has been uncompromising in its basic tenets. God is *Tawhid* (unity) and there is no other reality than Him. There is no Trinity. There is only One. Yet Islam has been embraced by millions in a region where life is typically pluralistic (it's profuse with spirits). Several currents encouraged both cultures to mesh into one of the world's great crossroads (more Muslims live in Asia than in the Middle East):

- Merchants first brought Islam into towns, including Malacca, Aceh, Banten, and Makassar, and the faith became associated with wealth. As traders throughout the Malay world networked with each other, Islam became a common frame of reference. They felt that they could trust fellow Muslims that they saw bowing to Mecca in mosques. The Koran emphasizes business ethics—people in the Arabian Peninsula lived by trading, and keeping promises was a life-or-death matter in the unforgiving desert. Islam allowed merchants in states throughout the Malay world to feel that they could depend on each other.
- Sultans of the growing commercial states could bolster their own prestige by adopting Islam. Their courts were flashy, and rulers often employed scholars to write about Islam and help

administer its law. In the Malay world's hierarchical societies, elites awed commoners with resplendent rituals, and the latter felt impelled to follow their superiors into Islam.

Royal ancestors had already been honored in the Malay world, as they were among the Khmers and many other Southeast Asian societies, but they now acquired some powerful additions to the family. Alexander the Great and kings in the mighty Persian courts became proud predecessors in genealogies of Islamic rulers; Malay sultans could add them to their own roots. Islam also introduced legal codes and provided stable procedures for royal successions.

- Some people in Malay societies were slaves, and they could free themselves by becoming Muslims. Forces from the top and bottom of the social hierarchy thus converged to establish Islam among Malays.

- Commoners who had to leave their ancestral lands as ocean-going merchants and warriors could find the universality of Allah and the portability of the Koran comforting. They could also share them as key aspects of their common field of meanings.

At the same time, the Malay language became more standardized as Islamic literature spread and pan-regional trading became more frequent. People's identities as Malays grew and they considered Islam to be a central aspect of their culture.[13]

- Sufis brought mystical varieties of Islam which found welcomes in Southeast Asia, where people had long believed that the world is profuse with supernatural powers. Malays who converted could feel connected to the power (*berkat*) of holy men and sultans. Even in modern times, many Malays seek the *berkat* of saints at their tombs. Many have believed that Koranic passages contain magical efficacy, and they've paid specialists to chant them to improve health and wealth. Some have displayed verses in their homes to promote the family's well-being. Certain passages are known to cure diseases, ease emotional problems, and ward off others' evil intents.

- The above reasons have been given by scholars, but Southeast Asian Islam has another dimension which can only be appreciated from an insider's perspective. Cozy family and *kampong* (*village*, or *neighborhood* in a city) life are basic in Malay society. Adibah Amin wrote a wonderful memoir called *As I Was Passing* in which she rhapsodized about the joys of being at home during Islam's fasting month, Ramadan. Old men read the Koran, wives cooked with chili powder, and children played. After the daytime fast, neighbors visited each other and shared dishes. Daily prayers and big events like weddings give people reasons to gather and enjoy each other's company. Malays take a lot of pride in their hospitality, and Islam provides many occasions for sharing warmth.

Though Islam professes unity, it adds yet more diversity to Malay society. The mosque expresses God's unity by rendering all the worshipers in the prayer hall and courtyard equal under Him and pointing them towards Mecca. But its vibrant forms and colors add even more wealth to Southeast Asia's landscapes. The golden domes and slim white minarets mix with the foliage as handsomely as Thai temples do. People can have it both ways in Malaysia. They can honor God's unity and enjoy its diverse manifestations in the world.[14]

The infinite variety in UIG allows fusions of cultures that seem radically different on the surface. They still have many points of contact. This encourages more growth of horizons, and this Growth enhances cultures' Unity—Islam became central in Malays' shared perspectives and identities.

Malaysia is more than Malay. Chinese people comprise much of its population, and they have created a distinct culture. Most live on the west coast and in southern cities. Some settled in Malacca in the 15th century just after China granted its monopoly, and more arrived when China's Qing Dynasty (1644–1911) was founded. This new government was especially unpopular in southeastern China because it often disrupted its beloved maritime trade. But most came in the 19th and early 20th centuries, when the British needed more laborers in their tin and rubber industries. They worked doggedly, and some prospered and rose to become middlemen and managers. Many others became merchants. True to their backgrounds as immigrant traders, Malaysia's Chinese were direct in their dealings with me. One taxi driver complained about privileges that the government grants Malays. He said that it allows them to enter universities and obtain loans for businesses more easily. "Malays are lazy and Chinese have to work hard!" he said in a bitter, gravelly tone.

Ismail Noor and Muhammad Azaham expressed a Malay perspective of this issue in *The Malays Par Excellence*. They said that British colonial administrators took economic initiatives away from Malays and forced them into agricultural settings while encouraging the Chinese to thrive in cities. In this way, they divided and conquered.[15] The authors claimed that Malays work best for someone that they know personally and are happy to please, and that toiling for a wage in an impersonal economic system is foreign to the warmth of traditional Malay life.

A fifty-something Chinese shop owner in Malacca told me that he resented his father for sending him to a Chinese school rather than an English one. He felt that this hamstrung him from finding jobs. Most Chinese feel that publically criticizing their parents is improper because honoring them is a key Confucian value. But many that I met in Malaysia quickly expressed themselves.

A colorful mixture of deities enlivens their traditional spiritual life. The gatekeeper of the main temple in Malacca's Chinatown invited me inside, where I found a who's who in the Chinese spirit world. Shrines for Confucius, Quan Yin, Daoist immortals, ancestors of locals, and gods specific to merchants nestled side by side in a pluralistic heaven that reflected Malacca's diversity.

Two men were smoking cigarettes while worshiping, and one took a puff while standing in front of the shrine. "That's disrespectful!" my guide in Cairo later declared when I told her about him (predicting that she would respond like that, I was being mischievous). In contrast to Islam's insistence on God's unity and uniqueness, traditional Chinese societies have seen nature as populated with an enormous number of spirits as though the afterlife is an extension of the community. Like many Southeast Asians, the Chinese have an ancient heritage of living in intimate societies and feeling that the departed are still close to the living. Some of their religious practices seem casual to many Muslims, but they struck me as equally sincere, but according to traditional Chinese views of the world.

Malacca's temple also accommodates a lot of forms and hues. Its red banners, dark wooden carvings, stone statues, red ancestral tablets, priestesses in black robes, stately white outer walls, upturned roof corners, and Daoist gardens that integrate rock and foliage mixed as spritely as its denizens.

I felt that being Caucasian gave me advantages in Malaysia. Many Malays and Chinese that I met didn't trust each other, but both trusted me enough to share personal matters, probably because I was more ethnically neutral. A Chinese taxi driver took me to Kuala Lumpur's airport to fly to the northeastern city Kota Bharu, and he warned me about its overwhelming Malay and Islamic majority. "Be careful! Don't walk on side streets at night. And if someone asks where you're from, say 'France' or 'Sweden' but not 'America' or 'England.'" But Kota Bharu couldn't have been more different from his suspicions.

The daily bazaar spread through the town's center, and it occupied a central pavilion and several old wooden buildings. Three young Malay men who ran little T-shirt shops in the upper floor of one of the wooden structures were sitting on stools in an aisle, and one was playing a guitar. I stopped to listen. They noticed me and I excused myself by saying that I play too. The magic kris's owner handed it to me. I stopped playing when I heard the call to prayer from the central mosque, but none of them reacted—they seemed entirely interested in playing music. My new friends soon asked me if I wanted to jam with a local rock band in the evening.

We entered a small studio on the second floor of an apartment building downtown. The studio was operated by a drummer who was wiry and taciturn. His hair hung four inches below his shoulders, and it framed a soft-featured face that made him look almost like a beautiful woman. His outer delicacy masked an inner restlessness—a rock drummer's soul. Let's jam, dude!

His playing was machinegun-fast and pinpoint-accurate, and he had great ears. On the spur of the moment, he repeated melodies I played during solos. The other two wanted to be bluesy but he wanted to rock, so I ripped into a fast Metallica song and a huge grin erupted on his face. I then tore into an even faster song by Megadeth and he gleefully banged away. The other two stood by the wall with ear-to-ear smiles. Right after our jam, one took me to a country fair with his wife and son to watch a shadow puppet performance. I enjoyed metal and Wayang Kulit in one night—Malaysian diversity in its full splendor.

Kuala Lumpur also bustles with variety. The Petronas Towers adapt old geometric patterns from Arabian and Persian mosque designs to modern skyscrapers. One evening, I stood under them to watch their windows light up against the darkening sky. A crowd of locals gathered and we all slowly strolled in the warm, thick air.

The streets winding around the towers sported old British colonial buildings, traditional Malay houses on stilts, more modern skyscrapers, snazzy shopping malls, and restaurants of every ethnicity. People sat on the sidewalk of a Middle Eastern cafe smoking hookah pipes. Chinese restaurants lined with hanging red paper lanterns beckoned nearby, and a Hawaiian eatery did thriving business down the road.

Figure 40. A hookah pipe and modern ads blend in Kuala Lumpur's cityscape.

One of the best Islamic art museums in the world crowns a hill with a panoramic view of the gleaming skyscrapers. The building is white, with large windows. All this brightness seemed like purity, which sanctified the rooms that housed the art. The museum devoted a section to each region with old Islamic traditions, except sub-Saharan Africa. The large collection of art from Southeast Asia gave me a revelation.

Islamic art in Southeast Asia would make up a great book. One of the most common traditional Malay patterns is called *awan larat*. The term means *continuous floating clouds*, and it has a copious range of meanings, from a dancer's hands to the energy that infuses life. Balanced flow is the main idea that underlies it—designs in an artwork are evenly distributed rather than concentrated on one body's mass. Patterns thus balance solid and empty spaces so that they seem to fuse into a harmonious field of energy that's both animated and graceful. The motifs usually include vines, flowers, and creepers, and they interweave well with Arabesques and scrolling Arabic letters. They provided yet more media for fusions of Southeast Asian and Islamic traditions.

Because cultures can share many ideas, images, stories, and texts, the world is full of glorious fusions, and Malaysia enveloped me in many blends of mindsets. This variety continues traditions of the proto-Malays who took to the sea thousands of years ago. More Americans are aware of Thailand, but those who explore its southern neighbor will find it equally fascinating.

I'm excluding Indonesia, Burma, and the Philippines from this chapter only because of spatial constraints. But each is as culturally rich as the other Southeast Asian countries.

So multiple cultures have comprised Southeast Asia. Each society is unique, but all have constantly been interconnected. They have traded goods, exchanged political envoys, fought wars, and shared art, ideas, stories, and religious customs. This multidirectional influence through many media has enriched all of these societies. It has also given them many commonalities even though they're also profoundly different (Thai and Cambodian societies have employed different aesthetics to unify themselves; Malays have been more oriented to the sea and they later embraced Islam; and Vietnamese have absorbed much Chinese influence). Some of the experiences and cultural traits that they have shared include wet rice farming, monsoons alternating with tropical heat, stilt homes, the prominence of rivers and boats, spirit cults, serpent cults and their prominence in art forms, aesthetics that fuse grace and energy, social hierarchy, betel chewing, massages in medicine, a multitude of rituals, the central importance of etiquette, and cuisine that mixes many flavors and which often includes rice and seafood. All of these countries have a Southeast Asian feel that's distinct from India and mainstream China because of all these commonalities.

Many women in Southeast Asia have had freedoms that women in traditional Indian and Chinese societies haven't been able to enjoy. The latter two cultures have often emphasized strong patriarchal traditions—the male head of the household has been sacrosanct in Hindu and Confucian cultures. But inheritance has often passed through female lines in Southeast Asia. Divorce has also often been relatively easy. In many traditional Indian and Chinese societies, it was common for a new bride to move into her husband's family and be confined to his household, laboring from dawn to dusk while some of his elder relatives criticized her. Anthony Reid noted that newlyweds in traditional Southeast Asian societies have often lived in the bride's family's village. Many old legal codes insisted that property be jointly held.[16] So Southeast Asians' concepts of the family have often been more flexible than Indian and Chinese ideas of patriarchies, and people have often moved between both paternal and maternal kin.[17] In addition, adoption has often been relatively easy in the region. Milton Osborne noted that the nuclear family has been stressed in much of Southeast Asia, as opposed to the extended family in traditional India. To me, these customs have also contributed to Southeast Asia's distinct feel. Instead of being strictly bound to the patriarchal household and to one's place in the extended family, social organization has often been looser and more flowing, adapting to circumstances as they change.

Reid also noted that women have often taken the initiative in courtship. Zhou Daguan was astonished by the sexual freedom of Khmer women, and I enjoyed the flirtatious security guard at Siem Reap's airport and the Thai woman who asked me if I'm gay. To be fair, I've met a lot of outgoing women in China and India too, but that might be because modernization has only recently allowed them to be so, and because many women in those two countries are attracted to Western men. Oppression has been common in Southeast Asia too (women have been banned from mainstream Buddhist monkhoods in Thailand, they're not allowed in sensitive places in several northen Thai temples because of fear of menstrual blood, and Vitenam's Le legal code, which has been praised for allowing women to inherit their shares of property, was ususually applied to favor patrilineal succession), but a lot of evidence suggests that, on average, women in Southeast Asia traditionally enjoyed more freedom. Women have often been out in the markets, doing the buying and selling. Zhou Daguan noted that they operated Angkor's daily market, and travelers to Ayutthaya wrote that they ran market stalls and permanent stores.

Victor Lieberman noted another type of social fluidity in Southeast Asia.[18] Before modern nations were organized, people often submitted to the person with the most political power, and they could transfer loyalties to another when circumstances changed. Even in the late 19th century, some people living near the borders between states paid tribute to multiple sovereigns.

Although many Indian ideas were imported in Southeast Asia, the caste system wasn't usually adopted deeply (Burma was an exception to some extent in places where its Indian population was politically prominent). When it was imported, it was often for ceremonial reasons rather than as a basic ordering principle for everyone in society, as it was in India. For example, a man in a temple in Bali told me that a priest that we saw was a brahmin and that he was a sudra (the lowest of the four castes). But he only invoked caste in the temple; he was casual everywhere else. Though Southeast Asian societies have emphasized social hierarchy and distinctions between elites and commoners, the levels of society have often not been as extensively and precisely stratified as they were in India's caste system, so people weren't as embedded in a permanent social class for life (Ayutthaya's system of social ranks was a temporary exception).[19] The line between elites and ordinary folks has been firm, but people on each side have often been able to change occupations, familial structures, and localities with relative ease.

Lieberman wrote that populations in Southeast Asia were sparse in most places before modern cities emerged. This has made labor a scarcer resource than land. Since people could change loyalties when another ruler acquired the power to attract followers from neighboring lords, politics in the region were often more characterized by ebbs and flows than by sharp borders.

The relative political fluidity, gender equality, and geographic flexibility have given people all over Southeast Asia shared meanings. They have often been able to agree that life is a flow—situations often change unpredictably. Loyalties are typically personal rather than based on enormous abstract institutions like a Confucian bureaucracy (outside of Vietnam) or India's caste system. People have often looked to their local worlds and adapted to circumstances while making their surroundings pretty and having fun whenever possible. They have often favored politeness and the enjoyment of little things more than big systems of abstractions.[20]

Southeast Asians have also shared culinary experiences. Rice and fish have been basic in most societies' diets, and many dishes mix ingredients. The Thai stir fries and curries, the Vietnamese pho bowls, the Malay fish soups, and the Khmer amoks all blend meats, vegetables, and sauces. All these types of dishes emphasize fusion of many flavors. They also encourage common aesthetics—each mouthful tastes different so that people enjoy a multitude of stimuli rather than a single object, like a turkey leg, a kabob, or a frankfurter.

Even when they have fought, Southeast Asian states have often shared assumptions and aesthetics by taking each other's residents captive and transferring them to their own territories as laborers, artists, and soldiers. Ayutthaya transported many people from the Khmer Empire and Sukhothai in this way, and David Wyatt, in *Siam in Mind*, wrote that its kings often settled people on the opposite side of the kingdom from where they were captured (for example, many that were taken from Sukhothai in the 15th century were sent to the deep south). The Burmese carried many of Ayutthaya's top performing artists to their own land after the 1767 sack, and this became one of the main wellsprings of Burmese performing arts.

Although each Southeast Asian country has been unique, all have shared many environmental, cultural, and political features which have given people from the different states a wealth of ways to interact and share assumptions about the world. The region is highly diverse, yet interconnected through many media so that all of its cultures have always been able to enrich each other. This often hasn't been taught in classrooms there, but this is largely because modern schools developed under colonial and local political regimes that wanted to train youths to serve their systems of extracting the land's resources without questioning the status quo. But for many previous centuries, people traded goods, art forms, faiths, ceremonies, stories, and foods.

This interconnectedness has also included ongoing dialogs with cultures beyond Southeast Asia. People adopted Hinduism and Buddhism from India and Sri Lanka. Though Islam originated in a profoundly different land, it entered the region through several media. Chinese immigrants imported their spirit cults and combined them with local deities into lively pantheons. There are always many pathways between any two cultures. Every location in Southeast Asia mixes places throughout the region and in much of the rest of the world.

The West has also synthesized many places. Greece, Italy, and northern Europe shared ideas, images, religious beliefs, and political traditions and used them to unify their worlds. Art forms and ideas that Europeans have considered fundamental have also been shared within wider cultural exchanges, particularly the Judeo-Christian tradition, which emerged in the Middle East.

There is thus always more to see and enjoy in any location than what is commonly perceived. Unity/Infinity/Growth is integrated through all places, as it is through all times. This integration of UIG through all locations and temporal periods enables us to see boundless potential in every place, just as we can see time as an infinitely creative now. There are limitless ways in which different places and times can be synthesized, and each place and moment can be a launching pad to ever more perspectives.

UIG has many different levels—there are several magnitudes of social systems in which certain ways of seeing the world emerge and coalesce, and all these levels permeate and influence each other:

1. Local societies can profoundly influence a whole region, as Florence, Angkor, Sukhothai, and ancient Athens and Rome did.

2. Areas that we identify as countries today, such as Italy, Thailand, Cambodia, India, and China, developed cultural traits that the majorities of their populations have shared.

3. An entire region, such as the West and Southeast Asia, has many common characteristics, which are shared through several media.

4. Many human traits are common to all cultures, including families, political structures, religious ideas and feelings, cosmologies (ideas of how the universe is structured), speculations about the origin of the universe and of society, humor, play, romance, sexuality, relationships between genders, friendships, economic exchange, music, dance, sports, visual arts, the use of technology, the progression from childhood to old age, and ideas about death and the afterlife.

UIG is thus richer than something that can be conceived as a single object. These levels are not like marbles, as Thailand, Cambodia, Malaysia, Laos, Vietnam, and Burma can appear to be on maps that make their borders seem solid. Instead, the different levels interpenetrate in ways that reinforce each other. For example, Renaissance Florence, Venice, and Rome added to many influences from the ancient Greco-Roman heritage and from Christianity. Sukhothai, Lan Na, and Ayutthaya had many common aspects that meshed into a cultural landscape which has been characteristically Thai and distinct from Cambodia, Vietnam, and Malaysia. At the same time, all these countries have shared many general Southeast Asian traits. UIG includes all levels of cultural commonality, from the local to the global, and all can enhance each other.

Within any space that people identify, all these levels are interconnected. As you explore how integrated places and times are, the world can appear bigger and bigger, and its size can grow in ever more directions as cultures interact in more ways. This growth can happen from any space and in any moment when violence, political oppression, ecological hardship, and willful mental narrowness don't constrain perspectives. The ability to see more is ingrained in geography—in all places and times that human beings have lived in, you can always see more beauty and more ways to combine new ideas and integrate cultures.

What can we conclude from this? I find four things especially gratifying:

- As this growth continues, people can increasingly appreciate each other's perspectives and become more sensitive to each other. This will encourage compassion to spread in all spaces so that it becomes a fundamental aspect of geography.
- The future of identity. We can free our identities from a single category or dichotomy, like Eastern versus Western, or black versus white. As we keep looking *At, With,* and *Beyond,* our identities can expand through more cultures and historical periods. As this happens, we can deepen our affinities with people in all times and places. As our personal identities expand, we can incorporate more people's perspectives into bigger and more creative views of the world. So Growth is a key aspect of our identities—we are always more than any label that can be attached to us, and this *more* can always develop further.

  This does not mean losing the identities of the cultures we grew up in. We can always use their conventional perspectives, and I think this is necessary because a person's original cultural landscape is so deeply ingrained in her that it's not possible to completely jettison it. She needs to look *At* in order to have a shared field of meanings with others. But we can liberate ourselves from our conventions for a while and then return to them and see them anew. As we keep traveling through the circle of looking *At, With,* and *Beyond,* our early home and other cultures can keep enhancing each other. We retain our cultural and personal identities, but they become more refined and multifaceted so that we have many ways to relate to each other and to enrich each other's identities even more. We thereby become more unified and increasingly varied at the same time.

  This mutuality can grow between cultures too. Each remains unique, yet all can keep appreciating and enhancing each other in more ways. Mutual enrichment can become a fundamental aspect of geography.

- We can control our thoughts—we don't need to slavishly adhere to our concepts. The more we look *At, With,* and *Beyond* to explore Unity/Infinity/Growth, the more we can choose the ideas we explore the world with. Instead of following our preconceptions and treating them like universal truths which completely bind our horizons and identities, we can endlessly explore different places and pasts and use an increasing range of ideas and perspectives from them as steps to ever higher perspectives, which can integrate even more cultures and viewpoints.

- Ideas can become sources of joy. They become part of an infinite dance that pulsates all over the globe. We can always arrive at new perspectives, and we can shift between them like steps in a dance. Each culture, and each space and time that people identify, has so much possibility for more meanings that our horizons can expand from one view of the world to an infinite dance of mindsets from all places and times. I am the dance and so are you. Its exuberance, playfulness, and joy can be partially expressed by Khmer temples, Thai wats, Italian Renaissance paintings, ancient Greek temples, and Indian art. Every culture can express it to some extent, but never fully. Nothing captures it completely—we can only join it, become better dancers, and make it even better and more evident in geography. We all grow more infinite, and infinity grows through us. I think, therefore I love.

How high can we go? It's always impossible to say because what we can envision is tied to our imaginations and ranges of experiences and ideas, and they will keep expanding as we continue to look *At, With,* and *Beyond.* But we'll widen them as much as possible in the conclusion and peer into our highest potentials for creativity and joy.

CONCLUSION

ARCHITECTURE OF PARADISE

How BIG IS our world, and how much can we enjoy it? In this chapter, we will learn as much as we currently can about how high our perspectives can soar. We'll cover a lot of material first in order to have a steep ascent. After this chapter, we'll return home, with a how-to guide for bringing the loftiest possible visions into our lives and sharing them with our families, friends, and coworkers.

In *Siam Mapped*, Thongchai Winichakul wrote about old and new perspectives existing side by side during and after Mongkut's reign (1851–68). Although the great king initiated a more scientific way of seeing the world, most people kept their old perspectives and mixed them with it. For example, they used the newly imported Western knowledge of astronomy and mathematics to improve calculations in their traditional astrology. Things haven't changed much since then. Bangkok's top universities, including Chulalongkorn and Thammasat, are renowned for their engineering and business schools. I visited both campuses and noticed that their buildings looked like those built in many of California's state colleges in the 1960s and 70s—the plain five-to ten-story rectangular boxes projected order and rationality. But Bangkok still brims with astrologers, amulet sellers, spirit houses, and people who counteract sorcery for a fee. I saw many glittering spirit houses in front of new skyscrapers, and the royal palace, Wat Pho, and Wat Arun still rise in the city's center.

Thai schools teach modern geography, but wats still bedeck the landscape with shimmering colors and flowing forms. Thailand is still full of sacred centers. The royal palace and all wats and Buddha statues seem to radiate goodness and protect communities. Theravada Buddhist traditions, animism, and old distinctions between *muang* and *pa* are still key aspects of Thai culture. They're deeply ingrained even though the digital world and recent clashes between the rich and poor have made it harder for many to fully appreciate them. They alternate with modern ideas of geography according to context. Many teachers feel deep respect as they pass wats on the way home to grade students' geography tests, and I often saw groups of school kids honoring their heritage in historic wats.

As one of the multiple ways of seeing the world in Thailand, modern geography has become part of its ancient heritage of combining a variety of views. Many perspectives have coexisted, and people can never reduce the whole environment to one vantage point.

The Khmers also integrated their world by fusing multiple perspectives of it. They combined magnificent monuments and royal pageantry with villagers' intimate communities, local spirit cults, and the natural environment. Vietnamese combined Chinese and local cultures. The Malay world first assimilated Hinduism and Buddhism and then embraced Islam, and yet has retained many of its own traditional customs. It may seem contradictory to say that people in all these countries unify the world with several views of it. They hold onto, not one geography, but multiple. Cultures in this region have generally been pluralistic, but is this thinking uniquely Southeast Asian? We have been exploring dominant perspectives and ideas that different cultures use to unify themselves with, but as we delve more deeply into these societies' ways of seeing, we will find yet more dimensions in them which can show us higher levels of the integration of Unity/Infinity/Growth, which can encourage ever more creativity and joy.

Alberti wrote his mathematical theory of three-dimensional perspective in the 1430s, and a detailed map of Florence was made in 1470. In 1500 a map was made of Venice, and by the end of the 16th century, every major European city was outlined by a map that allowed people to see it from a bird's eye view. They could follow every street on it and examine the outline of each building. These maps thereby helped initiate a new way of seeing the world, which was less oriented to the medieval hierarchy of beings and more to details in material life. The recent development of printing allowed these maps to be produced and disseminated quickly.

However, the historian A. Richard Turner, in *Renaissance Florence*, wrote that three-dimensional perspective didn't became the West's dominant way of seeing the world until much later. Alberti theorized it to give painters better techniques for realism, and maps were made for political and commercial uses by governments and leading merchants. But the displacing of older views was a long process; people used multiple perspectives to integrate their world for several centuries.

E. M. W. Tillyard, in *The Elizabethan World Picture*, wrote that people in late 16th and early 17th century England still used many of the ideas that Gothic cathedral builders did in the 13th century. From their standpoint, the universe is a great chain of being, with God ruling a hierarchy of elevated souls in the sky, humanity living beneath them, and beasts and plants existing in the bottom levels. All are in their set domains. Arthur O. Lovejoy, in *The Great Chain of Being*, wrote that this was still a dominant idea in Europe in the 18th century, even though that was also the age of The Enlightenment, when science's prestige spread.[1] In his 1733 poem, "An Essay on Man," Alexander Pope said that we and all other beings are in our proper places, and that,

> "All are parts of one stupendous whole,
> Whose body Nature is, and God the soul."

Masaccio painted the body as monumentally real in the early 15th century, but 300 years later Pope still favored ideas from the Middle Ages. These two perspectives of the world (one focusing on the body within three-dimensional space, and the other emphasizing a metaphysically based hierarchy) thrived together for a long time in the West. Like Southeast Asians, Westerners have unified their world by using many views of it.

However, cultures' most widely shared views of the world are not randomly assembled. Westerners haven't seen and represented nature as graceful and animated energy flows as much as Thai artists have. This Thai view of the world developed in a deep cultural landscape that was different from the West's. The Western tradition doesn't have the web of associations that would make Thai ways of seeing as central in it. Ideas of yin-yang patterns of energy didn't take root in Europe nearly as much as they did in China. Each culture emphasizes a unique mixture of ideas that make the most sense for the most people—they can structure their experiences with them and share a common field of meanings. These ideas fuse into perspectives that seem like basic reality, but these perspectives can show us more richness in UIG when we explore them more closely.

If the great chain of being was a central idea in the West from antiquity to the 18th century, how did it originate? It emerged over several centuries in a cultural setting that was already infinitely fertile. Before the Greeks lost their beloved freedom to the northern kingdom of Macedonia in the fourth century BCE, their civilization was largely centered on independent city-states, and people saw geography as a community of them, with each ruling its own domain. These states traded and often fought, but their residents usually focused on the world of distinct towns and their surrounding farms and shores.

Geography encouraged this orientation. The typical Greek island is small and it rises within a few miles from its closest neighbors. City-states emerged on these islands and in small valleys and plains on the mainland. The ancient Greek world was composed of many independent city-states rather than one empire, and they were distinct and clearly partitioned by coasts and mountains. But because they were near each other, it was relatively easy to sail between them. Many of these states specialized in certain goods and they constantly traded with each other. Their islands, mainland valleys, and colonnaded temples reflected the same reality: a field of distinct entities that are linearly related to each other.

I boated to several Greek islands in 2008 and 2013 and everything on them stood out. The white stone homes, red tiled roofs, clear outlines of mountains and craggy cliffs, sparkling blue water, dark coastlines, small fishing boats, and little olive groves were distinct. No single thing dwarfed the others; all things were in scale with each other. No towering Himalayan peaks or dense Cambodian jungles dominated the environment. Instead, a field of distinct entities that are proportionate with each other developed as a basic model of reality in ancient Greece. This idea was a key root of Michelangelo's *David*. Both the free-standing male nude and the Greek temple are distinct, complete, and finely proportioned.

I also experienced this predominance of clear distinctions when I sailed between the islands. A body of land appeared every few minutes. Because of this, I kept looking for coastlines. When land appeared, its clearly shaped mountains stuck out of the water as definitively as a Greek temple. For an untold number of ancient Greeks, this view was a model of well-being. It meant a return, or *nostos*. A return to firm land and civilized life resonated deeply enough to become the main theme of Homer's *Odyssey*, which recounted his wanderings and homecoming after the Trojan War.

Ancient Greeks' political centers reflected their islands and coast-lines. The agora was the town's hub, where everybody met, traded goods, and decided on public policy. The space was plain by Angkor's standards. It was open, unpaved, and surrounded by temples that were human-scale. So a key center of experience that ancient Greeks shared was an open area in which everyone was within clear sight and earshot of each other. There was no royal palace to awe everybody, and many Greeks were proud of this. Each person was like a point, and straight lines directly connected all points to each other because any two people could interact without a big institution or a king dictating the protocols. The temples around their agoras projected clear and proportioned lines of columns, which provided models of eternal order.

Ancient Greeks often structured religious experiences in terms of these civic centers. Delphi was the most popular pan-Greek religious cen-ter. People from all over the Hellenic area flocked to it to hear Apollo's oracle, and many thought it was the center of the world. But it seemed like the edge of it when I first got there in 2008. The ancients had to trek up a high hill to a place that's ringed by a rugged cliff for about 120 degrees. But they made this otherworldly landscape look like home by building colonnaded stone temples and carving friezes of muscled gods and warriors. Ancient Greeks made supernatural Delphi reflect their urban life.

City-states erected colonnaded treasuries at Delphi, and they stored offerings and equipment for rituals in them. Many well-proportioned buildings thus rose on the path that curved up the hill and led to Apollo's temple. Ancient pilgrims entered and received pronouncements from a woman sitting on a tripod who breathed vapors rising from below.

She supposedly went into a trance and provided oracular advice. People made their approach to this engagement with supernatural powers seem as tangible as a trip to the market in the agora.

The area above Apollo's temple looked just as civic. A large amphitheater rose on the hillside, and its circular form made people face each other as they did in their hometown theaters. They watched each other during performances, sharing emotions more intensely than people in modern auditoriums sitting in rows and facing the stage usually do. Ancient Greek towns were more personal than modern cities, and Delphi was just as communal. The Greeks made the whole area which was a key intersection with mysterious powers resemble their home turf. Their most sacred geography mirrored their worldly politics.

So land, sea, towns, politics, and sacred architecture converged into a common ancient Greek perspective of the world, which focused on distinct entities, clear boundaries, abstract shapes, linear relationships, and human-sized spaces. It was both intimate and fathomable. Literacy and trade increased after the eighth century BCE so that some people became more aware of lands and people beyond their own communities, and by the fifth century, the horizons of some folks expanded into hopes for the soul joining the gods in the afterlife, and into ideas of a long succession of reincarnations into many different species. But Walter Burkert, in his classic study, *Greek Religion*, wrote that most people in the Greek world still focused on what was tangible (dreams of joining gods were held by some followers of Orphic cults, and ideas of reincarnation were more common in Sicily and southern Italy than in Greece—most Greeks didn't express beliefs in it). Burkert wrote that Greek religion was an extremely public tradition because it was bound to the city-state— sacrificial processions, athletic contests, communal meals, temples with handsome proportioned exteriors, and demonstrative prayers and vows were regular experiences that dominated the field of meanings everyone shared.[2]

But after Alexander the Great expanded the Greek world all the way to India in the fourth century BCE, the area from Western Europe to East Asia became more integrated. More Westerners' horizons grew into lands beyond their own, and this was a key root of the great chain of being. But their new perspectives didn't displace the old views centered on cities. Both world-views coexisted for a long time and fused in many creative ways.

A second century CE writer in the Roman Empire named Apuleius wrote *The Golden Ass,* which recounts the journey of a man called Lucius, who accidentally turned himself into a donkey while experimenting with magic. He wandered around the Mediterranean to change back and was ultimately granted his wish by Isis (Romans had imported this popular Egyptian goddess, who was associated with salvation). Although the tale was fanciful, cities often dominated its geography. The Roman Empire's urban centers included a forum, public bathhouses, theaters, libraries, paved roads, and aqueducts. Lucius could travel to any city and assume that he would meet people who shared this world, and they conversed as though they knew its institutions and idioms. Characters debated in Roman oratorical styles, and they invoked legal procedures that Apuleius's urbane readers would have recognized.

This idea of geography as a network of cities flourished for several more centuries, particularly in the east, which was less affected by the invasions of Goths, Vandals, and Huns which brought Rome to its knees in the fifth century. In Jordan I visited the basilica of Saint George in Madaba to see a famous sixth century mosaic map of the eastern Mediterranean which spreads out on its floor. Cities are its most prominent features—tight clusters of buildings illustrate Jerusalem and all other towns, and areas between them are desolate beige spaces.

But in that century, bubonic plague outbreaks, more barbarian invasions, and a further decline in literacy beset much of Roman Europe. Ideas of geography increasingly focused less on cities and more on Christian sites such as cathedrals, monasteries, and shrines for saints, martyrs, and Biblical events. Near Madaba's basilica rises Mt. Nebo, which Moses ascended just before leaving this world. As he gazed at the land of Israel, Yahweh told him that he would never set foot in it but promised that his descendants would. This became a key event in Hebrew and Christian history because it was a landmark in God's covenant with humanity. The site's plain square church made me think of holiness when I stood in front of it. Its outer walls were undecorated and their tan color matched the barren land. Places that emphasized spiritual history were becoming more prominent in people's minds than colonnaded civic plazas, and this thinking became dominant in Europe until the Italian Renaissance. It was entrenched enough to remain strong in the 13th century, when towns had grown and people were building Gothic cathedrals.

This geography of holy places meshed with ideas of the great chain of being. Around the beginning of the sixth century, Pseudo Dionysius formalized the great chain by detailing its nine classes of celestial angels. Animals and plants make up the lower levels. But the West's cultural landscape was much richer than the replacement of one view by another.

Apuleius's *The Golden Ass* expressed both perspectives more than three centuries earlier. It portrayed an international community of urbanites and a world of magic. It then became spiritual when Lucius was introduced to Isis and she restored his human existence and taught him a lesson: Aim for higher things than base magic.

Mixing the physical and metaphysical wasn't new in the West in Apuleius's time either. By the sixth century BCE, the proportioned colonnades of Greek temples made the world and sacredness mirror each other. They embodied the universe's enduring order, and they graced both Delphi and cities. The Homeric epics portrayed Olympian gods as though they were human beings, right down to Zeus and Hera's marital roes and Aphrodite's spoiled brat pouts. As below, so behaved the gods above. In the early fourth century BCE, Plato made this mutual reflection a general philosophy by saying that the universe was created according to divine ratios. But *The Golden Ass* was a different beast.

Apuleius's book portrayed a world more out of joint. People's forms and fortunes transformed quickly, and magic could turn humans into animals. As a donkey Lucius suffered one mishap after another. He was forced to drive a grinding wheel in a corn mill and then had to pull an overloaded timber cart while the boy in charge of him beat his right hip until it was covered with blood. The historian of literature Erich Auerbach noted that even the writing style expressed a disjointed world. Apuleius used a refined Latin style to detail the open sores on Lucius's body after the beatings and to describe other grotesque scenes, including two women urinating in a man's face. So much for timeless Platonic beauty.

But Isis saved the day. After wandering through a world full of perils, Lucius met a divine personality who transcended the winds of change and turned him back into a man. What happened to the natural balance in those Greek temples? Why was the world so topsy-turvy before Isis put things right?

Apuleius struck a nerve that was already sensitive throughout the empire. More than a century before, the Roman poet Ovid wrote his *Metamorphosis*, which was full of transformations from Greek mythology. A horny Zeus changed into a bull to carry off Europa, and Daphne turned into a tree when Apollo ran after her. The Homeric epics had been central literary models for Greek and Roman writers, and they had unified themes (Achilles' impact on the Trojan War in the *Iliad*, and Odysseus' return home in the *Odyssey*). They gave these topics moral dignity, but Ovid irreverently told Greek myths as loosely related stories that ended in a sudden shape-shift. The world had changed between the time of those Greek temples and the Roman Empire. It had become integrated into an economic system that reached all the way to China and the Funan area. But it seemed disjointed to many.

A first century CE Roman writer named Petronius brings us into this world in his fictional story, *The Satyricon*, by letting us eavesdrop on a banquet. The host, Trimalchio, has recently become rich and he's eager to show off his new wealth. Two of his guests slander his wife, Fortunata, by saying, "All she cares about is money, but before their marriage, her work was so lowly that you wouldn't have even taken a piece of bread from her hands. But now she watches her husband's money like a hawk, and when she takes a rest, she gossips like a magpie." The visitors marvel at other people's sudden changes of fate. Some have suddenly made fortunes while others have been ruined.

Now it's time to eat and Trimalchio serves a round plate with dishes that resemble the 12 zodiacal signs. A hunk of beef lies over Taurus (the bull) and a pair of testicles and kidneys garnish Gemini (for being associated with twins). He picks his teeth with a silver toothpick and then makes a literary allusion that reflects the shallow learning of a parvenu. "Wine lasts longer than us poor humans, so let us drink it up and enjoy." Six hundred years before, Greek lyric poets sang this life-is-brief-so-enjoy-the-moment theme so much that it became a lit-erary cliché. Trimalchio thus tries to appear sophisticated but repeats what's been worn out for centuries. He then gets drunk and boasts about the tomb that he plans to build for himself, which will immortalize him with reliefs of ships that brought him his fortune, and of gladiatorial games that he sponsored. Everything he does and says is a laughable example of bad taste. But for him and his guests, the world is constantly changing. Fortunes are quickly made and lost and social positions are unstable. Nobody has the chance to become refined; people can only put on garish shows to show off their wealth. The guests observe the circus-like atmosphere with the wide eyes of country boys who have just arrived in the city.

Petronius strived to be different, and his cultivation became so renowned that Nero appointed him as his arbiter of taste. But work-ing for the boss from hell made him just as vulnerable to life's sudden changes. A jealous rival denounced him and he was arrested. Believing that execution was inevitable, he committed suicide by slashing open his veins. The fickle goddess Fortuna enriched the refined and the rustic, and then turned on both with equal indifference.

Fortune's cruelty wasn't just a literary theme; it was a fact of life in the city of Rome because grandeur and squalor were close neighbors there. Thousands of multi-story apartment buildings rose in it. One was so high that it was considered the eighth wonder of the world. Collapses and fires were so frequent that Augustus Caesar limited their height to 70 feet. Rooms not by the street received little light, but apartments and halls reeked with odors and writers suggested burning bread for relief from them. Because many buildings lacked running water, people had to lug heavy buckets up the stairs, and they often dumped waste from their windows. May the gods help anyone unpopular with his neighbors.

Streets were so narrow that it was illegal to drive carts on them during the day. People delivered goods in the evenings, shouting at each other to avoid collisions. Garbage piled up, dogs foraged, and thieves prowled. Between 300,000 and 400,000 slaves lived in the city, and they did most of the manual labor. Hoards of unemployed men thus hung around with nothing to do, so emperors regularly gave them bread and gory shows in the arenas to keep them from turning into subversive mobs. Streets were often so crime-ridden that only a fool would have ventured out at night.

Emperors built magnificent monuments and forums between the mazes of firetraps, creating a cityscape that alternated between splendor and shabbiness. Around 50 BCE, Julius Caesar erected a new forum that branched off the main one, which had been Rome's commercial center since the sixth century. Augustus then constructed another forum next to Caesar's and boasted that he had transformed Rome from a city of brick into a city of marble. Throughout the first century CE, more emperors erected their own forums. They also built public bathhouses, temples, theaters, stadiums, and victory arches. The perspectives that people had while walking through ancient Rome alternated between overcrowded slums and the grand marble colonnades and statues of gods and emperors in open public spaces (many of the rich lived in villas in the hills and countryside, sheltered in their private gardens). Slogging through crowded trash-laden streets, a person would have suddenly seen the towering arches of a theater, or the 1,000-foot frontage of the baths of Emperor Trajan. The disjointed perspectives in Apuleius's and Ovid's writings thus reflected Rome's cityscape (most of the remains that the 15th century Florentines saw were of the grand monuments—they idealized Rome as the model of civic order but weren't exposed to the ancient city's seamy sides).

The bathhouses were stupendous and they provided temporary relief from the social tensions. Rich and poor had access to both cold and hot baths, which were surrounded by gardens, sporting grounds, fountains, lecture rooms, libraries, and covered promenades. Some were as big as a modern shopping mall but more elegant, with coffered ceilings and niches for marble statues at regular intervals. Anyone could enter them for a break from the crowded streets, and for a while, enjoy beautiful surroundings in the company of friends, snack-sellers, and musicians.

But the Coliseum operated from morning to night. I first walked around its upper concourse and admired the size of the building, which sat more than 50,000 people—as many as a major league baseball stadium. Cavernous arches ringed the entire edifice, and they allowed it to be filled and emptied in minutes. But I then descended to the lower level, where thousands of people had suffered and died.

When I visit an archeological site, I linger in several places to imagine how people lived and thought. I usually love getting as close as possible to the ways people experienced the world, but the Coliseum became unbearable. To my left, victims quivered as leopards yanked out their intestines, and to my right, spectators ate figs and cheered. The word *arena* comes from *harena*, which was the sand that was spread on the ground to soak up the blood. I looked up towards the seats and thought, You assholes! How can you enjoy this?

To take my mind off the sadism, I looked up at the architecture but that only made me feel worse. The contrast between the arches' grandeur and elegance and the inhumanity that they framed was sheer madness—the building glorified the cruelty. I couldn't stand it anymore and stormed out of one those outer arches.

But within five minutes, I was walking past one of the ancient city's most magnificent public halls. This was the beginning of the original forum. As ancient Romans did, I saw dramatic contrasts between those that the goddess Fortuna smiled upon and the ones that she cast down.

Rome's bloody shows didn't catch on as much in the East—many Greeks and Levantines found them appalling. But Fortuna ruled there too. Gaps between rich and poor had widened since Plato's time, which was in the early fourth century BCE. Alexander the Great had conquered Persia in the late fourth century, confiscated its massive treasury, and allowed its gold to circulate in his empire's newly integrated world. Some people prospered and others were left behind.

Greek culture became the main standard of civilization in Alexander's wake, and many cities from Athens to Central Asia had an elite population who exercised in gymnasiums, attended plays in amphitheaters, and admired sculptures of heroes and Olympian gods. From Athens to the Oxus, upper class Greek boys competed in sports, studied Homer, and learned to play the lyre in colonnaded courtyards surrounded by lecture rooms. But the majority to the east of the Aegean spoke their local languages, labored in the fields, and remained illiterate. Differences between lifestyles and incomes had become more dramatic.

The world as most people knew it had grown, and it dwarfed the classical proportions of Greek temples and agoras. The environment of

self-contained and intimately sized cities turned into an integrated economic system which included mob-infested metropolises and widened
gaps between the rich and poor. Rome harbored about one million souls
and about half a million lived in Alexandria (Angkor was about the size
of Rome, but homes were single-story houses rather than towering tenements). The forces that affected people now seemed impersonal.

So people tried to humanize them. Greeks imagined them as a goddess called Tyche and Romans called her Fortuna.[3] People everywhere
imagined the unpredictable as a personality that they could pray to, and
they built temples for her in almost every city. But she was often more
fickle than merciful, and she could ruin people as easily as strengthen
them.

As the world expanded after Alexander's conquests, so did people's visions of the universe. More ideas besides the old community of
Olympian gods became common, and astrology spread from Babylonia
throughout the Mediterranean in the late first millennium BCE.
Babylonians had developed the 12-house horoscope and used it to cor-
relate the regular motions of heavenly bodies with events in the world.
Instead of human-like Greek gods, the universe's main forces were
impersonal celestial bodies. The sun, the moon, planets, and constellations that comprised the zodiac were the divinities that presided over
the world. Many Greeks' ideas of the universe had expanded from the
independent city-states' popular view of a three-part order of heaven,
earth, and underworld. This cozy cosmos fit a pantheon that had human
appetites. Gods in the sky and people on earth mirrored each other, and
the two Homeric epics portrayed this intimacy. But the regularity of the
stars fit the newly enlarged world, and the heavens were now so big that
their forces seemed less personal and more mechanical.

In the third century BCE, Aristarchus of Samos discovered that
the earth orbits the sun. However, Claudius Ptolemy (100–178 CE) still
saw the earth as the center of the universe, and this idea stuck until
Copernicus challenged it the 16th century. But Ptolemy's cosmos was
also larger than the older one, as well as more differentiated. His earth
rested in the center of a system of spheres that were nested within each
other. The moon was the closest to the earth, and progressively farther

out were the spheres of Mercury, Venus, the Sun, Mars, Jupiter, and Saturn. An area of fixed stars surrounded all the planets. The West held onto this view of the universe until the Renaissance.

Babylonians had applied astrology to the fortunes of their state, but Greek intellectuals in Alexandria combined it with a wider range of ideas and synthesized a view of the world that dominated the time between the independent city-states and Christianity's rise. The heavens' mechanics were applied to human lives, and a big network of ideas became associated with their orbits. Each celestial body had certain characteristics. The moon and Venus were feminine and the others were masculine. People associated each with a substance. They connected the moon with silver, Mercury with its namesake, Mars with fire, and Saturn with lead. The celestial bodies also had personalities. Mercury was unpredictable and playful, Venus was amorous, Mars had a temper, and Saturn was dull and lethargic. But how did all this stuff fit together?

Many people thought things were related by cosmic sympathy (*sympatheia*). In the third century CE, Plotinus (a philosopher who lived in both Alexandria and Rome) wrote that things that are alike have a natural concord. Things in different parts of the universe resonate with each other if they have the same characteristics. People are thus in synch with the celestial bodies that they're most like.

This was how a lot of people thought magic works, and its popularity increased in that uncertain age. All levels of Roman society practiced it. Julius Caesar uttered a spell three times to ensure a safe trip when he entered a carriage. Apuleius's interest in magic reflected his life—he had to defend himself against a claim that he had used it to make a rich widow marry him. Many people believed that they could affect another person from a distant place, and some tried to do this by manipulating things that had the same or opposite traits that he had.

Others applied words and formulas that supposedly compelled a god or planet to do their bidding. Some people specialized in this and they carried papyri with long lists of spells. Anyone could hire them to manipulate the supernatural to increase their wealth or health, or to harm a foe.

Both types of magic (manipulating objects and chanting powerful words and formulas) were more mechanical than the older Greek

Olympian religions. The latter had appealed directly to gods by offering a sacrifice, and people ate some of it in front of a temple in a shared feast (*eranos*) with the deities. But magic workers tried to force nature's hand—people resorted to less personal tactics than Greeks had used.

Some even wanted liberation from all of the universe's mechanics. A person who endures a workweek full of office politics, computer glitches, and cranky customers says, "I'm outta here!" when Friday afternoon comes. Some ancients began to think like this, but on a larger scale. By the second century CE, some people saw the whole cosmos as an impure form of a more spiritual reality. Gnostics had negative opinions of creation and thought it was a degeneration from original cosmic unity. The salvation of one's soul depends on knowledge (*gnosis*) of this unity, which is deeper than what the five senses can perceive.

Christianity clamped down on these ideas as it asserted that salvation comes only through Jesus and the Church. The new faith emerged within this cultural setting in which people were already envisioning an enlarged and impersonal cosmos and seeking deliverance. Isis, in Apuleius's *The Golden Ass*, appealed to this need when she rescued Lucius.

Isis was the divinity of one of the mystery religions that people in Hellenistic and Roman times embraced. Greeks had already developed their own mystery cults, particularly for Demeter, the goddess of agricultural growth. Some people associated her annual regeneration of vegetal life with personal salvation, and they conducted huge festivals near Athens for this. Orphic cults had grown back in the fifth century BCE, and some followers wrote about human souls joining the gods in the afterlife. People entered a mystery religion through an initiation rite that linked them with a god who was associated with dying and returning to life. By the third century BCE, people imported many more mystery cults from the East, and this made the West's spiritual landscape even more colorful.

Magna Mater (the Great Mother; she was also known as Cybele) came from western Turkey, and Rome's political leaders officially adopted her in 209 BCE when they were in an exhausting war with Carthage for control of the Mediterranean. Mithras came from Persia. He was an ancient god of the sun, justice, and war and was thus popular with

Roman soldiers. His followers saw the planetary spheres as a hierarchy of ranks of people's souls, which become increasingly spiritual through self-discipline. So mystery religions appealed to many mentalities in the varied Hellenistic and Roman worlds:

- Do you feel a need for feminine gentleness? Then come to Isis.
- Do you want undiluted male bonding? Hang out with Mithric dudes.
- Want to walk on the wild side? Cults for Magna Mater and Dionysos sometimes feature orgiastic dances, and some people who honor the former lacerate themselves with knives.
- Do you want quiet contemplation instead? Gnostic traditions, Plotinus, and the *Corpus Hermeticum* train people to look beyond the world's uncertainties and towards a more subtle spiritual unity.

But many folks just wanted company. A lot of women and immigrants joined mystery cults to have a group of friends in the midst of Rome's crowds and quick changes of fortune. They could now dine together and support each other when times got tough.

People's views of the universe thus expanded into metaphysical domains in several ways between 500 BCE and 100 CE, and they expressed them with many media.[4] A spiritual cosmos became a big part of Western thought—the great chain of being had many roots and it thus became a basic idea. But the emerging Christian faith was different.

The Gospels portrayed Jesus with a mixture of reverence and realism that no other religion came close to. Mithras was associated with creation, the constellations, and the universe's temporal cycles, but he was distant from daily life. Because Isis came from an exotic land that was already ancient, stories about her also often felt remote. Dionysos was good for a buzz, but he was too mutable and bizarre to be a reliable source of comfort. In contrast to them, Jesus ate bread with common people and healed the sick and lame, and the Gospels expressed his humanity with emotional immediacy. The downtrodden Mary Magdalene collapsed in front of him and he rebuked her accusers, "I came into your house, and you poured no water over my feet, but she has poured out her tears over my feet and wiped them away with her hair." Jesus sat with sinners and the poor rather than on an elephant as Suryavarman II did.

But he could also be rough. He upset the money changers' tables in the Temple in Jerusalem. Of course he got violent for a good reason. Those scorpions were cheating impoverished people who were coming to worship. They were mocking religion and taking advantage of the faith of the weak. Jesus was gentle when he could be and tough when he needed to be, but he always behaved like the ideal human being. The Gospels portrayed the man who was inspired by God with details that people could relate to. He was both spirit and flesh.

Yet he was ultimately treated like the lowliest criminal. He was punched, spat on, whipped, and nailed to a cross. Passersby jeered, "If you are God's son, come down from the cross!" Erich Auerbach noted that this mixture of high and low was unprecedented in Western litera-ture. The son of God was portrayed with a common writing style rather than with the elevated tones of Homeric poetry, Greek tragedy, and the Roman histories of Livy and Tacitus. The West's classical tradition taught that there should be unity of style, that each genre has its own style, and that different genres should be distinct. Tragedy, epic poetry, and national history must be dignified, with elevated language and poetic forms. Comedy and satire are about common affairs, so they're in down-to-earth styles, in language that people speak in their markets and homes. Everything is in its place—very classical. But the Gospels combine loftiness and commonness. They also mix sublime power and gentleness. These combinations make them seem inspired by a force beyond the command of emperors and whims of Fortuna.

This power is the Holy Spirit. Christians believed that it guided the authors so that their portrayals of the savior would penetrate all hearts. A new force was spreading through the world to tell people that the king-dom of God is at hand.

St. Paul took advantage of the great highway system that the Romans built and visited most of the key towns in Greece and Turkey. He spread the Gospels to more lands beyond Palestine than any other per-son, and he said that people connect with God, not through classical balance or an emperor's glory, but with faith. According to Paul, faith is much deeper than the respect that people showed traditional Greek and Roman gods—it's not just dumping meat and wine at a temple and walking away as the same old scamp. The type of faith Paul described entails abandoning yourself and completely trusting the Lord. A man had asked Jesus what the greatest commandment is and he replied, "You must love the Lord your God with all your heart, with all your soul, and with all your mind." He also said, "Anyone who finds his life will lose it; anyone who loses his life for my sake will find it."

The classicist Peter Brown studied the growth of this concept of total personal commitment to divinity. Many saw it as a conversion in which a person threw away his old identity and was reborn. Some left their towns for the desert in Egypt and arid hills in Syria and Turkey for lives in monasteries or as hermits. St. Anthony was one of the most famous. This son of well-to-do Egyptian peasants attended church and heard that Jesus said, "Go, sell all you have and give to the poor and follow me." Anthony took this literally and lived in the desert for many years, wearing a skin, refusing to bathe, and surviving on bread and water.

Literature about holy men began to circulate, and writers made sure that their spiritual prowess compared well with the deeds of heroes in the old Homeric epics. Wearing, eating, and drinking little under the relentless sun, they mastered their bodies, drove out snakes, and vanquished demons as soundly as pagan warriors had routed their foes. Brown noted that many men in Rome followed athletes, charioteers, and gladiators. Discussing their bone-crushing competitions provided relief in those crowded streets and tenements. Writers now portrayed holy men in similar terms—they were spiritual jocks.

A blood-and-guts story from St. Augustine of Hippo (354–430 CE) shows why the idea of the conversion of the whole person continued to spread. A young law student named Alypius detested the arena blood sports, but one night friends peer-pressured him into joining them. He protested, "You drag my body into that place, but you cannot force my mind into it!" He thought that old classical philosophies like Stoicism and Epicureanism, which expounded self-control and emotional balance, could keep him from getting swept into a crowd of louts, but he was in for a shock.

He took a seat and closed his eyes, but when a gladiator was struck down and the crowd roared its approval, he opened them. The audience's energy and the sight of glistening blood stirred him into the same frenzy, and he cheered with everyone else. Augustine was teaching that the mobs, ruthlessness, and immoderate vices of his day were too powerful to be overcome by the rational self-discipline of the classical world. A person needed to go further inwards, to the core of his being, and give it to a higher power.

Brown noted that features of the landscape in Egypt, Palestine, and Syria became associated with this higher power in the third century CE. People associated places in deserts and mountains with the lives of saints who inhabited them and with Biblical stories. The idea of the holy person became ingrained in geography.

I experienced the power of this geography in Ephesus, on Turkey's west coast. This had been one of the main ancient Greek cities, and it was renowned for an enormous temple for an Olympian goddess called Artemis, but Christianity gave it new landmarks. The Gospel of John says that Jesus addressed his mother and John from the cross: "Seeing his mother and the disciple he loved standing near her, Jesus said to his mother, 'Woman, this is your son'. Then to the disciple he said, 'This is your mother'." A traditional belief then emerged that John brought her to Ephesus. I went to the building that she was supposed to have lived in. The claim that she resided there is controversial but it hasn't been disproven, so there's a chapel in it now. The house is stone and in the shape of a T. Most of the building has been dated to the sixth century CE, but parts of some walls might have been built when she lived. The house rests high above the once-noisy central streets, and evergreen trees shade the area, giving it a morning-fresh aroma. Branches rustle in the gentle breezes. Because my mom had recently passed away, I was sensitive to elderly women's concerns for security and comfort. It felt good to think that Mary's last years were comfortable if she did live there. My eyes moistened, as many people's surely have over the past centuries. I felt that my heart was united with all those who had visited the place. The emerging Christian world embraced a geography of holy sites that stir deep feelings and inspire spiritual thoughts.

However, the new didn't immediately replace the old. Ephesus's center remained a busy cultural and commercial hub, and people invested a lot of money to beautify it. Its ruins are sometimes promoted as examples of timeless classical architecture, but many buildings and monuments were constructed from the late first century CE to the third century in a style that's so flowery that it has been called Baroque. The Roman emperor Hadrian, who lived from 76 to 138 CE, was a classical buff, and a governor's son during his reign built the town's famous library to honor his own father and maintain Greek civic culture. So not everyone was into conversions. Many still honored the traditional city-centered past and added new styles to it to make urbane living even more sophisticated. Both mindsets thrived together, and they fused in ways that have comprised much of the West's heritage.

Christianity spread in the cities where St. Paul had preached. The faithful initially met in homes and later built churches in their neighborhoods. The Gospels synthesized both views of the world. Supernatural portents bracket Christ's life, from the star and the magi at his birth to the afternoon sky darkening during his crucifixion. But Jerusalem formed a classic urban setting, with a trial and a mob of shouting idiots—two things that Rome's denizens knew well.

The Gospel of Luke has a classical perspective at times. It begins by depicting John the Baptist's birth and the archangel Gabriel's annunciation to Mary that she will become the mother of God's son. These two events, which presaged Jesus' birth, balance each other like the sides of a handsome picture frame. Luke then says that the savior was born during the reign of Augustus Caesar. By doing this he situates the greatest sign of God's glory and love within the Roman Empire's worldly framework.

Another central Christian mystery occurred within a classical setting. The Transubstantiation (bread becoming Christ's body and wine turning into his blood) occurred during the Last Supper, when Jesus and the twelve apostles ate together in the dining room of a private home. Jesus took a cup of wine and said, "Take this and share it among you, because from now on, I tell you, I shall not drink wine until the kingdom of God comes." Its transformation into his blood symbolized the new covenant between God and humanity (several Protestant sects that emerged in the 16th century rejected this idea, but it was central in the Christian world before then and still is in the Catholic faith). This sign of God's glory appeared among men eating food and drinking wine—people in the old Greek city states considered symposia of men dining and sharing wine and conversation to be the apogee of civilized life. The Last Supper's urbane setting encouraged new classical images when Italian Renaissance artists painted it. Leonardo da Vinci's *Last Supper* shows the apostles in a line as straight as a Greek temple's colonnade, within a room with equally measured lines on its walls and ceiling.

Many stories about the Buddha and Hindu gods took place in outdoor settings that were dramatically apart from urban life, including forests, mountains, and the field where the two armies slugged it out in the *Mahabharata* for the throne of India. Palaces were also common venues. All these places are ideal for zinging into cosmic realms because they lack civic settings that ground them in the world. They easily mesh with Indian ideas of a vast universe and of copious flows of energy that animate nature. These settings enliven Angkor Wat's walls, fusing cosmic vistas with royal majesty. But the Gospels' locations in common homes and urban streets have kept the West's horizons on speaking terms with where they were in the ancient Greek city states.

So about 2,000 years ago, these two ideas of geography thrived together in the West. One was dominated by secular life in towns, and the other by metaphysics. Civic and spiritual perspectives were both highly developed. They converged in the Gospels, and they have given life to stories and images that people have internalized ever since.

Ideas and art gradually shifted towards the spiritual side and usually remained there during the Middle Ages, but older frameworks were still kept and both enriched each other throughout medieval history. The Church had adapted the architecture of ancient Roman basilicas for its houses of worship. The pre-Christian basilicas were large public halls with a raised apse at the far end from the entrance and a colonnade along both sides of the middle. This became the most common design of churches in Western Europe.

Other church designs were also in simple classical forms. Two early churches in the city of Rome, Santa Costanza and Santo Stefano Rotondo, are stately circles with a colonnade forming a ring around the center. Baptisteries were in the form of an octagon because the number eight symbolized rebirth—since God had created the world within seven days, eight symbolized a new beginning. Simple classical forms were now combined with spiritual symbolism, but they were still central in people's ideas of the universe. When towns in Europe grew again in the 11th century and new and larger churches were constructed, the builders used the old arches, colonnades, and semicircular apses as ordering principles for the renewed urban life, synthesizing them into the new Romanesque style. Then as towns continued to grow from the 12th to the early 14th century, people kept blending metaphysical perspectives with the old classical world. They did this in Gothic cathedrals and in literature, including the *Divine Comedy*.

This book's chapter on Thailand's recent problems and the chapter on Laos, Vietnam, and Malaysia showed that many times and places are interwoven in any moment that people experience and any place that they inhabit. The latter chapter also explained that times and places are integrated through multiple levels of cultural commonality (for example, ancient Athens, the entire ancient Greek world, the Western tradition, and common aspects of people in all cultures). But in addition to being geographically wide and historically deep, this integration of times and places is very dense because it includes our most common ideas, art forms, images, and stories, and they all have a multitude of meanings which can be combined in limitless ways. Greek temples, sculptures, and myths; Roman arches; church architecture; stories and images of Biblical characters and events; and the great chain of being have been especially meaningful in the West and shared through many media over several centuries because they express and integrate multiple views of the world—their abundance of meanings allows them to apply to a wide range of experiences and perspectives rather than to only a few situations. People thus consider them fundamental, share them with each other every day, and pass them to the next generation. The density of this abundance strengthens the Unity of a culture's shared field of meanings—people relate to each other through all these stories, ideas, artworks, and images, and this strengthens their bonds and makes them feel that they're in the same world.

This plentitude of meanings makes what seems basic inherently creative so that you can find inspiration all around you. The creativity in what unifies societies and seems fundamental encourages perspectives to expand into new views. The mixture of ancient Greek civic life in the midst of proportioned forms and the medieval focus on Biblical events inspired Italian Renaissance artists to develop three-dimensional perspective. The Gospels' portrayals of personalities and town life are so vivid that Italian Renaissance artists had a rich stock of stories and images when their patrons wanted to see them more clearly. Masaccio's painting of St. Peter taking the coin from the fish's mouth and giving it to the tax collector is historic for its early mastery of three-dimensional techniques, but that tale had already been a Biblical narrative for more than 1,000 years. Florentines could thus portray details that fit their emerging world, in which collecting money was a central concern. The ancient narrative detailed scenes that Florentines at the cutting edge of business found meaningful. Masaccio, Brunelleschi, Alberti, and Ghiberti combined spiritual and classical urban ways of seeing and synthesized a new perspective. An artistic flowering followed which climaxed in the works of da Vinci, Michelangelo, and Raphael.

So the wealth of meanings of ideas, images, and stories that are treated as fundamental fosters both Unity of a culture and Growth of horizons. This multitude makes UIG densely interwoven, and this allows many pathways into other cultures and new perspectives of one's own. UIG is so full of creative potential, which is spread through all places and times, that we can see limitless potential as a basic aspect of geography, and we can see it in any commonly shared idea, image, or story.

Westerners continued to unify their world by fusing multiple perspectives of it. Many 16th century maps of cities were dotted with churches whose steeples were the tallest buildings in town. Their perspectives were both modern and medieval—they were on the cutting edge, yet still focused on the past. But that slowly changed. In the late 17th century, Isaac Newton showed how to quantify the speeds and locations of any visible body in motion. In the next century, the integration of latitudes and longitudes allowed people to plot any place on the planet onto a two-dimensional map and a three-dimensional sphere. Perspectives were becoming more strictly focused on a rational two-and three-dimensional world than ever.

However, this didn't happen for everyone. In the late 18th century, poets and artists of the emerging Romantic era criticized efforts to make mind and nature march to military music. They said that feelings and imagination matter more. The poet William Wordsworth wrote:

> Sweet is the lore which Nature brings;
> Our meddling intellect
> Mis-shapes the beauteous forms of things:—
> We murder to dissect.

In other words, we lose appreciation of nature by analyzing it—it must be felt. Richard Tarnas, in *The Passion of the Western Mind*, wrote that Western thought has often alternated between rationalistic and romantic mindsets.

In the late 19th century modern artists rebelled against three-dimensional space in more radical ways. Impressionistic painters focused on the moment. Showing how light flickers on a pool of water lilies mattered more to Claude Monet than lingering over every detail of the garden and locating all with pinpoint precision.

Perspectives then became even more radical. Paul Cezanne painted landscapes in which distant mountains appear closer to the viewer than nearby fields do. He was insecure, extremely shy, and disinterested in public issues and current scientific discoveries. He even developed a morbid fear of being touched and once became enraged when another painter put his hand on his arm. Perhaps because of his lack of social grounding, Cezanne looked for permanence rather than impressionism's focus on the moment's delights, and he tried to show how people have lived in their natural environments since prehistoric times. Because mountains are dramatic, they seem close and elicit strong emotions so that they seem sacred. Khmers knew this well when they built Hindu temples on their summits. The French philosopher Maurice Merleau-Ponty thought that Cezanne expressed experiences that are deeper and more primary than precise lines between spaces.

Then in 1907 Pablo Picasso's *Les Demoiselles d'Avignon* stirred things up even more. It's composed of multiple frameworks that seem incongruently juxtaposed. By having several radically different viewpoints, it turned one of the most honored genres in Western painting since Titian's career (the female nude) on its head, and in many formerly inconceivable directions. The faces of its five subjects are shown from several perspectives at the same time, and bodies and the surrounding scenery are fractured into planes of different colors. Rebellions against three-dimensional perspective and its all-seeing vantage point were becoming more abrasive.

By the 1920s many people's daily lives mirrored Picasso's painting. Movie theaters, mass-produced and affordable cars, radios, commercial aviation, jazz, emerging pop culture, and growing cities with skyscrapers, telephone lines, and trolleys splintered perspectives into moments that weren't ruled by one all-seeing framework. All these together encouraged people to revere Picasso as a creative genius. Back in 1909 the Italian journalist F. T. Marinetti wrote the "Futurist Manifesto" which proclaimed that omnipresent speed has replaced time and space. He said that he found a racing auto with a roaring engine more beautiful than a Greek sculpture. The shifting position was becoming more exemplary than the static viewpoint which Alberti said that people can see everything from.

But these clashes between traditional and modern perspectives occurred within a larger cultural unity. Impressionists, Cezanne, and Picasso reacted against the canonical importance of the all-seeing eye in a three-dimensional space, but they made their artworks in terms that were directly opposed to this idea—they deliberately created images that were against its rules and thereby affirmed its importance. Critics, connoisseurs, and fellow artists then took stances on this issue of following or flouting traditional Western perspective, so it remained central in theories about art.

However, the flouting was only partial. Picasso's *Les Demoiselles d'Avignon* was as focused on the human body as Masaccio's picture of Adam and Eve being expelled from Eden. In Picasso's scene, five nude women in a bordello pose and gesture. He turned away from two ideas that the West has emphasized (the unified three-dimensional framework and realistic imitation of the world), but he was still centered on the human body. Picasso pared it down to its most basic essentials: abstract forms that are stylized. Ancient Greek temple builders and Plato had emphasized the most essential and permanent forms in nature. The modern Spanish painter held onto this idea and made it a key focus as he was jettisoning other hallowed traditions. He didn't invent Thai flows or yin-yang patterns, but instead worked with the same ideas that Westerners had considered foundational for more than 2,000 years. Picasso's painting has seemed meaningful and was one of the most influential artworks of the 20th century because there has been a unified Western tradition that it's been viewed and debated within.

I showed a book of Picasso's paintings to a Laotian man in Silicon Valley, and he laughed because he thought they looked silly. He and his wife enjoyed thumbing through it, but the artworks didn't elicit strong emotions in them. They never lingered over any single picture; they just thought it was fun to see the flow of images that mixed forms and colors in ways they had never seen before.

One of the West's most radical early modern artists was Marcel Duchamp. He seemed like playfulness personified, with a wry grin and twinkling eyes. Lewis Hyde, in *Trickster Makes this World*, admired his constant searching for new forms that were so unconventional that they made people question their own definitions of art. However, many of his works still expressed the West's most hallowed artistic norms. For instance, he sometimes used a measurement he invented called *stoppages*. He dropped one-meter-long strings from a height of one meter, traced their wiggles after they had fallen, and used this form to position objects in relation to each other in some of his artworks. Duchamp asked, "Why should the straight line rule everything?" He didn't use principles of Thai or Chinese painting to compose these scenes; he invented a technique that he directly contrasted with one of the West's most emphasized ideas. This trickster often wasn't so radical; he remained in dialog with the ancient West.

This multitude of ideas in dialog with each other encourages perspectives to expand in more directions than a culture's own history—it encourages looking *Beyond* as well as looking *With*, and it does so in ways that can become increasingly creative. This is because cultures influence each other and each culture integrates ideas in a unique way so that as you explore another society, you find not only other ways to see things, but also other ways to unify perspectives of the whole world. For example, traditional Thais' *muang/pa* distinction, animism, meandering perspectives, etiquette, respect for social superiors, and emphasis on the sacredness of rice are easily associated with each other because they're ways of conceiving people's zone of safety and taming its flows of energy. All these ideas reinforce each other and fuse with Thais' flowing art forms and their ancient heritage of small communities that emphasized harmony with the many spirits in the environment. Thailand's whole cultural landscape and the ways that multiple views within it are integrated have reflected each other. All easily express harmonious flows of animated energy.

Westerners have often opposed ideas more directly than Thais traditionally have. Reason and romanticism, as well as reason and faith, have often been expressed in opposition to each other. This long heritage of debate going back to ancient Greece has allowed people to unpack meanings of ideas and refine techniques for asserting them. The English poet Samuel Taylor Coleridge expressed the Romantic Movement's view from the late 18th century when he wrote a classic putdown of the statesman William Pitt the Younger. Because of his father's wealth, political connections, and parental ambitions, little William grew up isolated from nature and human feelings. He lived in a world of verbal abstractions and had none of the imagination and interpersonal skills that Coleridge saw in George Washington. He said that a real human being develops in a slow and steady way that's rooted in his tradition and natural environment. But instead of growing organically like a plant, Pitt was cast like a piece of iron.

The Nobel Prize-winning physicist Richard Feynman, in *The Pleasure of Finding Things Out*, rebutted the old romanticist idea that science cuts people off from nature. He said that he could enjoy a flower even more because he knew the science behind it. His appreciation wasn't confined to what everybody can see; he could also savor the complicated actions in its cells. He also enjoyed its evolution—its colors have evolved to attract insects to bring pollen to it, and this made him wonder if insects have a sense of aesthetics. Feynman concluded that science only adds to the world's excitement and mystery; it never diminishes them.

Whether you relate more to analytic or romantic ways of thinking, the West has a rich stock of expressions that will confirm that you're on the best road to reality, and that "the others" are wrong. Firebrand Abelard and mystical St. Bernard tussled over the importance of reason and faith. With their eloquence and strong personalities, they added more wealth to the West's traditions of asserting viewpoints as direct antagonists.

According to a Chinese saying, a person is a Buddhist in the morning, a Confucian in the afternoon, and a Daoist in the evening. The Mahayana branch of Buddhism grew in China rather than the more conservative Theravada, and many young people have enjoyed its creative metaphysical speculations. But a middle-aged person is on the firing lines, with a family to feed, a public career to tend, and bills to pay. He follows Confucian teachings because they maintain social order. Uphold them and you're more likely to prosper in the world. But when he retires, he can say, "Forget it all! I'm gonna relax and just be me." He has become a fine Daoist.

While Westerners have often treated faiths as opposed ideologies, many traditional Chinese have seen them within a holistic process: the human life cycle. Like yin-yang patterns in nature and concepts of qi in traditional medicine, all things are part of a system of energies that flow smoothly. This flow is typically in a circle which repeats. A Chinese-American friend told me that he finds Western religions too edgy because they're contentious about ideas. Life is fundamentally whole—it's a complete process. Faiths can succeed each other and be seen as phases of a complete cycle more than as separate ideologies abstracted from it and at loggerheads over the whole shebang.

So there are more dimensions in the integration of Unity and Infinity than we saw in the previous chapters because this integration happens in patterns that vary with each culture. The different styles of these patterns influence the ideas, art forms, and religions that a society considers fundamental. The unity of each culture and its multiplicity of ideas, arts, and experiences pattern each other. The whole and the parts are in a mutual relationship in which they co-develop and characterize each other.

As another example, in *The Ramayana Tradition in Southeast Asia*, Singaravelu Sachithanantham noted that societies that adopted the

Indian epic saw it in their own ways and modified it. He wrote that Malays focused on loyalty to the king and family, and on contests of military and athletic prowess. This makes their *Ramayana* resemble the Hang Tuah tales in the Malay chronicles.

Khmers often used the *Ramayana* to project kingly splendor. Some of the most famous scenes that they carved on temples are of the monkeys in the battle to rescue Rama's wife, Sita. They project so much power that I felt it in my gut as I examined the friezes on Angkor Wat. But Suryavarman also showed elegant sides of royalty in his self-portraits on the same temple, where he identified himself with Vishnu. In both ways, Khmer elites used the *Ramayana* to appear as regal as the monsoons and Tonle Sap's flooding. They used this story from India to unify the world in their own way.

David Chandler noted that the epic also appealed at the popular level in Cambodia because its version stressed politeness and obedience to authority. Cambodians called their version the *Reamker* and they performed it in villages into the late 20th century. Chandler said that the shows' refined royals, elegant dances, stately music, opulent costumes, and speeches about following the order of things resonated with villagers because many of their old traditions emphasized social hierarchy. Sachithanantham wrote that Cambodians added Buddhist doctrines to the epic which complemented this social harmony—the *Reamker* stresses familial virtue and the rewards and punishments that various deeds bring. The epic appealed to elites displaying their power and elegance, and to farmers emphasizing cooperative village life. Cambodians have seen the *Ramayana* in their own ways.

Indians have often seen the *Ramayana* from other perspectives. The 16th century saint and poet Tulsidas translated it into Hindi, and he felt that the story illustrates humanity's oneness with the universe. Because Rama was an incarnation of Vishnu, he embodied the whole cosmos. Tulsidas emphasized Rama as divinity, which people can merge with when they become increasingly spiritually aware.

The Nobel Prize-winning economist Amartya Sen saw yet another side of the *Ramayana*. In *The Argumentative Indian*, he wrote about India's hard-charging business world in which people can be louder and blunter than what many Southeast Asians are comfortable with. Several

Southeast Asian small business owners in Silicon Valley have told me that they have a hard time with Indian customers complaining directly because they cannot defend themselves without jettisoning the etiquette that they were taught to adhere to. Sen said that this boisterousness isn't just a modern trait and noted that ancient Indian epics contain lots of arguments. He concluded that many Indians like to quarrel, and they often express themselves without reserve. Some people outside India find it rude, but it's part of the abundance in India's natural and cultural environment. Many people like to express themselves fully, in lots of syllables and decibels. Some even argue that this is spiritual because they're absorbed in nature's copious flows of energy instead of being artificially polite. I once teased an Indian friend about her loud chatter and she retorted, "It is life!"

However, I've known more than enough people who are excpetions to these observations to feel that Sen's views of India are one-sided. India has always been too diverse to be associated with one personality type. But the *Ramayana* accommodates both worldly and meditative orientations. Arshia Sattar, in the introduction to his translation of the story (Penguin Books, 2000, p. xlvi), wrote that Indian epics have what he called narrative hypercausality—many single events have several causes instead of one. There are of course relationships between the characters, but they interact within a vast metaphysical field that includes long chains of karma, the general order of the world (*dharma*), and the universe's temporal cycles (*kala*) which structure events differently as cosmic eras change. Any or all of these aspects of the universe can affect what characters think and do and what happens to them. This abundance of causal agents encourages all sorts of perspectives in the *Ramayana*, from spiritual unity to political contentiousness.

The Khmers thus didn't assimilate all of the perspectives that the *Ramayana* encourages. They focused on royal authority, refined behavior, and obedience, and they combined them with their own Buddhist beliefs and their own forms of sculpture and architecture. Indians and Cambodians used some of the same stories and fused them with unique aspects of their own traditions to help unify their worlds.

So when you follow a story to another land that assimilated it, it often takes you into another way of unifying the world, which you hadn't previously imagined. Many of the same themes are retained, but they are often combined with a unique mixture of other themes, and they're expressed with that culture's own art forms. When you let a story, or an idea, or an image, or a work of architecture, or a ritual carry you to another society, it can bring you into another system of ways in which all aspects of culture mesh. The growth in UIG thus happens in higher dimensions than what have conventionally been seen as objects (such as a single art-work or idea); it also expands into entire cultural landscapes. In other words, looking *Beyond* extends, not just into new views of things, but also into new ways of integrating the entire world. The Growth of horizons happens, not just as counting more objects one-by-one, but also in leaps.

This encourages yet more Growth of horizons because these leaps into other cultures' perspectives widen people's imaginations. They can appreciate other ways of seeing, not just particular aspects of a culture, but also other patterns in which all aspects can mix. As they become accustomed to flights into different societies' world-views, these flights can become frequent enough to be ordinary.

A story, an idea, a painting, a sculpture, a building, and a religious ceremony is more than what it is currently seen as because it can elevate our perspectives to ever more inspiring patterns in which people are interconnected. People's views of the world can thus shift to a paradise in which all people and cultures are related by grace—all people and cultures can always reveal more of each other's wealth.

How much more? Considering that UIG is integrated:

- Through all places and times that cultures have inhabited,
- Through multiple levels of cultural commonality, which range from local communities to the whole world,
- Densely—through the most common ideas, images, art forms, and stories,
- Through transcendence—through the ability to take leaps into other cultures' ways of integrating the whole world,

our horizons and identities can keep growing so that the more they expand, the more they're encouraged to grow further, and the more we can help other people's horizons and identities to grow.

PARADISE CHAINED

But this infinite possibility in a perspective has often become a powerful divisive force. Thongchai Winichakul wrote that the map of Thailand became a metasign—it acquired meanings that transcended its initial uses. For example, some Thais used their country's map for political statements. The Communist Party made its form into a poster and drew Laos as a crouching man in Marxist garb yelling at Thailand to wake up. McDonald's golden arches have become a sign of capitalism, with meanings that range from a safe and clean place for families to have a quick meal to images of bland mass-produced suburbia and soulless corporations that whet people's appetites for high-fat foods that clog their arteries.

Because a sign can acquire new meanings and work in several contexts, mapmakers hold tremendous power. This potency can blind people to much of the world's richness and force it into the patterns that the map's outline imposes. Winichakul noted that maps in Thailand:

- Created artificial divisions. They imposed lines between "Us" and "Them" that were not sharp before Chulalonkorn's reign. The border with Laos became firm even though most people in both countries are ethnically Tai, speak related languages, follow Theravada Buddhism, and share many artistic traditions.
- Took autonomy away from principalities in the borderlands that had their own lords, rituals, and spirit cults.
- Eliminated Tai traditions of holding loyalties to several larger courts at the same time and thereby finding safety in numbers. Everyone was now incorporated into one kingdom which hemmed in their identities.

The Japanese historian Hayashi Yukio said that when Chulalongkorn created provinces, Lao living in eastern Thailand were suddenly forced to call themselves *Thai*. This compromised their independent identities. Many minorities in Laos who aren't ethnically Tai have been marginalized since it became a nation. The map became a means for people in power to increase their authority by marginalizing and suppressing many societies.

Winichakul wrote that it turned human beings into its own servants—into means for its tendency to over-categorize and divide the world.

Maps have certainly allowed people to comprehend much of the world. John Noble Wilford detailed this history in *The Mapmakers*, saying that they have allowed us to envision and compare climates, population densities, election results, soils, vegetation, sea temperatures, metals, and earthquake epicenters all over the globe. But they also leave out a lot of its richness while giving the impression of comprehensiveness. They don't as easily express cultural fusions, multidirectional cultural influence, and oppressed cultures (including Islamic societies in Thailand; Celts, Basques, and Gypsies in Europe; and many African and Native American cultures). They also leave out most of the historical richness of places and the nuances in great works of art. Instead, they reduce the world to the few variables that the mapmakers focus on. But each country, city, culture, and natural environment that they locate is also infinite, and it's connected with other places in infinite ways. We can gain insights about how much greater our world is than one map by exploring more of UIG.

PARADISE GAINED

How can we avoid a map's tendency to define us as less than what we are? We can do so by realizing how rich Unity/Infinity/Growth is and how much it can encourage us to become more than what we are currently categorized as. UIG is big because it includes all cultures, places, and times, but it is also small and easy to relate to because it permeates family life, and it's within children. The psychologist Jerome Bruner, in *The Culture of Education*, described a British mother speaking with her two-year-old son. She told him that the woman on the back of a penny she showed him was the queen. He insisted that she was "Granny," and his mom replied that they're sort of the same thing. Since many British people feel a combination of respect and affection for their queen, Bruner concluded that intimate human interactions, including ones experienced in infancy and early childhood, are interwoven with background knowledge that's textured by the whole culture.

I saw many two-to five-year-old children in Thai wats imitating their parents by prostrating in front of the main altar and putting the palms of their hands together in surprisingly graceful motions. But they were also able to play as long as they didn't disrupt others. They learned that the Buddha rules, but benevolently.

I also saw how a culture is interwoven in developing children in China. In 2011, I shared an overnight sleeper car on a train from Xi'an to Pingyao with an elderly husband and wife and their two-year-old grandson. The latter two sat on the bottom bunk, across from mine. The boy kept wiggling and she said "Huaidan!" The expression literally means *bad egg*, and it has deep meanings in a culture in which people learn to conform with the group. Her tone was harsh, with the implicit message, "Knock it off!" Many Chinese children frequently receive messages that they shouldn't deviate from group norms or disrespect elders.[5]

So parents can see their cultural landscapes in their children and in their own interactions with them—in the words they teach them and the games they play with them. Unity/Infinity/Growth is within us from the get-go.

Being in little things makes UIG even bigger because this gives it more possible channels to grow through. Daily interactions in the family can be portals to exuberant explorations around the world. We always have reminders that our identities are far more magnificent than what any map says they are.

How high can we go? How infinite can we become, and how much can infinity grow?

We can always go higher because people conceive infinity according to their experiences and ideas, and the ranges of both can always expand as they explore more cultures. The West's great chain of being, Thai Buddhism, and many Indian philosophies have seen the universe as a hierarchy of levels that are increasingly creative and spiritual. But we can soar even higher than their visions. We can see the field of connections we live in as more than levels that extend vertically. We can appreciate and further expose infinity in more and more directions without a final limit to the number of them because we can combine different cultures in limitless ways.

For example, I loosely structured this book as a Thai stupa. Both are in three parts, and each successive part is increasingly liberated from one conventional way of seeing. This is a natural structure for this book since the first two countries in my round-the-world trip are Southeast Asian. But you can mix any combination of cultures. Mauritius was the next country that I visited, and my experiences there took a more African turn. Dance is a central art form in many traditional African cultures, and it will shape the sequel to this book, which will journey through such an unconventional range of cultures in Africa, India, and Europe that it will be patterned like an exuberant dance. You can shift between different ways of mixing cultures without a final limit.

Some people use ideas and aesthetics that traditional Chinese have emphasized to frame explorations of different cultures. Wang Ping grew up near Shanghai and teaches English at Macalester College in Saint Paul, Minnesota. She has lived along the Yangtze and Mississippi and feels that people are deeply connected with rivers. Ping sees analogies with biology and says that water makes up most of our bodies, and that our vascular system resembles riverine systems. Because people have settled by rivers and traded along them for thousands of years, they're ingrained in human consciousness. She led a group of students on a trip from Shanghai up to the Himalayas, where they could see the source of the Yangtze, Yellow, and Mekong Rivers. They read poetry, hung prayer flags, and played music everywhere they went in order to help build a sense of kinship among communities along the Yangtze and Mississippi. They then took a trip down the Mississippi and did the same things. The Chinese have conceived yin and yang, not as separate domains, but as complementary patterns that flow together in cycles that characterize changes in nature. Ping sees the two great rivers as complementary. Since they helped pattern the cultures of the two biggest economies in the world, she's working to create harmony between both nations.

Many other cultures haven't been unified by rivers; they have used other ideas to consolidate with. Islam quickly grew through deserts and then along the Mediterranean. It then spread through Northern India, Central Asia, and the Malay world. Its rapid growth seemed to transcend all geographic boundaries. This has made it seem miraculous, as though it has been ordained by Allah, who in His glory, towers over all of nature's features. Millions of Muslims live in China, but people in both cultures have had a hard time understanding each other, partly because they have unified the world with different ideas. Expanding the range of ideas for integrating the world will encourage mutual appreciation so that people in both civilizations can overcome mutual suspicions and develop dialogs that can ease today's violent and exploitive politics. Perhaps Chinese can expand ideas of yin-yang patterns to aspects of Islam (for example, God is both merciful and firm), and Muslims can see the grandeur of Chinese culture as yet another manifestation of God's glory. Visiting several mosques in China and the Islamic art museum in Kuala Lumpur taught me that Islamic art in China would comprise a book as great as one about Islamic art in Southeast Asia. Mixtures of yin-yang flows, Arabesques, and swirling Chinese and Arabic scripts meshed into a wealth of patterns that are both vibrant and elegant. Many ideas can thus be used to help harmonize these two cultures. Because each encompasses over one billion people, softening boundaries between them will mean a lot in world history.

The Mayans, Andean civilizations, Polynesians, Aborigines, Japanese, and many African and Native American societies also lacked a main river as a source of unity. All these cultures have used different ideas to allow themselves to cohere.

So you can choose any culture or metaphor from geography, or any mixture of cultures and geographic features, and let it pattern ways in which societies around the world reflect each other. You can then keep exploring new cultures to expand the range of your ideas to use for comparing them. There is no limit to the ways in which you can combine perspectives and synthesize bigger views. You can keep at it so that leaps between multiple cultures become more common. The world's societies can not only shine on each other; they can flow together, dance with each other, become a pair in a harmonious system, express Indian ideas of a vast universe, embody ideas of God's glory, and interact in many other ways. We can always discover new ways in which civilizations can mix. Geography can be seen as an infinite interplay of cultures that is ever more exuberant and joyful.

We can actually soar even higher than many people have imagined heaven to be. Dante integrated medieval and budding modern perspectives in his *Divine Comedy*, and he ended his monumental poem with an ascent to the apex of heaven. He first rose through the planetary spheres that Ptolemy outlined more than 1,000 years before, and past the nine classes of angels in the hierarchy that Pseudo Dionysius detailed. He then recounted an experience that extended beyond the traditions he inherited.

Dante saw a river between two banks that were speckled with flowers. He bent down to examine it more closely, and its linear form became round and transformed into a huge lake of light. What had seemed like flowers became souls of the Elect, and they settled into petals around the circle, which rose in tiers of levels. Dante likened the whole configuration to a giant rose whose petals were arranged in a precise geometry. Baptized children and saints from the New Testament were on the left side, and unbaptized children and the blessed from the Old Testament occupied the right. Mother Mary was at the top of the row of petals that extended vertically from the center. Adam was beside her and Moses was next to him. Dante then experienced an even higher vision, which he concluded his poem with.

He looked up and saw three rings that shared the same circumference, and each was in a different color. The circles represented the Trinity. He contemplated how they were unified and likened his effort to geometers trying to turn a circle into a square. A flash of insight then came to him, but he said that words failed him. So one of the West's most influential texts climaxed with a vision of heaven in terms of concepts of static geometric shapes: circles and squares. The ideas that the great poet used to imagine the apex of paradise have been emphasized in Western culture since ancient Greece.

Many people have imagined paradise according their own cultures' conventional perspectives. In *Heaven: A History,* Colleen McDannell and Bernhard Lang wrote that Westerners' ideas of the afterlife changed after the Middle Ages. Contemplation of the entire cosmos, which scholastics had enjoyed, became less popular and heaven was modernized. By the 19th century, it was common for people to imagine meeting parents and other departed family members there. The nuclear family had become more central than extended families, which many pre-modern Europeans had lived in, and people began to see paradise in its terms.

Our ideas of paradise can now expand to all cultures nurturing each other in ever more creative ways. We can always imagine more ways in which cultures can share their heritages so that our field of connections (Unity/Infinity/Growth) can become ever more benevolent and jubilant. These increasingly varied combinations can complement the main religions:

- God's love grows through us. Since He told Adam and Eve to be fruitful and multiply, we can increase our abilities to fulfill His wish by making our imaginations and cultures more fruitful. For Christians, Jesus' love keeps spreading in more ways. For Muslims, manifestations of God's unity become even more glorious. For Jews, all of His people are in a sacred conversation which becomes ever more multicultural and creative.
- The Buddha's compassion permeates the world more as cultures become increasingly sensitive to each other.
- The vast universe that Hindus have imagined becomes ever more abundant.
- The pluralism that many Southeast Asian cultures have favored becomes even more fertile, and the world continues to be a balance of many conscious beings. All join harmonious and vibrant flows of patterns.
- Many traditional African religions focus on interpersonal relationships and the community's traditions. We can now see all the world's societies as a community in which they share ideas and dance together.

You don't have to be religious to revel in UIG. Humanists believe that people should have faith in their own creativity and outgrow the past's myths and religious traditions. Appreciating our creativity by exploring world cultures is consistent with humanism's focus on our own abilities.

All these faiths and mindsets can work together to build a more rewarding world for everyone. Boundaries between them can soften and people can outgrow hostilities between religions. Instead, their belief systems can be in dialogs that bring out yet more creativity.

Our explorations of paradise can expand into even higher dimensions than this because people can vary the patterns in which they mix perspectives from different cultures. For example, they can first alternate between two civilizations. For about five years when I was in my twenties, I read about Western thought and history in the spring and summer, and then Asian cultures' thought and spiritual traditions in the fall and winter. I sometimes felt that my studies were in yin-yang patterns by being aligned with the seasons (subjects from Asia that saw the world in holistic ways seemed more yin, which predominates in the winter). After mixing two cultures for a while, you might choose to fly between societies with the joyful spontaneity of some African and Latin American dances. I still cherish the memories of a weekend 20 years ago when I read a book about New Guinean art and one about Aborigine art. The whirl of images and ideas from exotic cultures that are very different from each other was electrical.

So the very shifts between cultures' world-views can be patterned in multiple ways. We can choose from an unlimited number of possible combinations of these shifts between infinite landscapes. Not only can infinity grow in infinite directions; the patterns in which the directions can grow can be varied in limitless ways. We're only limited by our imaginations, and they expand as we continue to look *At, With,* and *Beyond.*

This infinity of ways to vary patterns of our shifts between cultures may be hard to conceive now, but the richness of the mixture of Unity, Infinity, and Growth encourages us to expand into it. UIG is integrated through all places and times, and all levels of cultural commonality, in ways that are dense and which encourage leaps into new ways of seeing the world. As these leaps become common, we can experiment with new patterns of shifts between perspectives. The patterns of our shifts can become ever more imaginative and joyful.

An image that can suggest the wealth in UIG is the ancient Indian idea of a web of jewels that Indra has. Each jewel is reflected in all the other gems. Some ancient and medieval Indians used this image as a metaphor for the universe. But, as with Dante's vision, we can soar even higher. We can see many things as jewels in this web, including:

- Different cultures' ideas, art forms, stories, common objects, and behavioral norms,
- All people in the world,
- The features of every natural landscape that a culture inhabits.

Furthermore, we can vary the patterns of these reflections in limitless ways. We can then vary the ways in which we vary the patterns so that our reality increasingly becomes a fusion of play, joy, and love. There is no established concept of this fusion; we can only become it, and it can keep getting better as more people join it so that it is ever more creative and effervescent.

Many explorations in this book and ideas from other people's writings are in line with UIG (humanity's field of connections) becoming an ever more abundant field of joy, play, and love which becomes increasingly evident in the world's geography:

- The future of identity. We can become increasingly integrated with people and cultures all over the world, and yet retain positive aspects of our own personalities and traditions. We're all unified and infinitely varied at the same time, and we can mix with each other in limitless combinations. As we do, never-ending growth in infinite directions and ways can increasingly become a key aspect of our identities.
- We can increasingly control what we think about, so we can regularly think of the highest ideals that we can imagine. As we do this more frequently, the idea that everything is in a paradise full of love can be increasingly exposed in the world.
- The dense integration of Unity, Infinity, and Growth allows a limitless variety of new perspectives to emerge. All pasts fertilize the moment and all places enrich a space so that any moment and place can be a launching pad to an expanded world-view. Since U, I, G, A, W, and B can continuously enhance each other, this expansion can keep growing in more people, and in more ways.
- We can leap into different cultures' ways of seeing the world, and these jumps can become commonplace. We can then vary the patterns of our shifts between different cultures in new ways.
- Our perspectives can expand from "It is" to "It's more." As they do, we can see more potential in everyone. The two apparent paradoxes (It is by being more than what it is; and, A perspective expands beyond itself) can become increasingly evident in the world.

- Martin Seligman wrote that being future-oriented, rather than mainly focusing on the past, can increase life expectancy. We can now see multiple pasts within the present so that it's an abundant field of meanings that generates an ever more creative future. What we see and think about indicates a future full of potential, and our future is especially fecund because ideas from all pasts and places can enrich it.

- Knowledge and love merge. The psychologist Erich Fromm, in his classic book *The Art of Loving*, wrote that knowledge is one of the four elements in all forms of love. But this isn't a dispassionate categorizing type of knowledge. Instead, it appreciates a person's full richness and understands what is most beneficial for him. This requires sensitivity to his perspectives and background. The other elements that Fromm saw are respect, care, and responsibility. All four of these conjoin in a way of thinking and acting that helps another person attain the greatest well-being that he can.

  The philosophy professor Irving Singer, in *The Nature of Love*, wrote that love is affirmation. Like Fromm's idea of loving knowledge, love isn't a slavish adherence to a system of categories, or an algebraic calculation of monetary values. It doesn't define a person according to one variable and then stop at that definition, assuming knowledge of everything about him or her. Instead, love allows the beloved to be seen in more ways so that hidden facets and capabilities are exposed and encouraged to grow. According to both writers' ideas, love sees *more* in people and helps it to develop.

  A perspective becomes increasingly loving as we explore UIG by looking AWB—the perspective reveals ever more of a person's, or an artwork's, or a culture's aspects and connections with the environment. It always encourages more of her or its potential to grow so that it becomes increasingly evident in the world and able to help others to develop their own potentials.

All these factors encourage us to realize that the highest flying we can imagine is actually our identity. UIG><AWB expands the perspective

beyond any single pattern and allows us to appreciate an ever-widening variety of patterns and synthesize them in more ways so that we can attain ever greater levels of freedom and joy. We can become like angels, increasingly imaginative and compassionate. We can keep flying higher and inspiring each other to reach even greater heights. Our essence is to soar ever higher and transcend our current perspectives so much that we can not only find paradise, but take it to ever greater levels of luminosity and love and establish it as the primary aspect of our geography.

But politics, economic challenges, and academic conventions have kept people's horizons close to what they can immediately perceive within their conventional ways of looking *At*. Appreciating that our identity is the ability to fly higher and farther than we ever have is an excellent way to diminish political corruption and exploitation because we can realize that the extent of our human wealth is much greater than a one-dimensional focus on social status and money. But it's hard to envision our full beauty and potential when we're taught that money is the most important thing in the world; when geopolitics, corporate greed, and prejudice plague most societies; when possible ecological catastrophes loom; when terrorists commit atrocities in many countries; and when we're overloaded with information and have little time to reflect on the richness of cultural landscapes, meanings, ideas, and histories. All these problems keep encouraging a self-reinforcing process in which people are discouraged from seeing beyond them. But all this wealth is around and within us, ready to be exposed when we're ready to explore and share it. Paradise is here, it soars as high as we can imagine, and our imaginations will keep growing as we keep exploring it. We'll thus finish this book with a manual for bringing it into our lives and spreading it in the world.

A MANUAL FOR FINDING PARADISE IN THE WORLD

HERE ARE 18 ways to shift your perspective to paradise and bring it into your home. You don't need to practice every one, but if you make several into regular activities, your view of the world can transform into an infinite landscape that keeps getting richer and more pervaded with love. All steps mix looking *At*, *With*, and *Beyond*, so they keep shifting the perspective in ways that continue to become more inclusive and creative.

ONE: GET BETWEEN THE COVERS

I emphasize reading books, but I'm not saying that it's necessary for reaching paradise. Many spiritual traditions have stressed the heart and said that love is the main road to bliss. But this book is about exposing paradise in the world, and you can spread paradise further by understanding more of the world. Since our planet is globalized, learning about its different cultures and their potentials can allow us to nurture people more and allow love to grow in more ways. Furthermore, looking *At*, *With*, and *Beyond* encourages knowledge and love to merge. Both can add depth to each other and thereby grow even more.

Many people have the impression that reading is cold and dry. Mark Twain said, "A classic is something everybody wants to have read, but no one wants to read." But reading in ways that look *At*, *With*, and *Beyond* can turn learning into a lifelong exploration full of enchantments.

I became a bookstore rat when I was a business student in college. I hung out in the shops around the campus and bought used books about world history, cultural anthropology, philosophy, and psychology. I started to build my collection according to a pattern:

- Half of my humanities books were about Western cultures, and the rest covered other societies.
- Seventy-five percent of my humanities books were about the West, the Middle East, China, and India. I emphasized them because each influenced over a billion of today's people.
- The other twenty-five percent focused on little-known cultures. Many of these societies are indigenous, and these books were written by anthropologists who had lived in them. Their studies gave me a lot respect for pre-literate communities. Because their intimacy with the environment and their mythic lives were very rich and largely forgotten by literate cultures, these books exposed me to a wider range of mindsets than ones that have emphasized writing.
- I also bought books about science. I focused on liberal arts because cultures fascinated me from an early age, but I found science equally absorbing, and it has been central in modern Western culture. Studying science can add more mental discipline to cultural studies, and exploring other cultures can increase the imagination for studying nature—the range of concepts that scientists use, the diversity of patterns they appreciate, and the types of questions that they ask can broaden. Mixing science and the study of world cultures can enhance both.

The combination of books that I bought encouraged my mental framework to keep shifting, but half of my humanities books were still about the Western tradition because I was born into it. I thereby learned where I came from and discovered the depth in things from my daily life, including religious art and the classical architecture on the backs of America's paper money. Becoming more grounded in my own culture enabled me to find more meaning in places outside the West than I otherwise would have because I had something to compare them with. I could then return to the West and see even more richness in it.

My life changed within six months after I started to collect books. Windows to different times and places kept opening up and I began to approach professors in the history and psychology departments, as well as students from different cultures, and discuss their backgrounds with them. My world transformed from one place and time to a wealth of places and times that reflected each other.

A different distribution of books might work better for you. You might be interested in a half-and-half mixture of science and humanities. As long as you combine all three ways of looking, your horizons will constantly grow.

TWO: SHARE THE WEALTH

Tell your family, friends, and coworkers about your discoveries and share them through social media on a daily basis. Because many of today's media focus on politics, business, popular entertainment, and the newest tech gadgets, it's crucial to put content about cultural wealth out there so that more people can appreciate it. Ideas become influential in a society when they're shared widely and constantly. This reinforces them, so share your discoveries with as many people as you can, as frequently as possible.

I've posted articles from my website in several groups in LinkedIn. You can easily form your own groups on LinkedIn and Facebook, or search these sites for groups on topics that you enjoy.

You can join face-to-face groups in Meetup.com. This site allows you to search different topics and find groups dedicated to them within a radius of your home that you can specify. You can also create your own group in this site.

I don't do much on Twitter because I prefer media that allow more than 140 characters, but it's still one of today's most popular websites, and it could work well for you, especially if you've already built a large following. Several new content sharing sites have emerged, including Gootle+, which is similar to Facebook, but it has more features for finding new friends. Pinterest is used for sharing pictures, and it's popular among women. YouTube is by far the largest video sharing site.

Studies have been showing that many young people now prefer other sites to Facebook, which they consider uncool because their parents avidly use it. A friend of mine said that her thirteen-year-old daughter doesn't have an account in it because, "A bunch of old people post pictures of their dinners and kids there." A lot of teenagers enjoy Tumblr because it gives them creative ways to share multimedia content. Many teens and young adults enjoy Instagram for sharing photos, and WhatsApp is a popular place for sharing mobile messages. Maybe some of the young will return to Facebook since it recently acquired WhatsApp.

Forming a book discussion group that spotlights a different culture each time will encourage an endless succession of interesting conversations. This can be done locally or online.

You can thus spread the world's cultural wealth through many media. Talk, write, and share online. Spark as much discussion as you can so that more people will learn about our human wealth and our astronomical potential for increasing it.

THREE: FAMILY MATTERS

I don't think there can be anything more enjoyable than sharing the world's cultural wealth with family. If you build a library of printed books, the well-stocked shelves surrounding you will constantly remind all of you of the rainbow of cultures around the world, and the covers will always invite you to explore them further. A great thing to do with kids is to read a geography book with them and cover a different country every day or two. In one year you'll have journeyed all over the world with them.

Parents can also take their kids to places where multiple perspectives exist side by side, including museums and ethnic neighborhoods and festivals. If you live in a remote place, you can still read books, watch YouTube videos and international films, and search the internet for cultures in every country.

You can also share wondrous stories about your past experiences, and you don't have to have traveled the world to impress kids. The tales my parents told me about moving from Detroit to California before I was born seemed larger than life when I was little. The young couple drove across the country and explored the Grand Canyon, the Painted Desert, and Virginia City. Those places seemed mythical to me when they described them, and they made me appreciate America's vastness and wonder about what's beyond our shores.

You can ask elderly family members about times when they were young and feel more connected to past eras. My Uncle Jimmy visited my mom and me after my father passed away, and I drove him up to San Francisco for a day of sightseeing. I peppered him with questions all day about their boyhoods in Detroit during the 1920s and 30s and their experiences as World War II soldiers. My uncle enjoyed the interest that a younger man took in his past, and I learned what growing up in a great American city during two epochal times was like.

Detroit in the 1920s felt like the top of the world to many people. The success of its automobile industry made Henry Ford proud enough to declare towards the end of his life, "I invented the modern age!" The greatest crop of skyscrapers outside of New York and Chicago was being built and it culminated in the majestic Penobscot Building, whose stacks of white tiers rose up to a beacon which seemed to project the city's greatness all over the world. Detroit was a masculine city, and tens of thousands of young men went there to forge their places in the world.

The Great Depression then hit Detroit especially hard because fewer people could afford new cars, so business for my dad's father declined to almost nothing. He was a big man. With a six-foot-two frame and a well-muscled physique, he didn't lose many fights—he once yanked a blacksmith off his stool and pummeled him for whacking a horse on the rump with a hammer (the local blacksmith was often the strongest guy around). He was used to bending his surroundings to his will, but his confidence plummeted with his income. He had already lost his former wife to tuberculosis (before my dad was born), and their first child had died in infancy. The combination of all the tragedies made him retreat into himself and become emotionally distant by the time my dad was growing up. He didn't show his family much affection, so my dad rarely spoke warmly of him and he developed disdain for unreflective machismo.

But my dad venerated his mom. She did all the cleaning and maintenance work in the three-story apartment building that they lived in, sold women's clothing in J. L. Hudson Department Store, looked after her three boys, and always wore a smile. She had a deep Catholic faith, and although prostitutes lived in their building, she treated all of her neighbors with equal kindness.

Though people were poor, they had a lot of good times together. Uncle Jimmy told me about a pillow fight with my dad in their apartment. My uncle threw it at him, he ducked, and the pillow sailed out the window. Uncle Jimmy had to run downstairs and out to the street to retrieve it. He found it draped over the radiator cap of a bus that had stopped to pick up passengers. They were all laughing. My uncle thus showed me two sides of life in Detroit in the early 20th century: the brawny optimism of the good times and the introspection, mutual support, and ability to enjoy the little things during hard times.

Ralph Lewin is the former president of Cal Humanities (it was formerly called The California Humanities Council), and he shared an article on Facebook that he considers the most important advice for families. It recommended developing a family narrative. By discussing their family's past with kids, parents can help them develop strong identities. Some families become wealthier over the generations, and that becomes part of the narrative. Others lose net worth, but their members can develop a story, such as, "We have had our ups and downs, but we've gotten through all of them by sticking together." Lewin says that the key thing is to develop a story that endures through the generations. Families can create a tradition of expanding their horizons by reading books and watching videos about cultures.

FOUR: MEET AND EAT

After graduating from college, I became a Silicon Valley headhunter and résumé writer, and I met engineers from all over the world. I examined their résumés and asked them about their home countries and personal interests. We often went out to eat and some introduced me to Thai and Indian food. After growing up on pizzas and cheeseburgers, I discovered the exotic combinations of flavors, and this gave me another reason to be curious about their homelands.

Persian coworkers and clients introduced me to their cuisine. The best single word I can think of to describe it is *noble*. It's ancient and many dishes are covered with fine rice. Every grain is separate and honey-sweet. The herbs that garnish it aren't used in extravagant quantities; a few are perfectly chosen to complement the dish. Like Angkor, ancient and medieval Persia created huge land-based empires that were run by an elite class of people who managed territory for a king that was associated with sacredness. They surely enjoyed their feasts. We enjoyed ours too—the food fueled many long discussions about philosophy and world cultures.

FIVE: LISTEN TO THE MUSIC

Music allows me to share emotions with people in different cultures more deeply. My headhunting boss was also Persian and we enjoyed a lot of world music together. I played guitar and he played the setar, which is a delicate Persian stringed instrument with a small pear-shaped resonating chamber and four strings (it's very different from the more famous Indian sitar). Its soft sounds make it ideal for accompanying subtleties of Sufi poetry. There are no English translations for all of the emotional nuances in Middle Eastern music. Many of its scales are based on the quartertone rather than the halftone, which Western music is based on. They mix feelings of happiness and sadness in nuanced ways that Western music can't because distinctions between some notes are finer than what scales in Western music allow. Sufi poetry is often sung with instrumental accompaniment, and it expresses both longing for deeper connections with the universe and the enjoyment of its divinity.

I enjoyed discovering Indian ragas, and they gave me one of my first introductions to Indian culture. My favorite sitar players, Nikhil Banerjee and Vilayat Khan, performed long improvisations whose tempos increased from slow to manic, but they kept a single theme as though the music expresses the unity of all of nature's diverse life forms and processes. A raga conveys an emotion which is believed to be in tune with the universe's fundamental vibrations, and it's maintained from the beginning to the end of the performance. Phrases that a musician plays thus seem to extend throughout the universe—they're continuous with the whole process of creation, from the origin to today's immense variety of forms and energies. Ragas transcend melodies of single notes and express the vast cosmos which Indians have often imagined.

I also enjoyed Javanese gamelan music. Classical central Javanese styles feature slow tempos, and musicians use hammers that are muted to soften the tones when they hit the gongs and xylophones. Bowed stringed instruments, bamboo flutes, and singers interweave with them, and these sounds fuse into an all-enveloping energy that's both gentle and animated. I first heard this music on a record when I was twenty-four and I was instantly allured by a world that I had no prior exposure to. The recording was of the orchestra at the royal palace in Yogyakarta, and it sounded as though all the notes were resonating through the heavens. When I traveled to Indonesia five years later and arrived at the palace, the same orchestra was playing while birds chirped overhead. I thought, Wow! This sounds just like the recording!

I don't just listen to the music; I try to get into the mindsets of the people in its cultural milieu. A college student recently told me that she doesn't like medieval European music because it's sad. It actually has its share of lively tunes which were played during festivals and in palaces and upper class homes, and many of the "sad" songs aren't entirely so. The most commonly played scales in the West today are the major and the natural minor. The third, sixth, and seventh notes in the latter are half a step lower than they are in the major. All these lower notes give the minor scale a somber sound. But many of the scales that medieval musicians played mix notes from both. So they didn't convey an all-out, in-your-face sadness, but a more reflective feeling. Since people in medieval Europe lived with concepts of the great chain of being, much of their music integrated the material world with spiritual realms by expressing stateliness and timelessness instead of overt happiness or sadness.

I played a recording of 12th century English songs after I returned from my first trip overseas, in 1987. I went to England, where Wells Cathedral made a deep impression on me. Because it rose in the center of town, perspectives from all of the surrounding neighborhoods converged on its towers. Both worldly and metaphysical domains seemed in perfect harmony in the building. The combinations of happy and sad notes in the songs gave the music an emotional balance. The music and the townscape reflected each other in an integrated vision of the universe.

Each variety of music can bring you into an infinitely rich cultural landscape. I've found it an ideal medium to mix with reading because I can explore other societies by both feeling and thinking, and this deepens my immersions in them.

SIX: DANCE TIL YOU DROP

Dance is another universal art form, and one of humanity's oldest. Animals used it to communicate and get in synch with each other long before humans emerged. The developmental psychologist Howard Gardiner has written that bodily motion makes up one of the most basic human intelligences. How different societies emphasize bodily experience is yet another one of their dimensions.[1] We saw that Thai culture has often emphasized slow flows. The anthropologist Herbert Phillips, in *Thai Peasant Personality*, noted that Thais are sensitive to the importance of the body in human relationships and that they're often more aware of physical bearing than Westerners are. Thais are taught that moving gracefully rather than abruptly is a sign of good character. Many African cultures have rich ways of categorizing bodily experience, and dance is one of the most central art forms in Africa.[2] A lot of Latin American cultures have also made dance a key art form. Ancient Khmer dance and Indian Bharatanatyam have symbolized patterns of creation. Ancient Greek city-states used dance to foster communal harmony and encourage crop growth. Native Americans have danced to harmonize with spirits and powers in nature. Appreciating dance is yet another way to experience another culture, and it's a lot of fun to mix it with reading.

SEVEN: CATCH THE SPIRIT

I try to participate in a culture's religious life whenever I travel. Religions convey deep emotions, express how societies think that the universe is integrated, and help communities cohere. I've enjoyed immersions in Thai culture by sitting on the floor and observing people in viharas.

But you don't need to go overseas to share other people's aspirations for connecting with divinity. I've had a lot of fun at Thai and Laotian New Year festivals in temples in California. They always included luscious food and ended with a water fight. Additionally, you can go to local mosques, Hindu temples, synagogues, and churches of different denominations and learn about other people's rituals and ideas about how the universe hangs together.

The day I arrived in Paris in 2010, I walked to the Seine River and entered Notre Dame Cathedral. A Mass was about to begin and I found a seat in the front row, where I basked in light emanating from the stained glass windows in both transepts. The choir sang and a young woman with a beautiful voice led it. She had a visage that I saw many times in France: an intelligent and sincere female face framed by dark hair. I then enjoyed the French language's music when the priest lectured, and the aroma of incense blended with it. I was thinking, "What a wonderful fusion of senses to greet me when I first get to Paris!" when a roughly sixty-year-old woman two rows behind me interrupted my reverie.

She sat alone and began to loudly rant to no one in particular in a raspy tone that was full of anguish. She continued for several minutes without pausing, and this made me think that she had a severe psychological problem. A middle-aged man sitting about six seats to my right finally turned around and pointed at her with a menacing expression. She quieted down for two or three minutes but flared up again. He then stood up, turned around, and was about to dart over to her.

An usher rushed over to him when he began to take the first step, put a hand on his shoulder, and said, "Monsieur!" His tone was equally firm and soft, as though he was saying, "Give a troubled soul a break." This was Mother Mary's house. Her cult had spread through Europe in the 12th century, when the construction of Notre Dame began, and many Gothic cathedrals were dedicated to her. It was as though she took the woman into her hands. After the savory mixture of perceptions, I witnessed the Catholic humanism in French culture.

EIGHT: GET NATURAL

Because the natural environment helps shape cultures' thought patterns, I take walks in the country whenever I travel. In Southeast Asia I never get tired of seeing the stilt homes with soft brown and tan colors, the relaxed people, and the all-enveloping greenery mix into soothing mélanges that seem to embrace me.

I've spent many afternoons hiking in the hills around Silicon Valley, gazing over their rolling fields, over the flat suburbs and freeways beyond, and towards the bay and distant mountains. Breezes caressing my face, hawks flying overhead, and stately deer take me away from the endless lines of asphalt and traffic lights that usually surround me.

The novelist, poet, and academic Wendell Berry, in *Life Is A Miracle*, wrote that every natural environment is unique. He has been a life-long farmer and his intimacy with the land taught him that no ecosystem can be completely reduced to any other, no matter how small it is. Every place has its own integrity, and it often profoundly influences a culture's ideas and art.

NINE: SEE FROM ABOVE

When I was nine I rode in a single-engine private plane over Vacaville, California, and magic ensued as soon as we took off. The view was no longer confined to the street lines, fences, and concrete and plate glass building fronts. I now felt free to see whatever I wanted to explore. Each town block and field of crops had its own shape and hue, and all fused into a tapestry that seemed luminous.

You can also go to rivers, as Wang Ping does. Oceans, lakeshores, and city, state, and national parks also encourage people to see multiple places in one perspective. If you visit them regularly, you can become used to seeing the world as a multitude of patterns and ecosystems.

TEN: BE A PERSON FOR ALL SEASONS

Relate to people of all ages. I have always enjoyed the elderly because they can share perspectives from another time. During my first overseas trip, in England, a retired schoolmaster with a full head of white hair ran the first guesthouse I stayed in. When I arrived he was grumbling that corporal punishment had just been banned in schools in France. He believed that caning builds character. With impeccable Kentish diction, he said, "I boxed my daughter's ears once. She turned around and hit me right here (pointing to his nose). Broke my glasses.

Bloodied my nose. From that moment on, we became closer." I thought, Only in England!

An elderly man and wife ran the second guesthouse I slept in, which was also in a small town in Kent. They were retired hops farmers and they invited me to "have a sit-down" with them in their living room after I returned in the evening. They had lived in the area all their lives and she told me that she stood outside during the Battle of Britain in 1940, watching the planes overhead until an engine fell out of the sky and landed a few yards from her. I said, "That's hard to imagine now because the countryside's so peaceful." I realized that their calmness and cheerfulness prompted me to make that comment as much as the rolling fields and hedgerows did. They seemed engrained with the land and its steadiness and serenity. I thus met contrasting personalities as soon as I arrived overseas for the first time, and I thought they all represented the traditions and landscape of a country that has engendered so many creative individuals over the centuries.

I often sleep in hostels when I travel, and I enjoy the young people who stay in them as much as the elderly. They're open, energetic, and eager for fun and new experiences. In Athens in 2008, I met a twenty-year-old man from Tennessee who had just come back from the ruins of Plato's Academy. Nobody else in our hostel had gone there and I wasn't planning to because very little of it has been preserved and it's out of the way. But he said, "It's amazing that nobody goes to such an important place." Realizing that he was absolutely right, I followed his footsteps a few days later. He sometimes reclined on his bed, reading a Bible that he carried with him, and his face was always serene, with crystal-clear eyes. He seemed idealistic and well-grounded at the same time—I felt that he would have been a wonderful student of Plato's.

More raucous but equally sincere were three roughly twenty-year-old men from Pittsburgh that I met in 2010 in a hostel in Brussels. They had never been abroad before and they hit the bars with full zeal. They were amazed that one place offered over 1,500 different varieties of beer and marveled that a person would have to have a different drink every night for nearly five years to sample every one. But they were equally wide-eyed when they saw their first Gothic buildings. Everything they saw was opening their horizons.

Conversing with people of all ages keeps perspectives fresh because it allows you to hear voices from many times. It reminds me that the past and future always exist in the present.

ELEVEN: BE NOT OF AN AGE BUT FOR ALL TIME

Studying history gives me deeper perspectives of what I see when I travel. Exploring ancient history provides insights about cultures' origins, and it makes me feel affinity with Richard Feynman's statement about appreciating flowers more deeply after learning how they develop. I enjoy the present all the more when I see pasts that have fertilized it. Because Thai processions and Italian street festivals reflect the heritages of their cultures, I delight in the crowds and lively colors and see depth in them at the same time. I especially enjoyed the political rally in Florence because it made me feel more connected with Michelangelo's time.

I also enjoy the present and mix it with the ageless, and this makes both of them more pleasurable. When I travel I immerse myself in pop cultures as well as the museums and temples. Pop cultures' focus on today helps prevent any past from becoming constricting. I can explore something historic, like a cathedral or an ancient Greek temple, and then return to the present and see the pasts with fresh eyes. I can alternate between deep appreciations of our human heritage and irreverence.

One of my favorite rock albums is Deep Purple's *Made in Japan*. It was recorded live in Tokyo and Osaka in 1972. The musicians blended the timelessness of classical music and the emotional immediacy of the blues into what feels like a full panorama of human feelings. At times it's as intense as anything Metallica ever recorded, and at other times it swings like big bands from my parents' days. The album unleashed so much power that its shock waves are still reverberating in Asia. The first thing that the guitarists I met in the bazaar in Kota Bharu, Malaysia asked me was, "Do you know any Deep Purple?" We became instant friends because I played a classic song called "Highway Star."

I wish I had received a dollar every time someone in China asked me to play the Eagles' "Hotel California" after I told them where I live.

I kind of like the song but I almost never play it because the number of times I've heard it probably exceeds the number of cars on the LA freeways. I was fourteen when it was released, and since it was all over the airwaves back then, it's probably burned into my nervous system for the rest of my life. I can always recall its chords, even when I haven't played it for years. In 2012 a young couple from Beijing that I met in a village near Yangshou asked me to perform it during a lunch break in the middle of our bike trips. They then invited me to ride with them for the rest of the day. Together we enjoyed views of old farm houses, rice fields, and dark, craggy rocks that jutted almost straight up for hundreds of feet. We shared pop culture and some of the most honored views of traditional China at the same time.

TWELVE: LOG ON AND OFF

I spend time online and offline every day so that neither the digital nor the analog world dominates my perspectives. I find that they enhance each other when I spend about the same amount of time in each.

I log off for a few hours and read books, play music, and jog. I then log on again and share new ideas with online friends. I look forward to being back in the cyber-buzz after the quiet time, and after being online for a while, I enjoy going back into my library and being more reflective. I try to log off at least an hour before I go to bed and then read. This gives me new perspectives at the end of the day and time to digest them. It also allows me to relax and fall asleep more quickly.

Some technologists say that human cultures are increasingly being uploaded into the digital world, and they justify this claim by stating that the information in it is growing at an exponential rate. Ray Kurzweil and Kevin Kelly are two of the best-known, and they cite a trend called Moore's Law, which has usually accurately predicted that computing chips shrink by one half in size and cost every 18 to 24 months. Kelly also says that this law of accelerating returns applies to other aspects of digital technology, including the amount of information that can be stored and the bandwidth for transmitting it. Because of this exponential growth, they conclude that the digital world will ultimately include all human thought and culture.[3] We'll examine this issue at length here because the recent proliferation of digital media is one of the most influential cultural movements in human history, and it will profoundly affect our well-being, for good or ill. I'll show how looking *At*, *With*, and *Beyond* can help us steer events towards the former.

The world is more than information because people also think about larger meanings and contexts, as well as canonical artworks, values, and concepts that integrate experiences. These aspects of thought and life become ever more rewarding as you study and compare more times and cultures that preceded the internet. Homer, Dante, Shakespeare, Italian Renaissance artists, and the builders of Greek temples, Gothic cathedrals, Angkor Wat, and Sukhothai were poor in information from today's digital world's standpoint because they lacked the technologies to store, process, and transmit as much of it. But they were so rich in meaning and context that their works have resonated with people in every subsequent era. So were the Indian priests, monks, and artists who brought their heritage to Southeast Asia. So was everybody else who created artworks, literature, and philosophies that have influenced people over many centuries.

Unity/Infinity/Growth (humanity's field of connections) has been integrated in many ways besides information over the previous several thousand years, including:

- Stories. Jerome Bruner, in *Acts of Meaning*, wrote that people largely think in terms of stories, and that this is so from early childhood on. Stories are more than bits of information because many of the ones that people find most engaging have several meanings. The Gospels have been so influential partly because Jesus is portrayed as both divine and human. He is not reducible to bits of information because he also represents integrating ideas, including God, the Trinity, spirit becoming flesh, the salvation of humanity, and the dawning of a new historical era. He is also meaningful in terms of values, such as love, mercy, and steadfastness. Ancient Greeks treated the Homeric epics as their Bible by referring to them for values and perspectives. These texts portrayed gods and warriors as both magnificent and petty, and they depicted them as physically lustrous. Their stories raised questions about the world and provided ways to debate them. The ambiguity of many canonical stories, the integrating ideas and human experiences they address, and the memorable personalities of their main characters give them depth and make them engaging enough for people to remember and discuss throughout their lives. They also allow people to identify with the characters. The combination of all these aspects of narratives gives them a central place in cultures.

- Shared histories. Societies use them to cohere. The Gospels were part of the West's in 15th century Florence, and the Chiang Mai chronicles detailed Lan Na's collective history. Shared histories are more than bits of information because they're meaningful as a whole process in which the past has unfolded into the present, and because people associate both their individual and communal identities with them. The collective past is meaningful as it pertains to the whole person and the entire community. This meaningfulness determines what people decide to store as information. Thus the Chiang Mai chronicles detail genealogies that link royalty with the Buddha and then switch to the doings of Thai kings, but they exclude stories about monarchs in Cambodia.

- Religion. People share a tradition of ways to connect with the unknown. Like shared histories, religion helps societies to cohere. Religious texts and ceremonies contain bits of information, but people's faith in them as bridges to the unknown and keepers of communal harmony enables them to endure in a culture. This is why the information in them is considered important enough to preserve. As with stories and shared histories, the context makes the information relevant, and the whole cultural landscape creates much of the context.

- Canonical artworks and art forms. Like stories, they often have many meanings, and new interpretations of them emerge as times change.

- Ceremonies. Births, weddings, funerals, and religious celebrations like Christmas and New Year also help societies to cohere.

They form memories that people share, and artists produce works for them.

- Music. From Christmas songs to gamelan orchestras in Javanese courts, music is often a key part of ceremonies. People don't just process it as information; they collectively perform it, emotionally respond to it, and incorporate it into their lives. They dance to it, woo each other with it, and use it to remember the good old days when they age.
- Bodily experience. Movement is central in many arts, including dance and rituals, and it deepens collective experience. Hugging, sex, and other types of affection are also central in most societies.
- Common objects. Family Bibles, 16th century dinnerware in the Louvre, Sukhothai ceramic figurines, and Thai cuisine are examples that we saw of things that people live with on a daily basis, which impart their cultures' aesthetics and values. They're more than objects and bits of information because they convey meanings that reflect the whole cultural environment.
- Values. Thai etiquette and 15th century Florentine commerce helped shape their societies. From ancient Greeks to today's Americans, many Westerners have been proud of their freedom.
- Integrating ideas. Westerners have often held permanent ratios and geometric shapes as fundamental. Medieval Europeans often treated the great chain of being as an integrating idea. Many Southeast Asian societies have integrated their worlds with ideas of religious and political centers that both project and tame animated energies.
- Purpose. People have ideas of what the goal of life is, whether it is to achieve a higher birth or nirvana, as many Buddhists feel, or to forge their places in the world as individuals. A culture helps shape these goals and people teach their children to strive for them.
- Families. We're not separate nodes that merely process information; we grew up in families. The bond between parent and infant characterizes the environment in which people first become

conscious, and Jerome Bruner noted that infants imbibe many of their cultures' traditions from their parents. Relationships with siblings, grandparents, aunts, and uncles are also important in many people's lives. Affection and feelings of belonging are usually first experienced in families, and psychologists say that both needs profoundly influence personality development.

- Childhood. People don't begin life by being booted up as fully grown adults. The psychologist Erik Erikson wrote that childhood is a key part of personality development and culture. Children see parents and other elders as role models, and relationships with these elders have strong formative effects on the personality. So do many childhood friendships.

- Relationships between genders are also fundamental, and many stories, ceremonies, and popular songs dramatize them. Romance, sexuality, marriage, and gender-based roles are key aspects of human experience and cultures' values.

- Humor and play are common in cultures all over the world. Not all meanings that people share are literal and factual. Fun often involves bending or temporarily suspending rules, and it strengthens human relationships. Many of people's most cherished memories are of good times they had with others.

- Physical meeting places. Southeast Asian markets, Thai wats, and Italian piazzas are places where people learn about their cultures. Children go to them, first with their parents, and they see examples of how to behave. Canonical artworks are often displayed in these places, including Michelangelo's *David* and Buddha statues from Sukhothai and Lan Na.

- The natural environment. This has helped shape cultures' shared experiences since homo sapiens emerged.

- Cuisine. Eating together is one of the most common ways in which people bond. It's often a central part of weddings, business relationships, and many religious ceremonies. And cuisine often reflects the cultural landscape that it originated in (Thai, Chinese, Indian, Persian, and Italian food are excellent examples).

The key thing about human life over the last several thousand years is: People have used all of these experiences to integrate their perspectives, societies, and personalities. All facets together have characterized our lives. This wholeness, with its multitude of facets, has always been our shared humanity. Our human bonds are multi-dimensional, and they're integrated with all places, times, and media (a person can thus grow up without a mother, be an avowed atheist, and have a private wedding without the big shindig—he is just as human because he still shares the majority of common experiences and thus has infinite ways to connect with others).

However, some technologists have recently spoken about computers and human minds in the same way, as though the mind is strictly an information processor. But people's memories are often tied to experiences with the above facets. Most of the memories of my trips include the cultural contexts that I was immersed in, the highly nuanced art that I enjoyed, the walks in the natural environment, savory meals (often in highly textured places, including Southeast Asian street cafes and markets, Italian piazzas, and French outdoor cafes), after-dinner jogs through neighborhoods, experiences of sharing music with people, romantic encounters, and long conversations with others about their lives. I've forgotten most of the experiences that were strictly focused on information. Looking at the departure schedule in the station in Vienna to see when my train was going to leave for Regensburg had little meaning once I boarded, so I don't recall the departure time, but I still remember the experience of being in a crowded train station in a great European city.

My earlier memories also have many facets besides information. As I remember boyhood walks along Northern Californian beaches with my father, I think of his gentle voice and our sense of wonder as we looked out to the ocean, imagining how people on the other side of the Pacific lived. I also remember the cool breezes, the misty air, the calls of seagulls, and the hot chocolate we drank upon returning to the car.

The many facets of our experiences and memories strengthen our human connectedness, and together they help integrate societies so that everyone in them can share similar meanings. People are related through touch, stories, familial experiences, feelings, romance, natural environments, human-made places (piazzas, churches, and temples), humor, ceremonies, political structures, music, artworks, cuisine, and ideas about how the world coheres. This abundance has also allowed infinite scope for creativity, as well as many points of contact between cultures. This densely connected fabric of UIG links us with all places, times, and experiences.

But the increasing prevalence of smartphones, wearable technology, emails, websites, artificial intelligence, and electronic games makes it easy for people who focus more on them than on our entire human heritage to conclude that the digital world is all there is and that it's the only field that integrates us. Jim Blascovich and Jeremy Bailenson, in *Infinite Reality*, say that virtual reality and robots that seem so human that people can treat them as surrogate girlfriends and boyfriends will become more commonly used. Newer and more sophisticated robots can sense pleasure and respond to it. In the near future, robots' appearances and bodily features and textures will be increasingly life-like and customizable according to a person's preferences. Though I wouldn't mind a harem of devatas dancing for me whenever I want, the authors warn that video cameras that can monitor our feelings by tracking eye movements and sending them to databases for permanent storage may increasingly pervade our lives. The seductiveness of these technologies, and the ominous power of the people who have access to information about us, require us to realize that the analog world is at least as rich as the digital world because of cultures' long and multi-textured histories and their immersion in natural landscapes. We can attain much more well-being by maintaining space in the analog world so that we'll always have imaginations and identities that flourish without depending on our digital gadgets. We can thereby enjoy both worlds, let all facets of human experience shed light on each other, and realize that we can always be more than what either world's conventions say we are.

Alphabet Inc's (Google's parent company) executive chairman, Eric Schmidt, said that people all over the world use Google to search many of the same celebrities (he has often cited Britney Spears as an example). He concluded from this that people in all cultures are the same. But that only says that we're the same when we look up topics in Google's search box. However, Thais don't traditionally do that when they're ambling through wats. Westerners don't usually do it while attending Mass in a Gothic cathedral or reflecting on the meanings of a classic novel while reading it. And Africans don't usually conduct searches while engaged in a communal dance. I don't do it when I'm offline, enjoying my library, or while playing guitar, spontaneously fusing musical styles and losing myself in the flow. I don't spend much time online searching the world's cultures because my library is already well-stocked with books about them, and they examine them more deeply than most websites do. I find Schmidt's reasoning circular because it pertains only to people at the moments when they're performing internet searches and it devalues the wealth of meanings in other activities, which are often rooted in histories that are much older than Google's.

Siva Vaidhyanathan, in *The Googlization of Everything: (And Why We Should Worry)*, wrote that Google encourages impressions that it's comprehensive by giving a user who conducts a search a list of items precisely numbered from one to several million. But compared with material about technology, business, and pop culture, there's not much content online about Cambodia's cultural roots, or Lan Na viharas and sculpture, or Thai painting, or Laotian folklore, or Vietnamese modifications of Chinese art, or Islamic art in Southeast Asia and China. Google will give you these results only if you specifically search for them, but it won't encourage you to do this. What seems comprehensive is actually skewed towards what most people put online and then search for. Google is less inclined to show us the tremendous wealth in the world's under-appreciated cultures and more ready to show us what its users' largest demographic groups are already aware of and want.

Vaidhyanathan noted that Google's search box is inherently conservative. It rewards the websites that are already popular by listing their addresses on the first page after you type in a search.[4] It also rewards the ideas that have been searched by the most people rather than ideas from cultures that most people don't know about, or new ideas that novel mixtures of cultures can inspire. What might seem like the entirety of human knowledge is thus often a self-reinforcing circle: What's already popular appears on the first page of search results because it's already popular. Vaidhyanathan wrote that Google indulges our wants and encourages us to believe that the list it gives us is everything under the sun.[5] It doesn't promote looking *Beyond* as readily; we have to take the initiative to do that.

Information is mainly oriented to looking *At*. Looking *At/With/Beyond* entails reflection too, and it's hard to have time for that when 100 unread emails from your clients and colleagues glimmer in your inbox and your smartphone continuously receives messages. It's also difficult to take time to reflect, or to discover Lan Na or Vietnamese art, when the increasing amount of information online requires people to specialize in fields and spend most of their time keeping up with developments in them. But the abilities to reflect on meanings, enjoy continuity with pasts, and discover differences between cultures have been some of the most universally human characteristics for thousands of years, and these reflections have inspired humanity's most influential art and thought for several millennia.

The psychologist Howard Gardiner feels that what makes us human is our ability to transcend and to be flexible.[6] I agree—we can always expand our horizons beyond our current context and gain higher perspectives. We can do this with our technologies too, and I feel that we must because we are in danger of becoming increasingly dependent on them for our contexts, identities, and integrating ideas as they increasingly dominate our economies and impel us to focus on them. They can define us with even more power than maps have had, and they're largely controlled by corporations that strictly focus on their own revenues and shareholder values.

Google is now trying to be the dominant place where people do their online shopping. Now that Alibaba, which is the biggest fish in China's huge online shopping market, has gone public, the competition in this business has become even more intense. Because more than 600 million people in China are internet users, Alibaba has a lot of cash and business to give it momentum for expanding into Southeast Asia's, Africa's, and Latin America's growing markets. Since the financial stakes in online retailing are enormous, the biggest internet-based companies with search engines are likely to focus on enticing people to buy more consumer products and to click on paid ads, rather than discover all aspects of the world's cultures.

But we can retain rich and independent human identities, be in command of our technologies, and use both to soar to ever higher levels of creativity by spending at least some time offline, even if our jobs require us to be connected most of the time. Read books about societies that thrived before the internet and then go back online and share what you discovered. Take a little time for nature walks, or a dance class, or to explore different cultures' music. Sit in a local Thai, Vietnamese, or Hindu temple and watch the flow of colors and forms. You can apply looking *At*, *With*, and *Beyond* to the digital world—use it (looking *At*), reflect on how you're using it (looking *With*), step outside of it and appreciate other types of experiences (looking *Beyond*), and then return to it and share what you've learned. This will increase the variety and overall quality of the material that's online.

Another way to look *With* and *Beyond* is to regularly search cultures you're not familiar with. This will prevent you from only being fed what Google's search engine dishes out. Search engines won't automatically suggest that we explore the Malay world, or Aborigine cultures, or Navajo traditions. We need to make a daily effort to look beyond the conventional uses of search engines. By regularly shifting between these three ways of looking, our perspectives will always be fresh and increasingly deep.

Another way of mixing the best of the digital and analog worlds is to use social networking sites to meet people with rich analog lives. You can contact writers, humanities professors, artists, and world travelers for discussions. Together, we can create more online content about the world's cultural wealth.

Alternating looking *At*, *With*, and *Beyond* enables us to transcend recent discourses about the digital world's influence on culture, which have often been polarized between technophiles and technophobes, as though the digital world is the entirety or the end of civilization. Instead, looking *At/With/Beyond* is a joint venture—it's positive about using technology, but in a reflective way which allows us to improve its uses by adding more variety and nuance to them. We can enhance the online world by discussing a bigger range of ideas, cultures, and experiences. If enough people regularly share their explorations, we can make the digital world even more dynamic than it is now, and we'll make it easier for other people to discover the richness of our human heritage. It will be win-win because perspectives of both the digital and analog world will keep getting better.

Larry Page, a co-founder of Google and the CEO of Alphabet Inc., is known to have told his employees, "You're not thinking big enough" when they've pitched ideas to him.[7] Considering the variety of human cultures and their infinite wealth, this statement also applies to strict focuses on information in the digital world. It's true of any one-dimensional focus because that devalues the other facets of human experience and ultimately retards our abilities to appreciate them. Our field of connections is infinitely big because it includes many media, cultures, world-views, human personalities, and types of expressions. As people explore more of them and let them reflect each other in more ways, our field of connections can expand in limitless directions and patterns.

Appreciating multiple aspects of our heritage, adding them to the digital world by sharing our ideas and experiences, and then using social media to meet each other can allow our full human potential and our uses of technology to develop in ways that keep enhancing each other. We're only limited by our imaginations, and they expand as we keep exploring more of our field of connection's facets, cultures, and historical periods. We can always think bigger than one medium by regularly shifting the focus and incorporating more perspectives to appreciate ever more aspects of our field of connections. We can begin by sharing our discoveries about little-known cultures.

Admittedly, balancing digital technologies and the analog world will be a challenge. Because the largest companies with search engines are corporations, they must increase their stock values for their shareholders. Their executives thus have reasons to want us online 100 percent of the time, clicking on every ad and website that strikes our fancy so that their revenue from advertising and online purchases will be maximized. We thus need to make a daily effort to increase the world's bigness in all possible directions. The world's future is literally in our hands, and I find this exhilarating.

THIRTEEN: FEED YOUR HEAD

I write terms and the names of people and places in a notebook and memorize them. If you write five things down each day and regularly review them, in one year you will know 1,825 new things. Sure, they can be googled, but when they're in your head, you can reflect on them and find new meanings in them. People are losing the richness of this kind of thinking because the digital world enables them to look up information as easily as scratching an itch. This makes them even more reliant on digital technology and more inclined to conclude that information makes up humanity's entire field of connections. But if you regularly review what you learn so that it gets stored in your brain's long-term memory, every subject you think about will keep getting richer because you can compare it with more and more other things and perspectives. You will then have more ideas and topics to add to the digital world.

Having a lot of ideas and cultural landscapes in your head makes looking *At, With,* and *Beyond* especially rewarding. It gives you more to compare your current experiences to and a bigger range of ideas for creative insights.

Since I add things from many cultures and times to my notes, reviewing them feels like a flight around the world. It also feels like meditating because all of the world's places and times seem to shine on each other as I flip through my notebook.

FOURTEEN: KNOW THYSELF

One of the most important aspects of well-being is finding employment that enhances your creativity while still allowing time to explore new cultures and fields. It's also one of the biggest challenges for most people in today's economy. I still write résumés for people because business is a key aspect of culture (we saw that it was an important factor in the development of three-dimensional perspective in Florence), it's an excellent arena for exercising creativity, and the last ten years of commerce and technology have profoundly affected ways in which people think and interact with each other. Balancing work in the here-and-now with explorations of other times and places allows me to enrich my perspectives of both. So these next three steps will show how looking *At/With/ Beyond* can help you develop a more fulfilling career.

We'll start with your résumé—it is one of the most important documents that you'll ever own because it's often the first impression that you make on employers, and you will never know when you'll find a job that you'll want to pursue. But the résumé writing field has greatly changed recently because many people now hire professional writers. What seems like an outstanding résumé at first is thus often merely average. But looking *At/With/Beyond* can help you distinguish yourself in a crowded job market. We don't have enough space to be comprehensive because résumé writing is complex. Each person is different, résumés need to be tailored to each job, and applicant-tracking software systems screen most résumés before they're seen by human eyes. But we can explore some ways in which seeing *more* can give you a competitive edge when presenting yourself to prospective employers.

For example, I once worked with a technical writer who was laid off from a computer company that he had been with for 15 years. Because its operating system was proprietary, he never had a chance to work with systems most employers looked for, like UNIX and Windows. But I realized that the system he had learned was as complex as UNIX, and that this enabled him to develop many skills that transferred to other jobs. He learned a complex operating system. He wrote manuals that simplified it for users. He planned entire sets of manuals. He worked closely with engineers while planning the doc sets. He also developed writing and formatting standards for the whole publications department. On the surface, he didn't seem qualified for any current tech writing jobs, but he actually had 95 percent of what employers needed, and he found a job in about one month.

I also looked at a new graduate from unconventional perspectives. He had just gotten a Ph.D. in chemistry but worried about lacking experience. I asked him about his university research. Did he manage a lab? Did he manage a budget? Did he complete any projects under budget? Did he finish them ahead of schedule? Did he supervise any lab assistants? Did he schedule tasks? Did he make decisions about purchasing equipment? Did he upgrade the lab's information system? Did he streamline communications within his department? Because he answered "Yes" to almost every question, we crafted a résumé that made it seem that he had at least two years of experience.

At the other end of the seniority chain, I worked with a client who was looking for a CEO position in the entertainment industry. The first accomplishment he mentioned on his résumé was about building a department in his most recent company. I told him, "That's great if you're applying for a VP position, but you need something bigger here." I then asked him questions about CEO-level accomplishments, like what he did to build an entire company, what innovations in management he spearheaded, what groundbreaking products he led his company to develop, and what impact he had on a whole industry.

So when you're presenting yourself to an employer, look at yourself from every possible angle. Be as flexible with concepts as you can while looking for your biggest competitive advantages. Never settle on one definition.

This is especially important in the top half of the résumé's first page, which is what employers first read or skim (most skim at first). It's common to write a summary of accomplishments and skills that is tailored to the job that the résumé is being sent for. However, Alexander Pope warned about damning with faint praise. Technically it's a compliment if an attorney says that his client never hit his parents, but it's actually an insult because it implies that a strength any average person has is his main virtue. It's easy to stumble into this in today's crowded job market in which many top performers compete against each other. Saying that you increased sales 20% within one year, or that you generated a budgetary surplus of 5%, might sound impressive on the surface, but not if it's the norm in your industry. Make sure that the accomplishments you list really are outstanding. If your competitors have done similar things (you can find this out by consulting with a good headhunter), you can consider all of your relevant selling points and craft a list so that the combination of strengths shows that you can bring extra value to the company.

I recently met a résumé writer who was planning to state in her client's summary that he had "cultural awareness" because he was applying for a job that required a lot of international travel. But considering today's globalized world, that's such faint praise that it's like saying, "He eats shredded wheat for breakfast." When I asked her about his background, she said that he had worked in several Arabic countries. Then did he learn any Arabic? Modern Standard Arabic has many intricate rules, so if he became proficient in it, he demonstrated the ability to learn a complex system in a short time, which is a skill that can be transferred to learning new technologies. The maqam (the modal system in classical Arabic music) is also complicated.

Her client might have done impressive things besides learning difficult subjects. Did he organize any cultural events? Did he help a local organization raise funds? Did he give lessons in a local school? Did he conduct any group tours for American, European, and Asian coworkers? Did he help local craftspeople to develop a business? There are lots of angles for taking statements in the summary beyond generic terms so that each item in its list shows that the accomplishments and skills are special. Look at everything you state in as many ways as you can and then formulate the strongest possible concise statement about it.

A lot of employers today look for extra creativity and initiative beyond the job duties. A manager in a San Francisco law firm said that when her company downsized, the people it let go were the ones who had only worked on the cases that were given to them. It kept those who proactively contacted past and prospective clients to develop new business. It's thus increasingly important to think of what you did above and beyond your job description, which helped a company make money, cut costs, save time, increase market share, or improve its customers' experiences. You can also ask yourself if anything you did was a company record, or a company first—or an industry record or first.

Seeing *more* and using extra creativity also apply to interviewing. Reading a few articles about the company's industry before the meeting will enable you to speak about issues that will affect the hiring manager, and it will show that you're more proactive than many of your competitors. A lot of companies post such articles on their websites (often on the "Press Release" page). While there, you might also see articles about the most recent product release, a talk that the CEO gave at a conference, or a new strategic partnership. You should never just focus on the immediate job; the more you learn about the company's larger environment, the more you'll be able to show that you think on a larger scale than your competitors do.

Thinking creatively can also be used to handle difficult questions during interviews. One of my clients worried that the employer was going to ask if she knew their software, since she had little experience with it. I told her that it's not always necessary to give a simple yes-or-no response. There's a continuum between zero and ten on a ten-scale. Instead of saying that you haven't worked with a company's technology, you can talk about what you do know and show that you have some knowledge rather than none. Then describe something you did with similar technology, or with equally complex technology.

Both résumé writing and interviewing increasingly require expanding your perspective, being flexible with concepts, and looking beyond conventions. Getting into the habit of shifting your mental framework can improve your odds in both.

FIFTEEN: KNOW THY NEIGHBORS

Regularly shifting your perspective will also help you thrive in a new job. Additionally, it will enable you to build a robust professional network for long-term security.

Michael D. Watkins, in *The First 90 Days*, wrote that there is sometimes a high failure rate among people who transition into new jobs, largely because they carry the mindsets from their old jobs with them. People often go into new companies without learning about all the facets of the environment. A company has several dimensions, but many new employees focus mostly on their immediate duties, their bosses, and their direct reports. Watkins says that relationships with people in other groups are also important to develop. Managers in finance know how resources are allocated. Project, program, and operations managers know how all the groups in the company work together. Engineers can explain how the products work, and people in sales and marketing know about the company's customers. Learning about coworkers throughout the organization will give you a big picture of how it operates and help you to build more political alliances.

Watkins also says that it's important to know the company's culture, including its history, its employees' shared assumptions about the world (such as how power is distributed, how decisions are made, and how resources are allocated), and shared stories about the company's founding and early growth.

Learning about a new company thus has many dimensions. Each time you join a new firm, and each time you're promoted within your current company, you're in a situation that requires an expansion of horizons in several directions.

This multi-directional growth is increasingly necessary in all employment situations, even if you're not planning to change jobs. Average product release cycles have been shortening, companies form and change strategic partnerships more quickly, groups within companies collaborate more frequently, and people quickly develop new applications for current products. It's now more necessary to regularly reassess your own job function.

So never stick to a single definition in résumé writing, interviewing, working in a company, or professional networking. All of these now must be looked at from new perspectives on a regular basis. If you constantly see *more* in each, you're more likely to find and maintain fulfilling employment.

SIXTEEN: KNOW THY HUMANITY

Many people now worry about increasingly intelligent robots and software programs based on artificial intelligence replacing human workers. Nick Bostrom, in *Superintelligence*, wrote that this is one of the most important and difficult challenges in human history. Artificial intelligence which new robotic systems use is becoming more powerful and less expensive. Robotic nurses might replace some human caregivers, automated logistics planning systems can manage inventories and schedule deliveries, and automated cars can replace human drivers. The development of more effective online courses may threaten many teachers' job security. A senior air traffic controller that I know recently lost his job because software programs can now monitor traffic more reliably and cheaply than humans can. Bostrom wrote that face-recognition systems have recently improved so that they're used at some automated border crossings in Europe. Artificial intelligence systems are also employed to diagnose medical problems and recommend treatments. The finance industry uses them to detect trends in markets. In 2013 researchers at the Oxford Martin School analyzed over 700 occupations to see how easily they can be automated and concluded that 47% of the jobs in

America are at high risk of being eliminated by 2033. To keep yourself happily employed for the rest of your life, you can:

- Assess your greatest strengths and the unique value that you can bring to employers and clients, and be able to articulate them in a succinct way that makes you stand out. Try to do this within 25 words to make it easy to repeat and remember. Your statement should not just be about you; it should say how you help people. For example, I say, "I expand people's views of themselves and the world around them to enhance their well-being." I can lengthen my statement a bit by saying, "Bringing 25 years of cultural studies, world travel, and high-tech business experience, I expand people's views of themselves and the world around them to enhance their personal lives and careers." Think about what you can do for people and what makes you uniquely qualified to do it, craft a short message, and put it in several media, including your LinkedIn profile, website, business card, and professional bio. Practice saying it too because this is your elevator pitch.

- Continuously build your professional and personal networks, and mix people in your field with those in several others. Also include professionals with rich lives in the analog world. This will provide you with a diverse range of associates who can expose you to many fields and ideas and give you access to more services. Your professional network is one of your greatest assets for promoting job security (most employers prefer to hire people they already know), but relationships need to be developed beyond connecting with people on LinkedIn and handing out business cards to everyone you encounter at conferences. Keith Ferrazzi, in *Never Eat Alone*, describes how building relationships with people by meeting them face-to-face has allowed him to thrive. His style might not work as well for everyone, since many people don't have the opportunity to meet everyone in their online networks. Charlene Li and Josh Bernoff, in *Groundswell*, stress building relationships over the internet. Whether most of your associates are in person or online, have discussions with them that become increasingly deep and multifaceted so that you develop lasting mutual trust.

- Take initiatives in your current job and be able to articulate your accomplishments by knowing the impact that they have on your company. The Oxford Martin study concluded that creative intelligence is more machine-resistant than skills for repetitive tasks. Generating new ideas, conceiving new services or products, penetrating new markets, landing new customers, deepening relationships with current clients, expanding business into other regions, and learning about other cultures and forming relationships with businesses in them are less likely to be able to be duplicated by robots and software programs. So are other interpersonal skills, including negotiation, management, sales, and conflict resolution. Taking initiatives and thinking creatively will allow you to develop a reputation for being able to do what machines cannot.

- Exceed people's expectations. Doing more than people expected (perhaps by giving a little extra service or a couple more innovative ideas) will make them more inclined to remember you in the long-run. It will also encourage them to recommend you to their friends and associates, and to give you excellent reviews in online websites like Yelp and LinkedIn.

- Learn about companies besides your employer and its current customers and vendors. This will give you more awareness of the larger business world so that you can spot emerging needs and markets. In *Ask the Headhunter,* Nick Corcodilos details how you can successfully approach the companies you have researched for employment when they're not actively hiring. Steve Dalton, in *The 2-Hour Job Search,* recommends expanding your list of target companies beyond the ones you currently favor. He advocates learning about organizations you currently don't know about and mixing them with your present hot list. Continuing to do this will expand your horizons beyond one narrow list so that you'll always have more possibilities for a new career.

- In the long-run, develop as many facets of UIG as you can. Economics has been called the dismal science because it analyzes how people behave in order to acquire resources that are scarce. UIG is infinitely abundant, but because its full wealth is little-known, most ways to appreciate this wealth are not highly

demanded in today's economy. Instead, most people are currently encouraged to buy more stuff on eBay and Alibaba—there
is a tremendous discrepancy between our full human wealth and
what the economy currently rewards.

So increase people's awareness of our infinite human wealth
on a daily basis. As you share your own discoveries of the world's
cultural riches, you'll continue to meet more people with similar interests, and opportunities for collaborative work can open
up. You can develop organizations that help businesses in other
countries grow. Or you can promote artists in different societies,
develop educational videos, write articles or books, do volunteer
work in other cultures, or help develop schools in other countries
or in disadvantaged neighborhoods in America (Wilford Welch's
book, *The Tactics of Hope*, is full of examples of how people have
combined their own professional lives with helping those in less
advantaged societies). You can educate technology-focused professionals about world cultures and teach disadvantaged people technical skills—you can build bridges between people with different
backgrounds so that they can enrich each other. As you do, you'll
become known to people in more fields, and this will increase
your own long-term employability. Every day, do at least a little to
integrate your professional life with facets of UIG besides information. UIG is a joyful science. As you continue to expose it over the
years, you will help to make more of its facets central in the economy, and you'll deepen relationships in your professional network.

Robots and software programs exceed people's abilities to analyze
information, but looking *At/With/Beyond* and appreciating all facets
of our field of connections are our own skills. As you develop them,
you'll be able to make yourself harder for machines to replace. You can
approach every day of your professional life as an exploration of new
horizons as much as you can in cultural life.

SEVENTEEN: WRITE ON

I write about ideas from my readings, travels, and other activities in
a journal. I usually don't outline what I'm going to write beforehand.

Instead, I let ideas of different cultures and historical periods spontaneously emerge, then I do research to verify or discard them. Thoughts immediately flow when I do this informal writing. Since I read about different cultures in succession, writing about them is another way for me to feel as though I'm flying around the world. If you establish a writing routine in which new ideas keep coming to you, you will have another space that's never bound to one way of looking at things.

EIGHTEEN: HAVE AN ART ATTACK

I carry an art book whenever I can. It not only lets me appreciate more beauty in mundane situations (like the dentist's waiting room); it also allows me to have more conversations. One month after I returned from my 2007 round-the-world trip, I came down with acute appendicitis and had to rush to the emergency room. I brought a few books with me, including one on 17th century Dutch painting. Two of the nurses had Dutch blood, and they told me how stirring it was to see works by Rembrandt and Vermeer in Amsterdam's Rijksmuseum. When I visited the museum in 2010, I enjoyed the experience more than I otherwise would have because I could relate it to people I had met. I also enjoyed some of my hospital stay because of the conversations with nurses and physicians about cultures. The ER doctor noticed that I had a book about ancient Chinese history, and this prompted a conversation about traditional Chinese medicine. The books and the talks made me feel that I was flying around the world instead of being stuck in bed. Just before being wheeled to the operating room, he told me that I would enjoy the anesthesiologist because she was from Vietnam.

I usually glance through an art book in the morning. This allows me to begin the day with beautiful images before I read the news.

All of these steps mix perspectives so that you can keep attaining bigger views of the world. If you regularly practice several of them, looking *At/With/Beyond* can become ordinary, and every day of your life can be enchanting. You can take these steps as high as you want and have fun in the process.

You don't need to implement all steps. Try four or five at first, but at least work on the first three. Reading will give you a constant flow of new ideas, and you can share them with the people you care about and enjoy more fulfilling relationships with them. Sharing your discoveries with family and with wider networks on social media will allow your findings to become even more visible in the world around you, and it will improve the lives of the people you're close to.

If your schedule's already bursting, read for at least thirty minutes each day. You can try ten minutes during breakfast, ten during lunch breaks, and ten before going to bed. Then in the course of your day, you can share your findings with your family and social network. You can listen to different styles of music and ask people you meet about their home countries.

Other mixtures of cultures and media might work better for you than what I've found most enjoyable. If you're Chinese you might want half of your books to be on Chinese culture. Music stirs me a lot, but some people relate more to painting while others find dance more engaging. The method UIG><AWB lets me be me and you be you. But I recommend some general guidelines:

- Mix multiple cultures.
- Read as much as you can and mix that with other activities, whether they include dance, music, or nature walks.
- Divide your reading time between civilizations that have influenced the most people (including the West, China, India, and the Middle East) and little-known cultures. You'll thereby be able to combine the best-known societies with ones that few people know about. This will continuously give you exciting new perspectives, and you will always be connected with the big civilizations to have many people to share them with.
- Study your own culture's heritage. Comparing different perspectives is richer when you know the roots of the one you were born and raised in (or the two or more if you were raised in several). Looking *With* gives you more ability to look *Beyond*.
- Frequently share your discoveries with your family, friends, professional associates, and online groups, and ask them to share with other people. This will spread interest in our cultural wealth, help the people around you become more creative and

happy, and enhance uses of the digital world. I'm doing my part on LinkedIn, Facebook, and http://brianholihan.com. Feel free to connect with me on them.

As you keep doing these activities, you will see more of the richness of UIG around and within you, and you'll be able to continuously increase it. There's the old saying, "The sky's the limit," but we can actually raise the heavens to heights nobody has imagined yet, and then raise them again and again. We're only limited by our imaginations, and they will increase as we keep looking *At, With,* and *Beyond.* We can fully embrace our human potential and build a global civilization based on wonder, joy, and love.

Paradise is right here in this world—we only need to work together to expose it.

ENDNOTES

CHAPTER ONE: ENCHANTMENTS OF SOUTHEAST ASIA

1. Marina Roseman, *Healing Sounds from the Malaysian Rainforest* (Berkeley, University of California Press, 1991), p. 136–7.
2. Robert Knox Dentan, *The Semai; A Nonviolent People of Malaya* (Holt, Rinehart, and Winston, 1968), p. 162–4.
3. Zainal Kling, "Social Structure: The Practices of Malay Religiosity," in *Islamic Civilization in the Malay World*, edited by Mohd. Taib Osman (Kuala Lumpur, Dewan Bahasa dan Pustaka, 2000), p. 77.
4. Andrew Walker, "The Festival, the Abbot and the Son of the Buddha," in *Tai Lands and Thailand*, edited by Andrew Walker (Singapore, Nias Press, 2009), p. 129 and p. 136.
5. Clifford Geertz, *The Religion of Java* (Chicago, University of Chicago Press, 1960), p. 232–3.
6. Nancy Eberhardt, *Imagining the Course of Life; Self-Transformation in a Shan Buddhist Community* (Honolulu, University of Hawai'i Press, 2006), p. 79–82.
7. William J. Klausner, *Reflections of Thai Culture* (Bangkok, The Siam Society, 1993), p. 255.
8. See *Legitimacy Crisis in Thailand*, edited by Marc Askew (Chiang Mai, Silkworm Books, 2010) for a discussion of many of the modern problems that Thailand faces.
9. Milton Osborne, *The Mekong; Turbulent Past, Uncertain Future* (New York, Grove Press, 2000), p. 235. Also see Michelle Nijhuis, "Harnessing the Mekong or Killing It?" *National Geographic*, May 2015, p. 102–129.

CHAPTER TWO: THE DEPTHS OF ANGKOR WAT'S SOUL

1. Eleanor Mannikka, *Angkor Wat; Time, Space, and Kingship* (Honolulu, University of Hawai'i Press, 1996), p. 41–2.
2. Vittorio Roveda, *Sacred Angkor; The Carved Reliefs of Angkor Wat* (Bangkok, River Books, 2007), p. 20.
3. Michael Freeman and Claude Jacques, *Ancient Angkor* (Bangkok, River Books, 2007), p. 61–2.
4. This is the most common interpretation, but others have been proposed. Paul Cravath, in *Earth in Flower,* wrote that a real Khmer sea filled with fish was depicted, rather than the ocean of milk from Indian mythology, and that Vishnu is sitting on a stone throne instead of the cosmic mountain. But the object that Vishnu sits on is unfinished, so it's probably not possible to definitively say whether it's a throne or mountain. Roveda, in *Sacred Angkor,* and Jacques, in *Ancient Angkor,* stick to the conventional mountain and ocean of milk (it's possible that the Khmers conflated the mythical ocean of milk with their own natural environment in which a fish-filled Tonle Sap represented prosperity and order). In either interpretation, Suryavarman II was pivotal in the universe's order. See Paul Cravath, *Earth in Flower; The Divine Mystery of the Cambodian Dance Drama* (DatAsia, 2007), p. 46–7.
5. Vittorio Roveda, *Sacred Angkor; The Carved Reliefs of Angkor Wat*, p. 81.
6. Chi Mgbako, Rijie Ernie Gao, Elizabeth Joynes, Anna Cave, and Jessica Mikhailevich, "Forced Eviction and Resettlement in Cambodia: Case Studies from Phnom Penh," *Washington University Global Studies Law Review*, Volume 9, Issue 1, 2010.

CHAPTER THREE: GOING DEEPER

1. Charles Higham, *Early Thailand; From Prehistory to Sukhothai* (Bangkok, River Books, 2012), p. 122.
2. Ibid., p. 84–5.
3. Helen James, "Trade, Culture and Society in Thailand before 1200 AD," *The Journal of the Siam Society*, Volume 91, 2003, p. 15. James

said that there is no evidence that people in Thailand didn't start growing rice on their own. It's possible that both types of communities coexisted.

4. Charles Higham, *The Bronze Age of Southeast Asia* (Cambridge University Press, 2000), p. 71.

5. O. W. Wolters said that iron working might have been underway at a site in northeastern Thailand in 1500 BCE, but Charles Higham wrote that the earliest iron in peninsular Southeast Asia is from the mid first millennium BCE. In either way, iron usage intensified around 500 BCE. See O. W. Wolters, "Early Southeast Asian Political Systems," in *Early Southeast Asia; Selected Essays,* edited by Craig J. Reynolds (Ithaca, NY, Cornell Southeast Asia Program Publications, 2008), p. 57. Also see Charles Higham, *Early Cultures of Mainland Southeast Asia* (River Books, 2002), p. 27.

6. Tony Day, *Fluid Iron*, (Honolulu, University of Hawai'i Press, 2002), p. 43.

7. Wolters cautioned against seeing an excessively sharp break between early communities and the new large ones. The latter weren't states with written constitutions; they clustered around a leader with charisma and resources. But leaders' resources had grown into larger rice surpluses and more prestigious drums, jewelry, and ritual paraphernalia, which allowed them to attract larger followings. See *Early Southeast Asia; Selected Essays*, p. 63 and p. 179–80.

8. W. Randolph Kloetzli, *Buddhist Cosmology; Science and Theology in the Images of Motion and Light* (Delhi, Motilal Banarsidass Publishers, 1983), p. 5.

9. In *Theatre in Southeast Asia,* James R. Brandon wrote that shadow puppetry might have originated as a way to communicate with tribal ancestors, whose images were produced as shadows on screens. He felt that this practice might have originated in China. People in Indonesia also used masks to embody ancestors. So it's possible that stories from the Hindu epics were later fused with traditions that were already ancient. See James R. Brandon, *Theatre in Southeast Asia* (Harvard University Press, 1967), p. 43–6.

10. Hiram Woodward, "Bronze Sculptures of Ancient Cambodia," in *Gods of Angkor*, edited by Louise Allison Cort and Paul Jett (Smithsonian Institution, 2010), p. 46.

11. Mannikka, *Angkor Wat; Time, Space, and Kingship*, p. 56.

CHAPTER FOUR: ROOTS OF GLORY

1. John N. Miksic, "The Beginning of Trade in Ancient Southeast Asia: The Role of Oc Eo and the Lower Mekong River," in *Art & Archaeology of Fu Nan*, edited by James C. M. Khoo (Bangkok, Orchid Press, 2003), p. 15.

2. Victor Lieberman, *Strange Parallels; Southeast Asia in Global Context, c. 800–1830, Vol. I* (Cambridge University Press, 2003), p. 217.

3. Miksic, *Art & Archaeology of Fu Nan*, p. 30–1.

4. Some historians have thought that only the southern group is from Isanavarman's reign. See Ian Harris, *Cambodian Buddhism; History and Practice* (Honolulu, University of Hawai'i Press, 2005), p. 8.

5. Some modern scholars see more integration than division in this period. See Dougald JW O'Reilly, *Early Civilizations of Southeast Asia* (AltaMira Press, Lanham, MD, 2007), p. 122.

6. Ian Mabbett and David Chandler, *The Khmers* (Silkworm Books, 1995), p. 87.

7. The historian Craig Reynolds wrote that common people also took initiatives in building barays. But kings and other elites controlled the most resources. They must have financed and directed most of the construction—the largest barays were as long as 25 ocean liners. Reynolds said that there is little evidence that the barays were actually used to store water for farming, and that people built them to display the kings' prestige by wrapping them in Hindu and Buddhist myths to increase their luster. See Craig Reynolds, *Seditious Histories; Contesting Thai and Southeast Asian Pasts* (Seattle, University of Washington Press, 2006), p. 35–6. But newer studies have found water lanes between barays and canals that irrigated rice fields, so barays must have been used for

farming to some extent. See Victor Lieberman, *Strange Parallels, Vol. I,* p. 228, and Richard Stone, "Divining Angkor," in *National Geographic,* July 2009, p. 49.

8. A small class of merchants traded with the interior, but goods were mainly luxury and bulk items. They exchanged forest products, including rare woods, elephant tusks, and bird feathers, for Chinese and Indian handicrafts. Silver and gold ingots were sometimes used as currency, but alongside cattle, copperware, and clothes. There wasn't a single abstract medium of exchange. Victor Lieberman wrote that the Khmer economy was overwhelmingly based on agriculture. See Lieberman, *Strange Parallels, Vol. I,* p. 222–3.

9. Khmers often raised three or four rice crops per year. They also grew onions, mustard, eggplants, melons, sugarcane, gourds, taro, oranges, pomegranates, peaches, bananas, plums, and apricots.

10. Victor Lieberman, *Strange Parallels, Vol. I,* p. 231.

11. Michael D. Coe, *Angkor and the Khmer Civilization* (Thames & Hudson, 2003), p. 145.

CHAPTER FIVE: BUILDING FOUNDATIONS FOR THE GODS' PALACE

1. Victor Lieberman, *Strange Parallels, Vol. I,* p. 224–5.

2. Some people were already living there in the seventh century, and the temple Ak Yum was begun around then. Though smaller than the first big Khmer temples from around 900, it still integrated several shrines into a symmetrical mandala-like pattern on a platform. The Angkor area was thus already creative, but it was outdone by many factors in the ninth century. See Thierry Zephir, *Khmer; The Lost Empire of Cambodia* (Harry N. Abrams, Inc., 1998), p. 29.

3. Michael Freeman and Claude Jacques, *Ancient Angkor,* p. 198.

4. Vittorio Roveda, *Images of the Gods; Khmer Mythology in Cambodia, Laos & Thailand* (River Books, 2013), p. 347 and p. 350.

5. Victor Lieberman, *Strange Parallels, Vol. I,* p. 219.

6. David Chandler, *A History of Cambodia* (Westview Press, 2000), p. 43.

CHAPTER SIX: THE PAGODA AND THE CATHEDRAL

1. Claude Jacques felt that the politics were more complex because some battles show Khmers and Chams fighting together against other groups of Khmers and Chams. See *Ancient Angkor*, p. 85. Also see Vittorio Roveda, "Reliefs of the Bayon," in *Bayon; New Perspectives* (Bangkok, River Books, 2007), p. 322. Roveda wrote that the scenes might be of a mock battle staged during a festival to commemorate the actual victory.

2. Others have also seen Tantric influence in Cambodia. See Ian Harris, *Cambodian Buddhism; History and Practice*, p. 7 and p. 21. Also see John Guy, "Angkorian Metalwork in the Temple Setting," in *Gods of Angkor*, p. 126.

3. Peter Sharrok, *Bayon; New Perspectives*, p. 234.

4. David Chandler wrote that Khmers might have felt that the face towers represented multiple deities, since they often mixed faiths. See *A History of Cambodia*, p. 67.

5. Ian Harris, *Cambodian Buddhism; History and Practice*, p. 22.

6. Michael D. Coe, *Angkor and the Khmer Civilization*, p. 130.

7. The location of both the home and church is actually controversial. A reconstruction of Dante's home was built in modern times in the area where his house might have stood, and the church that he might have attended is half a block away.

8. Michael D. Coe noted that the literature that people used in their daily lives was written on perishable materials that the tropical climate and insects destroyed, such as palm leaves and screen-folds from the inner bark of trees. See *Angkor and the Khmer Civilization*, p. 40.

9. See Emile Male, *The Gothic Image; Religious Art in France in the Thirteenth Century* for a classic study of Gothic art and 13th century European thought.

10. *The Bahir; A Translation and Commentary by Aryeh Kaplan* (Northvale, NJ, Jason Aronson, Inc., 1995), p. xi.

11. Chandler wrote that most merchants were Chinese, Cham, and Vietnamese. See *A History of Cambodia*, p. 44.

12. Although peasants couldn't understand the Sanskrit texts, and though they might have had little background in the Hindu myths, their worlds of farming, the village, and local spirit cults were integrated with elite culture in many ways. The monsoons and heat, collective rice growing, ancestral cults, awe-inspiring rituals, the prominence of temples, and the emphasis on social hierarchy gave people in both levels many points of contact.

13. Zhou Daguan did say that Khmers were frequently ill, that dysentery was common, and that over 80 percent of dysentery victims died. People had bowel movements in pits that they dug and then covered up, and some were probably flooded into rice fields during monsoons. Khmers, like Indians, avoided eating with the left hand because they cleaned themselves with it, and they laughed at Chinese immigrants for using paper to wipe themselves. Germs weren't understood as sources of infections until the 19th century, and Khmers seem to have used Hindu concepts to distinguish cleanliness from dirt. But Europeans were also highly prone to sickness in the Middle Ages—the bubonic plague would wipe out more than a third of them in the mid 14th century. Life was short for many in both societies, and lived in the midst of other people's dirt.

14. See Hiram Woodward's foreword in *Bayon, New Perspectives*, p. 6.

CHAPTER SEVEN: FROM HELL'S BASEMENT TO BUILDING PARADISE

1. Richard Stone, "Divining Angkor," in *National Geographic*, July 2009, p. 51–4, and Victor Lieberman, *Strange Parallels, Vol. I*, p. 239.

2. *Bayon, New Perspectives*, p. 42–3.

3. Thierry Zephir, *Khmer; The Lost Empire of Cambodia*, p. 21.

4. Ian Harris, *Cambodian Buddhism; History and Practice*, p. 30, and Lieberman, *Strange Parallels, Vol. I*, p. 237.

5. Victor Lieberman, *Strange Parallels, Vol. I*, p. 239.

6. John Tully, *A Short History of Cambodia; From Empire to Survival* (Allen & Unwin, 2005), p. 190. Also see Milton Osborne, *Sihanouk; Prince of Light, Prince of Darkness* (Allen & Unwin, 1994), p. 6.

7. David Chandler, *A History of Cambodia*, p. 189.

8. John Tully, *A Short History of Cambodia; From Empire to Survival*, p. 167.
9. Ibid., p. 179.
10. Milton Osborne, *Southeast Asia; An Introductory History* (Allen & Unwin, 2010), p. 261.
11. Tully, p. 230.
12. *The Economist*, August 3–9, 2013.
13. *The Economist*, January 11–17, 2014.

CHAPTER EIGHT: TRADITIONAL GRACE AND MODERN LIFE IN THAILAND

1. Sunait Chutintharanon, "Historical Writings, Historical Novels and Period Novels and Dramas: An Observation Concerning Burma in Thai Perception and Understanding," in *The Journal of the Siam Society*, Volume 88, Parts 1 & 2, 2000, p. 57.
2. See Niles Mulder, *Thai Images; The Culture of the Public World* (Chiang Mai, Silkworm Books, 1997) for an interesting description of the Thai education system.
3. Santi Leksukhum, "The Evolution of the Memorial Towers of Siamese Temples," in *The Kingdom of Siam; The Art of Central Thailand, 1350–1800* (Snoeck Publishers, Buppha Press, Art Media Resources, Inc., and The Asian Art Museum of San Francisco, 2005), edited by Forrest McGill, p. 61.
4. David K. Wyatt, *Thailand; A Short History* (Yale University Press, 1984), p. 137.
5. Victor Lieberman, *Strange Parallels, Vol. I*, p. 260.
6. Herbert P. Phillips, *Thai Peasant Personality; The Patterning of Interpersonal Behavior in the Village of Bang Chan* (University of California Press, 1974), p. 59.

CHAPTER NINE: THE WORLD IN A POINT

1. Leon Battista Alberti, *On Painting*, translated by John R. Spencer (Yale University Press, 1966), p. 106. Also see Ross King, *Brunelleschi's*

Dome (New York, Penguin Books, 2001), p 33–6. Roberta J.M. Olson wrote that Brunelleschi's biographer, Antonio Manetti, said that he created his painting around 1420. See Roberta J.M. Olson, *Italian Renaissance Sculpture* (Thames and Hudson, 1992), p. 61. King said that Domenico da Prato had already called him the expert in perspective in 1413. The date's a little hazy because the painting has been lost since the French invaded Italy in the 1490s and took many art works.

2. In this book, I define *perspective* more broadly than its Latin root, *perspicere* (to look through) and its technical meaning for artists trained in Western classical traditions (to arrange objects on a grid of lines). These meanings have been emphasized in the modern West. I define it more inclusively, as a general way of perceiving and understanding the world, which people in a culture share.

3. Florentine society became more oligarchic and then more autocratic by the late 15th century, but it retained cultural roots in its older republican traditions—the artistic conventions that were established in the early 15th century were followed and elaborated on.

4. See Ross King, *Michelangelo and the Pope's Ceiling* (New York, Penguin Books, 2003), p. 244–6 for a discussion of earlier images of God as an elderly man pointing to Adam.

5. Ross King, in *Michelangelo and the Pope's Ceiling* (p. 246), wrote that the finger was actually repainted a few years after Michelangelo died because cracks had appeared in the ceiling.

6. A. Richard Turner, *Renaissance Florence; The Invention of a New Art* (New York, Harry N. Abrams, Inc., 1997), p. 76.

7. Gene A. Brucker, *Renaissance Florence* (University of California Press, Berkeley, 1983), p. 116.

8. There were exceptions. Ghirlandaio painted an old man with warts all over his nose, doting on a young boy with rosy cheeks and long blond locks. I imagine that he enjoyed depicting the contrast between old age and youth while unifying them with familial tenderness. But Italian artists showed people's beauty more often than their blemishes.

9. Many of Titian's later works became more religious and impressionistic. He lived and painted well into his eighties and experimented with many styles.

10. A. Richard Turner, *Renaissance Florence; The Invention of a New Art*, p. 111.

11. Many Third World countries have recently used three-dimensional perspective for depicting scenes, but they don't emphasize it as much as the West does—they haven't experienced the West's long history of all these converging currents. Artists in Bangkok learned it in the 19th century as Western influence spread, but they usually didn't yoke everything in the scene to it. Instead, they portrayed linear frontages of buildings and mixed them with the old traditions of showing images of daily life which people can meander through—they didn't integrate everything in the picture within one overarching framework. Other cultures have also blended three-dimensional perspective with the ways of perceiving the world which their own traditions have emphasized. Japan's Okyo saw Western drawings or paintings in Dutch-influenced Nagasaki, and he painted nature with meticulous realism, but without reducing things to a three-dimensional grid. Instead, one of his scenes lingers over minute details of a snow-covered tree branch so that you can feel a profound affinity with every leaf. In this way, he retained the traditional Japanese emphasis on affinity with little things in the surroundings without reducing them to a commanding perspective. In the 19th century, Hiroshige created many prints of Tokyo, and some peer down a crowded commercial street from about 20 feet above so that you can see a line of shops on each side. But the perspective doesn't converge on a point; instead the far end of the street spreads into a crowd milling around shops so that even a modern urban perspective is experienced as an intimate immersion in each scene—no abstract grid is imposed on it.

CHAPTER TEN: GRACE AND SPICE

1. The paintings on the walls do follow an order. The west end of the hall, behind the main Buddha statue, typically has a mural

that depicts Thai Buddhist cosmology, with the Realm of Desire below (where souls are tortured by demons) and spiritual worlds above (where celestials reside). The side walls depict the Buddha's past lives from Jatakas, and the east wall, at the entrance, depicts the story of his enlightenment. But these stories are more loosely related than Biblical tales because the latter are bound to a theology that sees Jesus' life as a one-time occurrence. Because the Buddha lived an enormous number of past lives, it's more possible to linger on any scene because they're all about the same personage. People can thus scroll over any scene at their pleasure; their perspectives aren't as firmly pulled towards the main altar as they are in most Romanesque and Gothic churches.

2.   This old concept of the world has been changing among some modern urbanites. Many young Thais see their beautiful forests and uplands as endangered ecology, and some lobby for its protection.

3.   Herbert P. Phillips, *Modern Thai Literature* (Honolulu, University of Hawai'i Press, 1987), p. 46 and p. 307.

CHAPTER ELEVEN: THE DAWN OF HAPPINESS

1.   David Wyatt, *Studies in Thai History*, p. 52.
2.   Craig Reynolds, *Seditious Histories*, p. 296.
3.   Craig Lockhart, *Southeast Asia in World History* (Oxford University Press, 2009), p. 54.
4.   Betty Gosling, *Sukhothai; Its History, Culture, and Art* (Oxford University Press, 1991), p. 55.
5.   Ibid., p. 62–3. Many of Wat Mahathat's most graceful forms were erected in the 14th century.
6.   Carol Stratton and Miriam McNair Scott, *The Art of Sukhothai; Thailand's Golden Age* (Oxford University Press, 1987), p. 45.
7.   Victor Lieberman, *Strange Parallels, Vol. I.* p. 259. Also see Betty Gosling, *Sukhothai; Its History, Culture, and Art*, p. 23–6.
8.   David Wyatt, *Thailand; A Short History*, p. 68–70.
9.   Joachim Schliesinger, *Tai Groups of Thailand, Vol. I* (Bangkok, White Lotus Press, 2001), p. 22 and p. 28.

10. Victor Lieberman, *Strange Parallels, Vol. I*, p. 240, and *Strange Parallels, Vol. II*, p. 203.
11. John Clifford Holt, *Spirits of the Place; Buddhism and Lao Religious Culture* (Silkworm Books, 2009), p. 29–31.
12. Charles Higham and Rachaine Thosarat, *Early Thailand; From Prehistory to Sukhothai*, p. 269.
13. Hiram W. Woodward, Jr., *The Sacred Sculpture of Thailand* (The Walters Art Gallery, 1997), p. 46.
14. Higham, *Early Thailand*, p. 253.
15. Victor Lieberman, *Strange Parallels, Vol. I* p. 248–9.
16. Ian Glover wrote that Srivijaya might have been a network of towns rather than a centralized state. See Glover, *Southeast Asia from Prehistory to History*, p. 325.
17. The capital was later moved to Jambi. See Glover, *Southeast Asia from Prehistory to History*, p. 306.
18. Ibid., p. 240.
19. Victor Lieberman wrote that Thai culture consolidated as a complex of practices and dialects only in the 15th and 16th centuries, but if so, many art forms and patterns of daily life were already in place when Sukhothai built its center. The development of Thai culture was a long process, with many dimensions, as the development of three-dimensional perspective in the West was. See *Strange Parallels, Vol. I*, p. 330.
20. Hiram Woodward said that the calling-the-earth pose was popular in northern India and that Thais might have imported it from there, but if so, they added their own style to it. See Hiram Woodward, Jr. *The Sacred Sculpture of Thailand*, p. 115.
21. Carol Stratton and Miriam McNair Scott, *The Art of Sukhothai*, p. 133.

CHAPTER TWELVE: NORTHERN THAILAND

1. Sanitsuda Ekachai, *Behind the Smiles; Voices of Thailand* (The Post Publishing Co., Ltd, 1990), p. 126–31.

CHAPTER THIRTEEN: A METHOD FOR FINDING PARADISE IN THE WORLD

1. This isn't just potential infinity because the ability to be endlessly varied enables all these facets of experience to be shared throughout a society (in all common media) and treated as basic in the first place. Aristotle distinguished potential and actual infinity from each other, but there's not a solid line between potential and actual infinity in cultures. A society's ability to easily create variations enables these facets to spread through all media and to be meaningful for everyone, and this allows people to create ever more variations.

2. Michael A. Singer, *The Untethered Soul; The Journey Beyond Yourself* (Oakland, New Harbinger Publications, Inc., 2007), p. 57.

3. Mihaly Csikszentmihalyi, *Flow; The Psychology of Optimal Experience* (Harper Perennial Modern Classics, 2008), p. 49 and p. 58.

4. Mihaly Csikszentmihalyi, *Creativity; The Psychology of Discovery and Invention* (Harper Perennial Modern Classics, 2013), p. 323.

5. Csikszentmihalyi, *Flow*, p. 70.

6. Edward Nelson, "Warning Signs of a Possible Collapse of Contemporary Mathematics," in *Infinity; New Research Frontiers* (Cambridge University Press, 2011), p. 77.

7. Gregory Bateson, *Mind and Nature; A Necessary Unity* (Bantam Books, 1980), p. 49–53.

8. See Jadran Mimica, *Intimations of Infinity; The Cultural Meanings of the Iqwaye Counting and Number Systems* (Bloomsbury Academic, 1988) for an example of ideas of infinity in terms of nature's vitality. Many West African cultures stress open-ended play as a basic idea—see John Miller Chernoff, *African Rhythm and African Sensibility; Aesthetics and Social Action in African Musical Idioms* (University of Chicago Press, 1981). See Daisetz T. Suzuki, *Zen and Japanese Culture* (Princeton University Press, 1973) for ideas of spontaneously appreciating each moment's uniqueness—many Zen and Daoist traditions emphasize this type of experience.

9. Bruce E. Wexler, *Brain and Culture; Neurobiology, Ideology, and Social Change* (MIT Press, 2006), p. 154–5.

CHAPTER FOURTEEN: BETWEEN BAMBOO AND CONCRETE

1. David Wyatt, *Thailand; A Short History*, p. 144. Rama I's mother was Chinese, but he was from an old noble family that was respected. Taksin's Chinese business connections had provided his army with food while he was building his following.
2. Thongchai Winichakul, *Siam Mapped: A History of the Geo-Body of a Nation* (Honolulu, University of Hawai'i Press, 1997), p. 111.
3. Thongchai Winichakul wrote a study of this process in *Siam Mapped*, on p. 48, 53, 56, 64, and 100.
4. David Wyatt, *Thailand; A Short History*, p. 199.

CHAPTER FIFTEEN: A NEW DAWNING OF GRACE

1. Michael J. Montesano, "Four Thai Pathologies, Late 2009," in *Legitimacy Crisis in Thailand*, edited by Marc Askew (Silkworm Books, 2010), p. 288.
2. Marc Askew, "Confrontation and Crisis in Thailand, 2008–2010," in *Legitimacy Crisis in Thailand*, p. 40–1.
3. *The Economist*, May 17, 2014.
4. *The Economist*, August 9, 2014.
5. Michael J. Montesano, "Four Thai Pathologies, Late 2009," in *Legitimacy Crisis in Thailand*, p. 278–9.
6. Maurizio Peleggi, *Thailand; The Worldly Kingdom* (Reaktion Books, 2007), p. 19–20.
7. Walden Bello, Shea Cunningham, and Li Kheng Poh, *A Siamese Tragedy; Development & Disintegration in Modern Thailand* (Zed Books, 1998), p. 7–8.
8. Sanitsuda Ekachai, *Behind the Smile; Voices of Thailand*, (The Post Publishing Co., Ltd., 1993), p. 33.
9. Michael J. Montesano, "Four Thai Pathologies, Late 2009," in *Legitimacy Crisis in Thailand*, p. 291.
10. David Wyatt, *Thailand; A Short History*, p. 205–6.

11. Sanitsuda Ekachai, *Behind the Smile; Voices of Thailand*, p. 90–2.

12. Joe Studwell, *Asian Godfathers* (New York, Atlantic Monthly Press, 2007), p. 77. Also see S. J. Tambiah, *World Conqueror & World Renouncer; A Study of Buddhism and Polity in Thailand against a Historical Background* (Cambridge University Press, 1977), p. 190.

13. Anthony Reid, *Southeast Asia in the Age of Commerce, 1450–1680, Volume Two* (Yale University Press, 1993), p. 254–6.

14. Anthony Reid, *Charting the Shape of Early Modern Southeast Asia* (Silkworm Books, 1999), p. 226.

15. Anthony Reid, *Southeast Asia in the Age of Commerce, 1450–1680, Volume Two*, p. 286.

16. Ibid., p. 285.

17. David M. Engel and Jaruwan S. Engel, *Tort, Custom, and Karma; Globalization and Legal Consciousness in Thailand* (Stanford Law Books, 2010), p. 79.

18. Thongchai Winichakul, *Siam Mapped*, p. 168.

19. Niall Ferguson, *The Ascent of Money; A Financial History of The World* (Penguin Books, 2009), p. 5.

CHAPTER SIXTEEN: THE WORLD IN A PLACE

1. Mayoury & Pheuiphanh Ngaosrivathana, *The Enduring Sacred Landscape of the Naga* (Mekong Press, 2009), p. 60.

2. Keith Taylor, *A History of the Vietnamese* (Cambridge University Press, 2013), p. 2.

3. Milton Osborne, *Southeast Asia; An Introductory History* (Allen & Unwin, 2010), p. 45 and p. 79.

4. For Chinese influence in Cham societies in the early years, see William A. Southworth, "River Settlement and Coastal Trade," in *The Cham of Vietnam; History, Society and Art* (Singapore, Nus Press, 2011), p. 77 and p. 108.

5. Anne-Valerie Schweyer, *Ancient Vietnam; History, Art and Archaeology* (River Books, 2001), p. 9. Also see Michael Vickery, "Champa Revisited," in *The Cham of Vietnam; History, Society and Art*, p. 371.

6. John K. Whitmore, "The Last Great King of Classical Southeast Asia," in *The Cham of Vietnam; History, Society and Art*, p. 198.

7. Victor Lieberman, *Strange Parallels, Vol. I*, p. 348.

8. Ian Glover, *Southeast Asia; From Prehistory to History*, p. 28. Also see Darrell Tryon, "Proto-Austronesian and the Major Austronesian Subgroups," in *The Austronesians; Historical and Comparative Perspectives*, edited by Peter Bellwood, James J. Fox, and Darrell Tryon (The Australian National University Press, 2006), p. 37.

9. Ian Glover, *Southeast Asia; From Prehistory to History*, p. 29.

10. Singaravelu Sachithanantham, *The Ramayana Tradition in Southeast Asia* (University of Malaya Press, 2004), p. 122 and p. 133.

11. Some historians think *silat* came with Islam. There was probably earlier Indian influence, since many martial arts originated in India. There was probably also influence from local spirit dances. See Ruud Spruit, *The Land of the Sultans; An Illustrated History of Malaysia* (The Pepin Press, 1995), p. 21 for possible Islamic origins.

12. There is another popular version of the Hang Tuah story, with another childhood friend called Hang Jebat. Hang Tuah killed him, and he died in Hang Tuah's arms.

13. Mohd. Taib Osman, *Islamic Civilization in the Malay World*, edited by Mohd. Taib Osman (Kuala Lumpur, Dewan Bahasa dan Pustaka, 2000), p. xxvi. Also see Hussin Mutalib, "Islamic Malay Polity in Southeast Asia," in *Islamic Civilization in the Malay World*, p. 32.

14. Movements to modernize Islam emerged in cities and towns in the 19th and 20th centuries, and their leaders have tried to purge Islam of the old animistic traditions. People in Malaysia practice Islam in a rich variety of ways.

15. Ismail Noor and Muhammad Azaham, *The Malays Par Excellence* (Pelanduk Publications, 2000), p. 94.

16. See Craig Reynolds, *Seditious Histories*, p. 189 for an exception. He wrote that the 1805 Siamese law code allowed the husband to manage his wife's property. Also, official Buddhism in Thailand doesn't honor female monks. Some Buddhist traditions in northern Thailand have harbored fears of menstrual blood as a pollutant—see Shigeharu Tanabe, "Spirits, Power, and the Discourse of Female Gender," in *Thai Constructions of Knowledge*, edited by Manas Chitakasem and Andrew Turton (School of Oriental and African Studies, University of London, 1991), p. 183–207. But

Maurizio Peleggi, in *Thailand; The Worldly Kingdom* (p. 80), wrote that women in Thailand were freer than women in traditional India and China.

17. Milton Osborne, *Southeast Asia; An Introductory History*, p. 6–7. Also see Craig A. Lockhard, *Southeast Asia in World History*, p. 32.

18. Victor Lieberman, *Strange Parallels, Vol. I*, p. 399.

19. See Tony Day, *Fluid Iron*, p. 63, and Mohd. Taib Osman, *Islamic Civilization in the Malay World*, p. 16 for other Southeast Asian societies that have emphasized hierarchy—traditional Malay cultures also often emphasized distinctions between elites and commoners.

20. Even the splendor-loving Khmers didn't emphasize a caste system. Jayavarman VII's enormous temples projected his personal authority more than they expressed a permanent and detailed social order. The sakdina system in Ayutthaya categorized people, but it was abolished in the early Bangkok period.

CONCLUSION: ARCHITECTURE OF PARADISE

1. Arthur O. Lovejoy, *The Great Chain of Being: A Study of the History of an Idea* (Harvard University Press, 1936). Also see E. M. Tillyard, *The Elizabethan World Picture* (Vintage, 1959).

2. Walter Burkert, *Greek Religion* (Harvard University Press, 1985), p. 276.

3. An ancient Greek historian and statesman named Polybius wrote that the known world became integrated into one system when Rome took over the eastern Mediterranean in the second century BCE. He felt that Tyche had a lot to do with events, including Rome's quick rise. Sudden reversals of fortune happened frequently, and they were now often caused by things beyond a person's and a community's control.

4. Ra'anan S. Boustan and Annette Yoshiko Reed, *Heavenly Realms and Earthly Realities in Late Antique Religions* (Cambridge University Press, 2009), p. 4–6 and p. 9. They noted that Westerners in late antiquity had a large variety of ideas of a metaphysical universe, and that these ideas didn't just spread from one imperial center. Instead, every periphery was an important center with its own

culture. All places converged, as they did in the development of Thai culture.

A MANUAL FOR FINDING PARADISE IN THE WORLD

1. Greg Howes, *Sensual Relations: Engaging the Senses in Culture and Social Theory* (University of Michigan Press, 2003).
2. Kathryn Linn Geurts, *Culture and the Senses; Bodily Ways of Knowing in an African Community* (University of California Press, 2002).
3. See Kevin Kelly, *What Technology Wants* (Viking, Penguin Group, 2010), p. 161–73, and Ray Kurzweil, *The Singularity is Near* (Viking, Penguin Group, 2005), p. 56–72, for discussions about accelerating returns in digital technology.
4. Siva Vaidhyanathan, *The Googlization of Everything: (And Why We Should Worry)* (University of California Press, 2011), p. 59–60.
5. Ibid., p. 52.
6. Howard Gardiner, *Truth, Beauty, and Goodness Reframed; Educating for the Virtues in the Age of Truthiness and Twitter* (Basic Books, 2012), p. 15.
7. Larry Winograd, *Time*, April 21, 2011.

ACKNOWLEDGEMENTS

I FIRST OWE a world of gratitude to my parents, Robert and Edith Marion Holihan. I always felt safe while venturing into distant lands and times because they gave me a nurturing place to return to. My dad was fascinated by the ocean, and he often drove my mom and me to the beaches between San Francisco and Carmel. He and I would walk over jagged rocks towards the cliffs to peer over the water, and my mom, ever a homebody, stayed in the car where it was warm and dry. Soon I would hear her yelling, "You're getting too close to the edge!" They were a perfect pair. He always delighted in discussing distant places, and she ensured that I always had a cozy home to return to. Their spirits are with me in every mile I travel.

The thousands of people I met during my journeys also inspired me. No single person stands out from the others because I was always venturing to new places and meeting more locals. As I look back I see, not one dominant light, but thousands of sparks, which together have helped to make the world shine for me.

I owe special gratitude to the people of Cambodia, Thailand, Laos, Vietnam, Malaysia, and Indonesia for letting me into their lives so deeply. They showed me that their cultures are among the richest in the world and made me feel at home in them. They often shared themselves with a combination of directness and warmth that often made me feel as though I was one of them.

I also feel special gratitude towards the people of Greece and Italy. I initially went to both countries to immerse myself in the West's ancient heritage, but the locals shared their lives in the present with me so readily that it seemed as though we had been friends since childhood. I first visited their beautiful lands in 2008, just before the global financial crisis hit their economies especially hard. When I returned in 2013, most people were struggling to make ends meet, but they remained as gracious as ever.

Thanks to Rachel Blackbirdsong, who performed this book's initial edit and gave me much useful advice. She was the first person who read it from front to back. Being both intellectually and emotionally immersed in all the cultures that this book covers, I couldn't always objectively decide when I needed to explain something further. She often told me where I needed to make points clearer.

Cindy Millet Bowles, Tiffany Colter, Katherine Sullivan, and Jason Gooding also read the full manuscript. Each made suggestions about the flow of ideas—invaluable for a book about so many places and times. Cindy gave me advice about maintaining the flow of philosophic ideas. Tiffany, Katherine, and Jason offered pointers about keeping the flow as I transition between descriptions of cultures.

Thanks to Gayle Gross for her 10-Day Book Club. We initially met on LinkedIn and found that we have similar interests in travel. She introduced me to Rachel and the book's first readers.

Sharon Abbot and Beth Barany provided useful advice about the book market in my early stages of writing. Both are marketing consultants and they graciously gave me some of their time in spite of their busy schedules.

Last but not least, thanks to Michele D'amico and Ferdinando Ballaré of South Beach Cafe in San Francisco. For 15 years they gave me a home in The City whenever I took the train up from Silicon Valley. They always let me stay long after meals to read or write, often giving me free food and drinks. After enjoying their abundant hospitality, I often felt that I had never left home during my visits to their original country, Italy. I'm still exercising off the weight.

INDEX

ABOUT THE AUTHOR

Brian Holihan has relished exploring the different ways in which people think since he was seven years old, when the cultural mosaics of his native San Francisco Bay Area, its diverse natural landscape, and his father's subscription to *National Geographic* widened his eyes. Since then he has extensively studied and traveled in societies in Europe, China, Southeast Asia, India, Africa, and the Middle East.

He mixes his enthusiasm for different places and times with equal fascination with cutting-edge trends in business and culture. He has worked as a Silicon Valley headhunter and résumé writer, and he still writes résumés and speaks about résumé writing and career development. He loves learning about people's unique histories and using his abilities to see extra richness in clients to help them maximize their creative potential.

He also savors music from all over the world. His first instrument was the guitar and he collects other stringed instruments while traveling. He has found music to be an excellent inroad to other cultures because it allows people to immediately share emotions deeply. Performing in other countries has given him some of the greatest experiences in his life.

Combining travel, study, high-tech business, personal encounters, and art has given him unique breadth to see all cultures and people from new perspectives and expose their potential for maximizing their well-being. Expanding people's horizons into the full richness of both the outer world and the inner self is his biggest lifelong passion.

Brian is available for select seminars, lectures, and consultations about creativity, careers, and world cultures, and can be contacted at brian@fullhumanitypress.com.